CW00749715

Arklow

The story of a town

by

Jim Rees

Dee-Jay Publications

Published in 2004 by
DEE-JAY PUBLICATIONS
3 Meadows Lane
Arklow
Co. Wicklow
Ireland

e-mail: jrees@eircom.net

Text © Jim Rees 2004

Cover photograph © J.B. Murray
Maps © Brian McKay

All rights reserved. No part of this publication may be reproduced or transmitted in any form or by any means electronic, mechanical, photocopying, recording or otherwise, without the prior written permission of the copyright owner, or else under the terms of any licence permitting limited copying issued by The Irish Writers' Centre, 19 Parnell Square, Dublin 1.

Typeset by DEE-JAY PUBLICATIONS

Printed in Ireland by Woodprint Craft Ltd.

ISBN: 0 9519239 4 3 (hardback)
ISBN: 0 9519239 3 5 (paperback)

ARKLOW

THE STORY OF A TOWN

By the same author

Arklow – Last Stronghold of Sail
(with Liam Charlton)

The Life of Captain Robert Halpin

A Farewell To Famine

Surplus People – the Fitzwilliam Clearances 1847-1856

The author and publishers wish to thank Wicklow Rural Partnership for their support, which made this publication possible

"This project has been assisted by Wicklow Rural Partnership Ltd under the European Union LEADER + / National Development Plan 2000—2006'

ACKNOWLEDGEMENTS

In the course of writing this book, I have received the unstinting help of many people. I'd particularly like to thank Dolores Tyrrell who started me down this road twenty-six years ago. Noel O'Cléirigh deserves special mention for reading the manuscript, as does Pat Power who, as ever, was always on call for advice and material. I must also name Kevin Byrne, Liam Charlton, Bruce Elliott, Mae Greene, Billy Lee, Criostóir MacCartaigh, and Stan O'Reilly, who all contributed towards the finished product. The names of many more contributors appear in the source notes. Any shortcomings are all my own work.

Without the co-operation of the staffs of the Wicklow County Library Service, both in Ballywaltrim and Arklow, the National Library of Ireland, the National Archives, the Librarian and staff of Freemasons' Hall in Dublin's Molesworth Street, and the Department of Folklore, UCD, this book could not have been written. I am also grateful to Arklow Historical Society for their moral support and goodwill.

A special thanks is owed to

Joe Murray

who generously let me use his
photograph of the town on the cover

and to

Brian McKay

For allowing the use of his maps.

CONTENTS

FOREWORD

Every book should meet two requirements.

The first is that it serves a purpose not already served. This book is needed to pull all the strands of Arklow history together into a narrative. A great deal of research has been carried out into this town's past by individuals and groups, and the results of that research have appeared in book form or as articles in the journals of the Arklow Historical Society, and others. The problem a newcomer to the subject faces is how to fit all these disparate pieces together to get an overview. I hope that this book goes some way towards solving that problem. While it tells the town's story, its comprehensive source list and bibliography will help anyone who wishes to delve deeper.

The second requirement every book should meet is once its *raison d'etre* has been explained, it should speak for itself.

Jim Rees
March 2004

1

Stories and Stones:
c.3000 BC – AD 400

Writers of biography often begin their stories with an outline of their subjects' ancestries. It puts their lives into some sort of context, a framework which might help explain the way their subjects thought and why they acted as they did. Writing a history of a town is very similar. Even when an exact date of "birth" can be identified, the historian must place that birth into an historical context. He must deal with the protracted pregnancy of its prehistory, no matter how vague that prehistory might be. When there is no exact date of origin, as in Arklow's case, sketching a context is all the more difficult.

This opening chapter deals with a mixture of fantasy and fragmented artefacts from a period of which we know very little. In times past, myth was used to explain the origins and purposes of silent relics and even now, with new techniques and tools to wrest information from the debris of ancient activity, the old stories tell us as much as the stones do. So before I begin this tale of a town I will issue a warning. If you don't want to read conjecture based on legend, unprovable theories and half-baked "histories", skip to Chapter Two and be prepared to take parts of that with more pinches of salt than is good for the heart. That leaves you with the Normans as the starting point for this story – and that would be even more misleading and nonsensical than going with the flow and starting here, with a few stories and stones.

Pre-Christian Arklow, in common with the rest of the country, remains relatively free of indisputable "fact". Imagination is spurred on by small pieces of evidence that come to light from time to time, and is sometimes given too much rein. Having said all that, the national heritage authority and the County Wicklow Archaeological Society have done much in recent years to increase our knowledge and understanding of our prehistoric past, and what follows is a glimpse of an ever-changing picture.

*

On the north side of the Avoca river, stretching from the bridge almost to the by-pass, is the Marsh, or the Mash as it was called by many locals until fairly recent times. Perhaps best seen from Vale Road, just under St Saviour's church, it is home to a wide range of plants, insects and other wildlife that makes its conservation a matter of immense ecological importance.

It is a remnant of the once wide estuary that gave the area its Gaelic name, An tInbhear Mór. In times of major flooding, such as in the aftermath of Hurricane Charlie in 1986 and the severe storms which annihilated the sand dunes of North and South Beaches three years later, the Marsh acts like a huge sponge, protecting the town by soaking up the burgeoning flow. Sometimes the water level rises above the grasses, plants and reeds until the Marsh is a lake stretching from the river to the firmer ground on which are built the houses of Inbhear Mór Park. At such times it is very easy to see how extensively the Avoca river ballooned at this point and why it was called The Wide Estuary.

Who were the first people to see that *inbhear mór?* Where did they come from and what did they call themselves? The problem with trying to piece together a picture of prehistoric times is that they were *pre*historic. No one, as far as we know, sat down and recorded the daily lives of the earliest inhabitants of the area we now call Arklow, and in the words of Liam Price, one of Wicklow's best-known historians, 'there is very little to be said about the history of County Wicklow until the end of the sixth century'[1]. We must therefore rely on fragments of archaeology to give us all-too-tantalising glimpses of a distant past.

The western side of what is now County Wicklow has many archaeological sites, each bearing testimony to a vibrant prehistoric population. By comparison, the narrow strip of land that separates the mountains from the sea has little to offer. Price suggests that ancient tracks connected our remote region to the more populous, and presumably more prosperous, plains of Kildare and Carlow:

From Arklow the way led past Aughrim to Rathvilly, or by a route further south which would have been directed towards the important prehistoric site of Ballon.[2]

In the northwest of the county stands the impressive hillfort of Brusselstown Ring. Price believes that it was in ancient times called Dún Bolg, a stronghold of the pre-Celtic people we refer to as the Fir Bolg. The mythologies tells us that the Fir Bolg were later defeated and replaced by the Túatha dé Danaan, a people highly skilled in the arts and sciences. When the Túatha dé Danaan were themselves defeated and replaced by a Celtic race known as the Milesians, they reputedly went underground both physically and figuratively, to pass into folklore as the 'Little People', their supposed magical powers still intact.

Such stories seem to have emanated from the Celtic victors. In bestowing superhuman powers on the vanquished, the Celtic victory would seem all the greater. In truth, of course, neither the Fir Bolg nor the Túatha dé Danaan were any more magical, mystical, or mythical than the Celts who replaced them. They were flesh and blood, a link in the chain of human migrants to Ireland. The Fir Bolg have been tentatively identified as a group of Belgic tribes. Price suggests that:

> A body of warriors landing in the neighbourhood of Arklow or North Wexford would of course move in towards the inhabited lands of the central plain; the fort of Brusselstown may have been built by them, and the remarkable stone fort at Rathgall, twelve miles to the south, may have been another stronghold of theirs.[3]

This linking of the area we now call Arklow with the massive hillfort of Rathgall near Tullow was also explored by Goddard H. Orpen.[4] To cut a very long (and very speculative) story short, Orpen tried to show that this ancient fort was Dunum, one of the seven inland population centres marked on the Ptolemaic map of Ireland which dates from the second century. In the course of his argument, Orpen drew on ancient legends, genealogies, the derivation of placenames, and a host of other methods of bridging historical gaps. The upshot of all this analysing, theorising, and general wishful-thinking is the following story.

Cobthach Coel was not a particularly nice individual. He was jealous of his brother Loegaire Lore, who reigned as King of Erin. Cobthach killed him and seized the throne, and for good measure also poisoned Loegaire's son Ailill, who was King of Leinster. Ailill's son, Moen, would have fared no better except for the fact that he had not the power of speech, and so, under the rules of accession, was no threat to his evil granduncle. Then, as in all good legends, something strange happened. Moen began to speak, earning himself a name extension, Moen Labraid – 'The Dumb One Speaks'. Cobthach's position was no longer safe and he obviously panicked. I say he panicked because instead of killing the youngster, as he had callously killed the boy's father and grandfather, he merely banished him into exile, fit, healthy and with an understandable chip on his shoulder. This banishment brought a further change to the youth's name. He was now Labraid Loingsech – Labraid the Exile.

Perhaps modern living has made me cynical, but surely there have been enough stories based on this premise. We immediately know what is going to happen. Labraid goes into exile, wins the support of the people who shelter him, returns with an army, and regains his birthright. Hollywood has done it a thousand times. Poems, plays and novels all with the same storyline have been bending book shelves for years. The only one who doesn't seem to have been familiar with this overused plot was Cobthach. While he was obviously a dab hand at murder, we must assume that intrigue was not his forte.

The two main versions of this legend, one in the *Book of Leinster* and the other in a 'Scholium on the *Amra Choluimb Cille*'[5], agree up to the point of banishment, but this is where the accounts diverge. The former says Labraid settled somewhere in Munster, the latter has him sailing east towards 'the speckled youths of the land of Armenia'. Orpen feels both are wrong and that Labraid Loingsech fled to 'tír fir Menia', the land of the men of Menia, or Menapia, a region in what is now the border lands of France and Belgium. The people who lived there were known as the Menapii and this is pivotal to our story. This, we are told, all happened in the third century BC.

So, where does Arklow come into all this? One of the coastal settlements marked on the previously mentioned Ptolemaic map of about five hundred years later (second century) is Manapia, the slight difference in spelling is unimportant and Orpen argued that the settlement was called after the French/Belgian region which had sheltered Labraid Loingsech. Manapia has usually been identified with present day Wexford town, but Orpen, encouraged by Sir John Rhys in his *Studies in Early Irish History*, argues that Arklow is a far more logical location. This, and other possible associations that are far too complex to go into here, led Orpen to summarise the Labraid Loingsech legend as follows:

> We can imagine Labraid the Exile ... returning to his country with an army of Galls. They land at Inver Amergin, otherwise Inver Mor, now Arklow, where they construct a cliff-castle, probably on the site occupied centuries later by the Northmen, and still later by Tiebaut le Bottiler.[6] This cliff-castle and the port which it protected was called by the traders who informed Ptolemy, 'Manapia' meaning the town of the Manapians; but the people themselves became known in Ireland as Galiáin or Galions and their cliff-fort at a later period as Rath Inver. To conquer Leinster they would inevitably pass up the valley between the mountains of Wicklow and Wexford to the open country in the neighbourhood of Rathgall. Here they built their great *dún* ... called from them Dun Galion. According to the legend they slay their master's rival and plant their master on the throne of Leinster. They become known as "the best fighting men in Leinster".

Orpen refers to how these warriors, with their distinctive broad-headed spears (*laighne,* from which we get the Irish name for Leinstermen, *Laigin*), got involved in Queen Medb's conquest for the Donn of Cuailgne, and how they fought in the legendary battle of Rosnaree against the Ulstermen, and how they went on to form close ties with Foinn Mac Cumhall and the Fíanna. All entertaining stuff, and all as provable as Goldilocks and the Three Bears. That is not to say that it *didn't* happen that way, but you'll notice that the above excerpt starts with the get-out clause 'We can imagine ...'. In all honesty, that is about all we can do when dealing with the ages that constitute our prehistory. These eras are littered with probablys, possiblys, plausiblys and maybes, and festooned with an abundance of don't-knows. We can create as many mosaics and kaleidoscopes from the fragments as we wish, but the bottom line still terminates in a question mark.

Before leaving Orpen and his identification of modern Arklow as the location of Manapia, I must point out that his argument never really caught on and, despite his best efforts, most antiquarians still opt for Wexford. Nevertheless, as we shall see, over many centuries the wide estuary of the Avoca was the portal through which many foreigners entered Ireland in search of either peace or plunder, depending on their mood at the time.

*

There are, of course, several interesting archaeological curiosities in the Arklow area. The scientific study of such monuments began in the early 1800s, and over the past two centuries surveys and studies have been carried out with varying degrees of competence and success. The following is a brief round-up of the region's archaeological heritage.

While they withhold more secrets than they surrender, 'the presence of standing stones, burials and rock art in the Avoca area suggests an expansion of settlement in the Early Bronze Age'[7], that is about 2000-1700 BC. The nineteenth century antiquarian G.H. Kinahan referred to the 'particularly simple version of rock art to be seen in the Wicklow/Wexford area'.[8] Cups and grooves in rock faces are well weathered, but distinctive enough to discount their being the result of natural causes. Kinahan also recorded ancient graves, usually urn burials, at Killahurler, Kilninor, Ballynabarney and Kilcashel.[9]

The construction of the Arklow by-pass in the late 1990s significantly increased our knowledge of prehistoric Arklow. This stemmed from the legislative measures which demand archaeological monitoring of major public works. As topsoil was stripped away along the route of the new road, qualified personnel watched for tell-tale signs of ancient activity. Several sites were identified and deemed worthy of excavation, and by far the most interesting of these was a known enclosure at Johnstown South, at the northern end of the proposed by-pass.[10] This site had been recognised as one of archaeological interest in the early nineteenth century and was included on the first edition of the Ordnance Survey map in 1838 as a subcircular enclosure. It consisted of a series of low banks of earth about half-a-metre high and roughly ten metres wide, enclosing an area about thirty-six metres north-south and thirty-three metres east-west.

The excavation was carried out between January 13th and September 1st, 1997. Initial work showed that farming practices over the ages had greatly disturbed the upper layers of soil. Prehistoric pottery rested at the same depth as coins from the nineteenth century. Large boulders and swathes of stone were too disturbed and irregular to say if they had once constituted walls, but large amounts of worked flint and pottery suggested that this was a major site.

Burnt bones bore testimony to human cremation, and a stone-lined cremation pit, constructed of four uprights and a capstone, was uncovered. Two unlined pits were also found. Some of the pottery was cord-impressed, a form of decoration achieved by pressing cord into the still wet clay of a pot yet to be hardened by fire. The patterns formed are more attractive than this rather prosaic description of the process might suggest.

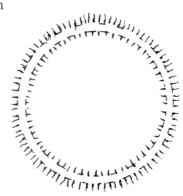

There is no need to go into every detail of the site here. The main point I'm making is that this was a major centre of activity. Over four thousand artefacts were recovered. The majority were mere fragments of coarseware pottery and various flint pieces, but there were quite a few intact artefacts as well. One of these was a bronze ring pin, another a bronze penannular brooch.

Ringfort at Johnstown South

While it may be hazardous to predict specific dates for Johnstown South based on the pottery, it appears that the pottery finds would agree with the dates given for other artefacts identified, i.e. principally Bronze Age with activity into the medieval period.

Preliminary sorting of flints prior to specialist attention indicates that the majority of pieces are flakes and cores; however, among the artefact assemblage there are hollow-based arrowheads, scrapers, blades, a barbed and tanged arrowhead and a leaf-shaped arrowhead. Flint finds were common throughout the site but were particularly concentrated in an area which extended from Quadrant C to Quadrant D. Here large quantities of flint débitage were recovered, suggesting that this may have been a flint-knapping area.[11]

Mould fragments show that cast wear was also produced along with the flint weaponry and tools. These, and the presence of two furnace pits and considerable heaps of slag (the solid scum on heated and worked metal), indicate just how active this site was three thousand years ago and place it well in the running as the region's oldest Industrial Park.

Nearby, in the adjoining townland of Johnstown North, another excavation in the summer of 1997 uncovered a *fulacht fiadh*. This was a pit which was filled with water in which the rewards of a good day's hunting were boiled. The animal carcase would be butchered into manageable pieces and a fire lit beside the *fulacht fiadh*. Close to hand would be a supply of stones. As the temperature of the fire increased the stones were placed in it until they became extremely hot, at which point they were transferred into the water-pit until the water reached boiling point. It might seem laborious and time-consuming, but experiments have shown the technique to have been almost as efficient as modern electric or gas cooking. These pits fell out of favour with the invention of cooking pots, and over the centuries they slowly filled with earth, disappearing from the landscape. What betrays them to the trained eye is the small mound of shattered stones, the discarded debris which split on the sudden transfer from the heat of the fire to the coldness of the water. These sherds would have been removed from the bottom of the pit and laid to one side, building over time into a small mound. At this particular site three troughs, eight fire hearths, and about a hundred stake- and post-holes were uncovered. No doubt the smell of boiling meat was carried on the breeze to the workers a few hundred yards away in Johnstown South, whetting their appetites as they watched the sun sinking towards knocking-off time.

Did these workers go straight home each evening, or did they stop off on the way? I ask this because two other pits and three troughs were also found nearby. Like the *fulacht fiadh,* they contained splintered fragments of burnt stone, obviously used to heat water, but the absence of animal bone or other debris associated with a cooking site suggests that our ancient ancestors were partial to the occasional sauna or session in a sweat-house.[12] So, imagine the scene three or four thousand years ago. Artisans knock off work after a hard day's flint-knapping and adjourn to the local sweat-house where they gripe about the basic wage, the unfair return for piece work, and the drop in the demand for arrowheads because of a Good Friday Agreement recently thrashed out between two local tribes.

Despite plenty of food and healthy saunas, death could not be kept at bay indefinitely and at Templerainey another 1997 excavation uncovered three sites, each containing evidence of burials.[13] Pits, some surrounded by stone protection, were found to contain charcoal and cremated bone. Pottery sherds and worked flint, perhaps from the local factory, are of the 'Beaker and Food Vessel' type associated with the

Bronze Age, and there were enough of them to suggest that this site may have been a cemetery.

Of course, some artefacts of archaeological importance had been discovered long before the Arklow by-pass was dreamed of. In the townland of Castletimon, lying by the roadside amid briars, brambles and nettles, is one of only four Ogham stones in the county. As such it is of immense archaeological importance, yet all that marks it out is a small, rusting metal notice warning all who come across it that the stone is a National Monument and that any damage inflicted on it will be avenged by the full rigours of the law. To accommodate potential vandals who may be bi-lingual, this decree is in both Irish and English. What the sign doesn't tell you is *why* this half-hidden stone is a National Monument, or what the lines on it mean. About seventy years ago, there was a debate in the chamber of Wicklow County Council as to whether the stone should be removed from where it lay on the roadside to somewhere safer, as 'it was only a matter of time before it would be unintentionally or wantonly damaged or broken'.[14] Some of the representatives felt it should be moved to Bray, others preferred Wicklow, but there was also the sound argument of leaving it where it had been for centuries, which is what happened. But couldn't it be kept free of undergrowth? And how much would it cost to have an explanatory plaque erected beside the useless threatening one?

Ogham stones are so-called after the ancient script which has been

Castletimon Ogham Stone (Commissioners of Public Works)

carved into them, and ogham script takes its name from Ogmios, the Celtic god of writing. It is based on the composition of straight, sometimes angled lines better suited for carving in hard materials such as stone or wood than for writing on skin or parchment. It is believed to have come into use in Ireland about AD 300. The Castletimon stone was first recorded by T.C. Tuomey in the early 1850s. A keen antiquarian, he carefully recorded all its dimensions, the many facets of its irregular shape, its size, and the position and sequence of the ogham marks in what was later described as a model piece of archaeological description. Mr Tuomey was meticulous,[15] but no sense could be made of the inscription. In a follow-up article,[16] it was suggested that he had copied the ogham script in reverse and the following text was then deciphered:

> NETACAR I SETACAG I   which can be punctuated as
> NE, TACAR ISE TACAG I   which means
> NE, BATTLE HE HAD PROSPERITY IN

NE was a personal name, so it would appear that this stone marked the grave of a warrior – one who had prospered in battle. Unfortunately, that is the extent of our knowledge, but should we let that stand in the way of a good story? I think not ……

There is something in the human psyche that dislikes blank pages. What we lack in knowledge, we are constantly tempted to compensate for with conjecture and imagined answers. This is where art comes into its own, and one of the oldest Irish art forms is storytelling. The gaps archaeologists and historians cannot fill become the space in which the storyteller thrives. Tuomey records a local legend which says that the ogham stone was kicked to the spot where it now lies by a sports-loving giant standing on Castletimon Hill, the ogham letters were the indentations left by his fingers. I suggest that his handling as well as kicking the stone shows that he favoured the Gaelic code over soccer – unless, of course, he happened to have been a goalkeeper.

A long-forgotten poet had another explanation, one more in keeping with the possibility of its being a grave stone. To him, the effort, time, and skill expended in carving the text could only be justified if the person it commemorated was nothing less than the princess lover of a warrior rather than the warrior himself. He even knew her name, Maeve.

The Grave of the Princess

Where Castletimon's rugged heights stand sentinel by the wave
Long, long ago a princess dwelt where still is shown her grave.
Her father o'er a verdant land for many years held sway,
And proud his banner floated on the shores of Brittas Bay.

Maeve's hair was like the ripening corn, a wave 'neath autumn skies
Her face was fair as any flower that in the woodland lies;
Her voice was sweet as mountain stream low rippling in its way,
Her brow was white as breakers' foam adrift on Brittas Bay.

And e'en the druid in his grave, sunk deep in mystic lore,
Dreamt of her smile when twilight crept o'er Castletimon's shore.
Like moonbeams on the glistening wave she inspired the poet's lay,
He saw her eyes in the stars that shone o'er lovely Brittas Bay.

From far and near rich suitors came and sought her hand to gain.
Strive as they might, she heeded not – their pleadings were in vain.
But one she loved, young Donagh bold, whose pennon led the way,
Where her father's war-boats cleft the waves of lovely Brittas Bay.

They met in secret when the moon sailed over land and sea,
They lingered where the shadows slept beneath a spreading tree.
Along the path of youth and love their willing footsteps stray.
'Twas like the path the moonbeams wore o'er lovely Brittas Bay.

But came the day when warriors brave were gathered on the strand,
'To ship! To ship!' the captains cried, 'for distant Albion's land'.
And foremost of that gallant band, young Donagh sailed away,
And left his love a-mourning him by lonely Brittas Bay.

Now, as the weary months went passed, from Castletimon Hill
The princess fair watched o'er the waves, her anguish never still.
Until at last far out to sea one golden autumn day,
She spied the war-boats speeding back to lovely Brittas Bay.

She hastened down the rocky slope and waited on the shore,
And soft her fond heart whispered 'My love, we'll part no more'.
But soon, alas, her hopes were crushed for gallant Donagh lay
Dead on the field of battle far from Brittas Bay.

She listened to the dreadful tale like one that's turned to stone.
She questioned not the tidings grim nor uttered cry nor moan.

One wild last look she cast around o'er land and tossing spray,
Then lifeless sank upon the beach of lonely Brittas Bay.

They hollowed out her quiet grave where stands the Ogham stone,
And left her in her long last rest beyond the breakers' moan.
And there upon the green hillside by moonbeam's sickly ray,
The druid carved her epitaph by lonely Brittas Bay.

Since then the centuries have rolled back the abyss of years,
And changing destinies have swayed this land to smiles or tears.
Yet when the moonbeams on the wave in magic beauty play,
The princess still her vigil keeps by lonely Brittas Bay.

When twilight shadows softly creep o'er Castletimon Hill
True lovers wander by her grave and dream as lovers will.
When the wind sings through the trees, sending forth a plaintive lay
They whisper 'Maeve still mourns her love' by lonely Brittas Bay.[17]

And there we have it; not a mention of Ne, nor does the brave-hearted warrior of the piece appear to have being particularly prosperous in battle. Why didn't Mr Tuomey's extremely detailed report tell us about the beautiful Maeve and her brave but beaten hero? Didn't he know there is more to life than measuring tapes, hand trowels and cold clinical fact?

The reference to 'the druid in his grave' at the beginning of the third verse probably alludes to the portal tomb, or dolmen, in the adjacent townland of Brittas, which I have been reliably informed is known to the locals – or at least those of them who know it exists at all – as The Druid's Altar.[18] Sadly, the poet was too wrapped up in the pangs of a love story to tell us more about the druid and his sacred table, but the seemingly indefatigable Liam Price wrote about it in 1934:

> ...... this was an isolated settlement being six or seven miles from any other site, even of the Bronze Age; it stands about a mile from the sand-hills which form the sea-shore, and was probably surrounded by uninhabited wood and marshy country. Such a site accessible only from the sea, and probably in a natural clearing in the wooded country, may have been chosen by the early settlers because they would get a plentiful supply of fish there.......[19]

> The Brittas dolmen has been very much damaged. The capstone measures twelve feet by twelve feet and is three feet thick. It has fallen into a sloping position on the north side of the uprights, four of which

The Brittas Dolmen   (N. O'Cléirgh)

are standing, forming a chamber seven feet by four feet. The tallest of
the uprights, that on the south side, is eight feet high above the floor of
the chamber. The stone to the north side of the chamber, on which the
capstone is resting, is a slab of white quartz shaped like a wedge or
mitre. The structure is so ruined that it is hard to say which way the
chamber faced.[20]

Despite its poor condition, Price did make a few educated guesses as
to the significance of the dolmen, although in the light of the more
recent discoveries of sites at Johnstown North and South some of these,
such as the supposed isolation of the site, must be called into question.

Less impressive, and equally mute, are two unclassified tombs from
the Bronze Age, one at Ballycoog and the other at Glenart. It is difficult
to date such ancient monuments as their style changed little over
centuries, but experts suggest that these date from sometime in the two
millennia before Christ.[21] Many ancient graves have been destroyed. In
1882, G.H. Kinahan recorded that a smith named Sullivan had been
digging in the Killahurler Moat. Sullivan expected to find treasure and
was no doubt disappointed to unearth nothing more financially
rewarding than a pottery urn. This was a time of field enlargements and
other developments which required the removal of ditches. In several

cases, the clearing away of hedges uncovered items of great archaeological interest, such as the Kish hoard mentioned below and Stone and Bronze Age burials. When it came to be known that many of these graves contained an urn, a belief was developed that if the urn was opened at the "right time", which was of course midnight, the finder would gaze upon gold. If, however, the urn was opened at any other time the gold would dissolve into ash.[22] In such cases the urns were smashed in anger, frustration or sheer bloody-mindedness, but at least the cats of the area could breathe a sigh of relief, for another belief stated that if treasure were found a cat must be killed to ward off bad luck.

One grave that deserves particular mention here is the one found at Kilmichael Point in June 2002. Pat Power, who has done so much for the history of not only Arklow but of the county in general, was one of a team of seven who excavated it. The following paragraphs are taken from, or based on, his four page interim report.

> For several months throughout 2001 an unusual pattern of stone was observed in an eroding sea cliff at Kilmichael Point... ... it [proved to be] a cist grave.
> Following the record breaking wet month of May it was noted that the cliff site of the grave was becoming very unstable and there was a danger that the whole lot would collapse into the sea. Historian and author, Fiachra Ó Lionáin, contacted Dúchas in late May... [who] gave permission for the grave to be excavated.
> Work commenced on the afternoon of June 17.[23]

The report goes into detail of how the excavation was carried out, the state of the grave, and what it contained, the types of soil, flint fragments and a matrix of marl. It is not possible to quote the four pages verbatim here, so I will get to the main item found.

> In a particularly wet part of the clay, under the protective cover of a large pebble lay what appeared to be a curiously marked rounded stone ... this was in fact no stone but portion of an Early Bronze Age burial artifact. The question now was the object still intact? ... Hemmed in by stone and clay it took over an hour of delicate brush and trowel work to ... fully expose the object which fortunately was intact, and considering its long interment, in pristine condition.

This was a remarkable find by any standards. The bowl measures five inches high, five inches across its mouth tapering to five-and-a-half inches around the middle before tapering again to three-and-a-half inches at the base. It was highly decorated. The bowl was taken to the National Museum for further examination and, at time of writing, the final report is still pending, but initial response is that it is approximately four thousand years old and in 'its excellent state of preservation was very important to the national collection of ancient artefacts'. There are plans to have a replica made for display in Castletown.

This rescue of such an important artefact reflects credit on all concerned. The team, consisting of Fiachra Ó Lionáin, Fr Eugene McCarney, Pat Power, Brian Byrne, Peter O'Toole, Pat Kinsella and Shane Kinsella, deserve even greater thanks for not smashing the bowl when it was found to contain no gold.

So much for the accommodation of the dead, let's get back to the needs of the living. Just south of the river at Arklow, a *fulacht fiadh* has been found,[24] while a hoard of Bronze Age artefacts were found at the Kish in the nineteenth century. A socketed spearhead, two axeheads,

The Kilmichael Bowl, discovered In June 2002.(Courtesy Pat Power)

and a knife were uncovered when a field fence was removed.[25] These artefacts are now in the National Museum.

Within the modern town boundaries, on or near the Ferrybank site now occupied by the Methodist church, there once stood a mound of earth. In his report to the Ordnance Survey Office written in Arklow on January 31st, 1839, Thomas O'Conor referred to a 'green mound in which, whilst it was digging and carrying away for manuring land, there were found some sepulchral urns containing ashes and bones partly consumed by fire. Several pieces of broken urns are still visible on the spot'.[26] This would appear to have been a Bronze Age burial mound and, as Pat Power has written,

> The Ferrybank mound was the oldest recorded man-made object we are aware of in the urban confines of Arklow, and its builders may have established for the first time continuous residence in and about that area.[27]

*

The Iron Age, the name given to that period which stretched from about 600 BC to the Early Christian Era a thousand years later, is the Age we perhaps most associate with the Celtic tribes of Ireland. It was during this time that these people crossed from Britain or France, bringing with them their technical skills with iron, with which they fashioned their agricultural tools and weapons of war. The bronze swords, daggers and spears of the indigenous tribes were no match for the newer, harder, sharper weapons of iron. Likewise, the relatively simple cup shapes and circles that decorated grave stones were primitive compared to the complexity of the Celtic style we call La Téne.

A typical Celtic homestead from the Iron Age consisted of a number of buildings grouped inside a defensive ring of earth, on the outside of which was a trench from which the earth to form the ring had been taken. Attackers would have to cross this trench, or ditch, before clambering over the ring, thus giving the defenders a double height advantage. Evidence suggests that the circular bank would have been topped by a wooden palisade. These features dot the Irish countryside and are variously known as ringforts, raths and raheens and they are remembered in many placenames. Thousands have been destroyed in recent decades, and the rate of destruction looks set to continue as the superstitious belief in their being 'fairy forts' is replaced by a modern scepticism fuelled by either economic need or greed. It is to be hoped that a new appreciation of these ancient monuments will encourage landowners to preserve them for their cultural and heritage value to the same degree as their forebears had been eager to avoid the displeasure of the fairies.

There are several ringforts within a ten miles radius of Arklow.[28] Most if not all are on private land. Those who are really interested can locate them easily enough with a bit of research, those who just want to tramp around other people's property won't get the chance of blaming me for guiding them there.

The foregoing is simply a mish-mash of fact and fable to show that there has been human activity in the Arklow area for thousands of years. That we know very little about those ancient people does not negate their lives one iota. They are as much part of Arklow's historical tapestry as we are.

And with that, I think it is time to venture into the ever-so-slightly less mist-filled Early Christian Era.

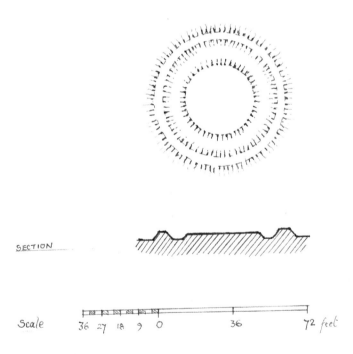

SECTION

Scale   36   27   18   9   0   36   72 *feet*

The Round-O Ringfort at Ballygahan

2

Saints, Septs and Scandinavians:
400 – 1169

Every year, on March 17th, hundreds of thousands of people up and down the country celebrate their Irishness. Across the globe, millions of Irish emigrants and descendants of emigrants take part in parades, dress in green, wear real or imitation shamrock, play Irish music, drink green beer and generally behave in a way that would make them cringe on any other day of the year. This is St Patrick's Day, this is Ireland's Day, a day in which the edges of nationality and religion blur and bleed into each other.

From our earliest schooldays we learn how a young Roman Briton was captured as a slave and spent six years on an Antrim mountainside herding sheep and pigs. We are also told how he made his escape by heading south to a small port where he boarded a ship bound for France with a mixed cargo which included wolfhounds. I once read that that small port was where Arklow now stands. Unfortunately, I read it a long, long time ago and haven't the faintest idea where. Could it be true?

In his paper 'Kings, Saints and Sagas',[1] Alfred P. Smyth quotes the seventh century writer Muirchú Moccu Machthéni as referring to pre-Viking Arklow as 'a harbour of some repute among us called Inber Dee'. Smyth believes this port benefited from a lucrative trade in goods exported to and imported from Britain. These goods were carried over the mountains to the richer centres of royal power at Naas, Rathangan and elsewhere. Such trade included hunting dogs, furs and wool being shipped out in exchange for 'luxury goods for the warlords of Leinster and beyond'. The transportation of slaves would have been part of this commercial activity. So, was the story I once came across correct? Did Patrick make his way south and escape through the port that would become Arklow? If it is true, why did he travel 150 miles or more? Surely there were other ports along the coast that offered the same opportunity for escape?

Wherever he left from is really irrelevant. What we do know is that he could not rid his mind of the people who had enslaved him. He felt called upon to return to Ireland and spread the Christian doctrine. He studied for the priesthood, was ordained, and returned in 432. From that time until his death in 461 or 493, depending on which source you choose to believe, he travelled around the country converting thousands of people to Christianity. He is now hailed as the Apostle of Ireland, an icon of unchallengeable stature.

When all the hype, stories, legends and assumptions are stripped away, there is really very little evidence to tell us when he was born, where he came from, when he died, or where he is buried. Conflicting opinion states he was either Welsh or from the north-west English town of Carlisle. The little we do know is taken mainly from his own *Confessions* and *Letter to Coroticus*, and although these are regarded as genuine fifth century works about a real personality, scholars over the centuries have argued and debated over who this man was. There are even grounds for believing that there was more than one Patrick. One thing is fairly certain – at least as certain as we can be about anything from that period – Patrick may have been the most successful Christian missionary to Ireland, but he was not the first.[2]

In 431, the year before Patrick returned filled with the zeal of a missionary, Pope Celestine I sent a man named Palladius as bishop to minister to the needs of Christians in Ireland. This not only suggests that there were already Christians here before 431 but also that there were enough of them to warrant the appointment of a bishop. The really important thing about this, as far as this book is concerned, is there must have been quite a few in the Arklow area, because according to the ninth century Tripartite *Life* of Patrick, Palladius is recorded as landing at Inber Dee, a former name for the area we now call Arklow.[3] That seems straightforward enough, but of course nothing is straightforward in the mists of prehistory. Not even the identification of Inber Dee with Arklow. One of Ireland's foremost nineteenth century antiquarians, John O'Donovan, stated that 'all who have written on the subject agree that Wicklow is the ancient Inbhear Deaa'.[4] O'Donovan, it seems, was not shy about making sweeping generalisations because a little research soon reveals that *not* 'all who have written on the subject agree that Wicklow is the ancient Inbhear Deaa'. There are those who say Wicklow and those who say Arklow, and this explains the rival claims of Arklow and Wicklow people when it comes to Palladian or Patrician legends. Arklow, however, would seem to have one major point in its favour when it claims to be Inber (or Ostium) Dee.

> In a Latin *Life of St Kevin,* it is stated that Glendalough was formerly known as 'Gleand Dée', the Glen of the Dée, the Dée being the Avonmore river, which runs into Arklow [5]

and, logically, Inber Dee, the estuary of the Dée, was a former name of Arklow. As we shall see, there are others who share this view.

The Tripartite *Life* tells us that Palladius established three churches in what is now County Wicklow. One is believed to have been at Donard, one at Redcross and the third went by the name of Tech na Roman. There seems to be more or less general assent regarding the first two, but Tech na Roman is more elusive. Liam Price wrote that 'If such a church existed, it does not seem to be possible to identify it'.[6] It has been suggested from time to time that Tigroney is a corruption of Tech na Roman, but Price believes that Tigroney is derived from Tigh Cróinin, meaning Cronin's house. 'Cronin was another name of Mochua, *Cill Mochua*, the present townland of Kilmacoo, adjoins Tigroney'. Whatever the truth of these conjectures, Palladius didn't hang around this area for long. According to the *Dictionary of Irish Biography*, he had 'little success and was forced to leave within a few months, dying in Scotland the same year'. It was time to bring on the big guns.

If we are to believe the legend that Patrick escaped through the port of Arklow, it seems a bit of a coincidence, to say the least, that when he returned as a missionary, he made landfall in exactly the same place. There is, of course, the possibility that he actually did this as a symbolic flourish, a dramatic statement that the place of his last contact with Pagan Ireland should also be the place of his first contact with Christian Ireland. As you will have gathered by now, the lack of hard evidence does not hamper speculation, it encourages it. For example ......

> In the year 432 Patrick came to Ireland as a bishop. At that time it took three or four months to travel from one country to another ...... During

their long voyage, their supply of water ran out. St Patrick was in much distress on hearing this but to their great relief they sighted land. They sailed towards it and it was Arklow Rock. St Patrick was the first to come ashore and where his foot touched a well sprang up. This is to be seen to the present day.[7]

This was St Patrick's Well marked on the Ordnance Survey maps and referred to in Price's *Place-Names of County Wicklow,* but it is not the only well he is supposed to have created or blessed in the area. Toberpatrick, on the west side of Croghan, and St Patrick's Well in Tinahely are also said to have direct contact with him. Unfortunately, these legends, unlike the wells in question, don't hold water. It is now generally accepted that St Patrick's mission took place across the northern half of the country and it is unlikely that he ever visited this area. If this is so, how did these stories come about?   There is a reference in a manuscript written in about the year 700 which states that

> St. Patrick arrived *in regiones Coolennorum* to a port called *Ostium Dee;* this was an old name for the place now called Arklow [8]

but some experts have placed the *regiones Coolennorum* at the time of Patrick in the plains of Kildare and that the people who lived there did not move into the Arklow area until about the eighth century. Once again, the bottom line is nobody *knows*. We can guess and we can summarise, we can theorise and hypothesise as much as we like. Nothing can be proved one way or the other.

But surely we can believe the best known of the Patrician legends in this area - the stoning of the missionaries until they got back into their boats and sailed further north? According to that story, one of the band was hit in the mouth with a stone, knocking all his teeth out. Deeming discretion the better part of valour, Patrick and his entourage took to their boats and headed north, stopping next at what is now Wicklow. Their reception there seems to have been kinder and the Dentally Challenged Disciple decided that it was here that he would build his church. Because of his new gummy state, he was given the name Mantán, Toothless One, and his church was Cill Mhantáin, which to this day is the Irish name of Wicklow town and county. Another version of the tale says that the attack and resultant injury took place at Wicklow – again based on the identification of Inber Dee as Wicklow and not

Arklow. Price believes that it never took place at all and the tale is 'an obvious invention, intended to account for the name Cill Mhantáin'.[9]

Whether all this is fact, fiction, or a tangle of both, Christianity had come to this neck of the woods in the fifth century and over the next few centuries Christian activity got under way. Five miles north of the town, at Ennereilly, St Dagan established a religious centre in the sixth century. Dagan is said to have been a member of the sept descended from Labraid Loingsech who, you might remember, returned from exile to claim his inheritance about 300 BC. Dagan's mother was Caoiltigherna, a sister of Caoimghín, better known to us as St Kevin of Glendalough. Noel O'Cléirigh has written

> The references to Dagan in other saints' lives show with what respect he was regarded and he is probably the Bishop Dagan who went to Britain about 608 AD to meet Italian bishops.[10]

There is a tradition that people with head or throat complaints pray to Dagan. This stems from the legend that Dagan was decapitated at some time in his life – but not, you will be surprised to learn, at the end of it. While decapitation can be normally depended upon to result in more or less instant death, this expected outcome was circumvented by the rapid reaction of a priestly colleague who is said to have prayed over the stricken saint until life returned. I can't vouch for whether the head or the body was the first to exhibit this miraculous regeneration, or if they both twitched at the same time, nor can I hazard a guess as to how the one was re-attached to the other, but perhaps it is best not to enquire too deeply into such inexplicable goings-on. Enough to say, Dagan got well, but such a literally hair-raising experience was bound to leave its mark and Dagan became the possessor of a circular scar around his neck, thereby marking him out as just the man to consult about your tonsillitis, sinusitis, headache or hangover. Remains of an ancient church, but highly unlikely to be old enough to have been built in Dagan's time, can still be seen at Ennereilly graveyard.

A little further north is Ennisboyne, a corruption of Inis Baoithin, or Baoithin's Island. Baoithin was another holy individual of high birth, reputedly being a grandson of Ronán mac Colmain, King of Leinster.[11] It is amazing how many of our ancient holy men were linked to principal tribal houses. This linking of spiritual and temporal riches seems to forewarn of the Norman habit of later centuries of first building a castle and then a monastery, as we shall see. Ennisboyne was well known to the compilers of ancient manuscripts, such as the *Book of Leinster* and *The Annals of the Four Masters*. From these and other sources, Noel O'Cléirigh has remarked

> It is recorded in the Life of St Patrick that relics of St Silvester and St Solonius, companions of St Palladius, were brought from the church of Donard in west Wicklow to Ennisboyne and were held there in great honour. Nothing is known of what subsequently happened to these relics. The people of the district have always had great veneration for St Silvester and his name has been widely used in the locality as a baptismal name.

The fame of these foundations, and the possible presence of relics, may well have been instrumental in their eventual downfall.

Other monastic sites, hermitages or early churches are recorded in such local placenames as Kilmacoo, Kilcashel, Kilmagig, Kilbixy, Kilmurry, Kilpatrick, Kilbegnet, Kildermot, Kilcavan, Kilowen, Killybegs and Kilgorman. There is, however, a danger of ascribing all placenames with the prefix 'Kil' to an ancient church, but in some cases 'Kil' is a derivative of *Coill*, meaning a wood, as in Killiskeyduff – *Coill an uisce dhuibh* - 'the wood of the black water', or Killeagh – *Coill liath* or *coilleach* – 'the grey wood' or 'wooded land'. Even when the association with a church is correct, some of them might date from a much later period. Having said that, many do date from the early Christian era. I have purposely omitted Kilbride from the above list, which may seem strange as it is the only one actually inside the modern town boundary, but I want to return to this most interesting and important of Arklow sites in due course.

*

Who were the septs who inhabited this area in the period under review, 400 to 800? Several of the ancient manuscripts of Ireland contain genealogies explaining the origins of various septs or *túatha* and their geographical areas of control. By the fifth century, the ruling dynasty in what is now County Wicklow, as well as parts of Carlow and Kildare, were the Dal Messin Corb. This was subdivided into smaller septs or *túatha*. By the seventh century, their star was in the descendent and some of the component septs were staking their own claims to land.

One of these subgroups was the Uí Enechglais Cualann who controlled the territory from roughly Ennereilly to Castletown-Inch. They probably came to this area from the western side of the Wicklow mountains, expelled from the richer lands of Kildare, in the early 500s. They are believed to have been descended from Enechglas, one of the sons of Cathair Mór. Enechglas received a gift of ships from his father, indicating that he and his followers were coastal dwellers.[12]

Texts dealing with the Ireland of that time, and with the conflicts and concerns of the various *túatha*, are general in their approach. There is very little, if anything, specifically to do with this region. On the other hand, there is no reason to suspect that the local situation differed greatly to what pertained nationally. To give a glimpse of Arklow life styles at that time, therefore, I can do no more than summarise Professor Donncha Ó Corráin's *Ireland before the Normans,*[13] which explains the political divisions as well as the social and economic structures of those long-gone people.

Any ideas of egalitarianism should be dispensed with immediately. Irish society was hierarchical with the 'upper orders' despising those they considered beneath them. The social strata of local lord, landlords, tenants, cottiers, serfs and slaves we tend to associate with other European cultures, and later times in Ireland under English and British rule, were as evident and as stringent in pre-Viking and pre-Norman Ireland as they were anywhere. These classifications and subclassifications were enshrined in the legislative code. Slaves were so common a feature in all communities that words denoting them were a recognised legal unit of value. A female slave was a *cumal*, and a male slave was a *mug* – are we picking up nuances of meaning echoing down the centuries when we say "no one's going to make a mug out of me"?

The trade in slaves was supplied mainly through the taking of prisoners of war or straightforward kidnapping. The vanquished on the field of battle were spared only if they were likely to be of monetary value to the victors. This value could be realised either through ransom, if the captive was an important secular or clerical figure to his people, or if he or she was strong enough, dextrous enough, or – dare I say it – attractive enough to fetch a good price on the slave market. The greatest supply of slaves seemed to have come from Britain, but other routes into slavery were also recorded in the annals. For example, in times of famine, 'fathers sold their sons and daughters for food'.[14]

Before we throw our hands up in horror at the grotesqueness of such an outrageous suggestion, perhaps we should give our ancient ancestors the benefit of the doubt and consider the possibility of those fathers taking the desperate measure to ensure that their children would be fed and thus survive the prevailing crisis. It is highly likely that an import/export centre such as Inber Dee/Inbhear Mór/Arklow would have seen not only its fair share of slaves passing between Britain and the richer regions of the Irish hinterland, but that a few would also have remained in this locality.

There was plenty of work for the slaves, serfs, cottiers, and farmers to do. Corn and milk were the staples, and we can assume that in Arklow fish was also a major part of the diet. Vegetable gardens were not unknown and livestock was vital not only as foodstuff but as currency.

> Land was measured in terms of the number of cows it could maintain, legal compensations were reckoned in terms of cattle; a man's standing in society was determined by his wealth and cattle-raiding was a recognised form of warfare and adventure for young nobles.[15]

Wild boar, badgers, birds and deer were hunted, but Ó Corráin believes that such pursuits were, in the main, for sport rather than economic necessity. Besides, the flesh of wild beasts was not as tasty as that of domestic animals. Rivers and lakes teemed with fish, and the Avoca was known as a salmon fishery right into the late Middle Ages. Sea-fishing was another source of food and means of barter. Ancient shells recovered from archaeological digs show that harvesting of limpets, periwinkles, oysters, scallops, cockles and mussels was common. Curraghs, not unlike those of the western seaboard today, were the favoured type of craft.

Apart from catching fish, these vessels were used to travel to England, Wales and Scotland. Irish monks had even sailed these boats to settle as far away as Iceland. Tales of these wandering clerics are recounted in old texts, the best known of these being the *Navigationis Brendani*, which records the voyages of St Brendan the Navigator. In 1977, Tim Severn proved that it was possible to reach Newfoundland in such a boat, using a stepping-stone route which would have been known to sixth century monks.[16] 'Secular society was equally sea-minded' and journeys back and forth across the Irish Sea were regular occurrences. Mention has already been made of Ptolemy's map, the compiler of which knew of Irish ports as early as the second century. These harbours were also known to the Roman historian Tacitus (c. AD 55-c.120), based on information received from traders, and it is clear that the Biscay ports were engaged in an extensive wine trade with Early Christian Ireland.[17]

This, then, was a well-organised society. Its people were aware of the wider world and, perhaps more importantly, the wider world was aware of them. Little wonder that their presence should attract the attention of unwelcome, as well as welcome, visitors. And the most unwelcome of all were about to make their appearance – the Scandinavian Vikings.

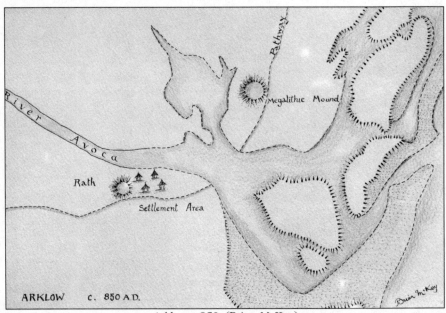

Arklow c.850 (Brian McKay)

*

From their settlements in the Orkneys and Hebrides, Norse raiding parties turned their attention to Ireland in the dying years of the eighth century. While there is evidence – and logic would also suggest - that the northeast coast was the first to feel the brunt, the first recorded raid took place on Lambay Island off County Dublin when the church there was burned in the year 795.[18] From their far north bases, it made little difference to them if they sailed south down the east coast of Ireland or around the top and down the west coast. What was important was their choice of target – monasteries. The religious communities on Inishbofin and Inishmurray were early victims. The Scottish island of Iona, with its famous Columban monastery, was attacked by them so regularly (795, 802, and 806, when sixty-eight people were killed) that the monks decided the time had come to seek a safer haven and they moved to Kells in County Meath. By 813 even the Kerry coast was no longer immune from Viking raids. There is no reference in the annals to Viking attacks on either Ennisboyne and Ennereilly, but such attacks were possible, even likely.[19]

For some reason, there seems to have been a lull in the Norse activities for the next seven or eight years, and it was not until 821 that accounts of further Viking high jinks resume with an attack on Howth. In fact, according to Ó Corráin

> In the first quarter-century of Viking attack, only twenty-six plunderings or other acts of violence to be attributed to the Vikings, are recorded in the Irish annals. In the same period the annals record some eighty-seven acts of violence which occur amongst the Irish themselves.[20]

Based on these rather surprising figures, Ó Corráin believes the Vikings have had something of a bad press. They were not angels, but could they really have been as blood-thirsty and barbaric as we have been led to believe? Does their long-standing reputation for mindless mayhem rest on an average of one outing a year? Today's football hooligans wreak more havoc than that. Nor should it be forgotten that this was an extremely violent age and it is quite clear from the above passage that the various *túatha,* which constituted the rather fractious people of Ireland, were far from being shrinking violets. Internecine strife and tribal warfare were rampant. Shifting political boundaries, cattle-theft, kidnapping, murder and general skulduggery led to pitched battles and skirmishes on a regular basis. Monasteries, tucked into the gently undulating folds of this Land of Saints and Scholars, were in constant danger of attack from Irish warriors long before the arrival of the Vikings and long after the Vikings had been absorbed into the indigenous population. The Vikings merely added a new dimension to the general axe-swinging tendency of the time, they did not introduce it.

Up to the 830s, Norse attacks were carried out by fast-moving raiding parties who remained seaborne or, at most, set up coastal camps. From that time on, however, they became sufficiently confident to make these camps substantial enough to spend the winter in them and this allowed them to penetrate farther into the hinterland along river routes. One of these camps was here at Arklow – Inber Dee. In fact, Inber Dee has the distinction of being the first Viking base identified by name in the annals,[21] and it was from here, in 836, that the *Genti* (pagans or heathens) attacked Kildare and burned half the church settlement. Other references to the Inber Dee Norsemen between 834 and 836 'accords well with the proposed siting at Arklow'. For example, there was a raid on Glendalough in 834, Ferns in 835, Glendalough again in 836, and Ferns again in 839. One of the most worrying attacks from the Irish point of view, however, was the attack on Clonmore, on what is now the Carlow border, on Christmas Eve 835 or 836. Not alone were many murdered in this raid and many more taken as slaves, but the fact that it occurred on Christmas Eve showed two new developments. One was it showed that the Vikings must now be overwintering in their coastal camp at Inber Dee and, secondly, they were sufficiently aware of the religious routine of the Irish Christians to pick a time when they would be most vulnerable to attack.

From about 840 things seemed to have settled down and a sort of uneasy peace reigned with just occasional glitches. Which brings us to the question, is this when the Viking town of Arklow came into being, sometime in the latter half of the ninth century? We know from the above that the Vikings had a year-round camp at Inber Dee from the late 830s, but there is simply not enough evidence to say when the transition from camp to permanent settlement took place. This presents us with the task of defining just what a "town" is and how it differs from a more or less permanent settlement. Is it the permanency of its houses and communal buildings? Is it its social and political structures? An environment in which families are formed and children reared? Is it the size and density of the population? A sense of community which sees a future for itself which is worth investing in? A quick glance in an assortment of dictionaries will tell you it is all of these things, which is about as useful as telling you it is none of these things. But, consciously or subconsciously, we all have our own ideas of what constitutes a town. Liam Price was satisfied that the criteria needed to meet his definition were in place at Arklow in or around the second decade of the 900s, and he suggests that the towns of Arklow and Wicklow were established following the death of the king of the local *túatha*, Cinéad.[22]

As mentioned earlier, the local *túatha* in the Arklow area was the Uí Enechglais. They, with other *túatha* of Leinster, including the Uí Garrchon based around Wicklow, fought the battle of Cenn Fúail in 917 against the second, and apparently more determined, wave of invading Vikings. The Vikings were seemingly successful enough to maintain their foothold at both Wicklow and Arklow, but the outcome was far from conclusive and subsequent references in the annals show that the power struggle between the Norsemen and the Uí Enechglais and the Uí Garrchon continued for some time to come. After a while, however, the factions began to integrate and there is a reference in the twelfth century *Book of Rights* which suggests that, by 1103, the king of the Uí Enechglais was a Hiberno-Norse ruler, named Glún Íarainn, a direct Irish translation of the Norse name Jarnkné, "Iron Knee", who was based in Arklow.[23] A later indication of this process of integration was the proliferation in the Arklow area of the surnames Dowell, O'Dowle, O'Doylle, and other varieties of Doyle in the late sixteenth and early seventeenth centuries.[24] This is a corruption of Dubhghaill, meaning Dark Stranger, and has been identified with the Norse settlers.

The name 'Arklow' is undoubtedly Viking and it is accepted that it derives from a combination of the Norse personal name Arnkell and the word *lo*, meaning a marshy ground or meadow near water – there are several variations of the translation, but they all roughly mean the same thing, and it is topographically appropriate in this place of wide estuary and soggy land at the water's edge. Wicklow has a similar derivation, Wyking-lo, the water-meadow of the Vikings, which perhaps refers to the Murrough.[25] These settlements were, of course, originally Norse-speaking – after all, in the early stages the only inhabitants were Norse – and it is difficult to say when this changed. While it is significant that the Viking names on the towns were the forms used in Norman documents, rather than earlier Irish names, it does not necessarily mean that the inhabitants were still Norse-speaking in the twelfth, thirteenth and fourteenth centuries. Trade and social interaction with the indigenous inhabitants were bound to erode the cultural differences between the Vikings and the Irish and it would have been difficult for the Norse tongue to have survived for many generations. A more modern example of such erosion can be seen in American cities of a hundred years ago, where ethnic enclaves eventually saw their language and customs fade as their children and grandchildren became part of the wider community. Nevertheless, some words of Viking origin, apart from Arklow, have come down through the ages, usually in placenames. Killahurler and Raherd may incorporate the names of long-forgotten Arklow Vikings. Templemichael and Kilmichael might be attributable to the fact that, unlike the Vikings who arrived on our shores in the early 800s, many of the second wave of Vikings, those who arrived about 917 and later, were Christian either before they got here or after they had been in Ireland for some time, and it is recorded that they had a particular devotion to St Michael the Archangel. Doubly interesting is the fact that an earlier name on Templemichael was Gluneren, which is remarkably similar to our old friend Jarnkné's Irish name, Glún Íarainn. The Priest's Gate, the old pathway leading across the top of the Rock, probably derives from the Norse word *gata*, meaning a path or road.[26]

The impact the Vikings had on Ireland as a whole, and on the environs of their enclaves such as the Arklow area in particular, was enormous. Once the initial blood-and-guts phase was over, they showed what remarkable traders and entrepreneurs they were. Their skills in building and handling ships and boats have almost become a cliché, but that doesn't make them any less valid. Their use of keels and other technical innovations transformed the methods used in Ireland up to that time. These advances are reflected in the many Irish words related to fishing and seafaring that are obviously of Viking origin. They also introduced coinage to Ireland, setting up a mint in Dublin, and standardisation of weights and measures. On the artistic side of things, an important aspect of Viking culture often overlooked, they enriched Irish literature and introduced new methods and motifs particularly in metalwork.[27]

Bearing this in mind, it is perhaps significant that the only Viking artefacts to be found in the Arklow area were not swords or battle-axes, but two tortoise brooches and a silver chain which are said to have been found in a woman's grave somewhere between Ennisboyne and Arklow.[28] Unfortunately, the exact location of the find is unknown.

> The gentleman from whom they were purchased was not able to furnish any particulars as to the find. They had passed through two or three pairs of hands before coming into his possession.

The brooches are very ornate and attached to the chain is a tiny silver case, suitable for holding pins or needles. Arne Emil Christensen of the Viking Ship Museum at the University of Oslo believes these brooches to be typically Norse and, as it was a firm rule in Viking burial custom that people were buried near their homes, we can be sure there was a Viking settlement or homestead along that stretch of coast, and that the settlers 'came fully equipped with a family'.[29] This settlement, and those at Killahurler and Raherd, would also indicate that the Arklow Vikings were beginning to move outside the protection of the town to set up homesteads among, or at least surrounded by, their Irish neighbours. The hoard dates from the early tenth century,[30] and is now housed in the National Museum.

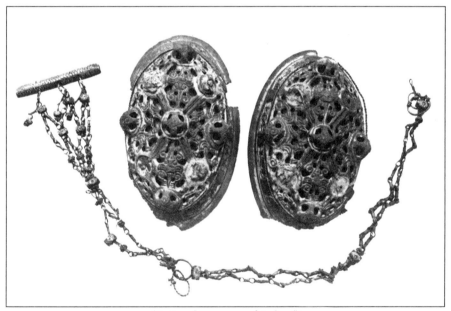

(National Museum of Ireland)

Also in the National Museum is a model of the Viking settlement at Wood Quay, Dublin. It is based on the archaeological evidence discovered during excavation and anyone interested in Arklow's history should have a look at it, for it offers an impression of what the town would have looked like at that very early stage of its development. While we have no direct evidence, logic suggests that Arnkell and his followers erected their stronghold roughly on the site the Normans later chose for their castle, overlooking that part of the river called Pollacholly or Poundacholly, which was deep enough to accommodate their low-draft ships. Pollacholly or Poundacholly is probably a corruption of the Gaelic *poll a chalaidh*, meaning 'harbour pool'. From that nucleus, the settlement grew.

By the middle of the twelfth century, integration with the Uí Enechglais would have made the port an important asset for trade between the hinterland and the markets of Dublin and perhaps further afield. Given a period of peace, the local economy might well have prospered, but no such peace was in the offing. A major shock was about to descend on the south east of Ireland; a shock that would deprive both the Hiberno-Vikings and native Irish of their political power. It was a shock that would reverberate down to the present day.

3

Businessmen and Butlers:
1169-1600

Hanging in the National Gallery in Dublin is the massive painting by Daniel MacLise depicting the marriage of Strongbow and Aoife. The artist pulled no punches in representing that marriage, that business transaction and political union, as the downfall of Celtic Ireland. Irish warriors lie dead or dying in the aftermath of battle, an ancient harper is too forlorn to play a lament. Even if he could summon the spirit the strings are broken, forever silent. Smoke engulfs a round tower, and a small church lies in ruins. The distinctive emblem of Celtic Christianity over the door – an even-sided cross inside a circle – symbolises that this is not simply a church, but the Celtic Church. In stark contrast to this desolation, Norman soldiers in gleaming armour stand proud and victorious, horsemen bear the banners of the new rulers, and trumpeters sound a fanfare welcoming the new age. And in the centre of all this mayhem and majesty, the young, optionless Aoife submits to her father's command and surrenders her hand to the Norman knight, Richard de Clare, Earl of Pembroke, known to history as Strongbow. Seldom has such a momentous occasion been caught in all its awfulness.

Aoife's father was Dermot MacMurrough, King of Leinster, a man with an amazing talent for getting himself into trouble. Dermot had been king of the province for thirty years when he was defeated in battle by the King of Connaught, losing his throne as a result. Not being the best of losers, Dermot decided to enlist the aid of mercenaries from England and Wales to help him regain his former position. He was aware that under the Norman feudal system which operated on the far side of the

Irish Sea, he would first have to ask the permission of the Norman overlord, Henry II. Henry was King of England, but was also the Count of Anjou and the Duke of Normandy, so he spent much of his time in France. In 1167, Dermot went there to put his proposal to him. Henry agreed, and he had several reasons for doing so. One was, such an enterprise would occupy some of his knights who might otherwise have too much time on their hands, time in which vague ambition might be shaped into dangerous strategy. Perhaps an even more enticing reason was, it gave Henry the opportunity to accept an offer made to him by Pope Adrian IV thirteen years earlier.

The Celtic Christian Church had long been regarded as something of a maverick by a succession of popes. While it owed nominal allegiance to Rome, papal writ didn't have much influence in this island on the edge of the known world. For decades, it was felt that something would have to be done to bring it under the heel of the Vatican. Perhaps it should not be surprising that it was an Englishman, Nicholas Breakspear, who pursued this cause with the greatest vigour. Breakspear, the son of a priest,[1] ascended the papal throne as Adrian IV in 1154. By coincidence, that was also the year in which Henry was crowned King of England. Adrian lost no time in proposing to the new king that Rome would award him the title of Lord of Ireland if he assisted in reorganising the Church there. At the time, however, Henry had enough to do to consolidate his own position in both England and France without taking on the extra burden of Ireland, and so left the offer in abeyance. Now, thirteen years later, not only was he in a better position to take it up, but here, out of the blue, was an invitation from a regional Irish king to send troops to Ireland. This was just too good to miss. Not only did he have papal approval, but he didn't even have to invade, he just had to accept an invitation to help out.

With Henry's consent, Dermot immediately sailed for Britain where he negotiated with Richard de Clare, "Strongbow". Part of the negotiated price was Dermot's promise of his daughter in marriage to Strongbow. Strongbow had never seen Aoife, so we can take it that his wish to marry her was not fired by love, lust, or infatuation. It was simply business. As a son-in-law, Strongbow would have a claim to the regained kingdom of Leinster when Dermot died.

The first detachment of Norman warriors arrived at Baginbun on the south Wexford coast in 1169. It was a small band, but their tools and techniques of war were far superior to anything the local Irish and

Hiberno-Norse had. Highly skilled archers clad in chainmail armour were more than a match for axe-swingers in woollen tunics. They quickly established a firm footing and Strongbow, now sure of success, followed this preliminary force with more knights and fighting men. It was at Waterford that he and Aoife were married. The MacMurrough-Norman warriors were unstoppable. Within a year they had taken Dublin and it seemed only a matter of time before Dermot, King of Leinster once more, would become High King of Ireland. Then, conveniently for Strongbow, Dermot died on May 1st, 1171, and Strongbow succeeded him as the Leinster king.

This development was more than Henry had bargained for and he quickly sent a letter to Strongbow to remind him not to get delusions of power. Strongbow replied,

> My lord and king, it was with your licence, as I understood, that I came over to Ireland for the purpose of helping your faithful leigeman Dermot in the recovery of his lands. Whatever lands therefore I have had the good fortune to acquire in this country, either in right of Dermot's patrimony, or from any other person, I consider to be owing to your gracious favour and I shall hold them at your free disposal.[2]

And so began the papal-sanctioned Norman conquest of Celtic Ireland.

The Normans were as efficient in the realms of business as they were on the fields of battle. With sharpened quills they divided up the spoils won by sharpened swords. The mercenaries had to be paid and that payment was funded by the redistribution of confiscated lands. The social structure in Ireland, no doubt chaotic in the eyes of the highly organised Normans, was revamped to reflect the values of the new regime. Ireland, or at least the substantial part of it that soon came under Norman rule, was divided up into baronies, usually based on one or more of the old Gaelic *túatha*. Although no longer generally used as administrative units, baronies are still referred to in legal documents as geographical areas. Meticulous records were kept, and it is at this point that the documented history of Arklow really gets under way.

*

To copperfasten his reminder that he was supreme overlord, Henry arrived in Ireland in October 1171. He confirmed Strongbow in his new position, but there were certain reservations. While acknowledging Strongbow's kingship of Leinster, Henry retained direct control of Dublin and several maritime towns and fortresses. Some accounts state that Wicklow, Arklow and Wexford were among the cherries Henry picked, but subsequent letters and grants would suggest that Strongbow retained Arklow.[3] When Strongbow died in 1176, his daughter was made a ward of court. In practice, this meant that Henry now had control of Strongbow's daughter's lands until she attained her majority or married, so whether Henry or Strongbow had retained Arklow was of little consequence - it was now in Henry's possession. In 1177, the year following Strongbow's death, Henry placed Arklow under the control of the Norman governor of Wexford.

Sometime around the year 1185, the exact date is not known, the name Theobald Walter became linked with the town and environs of Arklow. He sometimes appears as Tiebaut Walter, Theobald Fitzwalter, and several other versions of the name. He is a pivotal figure in Arklow's story, as he is the first recorded owner of the area and his descendants' deeds and land records give us a glimpse into the town's medieval history. A record of the original grant is preserved in the Ormond Deeds: -

> John, son of King Henry of England, Lord of Ireland, with the assent of his father, grants to Theobald Walter the castle of Arklow with the vill of Arklow and all lands pertaining thereto, to hold to him and his heirs by the service of one knight's fee, for all service.[4]

The Barony of Arklow can still be easily described. It stretches from Kilmichael Point to Wicklow Head, with its inland boundary roughly following the Croghan-Rathdrum-Glenealy-Wicklow line. The wording of the grant suggests that Theobald was awarded just the town and immediate hinterland, say a five mile radius, and certainly not the entire barony. Theobald was obviously a favourite of John's because, substantial as this grant might seem to us, it was inconsequential compared to other grants made to him, such as the baronies of Ormond Upper and Ormond Lower in County Tipperary. He was also appointed Hereditary Chief Butler of Ireland, an honorary position that brought a certain prestige at court. As such, he was

Honorary cup-bearer at the Monarch's coronation ... responsible for
giving the King the first libation of wine at the ceremony.[5]

Prestige was all very fine, but profit was better and the position was one
well worth conniving for as it entitled the holder to receive a tax
payment on all wine entering Ireland. This was in the form of two tuns
of wine out of every cargo of eighteen tuns or more. Theobald's son,
also Theobald or Tiebaut, thought so highly of both the honour and the
honorarium that he adopted the surname le Botiler (or Butler) and this
became the family name of his descendants. The Butler family coat-of-
arms includes three wine goblets to signify the importance of the title
and the tax.[6] The Butlers retained that tax entitlement until 1810, when
the government bought it back for £216,000, an enormous sum at that
time.[7]

The reference to an existing castle in the grant makes it clear that a
fortress of some kind had been built by the Vikings, probably of wood
and logically on the site of the later stone-built Ormond castle. There is
a case made, however, that before moving into the castle, Theobald first
set up home about one mile west of the town, at Ballyraine Middle. The
archaeological remains of a square earthen fort were excavated there in
1901. The scant evidence produced suggested that a fortified house of
substantial proportions stood on the site in or around the twelfth
century. Liam Price believed that it was here that Theobald Walter,
progenitor of the Butler family, first lived on his arrival in Ireland.[8]

In 1189, not long after Theobald received the grant, two things
happened that might have placed his tenure of the Arklow properties
in doubt. The first was the death of Henry II. The death of a king is
always an uneasy time, offering opportunity for the sidelined ambitious
and nervous uncertainty for those on whom the old king had smiled.
Who knew what power struggles might be played out? Grants might be
rescinded and redistributed. Theobald would not have been the first nor
the last to find himself a pawn in courtly machinations. The second
event was the marriage of Strongbow's daughter to William Mareschal.
It will be remembered that she had been made a ward of Henry's court.
Now, on the death of Henry and her marriage to Mareschal, all her
property, including the province of Leinster, passed to her new
husband. With a change of king and a change of immediate overlord,
anything was possible. But with the remarkable propensity for political
survival which later generations of his family would display time and

time again, Theobald emerged unscathed, and at some date prior to 1205, the following grant of affirmation was made:

> William the Mareschal grants to Theobald Walter and his heirs the vill of Arklow and the castle there, by the service of one knight; also Machatalewi by the service of four knights.[9]

This is more or less a repeat of John's grant to Theobald, with the addition of Machatalewi (wherever or whatever that was), but at least he now had all the bases covered. He not only had royal assent, but also the approval of the one man who might be in a position to mount a legal challenge. This butler was one shrewd businessman.

Theobald had already been busy expanding his lands even before Mareschal's grant to him. Sometime before the year 1200, but not long before, Theobald's Arklow properties were increased when he received the following grant from the abbot at Glendalough:

> Thomas, Abbot of Glendalough, grants to Theobald Walter and his heirs all the lands that belong to him in the abbacy of Glendalough, within the fee of Arklow, to be held by the service of one pound of incense yearly on the altar of Saint Kevin at Glendalough on that Saint's feast.[10]

This was a sad period in the long history of Glendalough. Even before the arrival of the Normans, the Church in Ireland had felt it was time to reorganise various dioceses through amalgamation. Glendalough seemed in particular need of reform. One of the Irish delegates to the Fourth Lateran Council in Rome, Archbishop Felix Ó Ruadhain of Tuam, reported that Glendalough

> ... had been held in great reverence from ancient times because of Saint Kevin who lived the life of a hermit there, but now was deserted and desolate for almost forty years, so that the church had been made a den of thieves and a pit of robbers, and more murders are committed in that valley than in any place in Ireland because of the deserted and vast solitude.[11]

This seems to have been the general opinion regarding the Glendalough diocese. In February 1216, just months after this scathing report had been made in Rome, Glendalough was joined to the see of Dublin. This merger was in reality a takeover. It had been on the cards for years. Did the abbot divest the Glendalough diocese of the Arklow properties rather than surrender them to his Dublin rival? Was it a touch of petulance from which Theobald benefitted? Or could it have been to encourage Theobald to grant some of his property to a religious order with the intention of establishing a monastery at Arklow?

It was the usual practice of Norman knights to secure ecclesiastical as well as military support for their new domains. One of the reasons for this was, perhaps, the knights' belief in the redemption of the soul through acts of charity to the Church. Largesse towards religious orders might go a long way towards remission of sins and an avoidance of eternal damnation. There was also a more material consideration. Soldiers, bristling with swords and crossbows, could keep control by threatening the mortal lives of the vanquished locals. Monks, armed with bibles and crucifixes, could keep even greater control by threatening the immortal souls of the vanquished. This dual power base was not new. It had been used many times before and it was to be seen again and again throughout history. Perhaps the image of the arrival of the conquistadors in South and Central America, with a cross in one hand and a sword in the other, sums it up best. Perhaps this is overstating the point, but it cannot be denied that the presence of a religious order in a newly subjugated region had a stabilising effect which military might alone could not achieve. The local knight got relative stability, the monks got land.

Theobald was an admirer of the Cistercian Order, and he was aware of their monastery in Furness in northwest England. According to Liam Price, before 1199 Theobald endowed these Cistercians with some of his lands at Owney in present day County Limerick. Within a short time of their arrival there, he also granted them some of his Arklow property so that a house might be established here as well.[12] A synopsis of the grant was recorded in the Ordnance Survey Letters.

> Theobald, the son of Walter, Butler of Ireland, for the love of God and the Blessed Virgin, and for the health of the souls of Henry II, King of England, King Richard and King John and those of Ranulph de Glainvill, Earl William Mareschal, the Lord Hubert, Archbishop of Canterbury, his (Theobald's) brother Henry Fitz-Walter his father, Matilda his mother, and for his own soul and for that of his wife Matilda, did confirm to God and the Blessed Virgin and to the monks of the Cistercian Order who came from the Abbey of Furnes in Lancashire, all his possessions in Arklow and on the south side of the river with the Burgages on the same side and all their appurtenances extending to the lands of Ada, the

Englishman, and then by the water which runs south between the lands
of the said Ada and those of John de Pencott; he also granted to them
the whole sea shore with all the salt-pits extending to the lands of
Maurice, the son of Maurice, with the right of shipwreck, that land and
salt-pit only excepted which belonged to the Abbot of Baltinglass and
further granted the Island of Arklow thereon to erect a house for monks
of the Cistercian Order with liberty to build the same in any more
eligible situation within the boundaries of his lands; also the fisheries
and hunting within the said boundaries and all the Irishmen with their
families residing there and their goods and chattels. He granted the same
in free pure and perpetual alms exonerated the monks from all secular
services and demands whatsoever.[13]

This was a generous offer, and although it is not possible to draw a line
on a modern map to show its exact extent, we can see that it went from
the river to beyond the Rock. The Baltinglass abbey salt pan is believed
to have been roughly where Roadstone now stands at what was later
known as Chapel Hogan, and there is evidence to suggest that Maurice
FitzMaurice's lands were around Castletown. This was definitely not to
be sneezed at. The Island of Arklow referred to was still in existence
until the development of the harbour in the mid-nineteenth century. At
that time it was just east of the bridge, roughly where the Bridgewater
apartments, Allen & Smyth, etc now stand. It was here that the river
became shallow and broke up into two main channels, and sometimes
several smaller ones, forming sandy islands, the main island being quite
substantial.

With such a carrot being dangled, it is strange that we have no direct
documentary evidence as to whether the Cistercians took up the offer.
But in 1839, Thomas O'Conor reported to his employers at the
Ordnance Survey Office in Dublin that -

An ancient graveyard with the site of a church was found on the north
side of the bridge of Arklow, in a sand bank in the Ferrybank townland
in this parish. Several graves containing skeletons were found here,
which were covered with large flags, the sides being built with stone of
various size and form. The surface of the place is still covered over with
human bones. A tomb stone ... was found here a few years ago, which
is six feet long, two feet broad at one end and one foot eight inches at
the other, and seven inches thick in the centre along the whole length,
whilst the edges on each side are but three inches in thickness.[14]

O'Conor concluded that the church which had once stood in the old

graveyard had been built by a community of
Cistercians in pursuance of Theobald's grant
to them. This is the only indication, slim as it
is, that the Cistercians did actually come to
Arklow. If O'Conor was correct, it looks as if
the Cistercians might have built in the sand
dunes adjacent to the island. The 'tomb stone'
(there is some doubt as to whether that's
what it was) is currently in the care of the
Arklow parish priest. As regards the
graveyard, during the summer of 1997
Arklow Urban District Council were carrying
out work on Ferrybank close to the Abercorn
Masonic Hall when several bones were
unearthed. They were not complete skeletons
and analysis of the fragments indicated that
they came from at least seven individuals,
both male and female and ranging in ages
from forty-five to possibly as young as three
months. Radiocarbon dating suggests that
they died between AD 1200 and 1300.[15]
While the presence of women and children

does not seem in keeping with this being a Cistercian foundation, it
should be remembered that at this period clerical celibacy was far from
being universally observed.[16] It can also be explained by the more likely
possibility that local people might have been buried in the consecrated
ground that constituted the church yard. One way or another, we are
no nearer to proving that the Cistercians ever came here.

*

Theobald Walter died in 1205, leaving a five year old son, Theobald II,
who was given in wardship to Geoffrey de Marisco until he was twenty-
one. It was this Theobald who took Butler as the family surname, and
it was during this period, the first quarter of the thirteenth century, that
Arklow really took on the identity of a Norman town. Burgages -
principal civic figures who were probably English or Welsh - were well
established and the Hiberno-Norse and Irish inhabitants reduced to
serfdom.

Similar displacement by other Norman lords pushed the O'Byrnes and the O'Tooles from their lands in the fertile plains of Kildare into the inhospitable terrain of the Wicklow mountains, where they nursed their grievances and over the next three centuries gave vent to frustrated rage. Arklow was one of the Norman strongholds continually under threat of attack from these less than happy neighbours.[17]

In 1274, these 'Irish enemies' pushed into the Norman-held, but largely unprotected, lowlands. Troops were organised to push them back into the mountains, but the Irish met the Anglo-Normans at Glenmalure and killed many of them. The Anglo-Norman king, Edward I, decided that these wild Irish would have to be subdued once and for all. A veteran of the crusades, Geoffrey de Geneville, was given the task and he arrived in Arklow where he left a force under Theobald Butler, great-grandson of the original Theobald. The presence of this force didn't deter the O'Byrnes and O'Tooles and skirmishing continued, so the following year a major offensive was launched on the mountain stronghold, but this proved equally disastrous for the Norman-English.[18] Many were killed in battle and others, trapped in the mountains for which they were ill-equipped, staved off starvation by eating their horses.

The O'Byrnes and the O'Tooles were not the only Irish septs who were peeved at the loss of their ancestral lands. The MacMurroughs weren't too happy either, although it is difficult to sympathise with them as it was their former leader, Dermot, who brought the Normans to Ireland in the first place. Their complaint was that their lands had also passed into Norman possession when the Normans had only been invited to help out in a local dispute. To them, it was a case of the hired help taking over the house and evicting the owner. The MacMurroughs were based in the north Wexford region, so Arklow also had to keep an eye on incursions from that quarter. The main instigators of trouble there were Art and Murchertach MacMurrough.

Throughout the 1270s, these MacMurrough brothers levied "tribute" from Anglo-Norman settlers between the hills and the sea, and generally upset Norman tempers. In 1274 and 1276, Norman troops mounted expeditions to rout these malcontents, but both expeditions resulted in victory for the Irish septs. Roger Bigod, the overlord for the region and possessor of lands in Carlow, realised that the only way to curb the MacMurroughs was to parley with them and agree on a treaty that would give them greater recognition as leaders of their people. When

Bigod proposed this strategy, Edward I agreed to grant safe-conduct to the brothers to go to England. These were issued on July 24th, 1280,[19] but the story gets a little complicated here with arrests, promises, releases, re-arrests, new issues of safe-conduct, and quite a bit of other toing-and-froing. The upshot being that it was two years later, in the summer of 1282, before the brothers accepted the invitation and it was agreed that they should move from one Norman haven to the next as they travelled to negotiate a treaty.

On July 21st, 1282 they were welcomed at Arklow castle. They were never to leave it alive. Despite the promise of protection, it had been arranged that Art and Murchertach MacMurrough would be murdered here. One account, dating from about 300 years after the event, claimed that the man who actually did the killing was a local landowner by the name of Pencoit.[20] There was a de Pencott landowning family listed in the document recording Theobald Walter's deed to the Cistercians. Pencoit might well have been a descendant. Even if Pencoit did the deed, the question remains who gave the order? The MacMurroughs were travelling under the king's promise of safe-conduct and a breach of that assurance was tantamount to treason. It was generally believed that the instigator was the Justiciar, or Chief Justice, Stephen Fulbourne. It is said that Fulbourne sent out word that 200 marks would be paid to the man who killed the brothers. To raise the money, Fulbourne levied the English-Normans in the area. As they were the people under threat from the MacMurroughs and they consequently would be the ones to benefit from the MacMurroughs' deaths, why shouldn't they be the ones to pay? There was an outcry when the deed was done, not over the murder itself, or even over the fact that the king's order had been ignored, but because Fulbourne had collected 500 marks and had paid out only 200, making a nice profit for himself into the bargain.[21]

Whoever carried it out, or had ordered it carried out, it was an act of unbelievable treachery, even in an age renowned for its brutality. Not only did word spread like wildfire, but it was remembered for generations to come. That day was used as a marker in the calendar, a day from which time was calibrated.[22] The deed was recalled in 1317 in a formal protest made to Pope John XXII regarding English crimes against the Irish people.[23] Needless to say, the papacy was not overly interested in the plight of the Irish people. The dual assassinations had been underhand, savage, cowardly, unmitigated murder and they were extremely effective in achieving an uneasy peace, at least temporarily.

Because of Arklow's vulnerability to attack, a garrison of well-armed soldiers was maintained here. From the castle walls, a view upriver led the eye into the mountains from which an assault may be made. Sometimes the garrison, led by Theobald Walter V, would venture into the interior, but in general both they and the mountain-based Irish each waited for the other to make a move. It is recorded that Edmund Butler had supplies for his troops arrive by sea in 1313, but this may have been for ease of transport rather than for security considerations.

In 1315, Edward the Bruce, brother of the more famous Robert, left Scotland to rally the Celtic nations against the English common enemy. The O'Tooles and the O'Byrnes needed no further prompting. This was the chance they had been waiting for. They attacked and burned the English settlements in the foothills and along the coastal plain, including Arklow.[24] The English recovered the castle and beat the Irish back to the hills. And so the see-saw fortunes ran for decades to come. In April 1331, 'the Castle was taken by treason of Irish Men', but it was retaken by the English the following year.[25] The ease with which the fortress could be successfully attacked pointed to weaknesses of either design or structure or both. The government took direct control of it from the Butlers and major renovations were carried out between 1332 and 1350.

The greatest clash was to come as the century closed when Richard II led the largest army ever to arrive in Ireland during the Middle Ages to subdue the Wicklow Irish, and his main adversary was Art MacMurrough Cavanagh.[26] It was 1394, and Art was following in the footsteps of the earlier Art and his brother Murchertach who had been murdered at Arklow castle in 1282. The English had found it expedient to give some status to some of the old Gaelic clans, such as the MacMurroughs, but it was as much to keep them in check as to acknowledge past claims to former possessions. Every now and then some of these acknowledged Irish leaders would assume too much in the eyes of the English overlords. Art MacMurrough Cavanagh was a case in point. He was imposing "tribute", better known today as protection money, on English settlers in both his ancestral lands and in territory in Kildare which had come to him through marriage. The more powerful of these settlers called on the king, Richard II, to curb Art's activities. Richard tried, but Art was too powerful in south Leinster to heed Richard's warnings. Skirmishing broke out between the various factions and Richard arrived at Waterford with a force of 30,000 bowmen and 4,000 men-at-arms.

Putting himself at the head of this formidable force, Richard struck out northeast across what is now County Wexford. Dense forest and impassable bog was not the type of terrain to suit such an army. In mountain passes, Richard's beleagured troops were attacked by Art's men on a guerrilla basis. Among the first targets of these attacks were the food wagons and soon Richard's army had enough to do to forage without engaging in warfare. By the time they reached the southern end of the Wicklow mountains, Richard's troops were already defeated in spirit and the king sent an emissary to Art to agree to a truce, during which a fuller peace might be reached. Art agreed, but according to one account once more treachery was afoot and it was only by quick thinking that Art escaped the fate of his kinsmen in Arklow a hundred years earlier. The war between Richard and Art continued.

The second campaign took place five years later in 1399. A record of it was made by a Frenchman who travelled with Richard's army. From that account, it appears that Richard and his advisers had learned nothing from their previous humiliation. They took the same route, fell into the same traps, and ended up the same way. Food supplies were early targets, and to compound the loss Art employed a scorched earth policy. After a short campaign, Richard realised that he had been

Ships bringing food to Richard II's army.

defeated once more. He offered Art generous terms if he would accept Richard as king, but to no avail.

> After some days of dreadful privation they reached the seashore at Arklow, where ships with provisions from Dublin awaited them. The soldiers rushed into the sea to reach at the food, fought for it ravenously, and drank all the wine they could seize. Soon after this timely relief, a still more welcome gleam of fortune fell upon the English host. A messenger arrived from Art expressing his willingness to meet some accredited ambassador from the king and discuss the matters at issue between them.[27]

The above extract of Richard's and Art's encounters is taken from A.M. Sullivan's account. Sullivan's continual reference to the 'vain-glorious Richard' and the 'invincible Irish prince' leaves the reader in no doubt as to whose side he was on, but he claims to have taken the kernel of the story from the French chronicler's writings of the events. For reasons that will soon become clear, I will continue with his account of the meeting between Richard's ambassador and Art.

> The earl of Gloster was at once despatched to treat with Art. The French knight was among the earl's escort, and witnessed the meeting, of which he left a quaint description. He described Art as a "fine large man, wonderfully active. To look at him he seemed very stern and savage and a very able man". The horse which Art rode especially transfixed the Frenchman's gaze. He declares that a steed more exquisitely beautiful, more marvellously fleet, he had never beheld. "In coming down it galloped so hard, that, in my opinion, I never saw hare, deer, sheep, or any other animal, I declare to you for a certainty, run with such speed as it did". This horse Art rode "without housing or saddle", yet sat like a king, and guided with utmost ease in the most outstanding feats of horsemanship. "He and the earl", the Frenchman tells, "exchanged much discourse, but did not come to agreement. They took short leave and hastily parted. Each took his way apart, and the earl returned to Richard".[28]

This meeting, we are told, took place in a wooded glen and if it took place shortly after Richard's bedraggled troops had reached Arklow, we can assume that it was not too far from the town. This very assumption was made by the 3rd Earl of Carysfort when he was enlarging Poulahoney Castle in the 1820s, roughly the same time as the Frenchman's chronicle came to light after centuries of oblivion.

Carysfort was intrigued with the possibility that the men had met in the wooden glen at Poulahoney and so he renamed the castle and the townland Glen Art, of which much, much more in due course.

The important point here is that even if the identification of Glenart as the location of Art's and Gloster's meeting is bordering on the realms of fantasy, the town of Arklow definitely featured as the supply base at which Richard's troops were saved from starvation. It is an indisputable milestone along our journey.

It was Richard's last campaign. When he returned to England he found that he had lost his throne while he chased Art MacMurrough Cavanagh through the woods and bogs of Ireland. Art, on the other hand, continued to hold sway outside the towns for twenty years to come.

*

I realise that I have made this entire era sound like one of blood-and-guts, a time in which every waking moment was spent trying to figure out how best to kill or avoid being killed. But between the dates of conflict listed above, one day followed another just as they do now. The very fact that specific dates can be pinpointed as significant in respect of war means that they were relatively rare. In between, life went on as usual. Food had to be produced, children reared, sickness treated. Land was tilled, crops grown and harvested, the sea gave up its fish, as did the river.

Perhaps the most important peacetime event was the arrival of the Dominicans in 1264. As mentioned above, Theobald Walter had been anxious to get the Cistercians to establish a house in Arklow. If they came, they did not stay long enough to leave firm evidence. In the early 1260s, however, Theobald's great-grandson, also named Theobald, invited the Dominicans to fill the gap. At the General Chapter of the Order held in London in 1263, it was decided that they would establish a monastery here, which was to be known as the Priory of the Holy Cross.[29] The fact that the first Dominicans arrived in Arklow the following year suggests that much of the ground work had already been done. The priory itself was erected a short distance from the castle, where Abbey graveyard is now, but the extent of the grant is believed to have been that offered to the Cistercians. Modern housing estates which contain the name 'Abbey', such as Abbey Street, Abbey Terrace,

Abbeyville, Abbey Heights, etc, and stretching out to the townland of Abbeylands behind the Golf Club and beyond, give some idea of just how much land the Dominicans controlled. Unlike the Cistercians, the Dominicans stayed and left an indelible mark on the area.

Aided, either voluntarily or otherwise, by the local serfs, the ordinary native people who had no legal or civil rights, the Dominicans developed the priory and cultivated the lands. Soon the foundation reflected the power of the Church and the generosity of the local lord. When Theobald died in the castle on October 6th, 1285, his remains were interred in the priory. His tomb was a reasonably elaborate affair, as was deemed appropriate for someone of his wealth and stature. His effigy laid upon the lid, in the manner of other prominent Normans in other medieval churches, such as in Kilkenny's St Canice's and in Dublin's Christchurch. Oddly, according to Lord Dunboyne's *The Butler Family History* (1966), the remains of both Theobald's father and grandfather (Theobalds II and III) were also buried in the priory.[30] If this is correct, they must have been disinterred from their original places of rest as both were long dead before 1264. Dunboyne also states that Theobald IV's tomb could be seen in the Abbey graveyard up to the beginning of the twentieth century, but no one seems to know what happened to it.

Although the foundation has long been referred to as 'The Abbey', it was officially a priory, a sort of outreach house subject to a more prestigious abbey. In this case, the Arklow priory was probably answerable to the abbey of Owney. The only tangible item associated with it is a fifteenth century bible which is inscribed to the memory of five members of the local Dowdall family, four of whom were dead and one still living. This bible is kept in Lambeth Palace Library in London. At one stage, during the 1980s, it was suggested that it should be returned to Arklow. It is an idea which deserves serious consideration, but only if the people of Arklow can prove the bible would receive the same level of security and the same degree of professional conservation it enjoys in Lambeth Palace Library.

A small stone cross, now the centrepiece in the Abbey graveyard, is believed to date from this period and is, in all probability, another survivor of the priory.

The early fifteenth century was a time of great turmoil in the Christian Church. Since 1378 there had been two popes, one residing in Rome, the other in the French city of Avignon, each excommunicating the

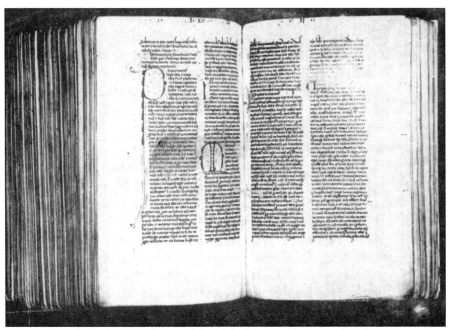

Bible from the Priory of the Holy Cross, Arklow, now kept in
Lambeth Palace Library, London

other, and each with his own college of cardinals. The whole of Christendom was split in two. For example, the King of England supported the Roman pope, the King of France supported the Avignon pope; universities and houses of business were also at loggerheads as to who was the real pontiff. After almost three decades of this situation, known as The Great Schism, the aforementioned universities suggested that Church unity was more important than allegiance to a particular pretender to the papacy. After all, surely the only true head of the Christian Church was Christ? It was decided to urge all protagonists to withdraw their support and lend it to a newly elected leader.

In 1409, Gregory VII of Rome and Benedict XIII of Avignon were both decreed heretics at the Council of Pisa, and a new pope, Alexander V, was appointed in their stead. This was the perfect solution – in theory. The problem was neither Gregory nor Benedict recognised the authority of the Council of Pisa, both remained unmoved and both excommunicated Alexander. The Council of Pisa had produced not a unifying single papacy, but a third pope. Whether through frustration, despair, or something more sinister, Alexander died after only ten months as Pisan pontiff, and was succeeded by Baldassare Cossa, who took the name John XXIII.

> When another Pope John XXIII was elected in 1958, several Catholic cathedrals had hastily to remove the fifteenth century John XXIII from their list of pontiffs.[31]

And where does Arklow's Priory of the Holy Cross fit into all this? By this stage, the priory was 150 years old and in drastic need of repair. To finance the renovations they needed papal sanction to sell indulgences. The question is, which of the three contending papal authorities did they apply to? Answer, John XXIII, the one whom many church historians today feel had even less claim to the title than his two rivals. Why they should choose him is not known. Perhaps they genuinely felt that he was the man with the greatest claim to the papacy. Perhaps he was the one they felt would give the best deal. Whatever the reason, the following Bull was issued at the Council of Constance in 1414,

> John, Bishop, Servant of Servants of God, to all the faithful of Christ who shall see these letters, Health and Apostolic Benediction, Desiring that the Church Friars Preachers in Arklow in the Diocese of Dublin, built in the honour of the Holy Cross, be frequented and supported with due honour. By the authority of the Blessed Apostles Peter and Paul, I confer on all penitents who visit the Church and contribute to its support, on the feast of the Nativity, Circumcision, Epiphany, Resurrection, Ascension, Corpus Christi, Pentecost and on the Annunciation, Purification and Assumption of the Blessed Virgin, the Nativity of St. John the Baptist, Saints Peter and Paul, the Finding and Exaltation of the Holy Cross and All Saints, and for six days following the aforesaid feasts, an Indulgence of Ten years and Ten quarantines.[32]

Just how much a penitent had to pay to have these ten years and four hundred days knocked off his purgatorial sentence was not stated, but it was either substantial enough or popular enough to allow the necessary work to be carried out on the priory, and it continued to operate for another 125 years.

The cause of its ultimate demise was the Suppression of the Monasteries in the 1530s, which resulted indirectly from Henry VIII's marital problems and the Vatican's refusal to see things his way. As with religious orders throughout these islands, the Arklow Dominicans were expelled from their priory, which by this time consisted

> of church, belfry, chapter house, dormitory, hall, three chambers, a store, kitchen, cemetery, and garden containing 2 acres with two parks and 3 acres of land of the great measure of Arklow and four messauges (i.e. dwellings and offices with adjoining lands) in the said town [33]

There were also other perks such as rent and a tax on all beer brewed in the town. Overall, it was a severe blow to the Arklow friars. Over the next few years these properties were leased and re-leased to various entrepreneurs such as Edmund Duffy (1540), Edmund Kenny (1541), John Travers of Dublin (1544) and Terence MacMurrough of Arklow (1547).

Despite their extensive properties and a certain degree of feudal control over the native people of the town and district, the Dominicans had not been the sole representatives of religious authority in the area. Arklow had been in the diocese of Glendalough from the early Christian period and when that see was amalgamated with the diocese of Dublin in 1216, the new authority divided the diocese into deaneries for administrative purposes. Each deanery was comprised of several parishes located within its designated area. Arklow was established as one such deanery.[34]

About 1275, a list of the churches in the Arklow deanery was drawn up. Earlier lists, dating from 1173 and 1179, also named several of these churches, but the 1275 list, known as the *Crede Mihi,* was the first complete one. Within a ten miles radius of Arklow, no less than twenty-two churches were named and many of these can be readily identified. The following is taken from the 1275 list, together with their modern equivalents where known. They are laid out in a roughly clockwise direction, taking Arklow as the quarter-past position:

Name in the Crede Mihi	Modern form
Arclo	Arklow
Killnevey	?, probably just south of Arklow Rock, perhaps where the ruins of St Ibar's church now stand.
Kilgorman	Kilgorman
Thursillan	?, probably near Tara Hill
Inchemehalmoc	Inch
Rathgallen	Rathgallen
Achederlar	Killahurler
Tachmayl	Ballintemple
De Leys	Templelusk
Kilcassel	Kilcashel
Balimackoynin	Ballykine
Mochrodan	Macreddin
Rossacheyn	Rosahane
Disirkevyn	?
Rathcrumcha	Rathdrum
Kilmecho	Kilmacoo
Stachlolach	Kilpatrick
Inverdeyle	Ennereilly
Glenerene	Templerainey
Dovenachrein	Kilmagig
Kineiny	Templemichael
Kilbride	Kilbride

Further lists were compiled in 1531, 1615 and 1630, by which time many of the 1275 names were no longer in existence, or at least no longer figured in the eccesliastical lists. The important point is that throughout the medieval period, there was a preponderance of churches in the area apart from the Dominican Priory of the Holy Cross.

*

Although the Butlers were still lords of this area, they had greatly increased their holdings elsewhere, particularly in counties Tipperary and Kilkenny. They had built castles at Cahir, Nenagh, Kiltinan, Kilcash, Roscrea, Terryglass, and Carrick-on-Suir, but the largest was the one in Kilkenny, and from the early 1300s this became the seat of the head of the extended Butler family. Because most of their properties lay in the

Upper and Lower Baronies of Ormond in Tipperary, the head Butler took the title Earl of Ormond.[35] Arklow had been the place where the family first settled in Ireland, but they had outgrown it. To them, it was now a political and economic backwater as the centre of gravity of their family fortunes shifted westward. That is not to say that they simply turned their backs on the town, port and environs. They appointed a constable, who lived in the castle, to look after their Arklow interests.

One of the first constables of whom we have a record was Elias de Ashbourne, who was put in charge of the castle in 1332. He was appointed by the government and not by the Butlers. The reason for this was the strategic importance of Arklow. The Irish had taken the castle and town in 1331 and lost it again in 1332, showing that the defences were wholly inadequate and it would seem that the government believed that much of that inadequacy lay with the Butlers. The government more or less commandeered it and put de Ashburne in charge. De Ashbourne, however, either wasn't up to the job or decided that he didn't want it, because three years later he was replaced by Gilbert de Moenes.[36] It was during this post-1332 period that major renovation work was carried out.

Just when the castle was returned to Butler control is not known, but we do know that on March 20th, 1357 Ormond appointed Thomas Talbot of Molaghyde (that is Malahide in County Dublin) constable for a period of twelve years. Talbot was to be paid £20 silver a year, as well as other fees associated with the position. In return, he was

> to keep and guard safe and secure for the use of the Earl and to return it (unless besieged, which God forbid, by the Irish enemies of the Lord King or other adversaries of the Earl), in sufficient state in which it now is.[37]

For whatever reason, Talbot did not see out his term and John de Ormy was appointed in his place nine years later for the same salary. His tenure was to last ten years, and as well as his £20 silver and other fees, he was given a robe worth twenty shillings. In return

> ... John shall keep the said custody against Irishmen and all other hostile people according to his power and his own costs; beyond which, if Irishmen or other enemies attain the castle, then the Earl or his heirs on notice made thereof shall immediately go to his help and if he do not come and the castle be taken against the will of the said John then he

shall be entirely quit and be excused in the matter. But if the castle be
taken owing to his neglect then he binds himself and his heirs in £100
silver to be paid to the Earl and his heirs. And while John has custody
of the castle the Earl will maintain it and all the edifices there.

Perhaps the reason for Talbot's early departure was non-payment or late
payment of his wages, because de Ormy's contract stated that if the
Butlers were forty days late with payment de Ormy had the right to
hand back the castle to them and be free of his contract. If they
persisted in not paying him, he could 'vacate and abandon the said
castle without challenge of the Earl or his heirs'.

As we have seen, concerns about being attacked by the O'Byrnes,
O'Tooles and Kavanaghs were understandable. Nevertheless, there is
evidence to suggest that Arklow was a relatively peaceful place between
1350 and 1530. Admittedly, the evidence is negative in that there is little
mention of fighting in the immediate area. Liam Price suggests that this
stability existed because of the 'comparatively good relations which
existed later between the Earls of Ormond and the MacMurroughs and
O Byrnes'.[38] He cites the earls as acting as interpreters in treaty
negotiations between the Irish chiefs and the English in 1395 and in
1425. Also the mother of a later earl, Piers Ruadh Butler, was Saidhbh
Cavanagh, a daughter of the MacMurrough leader.

It was practical politics that allowed the Butlers and the native Irish
to co-exist, at least up to a point. The Butlers knew they could never
totally subdue the MacMurroughs, O'Byrnes and O'Tooles as long as the
mountains and woods were so near, particularly in the wake of the
humiliating defeat inflicted on Richard II by Art MacMurrough. Likewise,
the Irish knew that while they could disrupt commerce and generally
make things unpleasant, the English were here to stay. Some sort of
accommodation had to be arrived at, and it would appear that the
compromise lay in the town of Arklow paying tribute to the Irish in
return for which local trading could proceed unhindered. In fact, by the
early 1500s, although the town and surrounding area were still
nominally under the control of the Butlers, it was the MacMurroughs
who were really in charge.

Throughout the 1400s, the Butlers had taken their eyes off the ball,
their sights being set on richer pickings. As Ormond earls and
associated junior branches, they had become one of the most powerful
families in the country. In 1525 Piers Butler, the 8th Earl of Ormond,

was appointed Lord Deputy of Ireland, and he felt the time had come to break the MacMurrough hold on the Butler lands and tenants at Arklow. Butler may have been bluffing, but MacMurrough was in no position to call it. In a written agreement between them, Butler recovered the Arklow estate without bloodshed. MacMurrough agreed

> for himself and his heirs and successors forever, to remit, release and quit claim to the said Earl and his heirs, all right, title, action, interest or demand which he had or by any means in the future should have, to the said Earl's lordship, manor and estate of Arckloe.[39]

That didn't mean that MacMurrough came away empty-handed. He was to receive

> all profits from the three Shires and almost half those of the town for his life, while recognising the Butlers' legal right of ownership.[40]

The 'three Shires' mentioned relate to the lands adjoining the town. The two shires on the south side of the river extended about two miles south and westward to about Woodenbridge. The north shire extended two miles north and from the coast to Shelton.

Butler wrote to the English government in London claiming this agreement to be a great victory over the MacMurroughs, recovering lands which had been 'in the possession of Irishmen in the space of theis 200 yeris'. He went on to say how he had risked life and limb to bring it about, showing that no better Lord Deputy of Ireland could be desired. One of the reasons for this self-glorification was the fact that the earl's greatest rival, the Earl of Kildare, also had his eyes on that most lucrative position. Not to be outdone, Kildare also wrote to the king to give the whole affair a different shade. He claimed that Ormond kept

> A warde of evill disposed personnes in a pyle adjoynyng to the see, called Arclow, which … robbe and spoyle the Kinges subgiettes, passing ther by.[41]

But the Fitzgeralds, the family of the Kildare earl, were on a collision course with the court of Henry VIII, culminating in the rebellion of Silken Thomas in 1536. With the Fitzgeralds' fall from grace, the Butlers, Earls and later Dukes of Ormond, were Ireland's most powerful family.

They were, however, a long-tailed family and some of the branches disputed which was the successor to the original Theobald Walter and therefore heir to the lands granted to him in the twelfth century. The dispute was settled when Henry VIII regranted the estates to Piers Butler in 1538.[42] Getting their Arklow properties back was more a matter of pride than anything else. Recognition of their authority was the important thing, but now they had increasingly bigger fish to fry and none of them were landed in Arklow.

In 1571, the then earl decided to restructure his Arklow properties and the means of payment of rent. For some time past, his tenants had had to pay not only rent to him but also tribute to the MacMurroughs. As the MacMurroughs were now no longer a serious threat, Ormond agreed with the tenants of Arklow town and the three surrounding shires to do away with these tribute payments on condition that the tenants' rents to him were increased. The agreement was signed and sealed in October of that year. Fifteen burgages, leading tenants and businessmen in the town, agreed to pay thirteen shillings and four pence a year, as well as other small payments in kind. They also agreed to repair the castle walls, have strong gates and outer ditches and pales made for the better defence of the town.[43] This reference to outer defences supports the general belief that Arklow was never a walled town. No illustration of the castle exists, but there is enough circumstantial evidence to suggest that it was rectangular or polygonal with a keep inside high curtain walls. Its extent can be gauged by starting at the single remaining tower at the Town Hall, following the wall into Parade Ground, up Upper Main Street as far as the western end of the Ormonde Hall. Presumably there was another tower here, at which point the northern wall ran along the top of the ridge known locally as 'The Alps' to rejoin the tower at the Town Hall. 'The citizens presumably took refuge inside the bawn (i.e. the enclosed area between the wall and the keep) in times of great danger'.[44] In return for the increased rents and work to be carried out, Ormond promised to try to get a royal charter for the town. This had several political and commercial advantages, such as the right to return a specified number of members to parliament and the holding of regular fairs and markets. Just how hard he tried to get the charter is not known, but it was never granted, although Wicklow town received one in 1613.[45] This apparent favouring of Wicklow may have been because it was the administrative seat of the new county established in 1606.

The earl's brother Edmund Butler was something of an embarrassment. He frequently went on rampages after perceived enemies in the Arklow area and even as far south as Ferns. One such foray took place at a time when hostilities had temporarily ceased between the dispossessed Irish and the English lords. Edmund's juvenile – some would say mad – behaviour was akin to a child striking matches in a room full of powder kegs. His penchant for burning and pillaging were frequent causes of complaint to the earl and the Ormond deeds refer to the 'miserable estate and decay' of the town and the three shires, presumably at least partly because of Edmund's antics.

Unfortunately, the deeds make no reference to the general living conditions or lifestyles and routines of the people, but from other sources we know that commerce continued over all those years of intermittent conflict. In 1402, for example, coastal trade between Dublin and Arklow was recorded,[46] and that as the sixteenth century drew to a close, Arklow trading vessels could be found as far away as the French port of La Rochelle.[47]

The manor of Arklow was leased to Richard Walshe in 1580. This meant that he probably resided in the castle and was in effect its constable. As with previous constables, he didn't keep the position for long and the manor was re-leased on April 20th, 1584 to Hugh Duff McDonell O'Byrne, a man who cannot be simply mentioned and passed over. It might seem strange that the earl should lease his manor to an enemy, but Hugh Duff McDonell O'Byrne's allegiance depended a great deal on what suited him at any given time. He had been an ally of Feagh MacHugh O'Byrne, but his loyalty to the clan had been suspect. The fact that Ormond leased the manor to him for a period of twenty-one years at £120 per year was all the evidence his clansmen needed that Hugh Duff was a turncoat. In October 1589, five years into the lease period, Feagh MacHugh attempted to enter Arklow castle and register his displeasure with his erstwhile supporter. The plan was foiled. Feagh escaped capture and Hugh Duff survived. He knew there was no going back and in 1595 he fought with the English against the O'Byrnes.

*

I will bring these medieval centuries to a close with an account of a battle which took place just south of the town in 1599. The politically unsettled Elizabethan era saw Wicklow in greater turmoil than it had been for some time. In the 1580s one of Wicklow's best known Irish leaders appeared on the scene. He was the Feagh MacHugh O'Byrne mentioned above, and his successes against the English gave new heart and hope to the O'Byrnes and their O'Toole and MacMurrough allies. When he was killed in 1597, his son Phelim MacFeagh O'Byrne took over and continued the fight.[48] The leader of the MacMurroughs at this time was Donnell Spanighe, 'the chief of the Cavanaghs, which in the Irish account is no less than to be King of Leinster'.[49]

Richard Devereux, Earl of Essex, was sent to head a large force to put an end to the perceived nonsense that an Irishman could possibly lay claim to the kingship of any part of Ireland. Like Strongbow in 1170 and Richard II in the 1390s, Essex landed at Waterford and headed northeast, through Enniscorthy and Ferns. He was aware of the disastrous expeditions of Richard II and had decided that before engaging the Irish in full battle, he would head for Arklow where he would leave some of the carriages and any sick or wounded men. On the way, they encountered bands of Irish watching them from a distance, but there was little attempt at serious attack. Just to show that he meant business

> his Lordship all the day long burned both in his way and on each side ...... The first resistance was at a village on our right hand, seated on the skirt of a great wood, and flanked on two sides with two groves of underwood ...... The village was burnt without the loss of a man.[50]

This last sentence could be either taken literally or it could mean without the loss of one of Essex's men.

They continued to head northwards, moving out towards the coast and came up by Castletown. When they reached Arklow Rock, on June 30th, Essex could see that his vanguard, under the leadership of the Earl of Ormond, was already nearing the town. The land that lay between this party and the main body at the Rock was comprised of sandhills and boggy ground. That wet ground would be drained by Arklow Golf Club three centuries later and had been known locally as the Warren Lough. On the west side of this wetland were woods which the Irish force, of an estimated 800 foot and forty horse, had used as cover until the time was right to attack the leading English group. Essex could see that his advance party would be annihilated by this Irish force and he immediately ordered 300 light infantry and all of his cavalry to attack the Irish and so rescue Ormond and the vanguard. When the Irish saw this small force sent against them, 'they came on with a louder shout and more speed than before'.

When the English cavalry reached the wetland, many of their horses got bogged down and the riders had to dismount. One of them, a Mr Coxe, was mortally wounded. A Mr Vernon managed to kill one of the Irish, but in the process his horse fell, trapping him underneath and he had to be rescued by a Mr Bellington. Essex's infantry went in with swords flashing and pistols firing. Behind them came musketeers and, on seeing these reinforcements, the Irish halted their attack. Essex assumed that their sudden cessation signified that they were also expecting reinforcements and he decided to force the advantage before their arrival. The break in momentum caused confusion among the Irish and allowed the English horsemen to bear down on them. Many threw away their weapons and tried to escape, but in their confusion they seemed to run into one or other of the different attacking groups of English. Some were

> so amazed that they stuck in the bog, and were overtaken and killed by our men ... His Lordship gave direction for following the chase; and we then marched away to Arcloe.
>
> The rebels' forces consisted of the Cavanaghes, the traitors of Co. Wexford and Low Leynster, the Burnes, the Tooles, the O'Moores of Leix, and all their bonnaghtes. Their leaders were Donnell Spanaigh, Phelim McFeach, and McRowry. Our loss was not above one or two common soldiers, besides Mr Coxe.[51]

It will be noticed that no estimate of Irish casualties is given, but that is not surprising as the writer could not even be bothered about the exact number of casualties on his own side, especially if they were 'common soldiers'. The victors quartered that night in Arklow. Unfortunately, we have no account of their behaviour in the aftermath of their victory, but it can't have been excessively bad or some account, even a folklore account, would have survived. It would also be almost certain that Essex, Ormond and the other leaders of the English force would have spent the night in the castle, before continuing on for 'Wyckeloe' the following day.

In the immediate aftermath of the skirmish, Phelim McFeagh sent word to the Lord Lieutenant that

He humbly craved leave to come to speak with him, with condition that
he might have his Lordship's word for his safe return; and prayed the
messenger to get him an answer. His Lordship's answer was that if he
sent to Arcloe for a passport only to come as a repentent rebel, to tender
his absolute submission to her Majesty's servant and minister, authorised
by her royal commission, he should have such a safeconduct; but if he
sent in any other form, or to any other purpose, he would execute the
messenger; for he would never suffer his commission to be dishonoured
by treating or parleying with rebels.[52]

I do not know the outcome of this exchange, but the proposed
surrender of Phelim O'Byrne signified the final years of Wicklow
resistance to English rule. The rest of Ireland had long been subjugated
and divided into administrative counties. The fact that the last remaining
place of defiance was on Dublin's doorstep had been galling to the
English, but that era was now over and the O'Byrne Country was about
to become County Wicklow, the last of the thirty-two to be so
constituted.

4

Century of Change:
1600-1700

The seventeenth century was a watershed in the political and social life of Ireland. By 1600 the Tudors had taken military control of the country, the last remnants of Gaelic Ireland fell apart after the battle of Kinsale on Christmas Eve 1601, and the romantically named Flight of the Earls set the seal on English rule here. The Wicklow septs were fighting a rearguard campaign and their dogged resistance fizzled out sufficiently to allow the English to establish Wicklow as a county in 1606.

Despite the impression made by the preceding chapter that Wicklow was in a relatively constant state of war between the Irish and the English throughout the 1500s, there were intermittent periods of peace and negotiation. Moves to have Wicklow made into a county had been mooted as early as 1542, and that was at the behest of Thady O'Birne,

> captain of his nation, and other nobles inhabiting 'a certain country between the Wynde Gates and the town of Arclowe in the county of Dublin'.[1]

Including Arklow in County Dublin was simply to place it somewhere under English control on paper at least. O'Birne and his associates were petitioning the king to have their lands recognised by parliament as an administrative region to be called County Wicklow. The Lord Deputy, Henry VIII's representative in Dublin, ratified this proposal provided that the king should agree to it within one year. Henry failed to sanction it with the result that the submission was not acted upon. However, within a decade three administrative regions corresponding to the territories controlled by the O'Byrnes, O'Tooles and Kavanaghs were established, each ruled by an English captain from a convenient fort. In 1578 the extent of a proposed County Wicklow was delineated, but the lack of suitable candidates for public positions in the region made it impossible to implement. It was not until 1605 that most of the logistical and political hurdles were overcome and County Wicklow officially came into being the following year. The centuries old English-versus-Irish conflict seemed to be over. The English had won, reality had to be faced and some form of mutual accommodation arrived at. But during the 1500s a new element of division had entered the equation - religion.

Butler lands at Arklow in Co Dublin.

Church allegiance has seldom been merely a question of religious affiliation, particularly in Ireland. It has usually been seen as a political stance as much as an expression of faith. We have seen how the Roman Church's desire to suppress the Celtic Church gave papal sanction to the Norman domination of Ireland. Likewise, the Protestant Reformation which spread through Europe in the sixteenth century divided the continent not only on tenets of religious belief but also politically, with most northern states adopting the new religion in various forms, while most southern states remained faithful to Roman Catholicism. This divide was reflected in the relationship between England and Ireland, with the former breaking away from Rome and the latter remaining loyal to Rome.

We have seen how in the 1530s, Arklow's Priory of the Holy Cross was one of the many religious houses closed as part of the General Suppression by Henry VIII. Henry had made himself head of the Church in England, and his daughter Elizabeth and her supporters widened the division between Catholic Rome and Protestant England even further. When she acceded to the throne in 1558 the chasm between Catholics and Protestants seemed unbridgeable. Leading Catholics were suspected of less than wholehearted loyalty to the crown, a suspicion exacerbated during the 1580s by the threat of Spanish invasion, and political expediency procured as many conversions to Protestantism as genuine faith did. This was particularly true in Ireland and a new depth of antagonism galvanised the already unstable relationship between the two countries. To complicate matters further, many of the Old English families in Ireland, such as the Butlers, remained Catholic and they feared that their claims on their lands would be vulnerable to the hardening anti-Catholic bias in London. So it was no longer a relatively simple English-versus-Irish conflict. The enemies of Gaelic Ireland, the Old English lords, now found that they had more in common with their fellow Catholics in Ireland than they had with the new Protestant regime in England. The Elizabethan plantations of Ulster and elsewhere, that is the confiscation of Catholic lands and their redistribution to Scottish and English Presbyterians and Anglicans, fuelled the concerns of the Old English Catholics even more, but it would be four decades before things came to a head.

In the meantime, life for those in Arklow already without property went on as usual. Most eked out their living from the land and fishing. As early as the fourteenth century the sea off Arklow had been identified as lucrative fishing grounds. An Italian map of that period clearly shows three fishing banks a few miles offshore.[2] These were the Arklow Banks which have claimed countless vessels over the millennia and are now the location for electricity generating windmills. In 1513 a map of Ireland in an atlas published in Strasburg shows Arklow as a seaport, and other references indicate that it was one of the main fishing ports in the country at that time. Significantly, when Captain Laurence Esmonde leased the manor of Arklow from the Earl of Ormond in 1601 for thirty years at £60 a year, he agreed to deliver twelve barrels of herrings to the earl during every fishing season for ten shillings a barrel. He also had to

> provide food and lodging for the Earl's horses and horseboys whenever they should be at Arklow, and to entertain the Earl and his company for twenty-four hours at his expense whenever the Earl should visit Arklow.[3]

but the main point here is the provision of fish. Arklow trading vessels were recorded in the French port of La Rochelle at the end of the sixteenth century. In the 1560s boards were shipped through Arklow, Wicklow and Dublin to Scotland for shipbuilding.[4] In 1612 Richard Mitten was appointed keeper of customs at the ports of Wexford and Arklow, which may have been a direct result of the growing business interests at Shillelagh, but much of this trade was later carried out through Enniscorthy.[5] At the time of Mitten's appointment, 1612, Arklow was a very ill-equipped port. Vessels as small as twenty or thirty tons could not land here because of the shallow, meandering estuary. Also the sand banks several miles out to sea were a navigational hazard that made shipping interests wary of using the port more than was necessary. Despite these problems, sometime in the 1620s, the Fowler brothers were appointed custom controllers for the port, again indicating substantial commercial activity.[6] Timber from Shillelagh woods and elsewhere were shipped through Arklow to England, the Netherlands, France and Spain.[7] A busy port was an economic hub. Not only did shipowners and seamen benefit, but dockers and carters were also employed. Shipwrights and riggers were needed to build and repair vessels.[8] The 1620s and '30s were relatively peaceful, but the religious/political tensions alluded to above had stretched to breaking point and were to have their effects on Arklow just as everywhere else in Britain and Ireland.

Charles I was crowned king in 1625, at a time when religious wars raged throughout Europe. Catholics were persecuted in many of the new Protestant states, while Protestants were persecuted in Catholic states. Charles was Protestant, but in the same year as his accession he married the Catholic Henrietta Maria, sister of Louis XII of France. This perceived alliance caused great unease and resentment in England. The Huguenots were being persecuted in France because of their Protestantism and many English parliamentarians felt that the marriage was not simply an insult to Protestants but was a potential danger on the basis that Henrietta's Catholicism might influence Charles's reign. Soon after becoming king, Charles requested money from parliament, they refused and he dissolved the assembly. Not only did this not solve his money problems, but it hardened attitudes between the king and the new parliament, which replaced the one he had dissolved. In 1628, parliament agreed to vote Charles money if he accepted a Petition of Rights, a list of civil liberties. Charles was prepared to accept any conditions. After all, he still had the power to dissolve parliament again after his finances had been sorted out. Which is exactly what he did the following year, and he ruled like the absolute monarch he believed himself to be until 1640. But Protestant power had not gone away. Leading members continued to meet in assembly and Charles, once again strapped for cash, was forced to reconstitute parliament. The members agreed to the reconstitution but again insisted on several conditions, one of which was the monarch could never again dissolve parliament without its permission. Charles had no option but to agree, although it altered forever the concept of absolute monarchy in England. In future ultimate political authority would rest with the king-in-parliament, a compromise in which, in theory, one body would act as a brake on the excesses of the other. The problem might have been solved on paper, but that was all.

While royalist and parliamentarian factions became entrenched in England, the religious divide also made itself felt on this side of the Irish Sea. Old English Catholics in Ireland, now allied with some of their erstwhile Irish enemies, decided the time had come to band together under Lord Mountgarret, an uncle of the Earl of Ormond.[9] I mentioned at the beginning of Chapter Three that the Butlers periodically displayed a remarkable propensity for political survival down the centuries. At no time in their history was this better demonstrated than during this crisis. The Butler family had remained Catholic during and after the Reformation, but there was one important exception. When Thomas Butler, eldest son of the then earl, lost his life in a shipwreck off Wales in 1619, he left behind him a young family, the eldest son of which was nine-year-old James, who had been brought up in London. As his father had been heir apparent to the Ormond title and estates, so now James became heir apparent. As such an important figure of the future, he was made a royal ward and brought up Protestant. When his grandfather, the earl, died in 1633 the twenty-three-year-old James acceded to the title, the first Protestant Earl of Ormond.[10] This meant that whichever religion was to emerge politically triumphant, the Butlers would have at least some family members on the winning side. James was later to write that his parents had

> lived and died papists, and bred all their children so, and only I, by God's merciful providence, was educated in the true Protestant religion.[11]

Such hedging of bets was far from unusual in leading political families, but in the case of the Butlers the situation could hardly have been more dramatic. James, as earl, was appointed commander-in-chief of the king's forces in Ireland at about the same time as his uncle was the *de facto* leader of a potentially rebellious coalition of Old English and Irish Catholics. That potential was realised in 1641 when the Catholics consolidated their strongholds around the country. Even allowing for contemporary and subsequent propaganda, accounts of one atrocity after another on both sides made the rebellion of 1641 one of the darkest dates in the Irish calendar. Some regions suffered more horrors than others. The northeastern counties of Ulster saw the worst excesses, supplying iconic images that would be indelibly imprinted on the minds of generations to come, even to the present day.

Arklow was lucky. When it was seized by Catholic forces in November, it was an apparently bloodless coup, despite unsubstantiated talk of local people being put to the sword.[12] By February 1642 'only a few scattered areas remained in Protestant hands'.[13] In May, the Catholic clergy came on board, holding a national convention in Kilkenny. Their aims were to

> restore the rights of the church, maintain the properties of the crown,
> and to defend the liberties of the nation.[14]

The alliance between the Old English lords of the land, the leaders of the native Irish septs, and the Catholic Church had been officially forged. An oath of association was drawn up and any Catholic who did not take it was excommunicated.[15] It was a George W. Bush style declaration of 'you're either with us or against us'. It was also decided at that convention to establish a provisional government in all but name. A further gathering was arranged to be held in Kilkenny in October of that year at which an assembly would be elected. From this date on, the new force was called the Confederate Catholics.

This was open rebellion. Neither king's proclamation nor parliament's writ was deemed binding in Ireland. Charles and his royalist supporters were too busy fending off parliament in England to deal with the situation here. That task was left to Charles's most trusted subordinate, his former ward, James Butler, Earl of Ormond.

By 1642, England was in the throes of a civil war between Charles's cavaliers and parliament's roundheads. A new military strategist named

Oliver Cromwell emerged to lead the latter. He brought new tactics and techniques which resulted in the formation of what was to become known as 'The New Model Army'. The battle of Naseby broke the royalists in 1645 and Charles went into hiding. Meantime in Ireland, Ormond had succeeded in getting the Confederate Catholics to cease hostilities in 1643. His trump card had been that the real enemy, the common enemy of Irish-based Catholics and royalist Protestants, were the parliamentarians and that other grievances would be best put aside until they had been beaten. A further agreement between the Confederates and Ormond in 1646, in which he agreed to grant religious tolerance to Catholics, shows how desperate Ormond was to win them over, especially now that the parliamentary forces had beaten the royalists in England. But it was a short-lived agreement. The Confederates reneged on this, siding with Owen Roe O'Neill after his victory at Benburb. When this happened, Ormond knew that the royalist cause was also lost in Ireland and he had no option but to turn Dublin over to parliamentary forces. He sailed for London soon after. After his defeat at Naseby, Charles went on the run and eventually made a treaty with the Scots. They invaded England but were repulsed. Charles was later captured and put on trial for treason, found guilty and was hanged on January 30th, 1649. Ormond had always been loyal to the king and, on the execution of Charles, he immediately pledged his allegiance to the Stuart dynasty and Charles's son, the future Charles II. This pledge of allegiance made it impossible for him to remain in England and he headed for France in 1650.

Arklow's experience of these very troubled times was, to say the least, low key. From the beginning, the Confederate Catholics deemed Arklow castle and the other Ormond properties legitimate targets and had taken control of the town and hinterland by the end of 1641. Once again in its long history, the castle seems to have proved useless as a citadel of defence and it would appear that it was held by the opposing factions at different times throughout the 1640s. Mention is made that it was in the possession of the Confederates in 1641, 1643, and that they re-occupied it on June 5th, 1647.[16] Perhaps they surrendered it to Ormond on the agreement negotiated with him in 1643 and retook it when they sided with the rebellion of Owen Roe O'Neill. One way or another, these exchanges must have been fairly tame affairs because there is no record of battles or even skirmishes associated with them. The only incident which suggests war damage was

in 1644 – Richard Dickson, an Arklow mariner, reported that as a result
of the rebellion, he had lost 2,500 feet of 12-inch planks intended for
ship building.[17]

But this relatively uneventful state was soon to end.

*

When the war in England between the royalists and Oliver Cromwell's
parliamentarian roundheads had drawn to a close, Cromwell turned his
attention to Ireland. This is not the place to give an account of his march
through Ireland, there are many books on that subject. What concerns
us here is how Arklow fared. On September 28th, 1649 the Cromwellian
forces camped along the high ground north of the Avoca river,
overlooking the town. The castle was in plain view. Cromwell himself
is said to have camped at Sheepwalk, and a large boulder in that
townland is still called Cromwell's Stone. I have heard that it is so called
because Oliver stood on it, dined on it, reclined on it, leaned against it
or in some other fashion bestowed on it a dubious posterity, but Liam
Price believes that it may have been associated not with Oliver
Cromwell but with a family named Cromwell who settled in the area in
1596, of whom more shortly.[18]

His force consisted of 4,000 infantry, 1,200 horse and 400 dragoons,
while the castle was defended by a garrison of one officer and twenty
soldiers[19] – or at least it would have been so defended had that officer
and his men not deemed discretion the better part of valour, and who
can blame them for getting out while they could? Cromwell had
established a reputation for sparing the defenders and inhabitants of a
town if the town was instantly surrendered. On the other hand,
resistance would guarantee slaughter of the garrison as well as many of
the citizens. News of the barbaric massacre at Drogheda a few days
earlier had no doubt reached Arklow and the small garrison decided to
abandon the castle and town to their fate. In fairness, resistance would
have been useless and, therefore, catastrophic. Apart from the soldiers'
understandably acute sense of self-preservation, the people of the town
must also have urged them to leave. They knew that their only hope of
survival was to offer no resistance to the roundheads. And so it was that

when Cromwell and his Model Army entered the town on September 29th, 1649 he found the way unbarred.

There was no bridge across the river at that time. About a mile upstream from where the bridge now stands was a crossing place still known as the Horse Ford. Most of his army would have crossed there, but Oliver may have used the ferry which crossed the river just a few yards west of the present bridge. The ferry was probably little more than a raft operated by rope-and-pulley between landing places. We have no image or description of it. The landing place on the south side was roughly where the backyard of Le Chef Food Emporium is now. On the north side, the landing place was known as the ferry bank, or Ferrybank as we know it today. Coincidentally, the man who owned and operated the ferry was Richard Cromwell, a namesake of Oliver's son, and a member of the family which Price believes settled in the area in 1596. That night, Oliver summoned this Richard to the castle, amused by the coincidence. He offered the ferryman anything he wanted, to which the no doubt much relieved Richard is reputed to have said that all he wanted was to be left in possession of his ferry. Oliver, impressed by the man's lack of greed, replied: 'A poor man I found you and a poor man I'll leave you', but granted him his ferry plots in perpetuity. The plot on the southern side was still commonly known as Cromwell's Plot until recent decades.[20]

While Richard Cromwell returned to his business, Oliver proceeded with his. He assigned a small garrison to remain in the castle while he, at the head of his army, headed towards Wexford, where he oversaw a repeat of the savagery perpetrated at Drogheda. Arklow, it seems, had escaped lightly. Recent revisionist interpretations of Cromwell's sojourn in Ireland suggest that much of the blame for the massacres at Drogheda and Wexford rests with the victims themselves on the basis that had they not resisted they would have been spared like the people of Arklow were.[21] Furthermore, the new argument would have it, by making examples of Drogheda and Wexford, Cromwell saved lives elsewhere. With a little more revisionism like that, Oliver Cromwell might soon be canonised patron saint of pacifists. As far as Cromwell himself was concerned, he regarded the massacre of Drogheda as

> a righteous judgement of God upon these barbarous wretches ...... it is good that God alone have all the glory.[22]

Three months later, the O'Tooles and the O'Byrnes attacked Arklow and Colonel Hewson set out from Dublin at the head of 1,000 men to retake it, which he did without even engaging in battle. It would appear that the sight of such a force was sufficient to make the O'Tooles and the O'Byrnes run to the hills. They attacked again in January 1650, but

> the garrison, commanded by Captain Barrington, made a sudden sally, and slew many of the assailants; the rest fled.[23]

This might be the incident referred to in a pamphlet published in London in 1662.[24] It stated that

> Captain Barrington, garrisoned at Arklow, murdered Donagh O'Daly of Kilcarrow and more than 500 others who had been received into protection by himself; and it is well known that most of the common people were murdered.

I have never come across any other reference to this mass murder, either in documented history or in the folk memory, which is very strange if it did happen. It should be remembered that the murder of the two MacMurrough brothers in 1282 entered folk memory and remained there for many years. Surely the mass murder of 'most of the common people' in the mid-seventeenth century would still be remembered in folklore at least? Most of the atrocities committed at that time have been recorded in the pages of history, why wasn't this one? We should not dismiss it because of the lack of collaborative evidence but neither should it be taken as gospel without some form of verification.

One way or another, it was the last time that the local Irish septs attacked the town, and it was soon after these forays that the Ormond castle at Arklow was destroyed on Cromwell's order. It was one of many Irish castles which were well passed their sell-by date. Useless as defensive strongholds, they merely offered a focus of resentment, reminders of humiliation and defeat. The cost of maintenance could no longer be justified. In short, they were more trouble than they were worth. The keep was razed, the curtain walls levelled. All that remained of Arklow castle was the solitary sentinel that had been the northeast tower, the lower half of which can still be seen in the Town Hall yard. Why that single tower was left standing can only be guessed at. It has been said that it was left to remind the owner, the exiled earl, that his

Ormond castle as it appeared in 1794, 145 years after its destruction

age was passed. If that was the reason, it was a declaration too quickly made.

Priest-hunting recommenced after the breathing space afforded to Catholics by the reign of Charles I,[25] and throughout the 1640s such persecution of the clergy was widespread. According to Denis Murphy, by 1651 'three-fourths of the religious were dead or in exile'.[26] No quarter was to be given to them and they were to be treated as enemies who had not surrendered.[27] One example of priest-hunting concerned the Arklow parish priest, Father Daniel Delaney. We do not know the exact date, but it was during the 1640s-50s period.

> The enemy came by surprise on Daniel Delaney, parish priest of Arklow and savagely massacred, before his eyes, his servant named Walsh, who was flying for his life with a packet of the sacred vessels and ornaments; but the priest himself, being a powerful man, drew his sword and defended himself so well against the attack that he compelled his assailants to promise him his life if he delivered up his sword. So far, however, from keeping their solemn promise, they immediately stripped the venerable man naked, and tied him to a horse's tail; the rider goaded his horse to full speed along a road covered over with brambles and thickets, and rough with frost and frozen snow, and dragged the priest to the town of Gorey. There the savage commander of those hunters condemned him to death in violation of the solemn promise. He was

covered over with blood, his sides torn and his whole frame exhausted; he was nevertheless delivered up to a guard of soldiers who were to watch him in turn during the night. While he lay there, naked, sleepless, frozen with cold, and livid with bruises, his guards amused themselves with twisting and plucking his long beard with a cane, and cruelly beating his sides with cudgels .... Next day he was three different times hanged to the bough of a tree, and three times let down to the ground to protract the agony of his torture, but he was strangled with a rope at last, and thus ended his life of suffering to reign triumphant in heaven.[28]

One of the main rooms in Áras Lorcáin, the new Catholic parish centre, is named in Fr Delaney's honour. Two more are called after Fr William Ryan, parish priest murdered in 1798, and Theresa Kearney who gained fame as Mother Kevin for her work in Africa in the first half of the twentieth century.[29]

*

If a week is a long time in politics, Cromwell was to learn that a decade is an aeon. His triumphant return to a republican England was reminiscent of Pompey's return to Rome. His mastery of the battlefield and his ruthlessness in victory, which as we have seen he deemed the work of god, placed him firmly at the top of the political tree. He became a monarch in all but name and he accepted the title Lord Protector offered to him by parliament, even to the point of being allowed to name his son Richard as his successor. When Cromwell died in 1658, Richard did succeed him, but he was unable to control the various factions within and outside of parliament as his father had done and he was forced from power the following year. The experiment with republicanism had degenerated into a virtual dictatorship and there were now growing demands for a restoration of the monarchy.

In 1660, Charles Stuart was invited back to England to accept the crown. The political wheel of fortune had turned full circle. Cromwell's body was taken from where it lay in Westminster Abbey and hanged as that of a traitor. His head was cut off and placed on a pole over Westminster Hall and his body buried at the foot of the gallows. A grateful Charles rewarded those who had been loyal to him, particularly James Butler, who had been prominent in the negotiations leading to the restoration of the monarchy. He was given a step up the aristocratic ladder from earl to become the 1st Duke of Ormond, and was appointed Commissioner for the Treasury and the Navy and, in 1662, was once again Lord Lieutenant of Ireland.

It was about this time that the new duke restructured his estates. The family's economic centre of gravity had long since shifted to Kilkenny and the Arklow estates were of diminishing importance. It was decided to lease the North Shire, the 4,000 acres stretching north of the river between the coast and about halfway to Woodenbridge. The lease was taken by Ralph Howard who arrived from England. His father had recently died and Ralph sold the family property there and brought his mother, Dorothea (née Hassels), to live here. She moved into the main house at Shelton, while he studied at Trinity College, Dublin. He graduated as a MD in 1667. Two years later he bought a house in Great Ship Street and was appointed Professor of Physic.[30]

The building his mother occupied was not the Shelton Abbey we know today. That was not built until the 1820s, but her home was a substantial house. We know this from the Hearth Money Rolls. In 1660 a tax on domestic fireplaces was introduced in England. The revenue from this was called the Hearth Money. It was not extended to Ireland until three years later. Although it was abolished in England in 1690, it was still levied here until 1793. As most habitations had some form of fire hearth, the lists of people liable are quite extensive. These lists are known as the Hearth Money Rolls. The 1663 rolls name those liable for the two shilling per hearth tax. This was payable in two instalments, Lady Day (March 25th) and Michaelmas (September 29th), but in subsequent years the entire sum was to be paid on January 10th each year. Wicklow historian Stan O'Reilly has researched and analysed the 1668 Rolls.

> The town of Arklow was prosperous enough according to the number of houses which had hearths in them, of 68 many are listed as having more than one hearth ...... [for example] Fleming, Vaughan, Stephens, Washington, King, and Cromwell ...... Major West who lived in one of the five houses at the Rock enjoyed the eight hearths in his home, his near neighbour Garret Cavenagh paid tax on two, at Ballirahin [Ballyraine] John Ward lived in one of the three houses listed and paid tax on two hearths ...... there is one house listed in the townland of Shelton, this was occupied by Rob. Hussels, Esq [i.e Robert Hassels] who was paying tax on nine.[31]

The nine hearths taxed in Hassels' house give some idea of its size and importance in the Arklow area. It is interesting to speculate just who 'Robert Hussels' was. He may have been Dorothea's brother who might have been in charge of the estate while Ralph Howard was in Dublin. It is also interesting to compare the towns of Arklow and Wicklow using the Hearth Money Rolls. While there were only sixty-eight houses listed with a hearth in Arklow, there were 140 in Wicklow, perhaps 'indicating that the county town enjoyed a higher degree of prosperity'.[32]

The name of Sir William Petty crops up in relation to Arklow about this time. In 1652 the London parliament instituted the Civil and Down Survey of Ireland. This was to identify the property of those who were deemed rebellious, which would be confiscated and redistributed to Cromwell's soldiers in payment for their services. Maps of various scales covering baronies and parishes, as well as inventories, were to be made.[33] The Wicklow maps and inventories were made in 1654 under Petty's direction. Unfortunately the detailed parish maps and accompanying inventories have not survived, although the barony maps are now housed in the Lansdowne Papers in the National Library of Ireland.[34] No doubt, these maps and inventories proved extremely useful when it came to imposing the hearth tax. Petty is recorded as having estimated that there were a total of 300,000 hearths in Ireland, representing a population of 1,300,000 people.[35]

But Petty might have another connection with Arklow. In his excellent *Maritime Arklow,* Captain Frank Forde wrote

> One of the earliest European catamarans was built at Arklow in 1663 to the order of William Petty, a Cromwellian settler and ancestor of the Marquis of Lansdowne. As a young man, Petty had served at sea and heard of the twin-hulled "Katta-maram" of the Indian Ocean. On his arrival in Ireland, he put his dreams into practice and placed an order at Arklow for his strange craft. Sadly we do not know the name of its builder.
>
> It consisted of two wooden cylinders, 20' long and of 2' diameter, hollowed out and plugged at each end. They supported a platform 20' long and 9' wide which carried a 20' high mast. Forty men could be accommodated on board. A model of Petty's craft is in the Science Museum, London and a photograph forms the frontispiece of The Double-Bottom Ship of Sir William Petty by the Marquis of Lansdowne (Oxford Press 1931).
>
> Her trials were conducted between Holyhead and Dublin in July 1664 and Petty recorded:

In her coming back with an extreme wind (to the west) she ran ye best Packet Boate quite out of sight in less than a watch, and left her to leeward. She arrived at this port (Dublin) at 5 o'clock this afternoon. It is night and ye Packet not yet heard of, although they set sail at ye same moment. It was early next morning before ye ketch came to Dublin.[36]

A replica of this catamaram was constructed by businessman Hal Sisk in the late 1980s, but I am unsure of its current whereabouts.

The 1670s and '80s seem to have been fairly quiet in Arklow. Dorothea Howard died at Shelton in 1684 and was buried in the ancient graveyard of Kilbride. Kilbride is listed in the Bull of Innocent III in 1216 as 'St Brigid's near Arklow', a church of the diocese of Glendalough. The small church was ruinous by 1630[37] and Dorothea was buried within its crumbling walls, a partial gable and general outline can still be seen.[38]

The relative relaxation towards Catholicism after the restoration of the English monarchy prompted some Dominican friars to return to the priory grounds, but it is impossible to say how much of the structure was still intact and Dominican archives show that over the next four decades, the friars were present in the town, although the community did not exceed seven members at any time and was often as small as two.[39]

The fact that the monks could live and preach in Arklow reflects the wider political picture at that time. Although Charles II was a Protestant, he was not as anti-Catholic as his parliament was and he still had enough constitutional power to have many of his wishes carried out. The tension this created increased drastically when his son James publicly announced his conversion to Catholicism. In 1683 there was a plot to murder both Charles and his Catholic son. It was foiled, some of the conspirators were executed but the leader, Rumbold, escaped to Holland. That Holland should have been his safe haven is interesting, because James' daughter Mary had married Dutchman William, Prince of Orange, only six years earlier. Is it not strange that her father's and grandfather's would-be assassin should find protection in her husband's country?

Two years later, in 1685, Charles died and was succeeded by James, the first Catholic British monarch in a hundred years. James ignored the Test Act – legislation designed to debar Catholics from becoming army officers – as he began to build military support for his reign. The following year he tried to dispense with all law emanating from parliament, the year after that he replaced the Protestant Lord Deputy of Ireland with a Catholic. Discretion had no part of James' strategies. The disquiet expressed on his conversion had grown to rumbles of volcanic proportions on his accession and now his autocratic approach to monarchical rule brought those rumbles to the point of eruption. The Protestant parliament could foresee a return of Catholic rule, a regime under which they would be persecuted just as they had persecuted Catholics and Dissenters. James II would have to go, but the monarchy was enshrined in the constitution as being independent of parliament. They had no legal right to overthrow James. However, another claimant to the title could, particularly a Protestant claimant with at least some familial entitlement to succeed James. In 1688, William of Orange, James' son-in-law, was invited to throw his name into the crown. He accepted, becoming William III, 'King Billy', and England was once again in the throes of a religious war, and once again that religious war spilled over into Ireland with the major flash points at Derry, the Boyne, and Limerick. And once again, people in the Arklow area were affected.

The Dominican friars were forced to keep a low profile, but they were not the only ones. At Shelton, Ralph Howard was known to support the Williamites and was forced to flee with his wife and children to England. The estate was put in the hands of a Jacobite named Hackett or Hatchett,[40] and Shelton was to be a safe resting place for the fugitive James after his defeat at the river Boyne.

Through the townlands of Kilpatrick, Ballyrichard, Templerainey and Coolboy, which lie to the north of the town, lie the fragmented traces of what was once an important road. On the day after the battle of the Boyne, July 1st, 1690,[41] a group of riders travelled this way in a bid to escape the Williamite victors. One of the group was the deposed king, James II. Leaving his followers to their fate, he had fled the battlefield and high-tailed it towards Waterford for a ship to France. They followed the road until they came to Shelton, where Hackett supplied the group with food and rest. There is a tradition that while there, James sneezed heavily, causing his nose to bleed profusely, staining a wooden upright on the porch. It was not a serious affliction and the flow was soon staunched. James and his small group continued on their journey, crossing the Horse Ford, along the Granny Well Lane through Ballyraine, emerging at the west end of the town close to where Arklow

Tennis Club now has its premises. They carried on down through the town and reached the last of the houses at what is now called King's Hill in Lower Main Street. One of the reasons put forward for this placename is that it was here that the people catcalled the scurrying king.[42] They would have had little to gain from a Jacobite victory, but were to suffer greatly with the Williamites in control.

One family who was glad to see the end of James were the Howards. With William and Mary on the throne and the Stuart dynasty hiding in France, the future augured well for loyal Protestant landowners, particularly as new anti-Catholic legislation was introduced to copperfasten Protestant ascendancy. This new penal code was so severe that it was deemed to have plumbed the depths of 'the perverted ingenuity of man'.[43]

5

Repression and Rebellion:
1700 - 1798

There had been anti-Catholic legislation in Britain and Ireland since the Reformation. Most of the laws were restrictions on religious observance without actually banning Roman Catholicism outright. Impositions such as Catholics having to pay tithes for the upkeep of Protestant churches and clergy meant that Catholics had to pay twice for religious obligations, once by law to the Protestant Church and secondly by personal conviction and ecclesiastical dictat to help maintain their own clergy. They were also virtually barred from entering politics, but they were entitled to hold land.[1] Under William and Mary, things were to get very much worse.

May 1st, 1698 was the deadline for all members of religious orders to get out of Ireland. Any monks, friars, or non-secular priests found in the country after that date would be deported. If they returned and were caught they would be put to death being deemed guilty of high treason.[2] Secular priests could stay if they registered, but registration included taking an oath which would be repugnant to Catholic clergy, with the result that no priest could in conscience register. Bishops were also exiled, which meant that when those priests who were allowed to stay grew old and died, no young priests could be ordained to replace them. In effect, Catholicism was to be eradicated from Ireland even though the Catholic religion was not actually banned by the Penal Laws. It would, it was believed, die out in the course of time. And that was just the tip of the iceberg.

> [Catholics] could not set up Catholic schools, nor teach in such, nor go abroad to Catholic schools. They were excluded from Parliament, from

the corporations, from the army and navy, from the legal profession, and from all civil offices. They could not act as sheriffs, or under-sheriffs, or as jurors, or even as constables. They could not employ more than two Catholic apprentices in their trade; they could not carry arms, nor own a horse worth more than 5 pounds ... To bury their dead in an old ruined abbey or monastery involved a penalty of ten pounds ...[3]

The list goes on. Trying to eradicate Catholicism was only one of the purposes of the Penal Laws, the other was to transfer landownership from the native Irish to English and Scottish Protestant settlers. There was little chance of wiping out the religion of the vast majority of the population. People are very resilient and usually find ways to circumvent repression. In this case, young men went to Irish Colleges in Belgium, France and Spain to become priests, returning to Ireland after their ordination despite the death sentence they would face if discovered. Also, after the first thirty years or so, the laws restricting the participation of Catholics in the commercial life of towns and cities were more honoured in the breach than the observance. The land policies, however, were far more effective.

A Catholic could not acquire land, nor buy it, nor hold a mortgage on it; and the Catholic landlord was bound at death to leave his estate to his children in equal shares. During life, if the wife or son of such became a Protestant, she or he at once obtained separate maintenance.[4]

Little wonder that within a hundred years less than five per cent of the land of Ireland was owned by Catholics.

It is estimated that over half of the Catholic landed families of 1700 shifted religious allegiance during the course of the century.[5]

By 1703 the new hard-line Protestant regime was in place and in Arklow it seemed incongruous that the Protestant community had no place of worship inside the town limits. They did have a church in the vicinity of Kilbride, but that was a mile or more away. They petitioned the Protestant Archbishop of Dublin, Dr King, for permission to build a new parish church in the town itself and the site they preferred was that of the old abbey.

As we have seen, since Henry VIII's Suppression of the Monasteries in the 1530s the abbey lands had been leased to a succession of holders, with Captain Laurence Esmonde taking charge in 1601. Esmonde, by then Sir Laurence, died in 1646 and left the property to his son, Sir Thomas. Because Thomas became a Catholic in arms against Cromwell's forces, the abbey lands and his other properties were taken from him in 1649 and given to Colonel Monk. The restoration of the monarchy, however, put the Esmondes back in possession in 1666, and by the time it was proposed to erect the Protestant church there in 1703, the owner was Sir Laurence Esmonde, son of Thomas. This Laurence might have been Protestant, or he might have simply thought it expedient to co-operate in the venture. Whatever the reason, and whatever his religion, he agreed to the transfer of the property to the Protestant parish and the new church of St Mary's was built on or near the site of the once proud Dominican Priory of the Holy Cross. The transfer referred to the church site only and Esmonde retained the many lucrative acres that surrounded it. The church was completed three years later and remained the Protestant parish church for the following 120 years. The Catholic church in the town was a small, mud-walled thatched structure not far away in what is now appropriately known as Old Chapel Ground.

*

As the eighteenth century dawned, the Duke of Ormond decided to rid himself of his remaining Arklow estates. Forty years earlier he had first leased and later sold his property north of the river to Ralph Howard, now he looked for someone to take the town and the lands south of the river off his hands. That someone was to be John Allen.

Like William of Orange, John Allen came to Ireland from Holland at the end of the seventeenth century.[6] He may have been a Williamite soldier or financial backer, as his rise in the business and political circles of the period suggests he knew on which side his political bread was buttered. He was one of the leading builders and architects of his day and used his political connections to be made a Privy Councillor. He purchased property in Stillorgan and other parts of south Dublin, but was also interested in acquiring a country estate by either lease or purchase and Ormond's remaining Arklow properties fitted the bill perfectly. The dates and form of acquisition are open to question, with some sources saying the transaction was completed on July 30th, 1700, and others saying that the deal was not finalised until April 1714.[7] Perhaps Allen, like the Howards of Shelton before him, initially leased the property before purchasing. The accounts agree on the size of the holding, 8,528 acres stretching from the sea to Woodenbridge, but not on the price, which ranges from £1 an acre, that is a total of £8,528, to £1,140 for the lot. The important point is that the 520-year association of the Fitzwalter/Butlers with the town and environs of Arklow was over. Some of their descendants can still be found here, but the ownership of the area had passed to new hands.

The Allens' social standing was raised to new heights by this acquisition. To have money was one thing, but to have a rural estate was the true mark of nobility, or potential nobility. Apart from their properties in Stillorgan, Carrickmines, Blackrock and Merrion, they acquired further property in Dalkey and Kildare. John Allen's eldest son, Joshua, became a member of the Corporation of Dublin, then sheriff, and then mayor. By 1717, Joshua's son John was rich enough and respectable enough to be awarded the titles Baron Allen of Kildare and Viscount Allen of Stillorgan. As well as land and rent revenues, the Ormond estate – now the Allen estate – carried with it the right to nominate two members to parliament for the borough of Carysfort, the virtually non-existent village in the Wicklow mountains at Macreddin near Aughrim. This was a typical "rotten borough" which allowed vested interests to retain political power. In 1622, Lord Falkland had built a castle at Macreddin, which became known as Cary's Fort. Seven years later, probably for financial reasons, Charles I made the 'town' of Macreddin and surrounding area into 'the free borough of Cariesfort' with the right to return two members to parliament. That right now passed to the Allen family and was valid up until the Act of Union in 1801.

The seat at the centre of the Allen estate was at Poulahoney. A map from 1726[8] shows a large hunting lodge on or near the site now occupied by Glenart Castle. Surrounding it are fields for cultivation and pasture, woodlands and parklands. As on most estates such as this, a central core of farmland was retained by the estate, a "home farm", to be worked by employees. A manager, or estate agent, was hired to oversee its day to day running, as well as ensuring rents were paid by tenants on leased properties and that estate rules and regulations were adhered to. Unfortunately, there are no documents from this period stating that that is how this estate was run, but it was the system used later. What we do know is that most of the 8,528 acres were leased out to farmers, many of whom sublet to smaller farmers and labourers.

Many, if not most, of the principal tenants were Protestants and this became the norm as the land-holding restrictions of the Penal Laws took affect.

A typical lease was one taken out on March 26th, 1736 between Joshua, Lord Viscount Allen and Ashley Hunt of Ballyrean (i.e. Ballyraine). It was a lease renewal, Hunt had already been in possession of the holding and his name appears on the 1726 map as a tenant in Ballyraine. The holding was of 143 acres and the annual rent was £23, plus 'sixpence per pound and two fat capons or three shillings in lieu'. Capons were castrated cockerels fattened for eating. Perhaps even more perplexing to modern eyes than the reference to the two unfortunate fowl is the unspecified duration of the lease. It was the norm at that time not to stipulate a definite time period in a lease. Instead the agreement would terminate on the death of the third of three named lives. As was usual, Ashley Hunt chose his own life and those of two of his family members, his wife Elizabeth and his son Matthew. Unfortunately, it doesn't record their ages.[9] One way or another it was a gamble. A fatal epidemic might wipe out the nominees within a year, leaving the other family members homeless. On the other hand one of them, not necessarily the youngest, might live for sixty or seventy years from the date the agreement was signed. Leases of specified duration did not become widespread until the nineteenth century. Because of the recorded names and family relationships, such leases are now very useful to family historians.

On the north side of the river, on the Howard estate, life mirrored that of its southside counterpart. The Williamite war, and the consequent political and financial straitjacketing of the vast majority of the Irish people, brought a stability that bordered on stagnation. The land was tilled or grazed, the sea was fished but there was little evidence of investment in the future. Rents were paid and the Howards and the Allens were content with this return on their expenditures. The only building of any note to be erected at this time, apart from St Mary's parish church, was a military barracks which was built about 1720 on the site of the old castle. The barracks survived until 1922, of which more anon. It has been suggested that the original Queen Anne barracks was a modest affair, 'low and draughty', which was added to in Georgian times, transforming it into a fine two-storey building.[10] Whatever the size and shape of the barracks when it was first built, it is reasonable to assume that much of the debris from the castle, destroyed on Cromwell's orders seventy years earlier, was quarried for building materials. The street widened slightly at this point, allowing room for the soldiers to drill on the open area and so give it the name by which we know it today, the Parade Ground.

Things started to pick up around the halfway stage of the century. In 1750, Elizabeth Allen married John Proby. The Probys had an estate in Huntingdonshire in England and their country seat was Elton Hall near Peterborough. As part of the marriage settlement, the Allen properties at Stillorgan and Arklow passed into John Proby's hands, as did the right to nominate the two Cariesfort/Macreddin members of parliament. The new lord of the land and of the town of Arklow had arrived and the name Proby was to be become inextricably linked with its development for the next 150 years.

In preparation for the transfer of the Allen estate into the Proby name a new estate map was drawn and this map now gives us a good idea of what the town looked like at that time.

> Arklow parish church, the militia barracks, an eight-arched bridge, and nineteen houses are illustrated in a layout consistent with the true position of the urban building circa 1750. The only ornament of note on the map is a beautiful rendering of a flotilla of ships.[11]

The depiction of an 'eight-arched bridge' is interesting in that the present bridge, the Nineteen Arches, is generally believed to date from the mid-1750s, although the exact date of construction has not yet been found. While it might be a mistake to take the number of arches in the map as accurate rather than representative, there is a tradition that a wooden bridge replaced the ferry sometime towards the end of the seventeenth century and this could well be that bridge. If that is the case, perhaps it is not surprising that after fifty or sixty years of service, it was decided that a new, stone bridge was needed. Many of County Wicklow's stone bridges were built at this time as part of the public works carried out by the forerunner of the County Council, the Grand Jury.[12] There are a couple of legends concerning the Nineteen Arches and both concern its architect Andrew Noble.

The bridge was a fine example of mid-eighteenth century engineering. Any designer/builder would have been proud of it, but that was not enough to satisfy the storytellers. To make Noble's achievements even more admirable it has been claimed that he was untutored in the engineering arts. Logic does not bear this out. This was an important bridge, a major undertaking. Why would the Grand Jury or anyone else entrust it to a gifted amateur? I think substantial proof of Noble's "ah sure, I'll have a go at it" status is required before we strip him of whatever academic qualifications he may have had. The second legend is that after it was built Noble saw a flaw, one he felt was so fundamental that he could not live with the shame and so committed suicide. I have heard that the flaw was he forget to incorporate small recesses along the parapet to allow pedestrians to stand in out of the way of passing wagons and animal herds. Even if no such recesses were incorporated, would that really have been sufficient cause for Andrew Noble to kill himself? Even if it can be considered an error, it didn't call for such overreaction. He might have been slightly peeved, he might even have stamped his foot and said: "That's it, no more bridge building for me". But suicide? Hardly.

Andrew Noble's 'Nineteen Arches'. (National Library of Ireland)

The fact that Andrew Noble is buried in the ancient graveyard at Ennereilly also makes a nonsense of the tale. At that time, suicides were considered to have died in a state of mortal sin and could not, therefore, be interred in consecrated ground. Noble's grave is well inside the cemetery wall, not just outside as it would have been had he killed himself. Apart from telling us that he died on December 7th, 1759 in his fifties, his headstone bears the square and compass symbol of Freemasonry.[13] It has been suggested that this proves his credentials as an engineer, but even by that time Freemasonry had little to do with the honourable craft of working in stone and is evidence of nothing more than his possible membership of a Freemason lodge. He may have been qualified, he may not, but on balance I doubt that the Grand Jury would have put someone "with a fair grasp of the principles" in charge of such an undertaking.

One of the reasons for building the new bridge may have been the mining operations at Avoca. Mining in Wicklow can be traced back to pre-Christian times, but the first modern reference dates from the end of the seventeenth century when John Howard of Shelton came into possession of a copper mine in February 1691.[14] As part of a marriage settlement it passed into the hands of John Howard Kyan in 1766.

While these developments might signify economic progress in the region, the town remained an unimpressive sight. Richard Pococke was a man who travelled far and wide and wrote extensively about his sojourns. In 1752, he published his account of his tour of Ireland, during the course of which he approached Arklow from Coolgreaney, having passed through County Wexford. The first building he came to was the

> ... Charter School for twenty boys and twenty girls on Lady Allen's estate, which I visited and went on a quarter of a mile to Arklow, a poor fishing town without a Custom House, pleasantly situated near the mouth of the river. They formerly had much fish in the river, but the coperas of the mines has corrupted the waters, so that most of the fish are destroyed. They have a good hard marle here which lasts a considerable time. There is a foot Barrack in this place and there was a convent here of Friar's preachers founded by Tibald Butler in 1264. It is said his statue is in the church of it, where he is buryed.[15]

The hard marl was the main material used in building the cabins in which the majority of the population lived. It was also considered a fertilising agent on farms. Pococke's assurance that it lasted a considerable time will meet with total agreement from anyone who has ever tried to knock down one of those cabins without the benefit of a JCB.

The Charter School Pococke refers to was established by the Incorporated Society for Promoting English Protestant schools in Ireland at the behest of Lady Allen.[16] The aims of the society were twofold, to proselytise poor and orphaned children, and to educate them to be useful apprentices in 'the offices of low life'.[17] The school was built on the corner of Yellow Lane and the road to Coolgreaney, then being the main Wexford road, opposite the fields later used as the town cemetery. She donated £50 and a lease of twenty acres at 8/2d (about 52c) an acre per year in perpetuity. This "school" was to operate until 1812 and was nothing more than a child labour camp. At first it accommodated twenty boys and twenty girls, all of whom had to pay their way through profit made on their work, either in-house through knitting or as out-of-house workers as domestic servants or farm labourers. The Society had strict rules of conduct for both children and masters, but these were seldom adhered to in any of the Society's schools, known as Charter Schools. The Arklow school was so bad that the Society at one stage sent an inspector to record all the breaches so that a new code of conduct could be enforced and an example made of the local committee and master as a warning to their other schools in Ireland. Mismanagement was the least of the problems. Abuse of the children, short rationing of food, manipulation of financial returns and/or number of children out working, used fuel records and other discrepancies were constantly exposed and never seemed to be overcome despite changes of personnel. It was eventually closed in March 1812.

In the same year that Pococke's account was published, 1752, and just two years after his marriage into the Allen properties, John Proby bought himself a peerage. Faced with the dilemma of thinking up a catchy title, he remembered his nomination rights for the Macreddin members of parliament (or Cary's Fort or Cariesfort MPs – the spelling changes constantly in the sources) and he took the title Baron Carysfort of County Wicklow.

The Proby estate and the Howard estate faced each other directly across the river. Poulahoney Lodge and Shelton House could have been seen from each other had it not been for the trees. Only the narrow river separated them and it was understandable that a degree of competitiveness should have been part of their co-existence. If the

Probys could have a title, the Howards felt that they should have one too. Although they had to wait a little longer for their bauble of nobility, the Howards had not been wasting their time. Ralph, who had arrived from England with his mother in the mid-1660s, died in 1710 and was succeeded by his son William. William entered public life and was MP for Dublin in 1727. When he died in 1728, he was succeeded to the estate by his brother Robert. Robert also had interests other than Shelton. He had become a cleric and had risen through the ranks to become Bishop of Elphin. He died in 1740 and was succeeded by his son Ralph, who became the first Howard to take up full-time (or at least lot-of-the-time) residence at Shelton since James II's nasal mishap in 1690. He too liked public life and was elected MP for Wicklow in 1761 and again in 1768. In May 1770, he was made Privy Councillor. All this public service, and whatever else was needed to oil the wheels of preferment, finally paid off on July 12th, 1776, when Ralph Howard became Baron Clonmore.[18] Granted, it was only a baronetcy, the lowest rung on the aristocratic ladder, but it was a start and perhaps more to the point, it was as much a peerage as the "Joneses" of Poulahoney Lodge could lay claim to.

The tenants on the estates of the neighbouring barons had more pressing matters to contend with, such as putting food on the table. As early as 1752, Pococke had referred to the loss of the fish stocks in the river because of pollution from the mines. Not only that, throughout the 1760s and 1770s the Irish seafishing industry experienced a drastic decline, and by 1773 things were so bad that the government felt it necessary to introduce an incentive for boatowners to enlarge their fishing fleets and to encourage more fishermen to upgrade their operations. This took the form of a bounty of £1 per registered ton of boat. The vessels which were listed for this bounty varied in size from twenty to seventy tons, most of them being between twenty-five and forty tons, and roughly reflecting a ton per foot of overall length. The smaller vessels had a crew of six while those in excess of seventy tons employed ten or even twelve men. Twenty-one Arklow boats received the bounty and these employed a total of 142 fishermen.[19] Eleven years later, in 1784, a similar incentive was offered and this time twenty-seven Arklow boats, employing 205 men, received the grant.[20]

It was undoubtedly a help, but the extra revenue generated does not seem to have been spent on giving the town a badly needed facelift. In 1775 Richard Twiss merely mentioned that he passed through here on his way to Wicklow. Obviously, he did not share Pococke's interest in education, pollution, or building materials. A kindred spirit was the famous Arthur Young who toured Ireland up hill and down dale between 1776 and 1779 and the only mention he made of Arklow was that he took the Arklow Road from Courtown.[21] In 1780 an anonymous commentator remarked

> ... Arklow on the river Ovoca, a pretty market town ... where are the ruins of a castle of the late earls of Ormonde. Here are barracks for two companies of foot ...

then he talks about the Avoca mines before turning his attention to Gorey.[22] At least he did say it was pretty. Eight years later, in 1788, the very same complementary remarks expressed in the very same way were published anonymously in London in *The Compleat Irish Traveller.* Were efforts finally afoot to clean up Arklow's image, so that now it had the appearance of 'a pretty market town'? Perhaps having two members of the minor aristocracy in the district helped. If so, this impetus towards developing a tidy town received a further boost in 1785 and again in 1789 when the said barons both received a step up the social ladder. The Howards, in addition to being barons of Clonmore, became Viscounts Wicklow on June 23rd, 1785, and John Proby, baron Carysfort, became the 1st Earl of Carysfort four years later.

Ralph Howard felt that his family's exalted position ought to be visibly reflected. No longer was a departed Howard to be buried in the cold clay of Kilbride graveyard. Their bodies would be housed in an edifice more becoming of aristocracy, an edifice that would be easily seen from most points within a radius of a mile. This mausoleum would take the highest position in the ancient cemetery and would dwarf the ruins of the medieval church. The views from Kilbride of the town, the hinterland and the bay make it easy to understand why this spot has been accorded special status since early Christian times, and possibly even before that. The location, then, was something of a given, but other factors offered a wider range of choice and the next thing to be decided upon was the architectural style of the mausoleum.

The late eighteenth century was a time of Philosophical Enlightenment. Knowledge was deemed the true basis of individual happiness and source of common good. Received information could no longer be taken at face value and science became the new religious touchstone. Society was believed to have lost its way in a morass of superstition and Enlightenment thinkers pointed to the glories of classicism as the markers along the road to a new age. Voltaire, Diderot, and Rousseau were its heroes in France, David Hume, Samuel Johnson, and others promoted the new thinking in England. References to ancient Greece and Rome littered the worlds of politics and art. Joshua Reynolds strove to incorporate classical allusions in his portraits of the rich and famous.[23] To speak of Athenian architecture or the colosseum of Rome was to display not only education but good taste. Many of these Enlightenment thinkers were Freemasons, and Freemasonry symbolism was replete with geometrical images such as obelisks and pyramids.[24]

A rising member of the aristocracy was bound by fashion, if not by affiliation, to display such education and appreciation of the "higher things". The new mausoleum for the family of the viscount was to be a pyramid. Having said all that, maybe Ralph Howard just liked pyramids. That's the problem with symbolism, there's a danger of reading too much into a perceived icon, a risk of assigning meaning where none exists. Apart from anything else, the Grand Lodge of AF&A Masons of Ireland have no record of Ralph Howard ever having been a

The Pyramid at Kilbride

Freemason,[25] although that doesn't mean that he wasn't. Their records are being computerised and at time of writing the database encompasses the counties of Dublin, Wicklow, Wexford, Kildare, Carlow and Cork from c.1758 to 1860 only. It is possible that he joined prior to that time or was a member of a lodge outside those counties. So, for now, let's forget symbolic significance and stick with architectural details.

The base is approximately twenty-seven feet square, the walls are perpendicular until they reach the height of six feet, at which level the slopes of the pyramid begin, meeting at the pinnacle about forty feet above ground level. The outer cladding is granite blocks. It is, in short, a fine structure and cost about £1,800, a huge sum in 1785.[26] This makes it all the more curious that it was only half-full when it was closed to further burial. Access was gained by a small door in the north wall. A corridor of about eight or nine feet led to a chamber ten feet square which has a curved brick roof, about twenty feet from the floor at its highest point. The wall facing the short corridor and the walls to the right and left each contained nine niches for coffins, three rows of three. The coffins were to be inserted lengthwise so that each niche opening was only two feet six inches square, receding seven feet.[27] When a coffin was inserted, a slab was fitted at the edge of the opening and sealed. The biographical details of the interred were carved on these, just as they are on ordinary headstones. The fourth wall has only six of these niches, three placed vertically either side of the chamber entrance, making a total of thirty-three coffin spaces in all, yet only eighteen were ever used. The first interment in the pyramid was Ralph Howard's daughter Isabella.

She was only nineteen when she died in December 1784. Considering that the pyramid was not built until the following year, it is reasonable to assume that she was buried in the graveyard and re-interred in the mausoleum when it was ready. The last interment in it of which we have a record took place in 1823, but tradition has it that one more did take place. A young female family member, a small child, died and was buried in the pyramid. For weeks after the interment, tenants living at Kilbride reported the sound of a crying child at night. The body was, we are told, removed and interred elsewhere after which the crying is said to have stopped.

Enough hardheaded detail. Let's get back to symbolism. Why thirty-three coffin spaces? The same layout with either one tier of niches more or less would have given a total of forty-four or twenty-two, but thirty-three was the number decided upon. The practically minded will say that Howard just liked things in threes, many people do, just as he might simply have liked the pyramidal shape. However, the more conspiratorially minded might see that the numbers three and thirty-three echo the number of degrees in Craft and Advanced Freemasonry as recorded by both Stephen Knight and Martin Short[28]. Much of the work of these writers has been poo-hooed by some, mostly masons, and given credence by many others, mostly non-masons.

↑ *North*

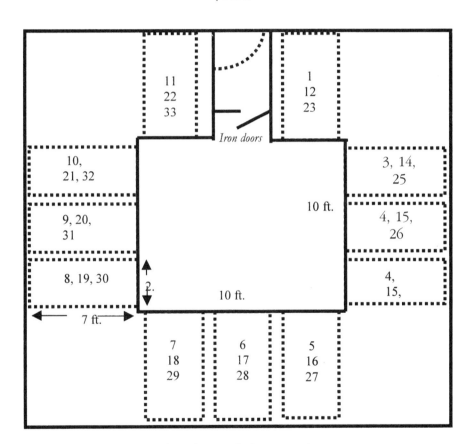

Floor plan inside the Pyramid

Interior of Howard Mausoleum

Entrepreneurs were beginning to make their mark in the area as well. A new mining concern had been formed in Avoca, the Hibernian Mining Company, and it was proposed to connect the mines with the port of Arklow by canal, with a branch to the company's lead mines at Glenmalure and another to the coal mines at Castlecomer in Kilkenny. It was an ambitious plan and the company was given the green light not only to build the canal but was also given control of the operation and development of Arklow harbour.[29] William Chapman surveyed the bay and harbour entrance in 1791 and made his report the following year.[30]

Because of the low tidal variation at Arklow (from eighteen inches on a neap tide to only four feet on a spring tide) and the fact that the river separated into shallow channels between the bridge and the sea, only small boats could enter the river. Larger vessels had to lie at anchor in the bay. This necessitated the use of lighters for loading and discharging. Lighters were small boats which would take cargo from the port to the ship, or vice versa. This involved additional handling and was extremely dangerous. Chapman proposed that quay walls be built to control the flow of the river, thereby creating a single channel deep enough for larger vessels to enter and leave port and so negate the use of lighters. He also intended to build canal locks at the bridge, a double lock at 'Poolahoney' (i.e. Poulahoney, Glenart), a seventy-eight foot span aqueduct in three arches, a staircase of six locks between Woodenbridge and the Meetings, several lock houses, weirs, tunnels and footbridges. He estimated that the cost, not counting the harbour development, would be £15,194-7-7. Nothing came of it. Perhaps it was a pipe dream, perhaps it could have worked, stimulating work in the area. The report, like so many others since then, was left on a shelf to gather dust.

The Relief Acts of 1782 and 1793 repealed some of the Penal Laws. These measures were not genuine attempts to establish civil liberties for Catholics and Non-Comformists, but were merely cosmetic measures to win their support for the London and Dublin parliaments in times of national crisis. The 1782 reliefs were brought about because of Britain's war against the American colonists, and the 1793 reliefs were a direct result of Britain declaring war on revolutionary France. At both times the last thing Britain needed was a disgruntled Irish majority snapping at its heels. Better to throw it a bone or two. Slight as they were, these measures encouraged the Catholic clergy and leading members of the laity in Arklow to form a committee to fundraise to build a new chapel to replace the one on Chapel Ground.[31] They set about their task in late 1794, but there is no record to show how successful their efforts were, but a most unexpected event the following year must have made them rub their hands in expectation.

Accounts of gold being found in the Wicklow mountains have a very long history. Many people believe that some of the ancient gold artefacts housed in the National Museum were made from ore mined in south Wicklow, although some experts doubt this. What is beyond doubt is that sizeable nuggets have been discovered on the slopes of Croghan Kinsella from time to time, and in 1795 something of a gold rush took place. There had been rumours of finds for twenty years beforehand. For example, an old schoolteacher is said to have discovered several pieces in 1775.[32] Ten years later,

> a local boy John Byrne who was fishing in the river found a nugget of gold weighing ¼ of an oz., which was sold in Dublin. However, this did

not attract much local attention as the gold was thought to be lost
property.[33]

Some took the story of Croghan gold seriously – and sensibly. An
unnamed local would go to Dublin every year for about ten years. On
each trip he would sell four or five ounces of gold to a jeweller there.
Some of his neighbours suspected that his fondness for solitary walks
on the mountain may have been the source of the relative affluence he
displayed when he returned from his annual outing to the city. One
day, he was followed as he trekked across the slope and he was seen
searching for gold in the stream then known as the Aughatinavought
and now called the Goldmines river.

> Immediately all other work ceased as gold fever swept the countryside.
> About 300 women besides huge numbers of men and children were at
> work ...... they used sieves, skillets broken in two and household tools.
> In their efforts to work as much ground as possible they missed much
> gold. So much so that later a profit could be made on the waste heap.
> This state of affairs continued until the 15th October 1795 by which time
> crowds were streaming into the area from as far away as Wicklow town.
> By now however the authorities were beginning to get worried and a
> party of Kildare militia were dispatched from Arklow to take possession
> of the river.[34]

In the two month free-for-all an estimated 2,666 ounces of pure gold
worth £10,000 was taken from the river.[35] This is the recorded figure
and does not take into account the quantity not reported. Although the
government's takeover did not meet with resistance, there must have
been some degree of resentment. For once, the ordinary working
people were coming out ahead. For once, they sensed opportunity and
the freedom to chase it. They had left their humdrum lives back in
Arklow or in the surrounding villages or on the farms they worked for
others' benefit. A lucky strike, or even a series of small finds, could
change their lives forever. Perhaps the ease with which they allowed
their dreams to dissolve, the ease with which they surrendered to
officialdom, reflected their lifelong subservience to the seemingly
inevitable.

Government interference was prompted by two factors. The first was
greed. Why should unruly peasants benefit when revenue from mining
the gold could accrue to those in power? The second was normal work

in the area was greatly curtailed as farm labourers, carpenters, carters, herdsmen and servants decided to take their chances in the hills. Local businessmen, who favoured steady profit over prospecting, set up makeshift supply stores and bars to separate the motley crew of miners from their finds. Camden, the Lord Lieutenant in Dublin, used this as one of the reasons for sending in the militia.

> Booths are erected for the sale of Whiskey, and a spirit of animosity begins already to appear among the different parties employed in gathering the Ore. I have therefore thought it necessary without the loss of time to direct the Commissioners to order the Collector of the King's Revenues for the district of Wicklow to take charge of the Mine, with assistance of the military force, to prevent the plunder of the Ore, and to preserve the peace of the country.[36]

Over the following two and a half years, the government searched for more nuggets and for the mother lode. The lode was never found and only £3,675-7-11½ worth of ore was recovered. The workings closed on May 26th, 1798 when many of the workers deserted to join in the rebellion which had just erupted and which will be dealt with in the next chapter.

When the Chevalier M De Latocnaye visited the area in 1796-7, the gold rush at Croghan had taken place only a year or two beforehand and it was natural that he should pass some remarks about this singular piece of excitement in the locality.[37] He visited the site and his questions 'about its location aroused so much curiosity' that he got 'a thousand questions in return', wishing to know if he was going to work the mine, if the Government had sent him, etc. He heard all about the lucky finds but nothing of the disappointments. He then headed for Arklow with as little information about the gold mines as the locals would tell him.

> I came to Arklow, where I was received with great kindness by the Rev. Mr. Bailly, rector of the village ... The country around the town of Arklow is pretty, well-wooded and diversified by mountain and plain. The company working the copper mines has the intention of making it [the river] navigable as far as Rathdrum.

De Latocnaye doubted if such an undertaking could succeed without government aid. As mentioned above, no aid was forthcoming and all we have to show for Chapman's work is his survey report.

The port of Arklow, besides, is bad; rather, indeed, it is a roadstead, for
the shore is flat, and vessels are obliged to remain nearly a mile out at
sea and to set sail on the least appearance of bad weather.

Another visitor to the area was G. Holmes who described the hinterland
in much the same way as everyone else did - beautiful, magnificent, etc,
etc - but couldn't be bothered even getting the name of the town right,
spelling it Acklow. To be fair to the intrepid Holmes, perhaps it was a
misprint, but more likely "Acklow" just didn't impress him enough to
warrant correct mention.[38]

*

As the eighteenth century came to a close the town was little better off
than it had ever been. It was bigger, but still nothing more than a village
that depended on the sea and the surrounding countryside. The mines
at Avoca were working and that created hope for the development of
the harbour, but when - or if - that hope would be realised was
anyone's guess. At least there had been some moves to stimulate the
fishing industry. The town itself and its hinterland on the south side of
the river was the property of the Earl of Carysfort, whose seat was at
Poulahoney Lodge a mile or two upriver. The land north of the river
was in the hands of the Earl of Wicklow who lived at Shelton House.
With the great exception of the Croghan Gold Rush, nothing much
happened to upset the mundanity of leisurely life for those who could
afford leisure, and nothing much happened to relieve the drudgery of
poorly paid toil for those to whom 'leisure' was another word for
unemployment. But before the eighteenth century closed, Arklow was
to play a decisive part in one of the most catastrophic episodes in Irish
history.

6

The Battle of Arklow[1]:
Saturday, June 9th, 1798

> Thus prepared about 4 o'clock, all of us at our posts I first saw in a
> moment thousands appear on the tops of the ditches, forming one
> great & regular circular line from the Gorey Road through the fields
> quite round to the sand banks near the sea, as thick as they could
> stand. They all put their hats on their pikes & gave most dreadful
> yells.[2]
>
> *Henry Lambart Bayly*

In 1798, the town of Arklow stretched from roughly where St Saviour's
now stands to where we now call Old Chapel Ground. The houses and
whatever inns and shops it possessed lined the single main street and
its adjoining lanes. The bridge of nineteen arches crossed the river
about two-thirds of the way down the main thoroughfare, leading to
Ferrybank and the road to Dublin. There were few, if any, houses on
that side of the river. The Coolgreaney Road was the main artery which
connected Arklow and Gorey, the Wexford Road we know today was
not built until the 1820s.

Anyone travelling from Coolgreaney would come to two junctions
about a mile before reaching the town. The first was at what we now
call McGrath's Cross at Ballynattin. If the traveller took the right turn
there, he could reach Arklow Rock via the Kish and could enter the
town across what is now the golf links. If he ignored this junction and
continued on to the next, the last one before the town was reached, he
had a choice of entering the town from two different directions. If he
stayed on the main road, he would pass an occasional house, continue
on past Lamberton House, the imposing dwelling of the local rector, the
Rev Edward Bayly, and reach the town at Upper Main Street. If he took

the right turn and travelled along a mud-surfaced laneway, he would skirt the town in a wide arc and enter it at the lower end. The locals called this route the Yellow Lane, probably because of the colour of its heavy marl. It is now called Cemetery Road or St Gabriel's Road or Emoclew Road. Take your pick. The first dwelling to be encountered along the Yellow Lane was Emoclew House. It had already been known by that name (which is the word 'welcome' in reverse) for some time. In the late 1980s, the name was changed to Glastnost. Yellow Lane continued down by Knockenrahan until it reached the spot now occupied by the Navvy Bridge. From this height, the lower end of the town, called the Fishery, could be seen with the expanse of Arklow bay lying beyond. There was still a great deal of greenery before the first line of thatched cabins would be reached at Old Chapel Ground, and Main Street lay hidden behind grassy fields some distance to the left.

At the lower end of town was the small Catholic chapel which the fundraising committee of 1794 had hoped to replace. Surrounding it was the dense cluster of fishermen's houses. A stream, draining adjacent fields, flowed by the last of the tiny mud-walled thatched cabins, across South Green before spilling into the river. This stream, which has long since been covered in, was crossed by a small causeway, or *tóchar* in Irish, giving access to the road that led across sandbanks to the Rock and on to Castletown. This had been the main coast road along which the Earl of Essex had entered the town in 1599, and along which James II had scurried in 1690. In 1798, there were few houses beyond the Togher, as *tóchar* was anglicised, and the locals called the waste ground of sandhills the Frolic. This would be built on in the following decades and is partly occupied by the area we generally refer to as the Fishery today and partly by Arklow Golf Club.

To modern eyes it was an unprepossessing, insignificant village. We have seen how even contemporary visitors dismissed it in a few words or ignored it completely during their travels around Ireland. But its mercantile activities, such as its fishing fleet and its growing importance as a hub for the surrounding area, made it 'a considerable place' on the cusp of relative prosperity.[3] Whatever status we might assign to it, grubby fishing village, pretty market town, or embryonic commercial centre, it was in its streets, along the Coolgreaney Road and Upper Main Street, the Yellow Lane and Old Chapel Ground that a fierce battle involving approximately 15,000 people[4] was fought on Saturday, June 9th, 1798. That battle lasted six hours. They were arguably not only the most important six hours in the long and convoluted history of this town, but they were also to have a tremendous effect on the course of Irish history.

Improbable as it may seem, that battle had its origins in the American War of Independence twenty years earlier. The ideas of republicanism and civil liberties as espoused in Tom Paine's *Rights of Man,* Jean Jacques Rousseau's *Social Contract* and other political writings, were gaining ground on both sides of the Atlantic. The American colonists had shown that Britain's imperial might could be defeated and a new order established. The French Revolution, with its cry of 'Liberty, Equality, and Fraternity', showed that monarchies and aristocratic oppression could be toppled in Europe as well as in America. Such principles had a strong emotional and intellectual impact on an Ireland ruled by Britain, an Ireland controlled by a Protestant Ascendancy under which the vast majority of the people were denied many basic civil rights.

In 1791 a group of young men with radical ideals formed the Society of United Irishmen in Belfast. Their aim was to unite all Irishmen, Catholic, Protestant, and Dissenter against the common enemy. The following year Anthony Perry of Inch formed the first United Irish Society branch in this area, albeit it was based in north Wexford. When war was declared between Britain and France in 1793, the United Irishmen recognised the opportunities the new situation offered. A major recruitment drive got under way and it is at this time that reports of United Irishmen societies in Wicklow appear. As a measure against invasion by the French and possible insurrection by the disaffected Irish, the government introduced the Militia Act. Each Irish county was to organise a military corps in which Catholics would be allowed to enlist, but only as common soldiers. To avoid undue fraternisation between the militia and civilians, no corps was to serve in its own county. For example, the Wicklow Militia served in Westmeath and elsewhere, while the Antrim Militia and others served tours of duty here. To ease Catholic disquiet with the ruling Protestant government, a Catholic Relief Bill was introduced, restoring some, but not many, civil rights to Catholics.

In 1796 Yeoman Cavalry corps were established. These were loyalist (but not necessarily Protestant) civilians who were to act as military police and as support to the militia and regular army units when called upon. At the outset, the Yeomanry corps were not overtly sectarian.

Catholics were welcome to join – but not as officers – and many did. However, many of the Catholics who did join had United Irishmen sympathies and they saw the corps as a means of being trained in the use of weaponry and military tactics.[5]

Some of the leading members of the United Irishmen were already officers in the French army at this time and they tried to persuade the French Directory to support Ireland's cause, thereby creating a useful ally on Britain's western flank. The man mainly responsible for the success of these petitions was a young Dubliner named Theobald Wolfe Tone. In December 1796, a fleet of forty-three ships carrying 15,000 seasoned troops arrived in Bantry Bay,[6] but terrific storms made landing impossible. Twenty ships were driven back out to sea and were unable to regain the shelter of the bay. With each passing day the gale grew fiercer. Sleet and snow squalls made matters even worse and the

remaining fifteen ships slipped their cables and headed back to France. A disspirited Tone later remarked, 'We were so near I could have tossed a biscuit on the shore'. It had taken the British political and military leaders by surprise and was later to be described as their luckiest escape since the Spanish Armada two centuries earlier. The government realised they had seriously underestimated the danger the United Irishmen posed and steps were taken to curb, and if possible destroy, them.

Theobald Wolfe Tone

As 1797 dawned, the authorities began gathering information about the movement in a more determined fashion. A network of spies and informers was set up to infiltrate the society itself and their findings surpassed the government's greatest fears. Martial law was declared in those areas deemed the most disaffected. Troops were quartered in Kildare to terrorise the populace into submission. In March 1798, the authorities became aware that a meeting of the National Directory of the United Irishmen was to take place in the house of Oliver Bond in Dublin's Liberties district. They arrested most of those present and, in one fell swoop, left the United Irishmen virtually without leadership. To prevent the formation of a new directory, the government pressed the advantage. Interrogations became more widespread and merciless. In the Kildare town of Athy a triangle was erected on which victims were flogged until they gave information about the United Irishmen or surrendered caches of arms. Some people stole weapons just to have something to surrender and so escape torture. One soldier, Sgt Tom Swayne, is credited with inventing the pitch-cap. Pitch was rubbed onto a victim's head and gunpowder added to it. This mixture was then torched and the melting pitch burned the scalp, trickled into the eyes and down the face. Half-hanging was also used in this reign of terror. Victims were hanged until life was almost extinguished, at which point they would be taken down, revived, and the process repeated until information was forthcoming. Lt Edward Hepenstall of the Wicklow Militia perfected his own version of this. A man of exceptional height, he stood back-to-back with the intended victim, who was invariably quite a bit smaller. A noose was placed around the victim's neck and the rope draped over Hepenstall's shoulder. Taking a tight grip on the rope, Hepenstall would take up the slack, then lean forward, lifting his victim off the ground and strangling him on his back. Appropriately, Hepenstall has passed into the folk memory as 'The Walking Gallows'.[7]

Such atrocities were also carried out in County Wicklow, where martial law was declared in November 1797. In spite of the original intention that no militia should serve in its own county, the Wicklow Militia were called upon to serve here because of the belief that the county was ripe for rebellion and all government forces would be needed to nip it in the bud. The Wicklow Militia had already earned a reputation for brutality in Westmeath and being on home ground did little to curb their enthusiasm. Despite these measures, the United Irishmen in Wicklow were at their peak in early 1798 with 14,000 members, at least on paper.[8] In Arklow, members of leading Catholic families, such as the Grahams, O'Neills, and Murrays, held posts of responsibility within the organisation. Matthew Doyle of Poulahoney (later known as Glenart) was also prominent, particularly on the field of battle throughout the course of the coming rebellion. The numbers of United Irishmen in the mines around Avoca were also considerable, leading to the disbanding of the Cronebane yeomanry because of the high percentage of suspected United Irishmen in its ranks.

While this was going on, loyalist members of communities in towns and villages throughout the country were encouraged to monitor the state-of-the-nation and to send reports to Dublin Castle. In Arklow, the most ardent correspondent was the local rector, Rev Edward Bayly.

Time and again he urged the government to take a firm hand in Arklow where

> all, or nearly all, the fishermen in the town, amounting to from 200 to
> 300, have been or very soon will be sworn United Irishmen.[9]

Major Joseph Hardy of the Antrim Militia was also in constant communication with his superiors in Dublin. Hardy was the senior military figure in Wicklow and it was his responsibility to keep the entire county in check. Like Bayly, he believed that Arklow's 'whole body of fishermen, 500 stout fellows [are] to a man united'.[10] It is interesting that Hardy believed the number of sworn fishermen in Arklow to be twice that of Bayly's estimate, an indication of how little hard information they had. It was reported that there were caches of munitions and guns in the sand dunes between Arklow and Kilgorman near Castletown, brought from England and Wales by Arklow fishermen. Hardy was so convinced of the strength of the feelings of the fishermen that he wanted to place 'a navy-enforced embargo on all sea traffic off Arklow' to stop further smuggling of weapons and ammunition. Such an embargo was impractical, it would affect the livelihoods of too many people, loyalist as well as republican. If these caches did exist, it would appear that they were never retrieved and are still lying where they were buried. Sir John Parnell of Avondale, great-grandfather of Charles Stewart Parnell, reported a swearing of United Irishmen in Arklow in August 1797.[12] The following month Bayly again put pen to paper. This time he wrote to Parnell outlining the state of affairs in the Arklow area. He said that the United Irishmen had

> made of late a rapid and alarming progress in Arklow and its vicinity.
> There is every appearance of approaching disturbance - arms are
> preparing - pikes making.

He added that the respect to which he had become accustomed was now replaced by 'a gloomy reserve'.

Bayly had been instrumental in forming the two local yeomanry corps, the Arklow North Shires and the Arklow South Shires, and his repeated sectarian outbursts did little to endear him to the majority of the population. Typical of his paranoia at that time was his remark

> I understand that the Roman Catholics to a man are sworn United Irishmen.

To appease this growing distrust of all Catholics, the parish priest, Fr William Ryan, added his name to those of other priests in the region to a loyal address, stating their allegiance to the authority of Dublin Castle and their abhorrence of the United Irishmen movement.[13]

Reports such as those submitted by Bayly and Hardy had one thing in common, they were made by people who were loyal to Britain and who could only surmise the real extent of the United Irishmen in the town. Even Bayly admitted in one of his letters that '... it is next to impossible to obtain any precise information ...'. Interrogations were widespread.

> Miles Byrne said that rebel families in the Arklow area 'suffered the most cruel tortures and persecutions' which had begun in earnest in early May 1798 and intensified until the rebellion commenced.[14]

Despite these measures, there was little or no definite information forthcoming. What was needed was someone on the inside. On May 21st, 1798 - just two days before the outbreak of the rebellion - they got the source they were looking for.

As the date of insurrection drew near, one of the leading United Irishmen in Arklow was having second thoughts. He decided to meet the local magistrates and confess his role in the society. To protect his identity, he was given the initials W.A.B.[15], but it is now accepted that he was Thomas Murray Jnr of Sheepwalk. It was Garret Graham who initiated Murray into the Society in May 1797,[16] and there is evidence to suggest that other members of the Murray family were also United Irishmen.

Murray told Bayly, Thomas Atkins and Thomas King, 'three of the secret committee of magistrates appointed for receiving private information',[17] how he had joined the United Irishmen and how the members were organised in cells of twelve, how groups of cells formed larger units, etc. It is too detailed to go into here, but enough to say that what he told the magistrates fitted exactly with what had been known and suspected. The principal United Irishman in this region, Anthony Perry, was arrested that same day. We do not know the time of day Murray made his confession, nor do we know the time Perry was arrested, so it is impossible to say which came first. Was Perry arrested on Murray's evidence (although there is no mention of Perry in W.A.B.'s recorded confession), or did Murray decide to confess because he had heard of Perry's arrest? We may never know. What we do know is, Murray's involvement caused his brother Daniel a great deal of embarrassment. Daniel had been educated as a priest in Salamanca in Spain. He was an avowed pacifist and five

Anthony Perry

days after his brother's confession, Daniel swore an oath of allegiance to Bayly.[18] His protestations of loyalty were accepted and he was free to go. Daniel Murray was later to become Archbishop of Dublin and was so eager to comply with government wishes and policies that he was to become known as the Castle Bishop.[19] Another brother, Peter, was arrested and remained in Wicklow Gaol until November 1798.

Despite Thomas Murray's confession and that of Anthony Perry, who confessed only after being tortured and pitch-capped, there was a growing sense that nothing could avert open rebellion. It came within days.

*

The United Irishmen decided they could delay no longer. They had lost much of their leadership, arms were being surrendered, members tortured and killed. In some ways, government excesses brought on the outbreak of war instead of halting it. On May 23rd, the rebellion was launched in counties Kildare and Carlow. In County Wicklow the following day, Catholic yeomen were suspected of being covert United Irishmen and were taken out of the ranks and murdered by their erstwhile comrades-in-laws on Dunlavin Green.[20] On the 25th, insurgents attacked the village of Carnew. They were repelled with heavy losses. A few hours later, twenty-eight insurgent prisoners were executed near Carnew castle. This part of Ireland was now in a state of war, with atrocities being perpetrated by both pro- and anti-government factions. Rural Protestants sought the protection of garrisons in towns such as Wicklow, Rathdrum and Arklow. Rural Catholics, especially families who had at least one member "out with the rebels", had little option but to leave their homes and travel with the insurgents to avoid retaliation by yeomen. Yet, surprisingly, the main eruption did not take place in County Wicklow, a relatively well organised United Irishmen county, but in Wexford.

Wexford had been a quiet county. The United Irishmen movement had made little headway there. Nevertheless the government sent in the North Cork Militia to continue its search-and-destroy operation. Many local loyalists joined in the persecution of neighbours and rampant sectarianism ensued. In the village of Boolavogue, the local priest, Fr John Murphy, had been adamant in his denunciation of the United Irishmen movement and had constantly encouraged parishioners to surrender any hidden weapons they possessed.[21] Like Fr Ryan in Arklow, he had signed an address of loyalty in April.[22] He believed co-operation with the military and civil authorities would defuse the potentially explosive situation. Many of his parishioners were won over and surrendered pikes, flintlocks and other weaponry in considerable quantities in exchange for protection. For a brief period it looked as if Wexford would remain in uneasy peace.

But then something happened which made Murphy do a u-turn. While indiscriminate floggings and other punishments inflicted on the people could not goad him to rebellion, the burning of his church did. In the wake of this event, and the result of the almost haphazard skirmish of Bookey's bridge, Murphy found himself the leader of a growing band of rebels-in-arms. Within a few days they won a victory over the notorious North Cork Militia at Oulart Hill. Their numbers swelled as hundreds joined them, either encouraged by the news of success or fearful of reprisals if they remained in their homes. United Irish cells from around the county and from Carlow and Wicklow rallied towards central Wexford. There was no turning back, and the rebel force then attacked the important town of Enniscorthy. Their remarkable success in taking it further increased their numbers.

Despite these successes, the rebel force was not a unified, disciplined army. Many were there out of fear, pushed to rebellion by the terrorising actions of local Orangemen[23], the North Corks, and other government forces. Others were avowed United Irishmen, men to whom Fr Murphy and other priests had refused the sacraments in the preceding weeks. And there were those who had old scores to settle or who simply revelled in the opportunities presented by the anarchy to come. Internal dissension was rife, reflecting this wide range of political opinion and none. Yet this diverse hotch-potch of an insurgent force took control of the county within a week. Some authority had obviously been exercised and that controlling agent increasingly appeared to be the Society of United Irishmen. Beauchamp Bagnel Harvey had been a United Irishman since the society's inception and was now in the thick of things in Wexford. He was appointed commander of the rebel forces there in the hope that he could instill some level of discipline before the British could mount a well planned counter offensive. Unfortunately, he proved ineffectual, but the United Irishmen in the lower officer ranks commanded more respect from their respective corps. It was decided to form two Wexford armies, one to control the southern half of the county and to strike into Waterford through New Ross, the other to head north and move on Dublin. The major obstacle this latter force had to face was Arklow.

Throughout the first week of June, as the north Wexford insurgents took Camolin and Gorey and prepared to attack Arklow, refugees fled the countryside, keeping ahead of the insurgents as best they could. Each new arrival in Arklow brought harrowing stories of what they had seen or heard, and each new account placed the rebels nearer the town. On Saturday, June 2nd, Rev Bayly decided to leave Arklow and head for the safety of Dublin. He cited his decision to leave as being '[t]he horror and agony of Mrs Bayly was such that I could not resist'.[24] One of his parishioners, Kearon, put his boat at the rector's disposal. As they sailed out of Arklow bay,

> the men said they saw numbers coming over the Rock at Arklow; they were perhaps like ourselves desolate fugitives, but they might be a party of the rebels pushed on by that back way ... no person of Reflection can censure my retreat, which I deferred to the last moment ... & which I then resolved on to save a hapless family ... and my Dearest wife and sisters, who swore they wd. not go without me ...

The letter mentions other people who also decided to escape to the relative safety of the city, but also some who refused, such as Mrs Rowan, wife of the garrison captain. The letter was addressed to Bayly's son Henry Lambart Bayly, whom the rector always called Lambart. Lambart had opted to stay and defend the town and his father urged him that

> living or dying be a serious and zealous Christian ... & if we are never

to meet again here, May we meet in the presence of our Saviour in
Heaven.

Surprisingly, fully aware of the dangers Lambart faced by staying in
Arklow, Bayly remembered to ask him to

> tell Manifold I depend on him to see that it [Lamberton House] is not
> plundered. Old Percival & Rogers always to sleep at the house ......
> send us by water –(not by land) some salt meat, Bacon, Ham & butter
> ... above all, if ever you have an hour leisure, pack up with Marten the
> choicest of my poor books.

While Bayly was thus wishing his son well in the life-and-death battle
ahead, the rebels argued over the timing and method of attacking
Arklow, and while they wrangled they missed a golden opportunity.

The garrison at Arklow was kept informed by refugees and others of
the rebels' progress and of their ever growing numbers. One story after
another fed this fear until it was finally decided that the town could not
withstand such an onslaught. The last straw came with the defeat of
Colonel Walpole at Tubberneering on June 4th and the resultant fall of
weapons, including several cannon, into insurgent hands. Terror swept
through the hearts of Arklow loyalists. Within hours of that British
defeat the garrison and loyalists of Arklow were packing up,
commandeering carriages and heading for Wicklow. By dawn of June
5th the exodus of would-be defenders was more or less complete. Had
the insurgents moved on Arklow at that time, they would have walked
in and the road to Dublin would have been open. Instead of pressing
on and taking this vitally important bridgehead out of County Wexford
they lingered on Gorey Hill.

What caused that delay has been argued about ever since. The truth
probably lies in a combination of reasons. Hayes-McCoy summed it up
when he wrote that the rebels lacked 'leaders, a plan of operations,
money, arms, ammunition, supplies'.[25] There were simply too many
opinions and not enough authority. For several days they rested on the
laurels of Tubberneering. When some of them did decide to move they
attacked Carnew, a strategically unimportant target suggesting that it
was an attack motivated by revenge rather than military logic. Finally,
at about ten o'clock on the morning of Saturday the 9th, they assembled
in their various corps and headed for Arklow.

At the head of this massive serpentine force was Billy Byrne of

Ballymanus, near Aughrim. Byrne was to prove his courage in the coming battle, but his prominent position on the march was because of his leadership of the Ballymanus Corps. The Ballymanus Corps was the generic name given to the Wicklow United Irishmen and comprised several companies from throughout the south county, amounting to about 1,800 men. Two of these were the Arklow North Shire and the Redcross. It was fitting that they should lead the insurgents into their home county. Other leaders of the insurgent army were Anthony Perry, still suffering from the torture inflicted on him two weeks earlier, Esmond Kyan, Matthew Doyle and Michael Dwyer.

Shortly after midday the makeshift army reached Coolgreaney. There is a piece of historical and logistical nonsense which says that these thousands of rebels and their followers lost further time here while they plundered the village pub. This was a coaching inn and no doubt had stocks of spirits and beer, but surely it didn't have enough to keep such a vast crowd in the jigs for several hours! It is not possible that the entire rebel force spent half the day drinking on the volume of alcohol stored in a single village pub. It is quite reasonable to assume that whatever stock was there was taken and consumed. That stock could have kept several dozens, perhaps even a hundred people happy for a while, or several hundreds might have had a couple of drinks each, but widespread and prolonged drunkenness was logistically impossible.

The real cause of the delay was far more shameful. There was still no one in overall command. United Irishmen argued with non-United Irishmen, questions of social rank and several other factors got in the way of seeing and achieving a common goal. Fr John Murphy of Boolavogue believed that, as a Wexfordman, his job was done. Wexford was in Irish hands, therefore his rebellion was at a successful conclusion. He refused to lead his followers into another county. He headed east towards the village of Castletown. He had stated before that such was his intention, but it was hoped that he would change his mind. His desertion weakened the authority of the other officers even further.

Unlike the insurgents, the British did not waste the days that followed Tubberneering and the retreat of the Arklow garrison. When they had reached Wicklow, General Francis Needham confronted them and ordered them back to their posts. Over the three days of the 6th, 7th and 8th, the Arklow garrison was re-established and strengthened by more troops arriving in commandeered carriages and carts. By the time the insurgent army left Gorey Hill, Needham had set up his base in Arklow and had under his command 1,360 infantry and 164 cavalry, made up of elements of the Royal Irish Dragoons, Gordon Highlanders, Ancient Britons, the Antrim, Derry, Armagh, Tyrone, North Cork and Cavan Militias, and the Suffolk, Durham and Dumbarton Fencibles. These were supplemented by the Arklow North Shire and South Shire, Camolin, Coolgreaney, Castletown and Gorey Yeomanry Corps. Numerically, they were vastly outnumbered by the approaching insurgents, but they were better armed, better trained and better disciplined. They also had the advantage of defending entrenched positions rather than having to attack across open ground. Feeding these numbers was impossible in a town the size of Arklow and widespread pillaging and commandeering was reported. The indiscriminate burning of houses attributed to the approaching rebels was echoed in the antics of local yeomen. Empty houses were deemed proof that their owners were with the insurgent army and therefore deserved destruction.

Barricades were erected in Lower Main Street and in Upper Main Street near the barracks. St Mary's church, at the old abbey, was used as a temporary barracks by the Gordon Highlanders. Wooden platforms were erected in the yard of the main barracks and cannon placed on these for clearer lines of fire. In the fields now occupied by St Mary's Road, St Mary's school, the chapel, the new parish centre, St Peter's school, the Medical Centre and around to the ESB offices, was a field encampment. On Ferrybank, the cavalry were kept in reserve. With all these preparations only one thing was certain of the coming battle, whatever the military outcome, the cost in human suffering would be immense. At the river end of Doyle's Lane, off Lower Main Street, Philpot's premises had been commandeered as a field hospital. Not only was it central and suitable for the purpose, but its owner was a known United Irishman, which made its confiscation all the more satisfactory.

Preparations completed, it was now time to wait. Those who had remained in the town in the hope that the insurgents would be stopped were now faced with the choice of fighting, on one side or the other, or making their way to safety. There is a story that the Arklow fishermen took their boats, their families and themselves out to the safety of the bay in the days preceding the 9th. It tells how they put in to the beach at Seabank, two miles north of the town, at night and sailed out into deep water again in daylight. This has passed into folklore as the cowardice of the Arklow fishermen. It is a story with which I have a great deal of difficulty. I have no doubt that when the insurgent army arrived on the high ground above the town, they could see fishing boats in the bay, but it is irrational to accuse the Arklow fishermen *en bloc* of cowardice. Several points need to be made and understood in this matter. The first is the natural wish of any man to protect his family. The fact that there were boats in the bay does not mean they were manned by able-bodied fishermen. It was the women and children and the old on both sides of the conflict who understandably sought the safety of the sea. There may have been some able-bodied men in those boats, but no one can say how many. There is ample evidence to show that able-bodied loyalist fishermen stayed in the town and fought with the garrison. Are we to assume that able-bodied Catholic fishermen were more cowardly, or more disinterested in the battle than their Protestant counterparts? Let's not forget that these were the men that both Bayly and Major Hardy had branded sworn United Irishmen. These were the men who had smuggled guns and ammunition into Arklow in 1797 and early 1798. Is it logical that, having run those risks, these same men would now turn tail and run when 15,000 of their fellows marched on Arklow, flushed with success? Nor should it be forgotten that in the insurgent army, as part of the Ballymanus Corps, Matthew Doyle of Poulahoney had 'raised an ad hoc company of up to 200 men based around a core of Arklow fishermen'.[26] Like the alleged booze-up at Coolgreaney, the *en bloc* branding of Arklow's fishermen as scurrying rats simply makes no sense.

It was three o'clock when the insurgents made their way from Coolgreaney. When they reached what we now call McGrath's Cross, one column turned right and headed for the Rock, to approach the town across the old coast road along the sandhills into the Fishery. A couple of hundred yards further on, another column turned right down the Yellow Lane to reach the Fishery that way and the main column continued on down Coolgreaney Road.

It was at the junction of the main road and the Yellow Lane that the first shots were fired. A detachment of soldiers had an outpost in the schoolhouse there,[27] but fled back to the barricade in the upper part of the town when they saw the strength of the insurgent force. The shots were merely token resistance or perhaps signals to the garrison in the town, rather than any serious attempt to engage the rebel mass.

The appearance the enemy made was astonishing, they seemed to cover the face of the earth.[28]

As the main insurgent body continued towards the first houses of the upper town, small groups splintered from it. Some of these manoeuvred the cannon guns they had taken at Tubberneering into position in the fields near where St Kevin's Secondary School now stands.

The clock ticked towards four. Anyone behind the barricades or in a central location in the town would have seen the masses of insurgents forming a wide arc. It was an image that was to remain with Lambart Bayly the rest of his life and he preserved that image in a letter he wrote to his father the day after the battle.

> Thus prepared about 4 o'clock, all of us at our posts, I first saw in a moment thousands appear on the tops of the ditches, forming one great & regular circular line from the Gorey Road [i.e. the Coolgreaney Road] through the fields quite round to the sand banks near the sea, as thick as they could stand. They all put their hats on their pikes & gave most dreadful yells. I could clearly distinguish their leaders riding through the ranks with flags flying. One of our guns was placed on the road above the barrack, two in the fields to the left of that, & a fourth further still to the left, opposite the Little Rock. This last first opened on the rebel line, and I had a fair opportunity of seeing the effect of grape shot as I was within 10 yards of the cannon. It tumbled them by twenties. – I could see large opens made which were as quickly filled up. This awakened them from the seeming astonishment into which our appearance had thrown them for a few moments – not having expected to find us so prepared. They then rushed on like madmen, & their cannon began to play – two in the front of our line and a third more to the southward, which advanced very near us. They fired them quick but two of their gunners (privates of the Antrims whom they forced to serve the cannon fired rather high, by which means many lives were saved) but our cannon was fired by a rascal who had deserted from the Antrim, & was determined to do mischief. He planted it for half-an-hour opposite our line of cavalry, & how we all escaped unhurt, Providence alone can tell – the balls went through our ranks, & close over our heads for a great time. At last, the General seeing we were the object, order'd us about an hundred yards to the rear; there we were more covered – but we heard them over our heads as clear as possible – they struck several houses, & the barrack during the cannonade; they also kept up a very brisk fire of musketry from all quarters & the pikemen who were the most numerous rushed forward on all sides to take the town, skulking along the ditches. At first our troops from too great eagerness fired at random,

and at a great distance, latterly they reserved their fire until they [the insurgents] came to within one hundred yards and then every shot told.

The North Arklow, & our dismounted Cavalry made a gallant defence & fired briskly at the line and even pursued them – their attacks were well concentrated and most desperate. They rushed on in every quarter from the Chapel [in the Fishery] quite round to the river above the town – they forced in the Fishery which they immediately set on fire – however, they were soon driven from thence by the Ancient Britons, & poor Knox's Corps[29] who charged them out, and dashed up the lane after them. Poor Knox from his eagerness went too far, & getting into our line of shot, a six pound ball killed him, & two of his men. At the Upper town the rebels rushed down into the very mouths of three Cannon, which opened them up with grape & soon cleared the road of men and Horses – for the leader, Father Murphy rode at their head with a fine standard in his hand, & on it a Cross with Liberty or Death. He made them kneel several times between Gorey and Arklow to pray for success & told them he wd catch the Bullets in his hands – which they firmly believed, but I suppose he only vouched for Musket Balls, as a six pound Ball struck him taking off his head.

There is more of Lambart Bayly's account to come, but there are several points in the foregoing narrative which need comment.

He wrote how the gaps made in the rebel lines by cannon grapeshot were as 'quickly filled up'. This determination of the rebels to storm the barricades irrespective of what weaponry they faced was also evident in the actions of some of their mounted officers who 'courageously rode into the cannon positions to discharge their pistols at the gun-layers'.[30] In the face of such an onslaught, it was only a matter of time before the defences would be swamped and the town taken. Only disciplined troops could withstand such blind courage and it was up to the British officers to enforce that discipline. None was more successful than Colonel Skerret of the Durham Fencibles. His men were in the front line, greatly outnumbered and physically tired. They were among the last of the re-enforcements to arrive, reaching the town at two a.m. on the 9th, just fourteen hours before the battle began.

Bayly also refers to the attack on the Fishery. This was the spot of first engagement, but there was little headway made by either side. The insurgents set fire to the houses there, but some accounts state that this action was not indiscriminate as one row was spared because in one of the homes was a dying man. He also describes how the first rebel attack at the Coolgreaney Road was repulsed with great loss of life, and how

The Battle of Arklow (detail). National Library of Ireland.

a second attack was launched soon after with equally devastating results. The insurgent officers, seeing the demoralised effect these losses were having on their men, decided to send a detachment of pikemen across the parkland between Lamberton and the river, presumably across what is now Arklow Town Football Club or perhaps nearer the Boys' National School, across what is now the Glendale estate or thereabouts and down to the water's edge either at that point or by using the Old Coombie Lane. By this tactic they hoped to flank the barracks and gain access to Main Street. But it was soon spotted and a detachment of Dumbarton Fencibles was despatched to cut them off with heavy musket fire. Many of the pikemen were killed or injured and the attempt was aborted.

Esmond Kyan

Bayly mentions the strange situation that both sides had gunners whose sympathies lay with those on whom they were supposedly firing. In the garrison a gunner with the Antrim Militia fired short of the insurgents, endangering garrison soldiers and combatant civilians. Likewise, the gunners who had been taken with their cannon at Tubberneering also purposely misaimed. When this became obvious to the insurgent officers, the gunners were replaced by Esmond Kyan. Kyan had been a committed United Irishman for some time before the rebellion, but before that had served in the British army and had seen action as an artillery man in which he had lost an arm and now wore a prosthetic made of cork. His training had not been forgotten. With a couple of well-placed shots, he blew the wheel off a gun carriage, thereby immobilising it, and hit an ammunition cart, killing thirteen gunners and Fencibles. A third narrowly missed the barracks and carried on to knock off the corner of Charles Sterne's house. Sterne was the local postmaster and was also Carysfort's agent in the town. Had Kyan been able to continue in this fashion who knows what the outcome might have been. But there was an equally accurate gunner on the garrison side and Kyan's cork arm and flesh stump were ripped from his shoulder. This severe injury ended his participation in the battle.

The loss of Kyan, the badly mauled detachment of pikemen, and the huge toll taken during the direct attacks on the cannon made up the minds of many that further attack would be little more than committing suicide. They decided to escape while they could. Some of these fleeing insurgents were met by Fr Michael Murphy. This was the priest from Ballycanew and should not be confused with Fr John Murphy of

Boolavogue. As mentioned above, John Murphy did not take part in the battle of Arklow, choosing instead to stay in County Wexford at Castletown. It is not known why Michael Murphy was so late in leaving Coolgreaney and getting to Arklow. By all accounts, the battle had already been in progress for several hours before he arrived on the scene. As he made his way from Coolgreaney he was amazed to see so many insurgents deserting. He urged them to regroup and follow him to the front line. Each insurgent unit had its own banner, around which the members of the unit, based on district, could rally. Michael Murphy is said to have carried such a banner that day. On it were the words 'Liberty or Death'. Murphy managed to persuade the men to try one more assault. His personal charisma and his standing in the community as a social and spiritual leader were strong factors in his favour, but he is also said to have used a stratagem, which is also accredited to other insurgent priests. As Bayly claims, Murphy is said to have produced spent musket balls, displayed them in his palm, with words such as 'Look, the heretic bullets can't harm us'.[31] The men rallied and he led them in a charge into the mouths of the cannon. Michael Murphy was killed, not by musket balls, but by cannon fire. Some accounts, like Bayly's, say a six-pound cannon ball took off his head, others say it was canister shot. Whichever it was, it was enough to end the third and final attack at the upper end of the town. The insurgents felt they were already beaten and they scattered in all directions. The cavalry was ordered to pursue them. 'The carnage was astonishing'.[32]

This "astonishing carnage" could well have been even greater. Lambart Bayly described the immediate aftermath as follows:

> Had we one hours light the Cavalry would have cut thousands off, but at night when they retreated it was quite dark. They carried off nine cartloads of Dead, which with those we found here, & the numbers we hear are dead of wounds in the Woods, & ditches cannot amount to less on the whole than 1000 men ...

Colonel Skerret estimated the rebel losses at 1,800 men, and General Needham believed that at least 200 to 300 of these had been mowed down by cannon fire.

The Battle of Arklow had been a major engagement by any standards. Such losses were particularly heavy for eighteenth century warfare, but worst of all, the Irish Rebellion of 1798 had been dealt a devastating blow. The insurgents had been aware that their ammunition was getting extremely low; what they did not know was that the garrison was facing the same problem. By the time the insurgents retreated, the soldiers had only eight musket rounds each and no more grape shot. A fourth push could possibly have carried the day. As it was, Edward Bayly was able to write six days after it had taken place that the battle

> was in truth a most Glorious & providential one for the Kingdom. I trust in Heaven it was the turn of their current, & that they are now completely on the ebb.[33]

The Battle of Arklow remains one of the great What-Ifs of Irish history. It halted the rebel progress and many commentators are convinced that it altered the course of the entire rebellion.

At some stage in the battle, Lamberton House was set on fire. By all accounts it was empty at the time, Bayly's servants understandably feeling their lives were more valuable than their master's 'poor books' and other possessions. Lambart Bayly wrote to his father that it was the work of looters, but it seems fairly clear that it was targeted because it was the home of Edward Bayly, who had earned the opprobrium he had complained of in one of his letters to Dublin Castle. One of those later accused of ordering its destruction, if not actually taking part in it, was Billy Byrne of Ballymanus,[34] whose courage and discipline throughout other phases of the battle are well attested. One of the reasons put forward for this vindictiveness was that the Bayly and Byrne families had been involved in an acrimonious legal battle some years earlier. It may well have added more fuel to the fire, so to speak, but Bayly's home was probably targeted because he had made himself an archenemy of the United Irishmen, and his sectarian outbursts had won him no friends even among non-United Irish Catholics.

*

Sunday, June 10th, 1798 dawned early. It was another day of fine weather in what had been a remarkably good spell. It is generally believed that the dry warm weather had contributed to the success of the insurgents. It raised their morale and made sleeping in the open no great hardship. But now, as the devastation became apparent in the wake of the whirlwind, it would take more than a clear sky and a bright sun to raise anyone's spirits.

The acrid smell of gunpowder and smouldering houses hung in the air. Worst of all was the stench of blood. Twisted bodies, many mangled and mutilated, lay where they had fallen the previous evening. One of them was headless, some say decapitated by a yeoman whose trade in peacetime was that of butcher. The corpse was nevertheless identifiable by where he lay and by his garb. It was what remained of Fr Michael Murphy. Several stories have grown up around the disrespect shown to Michael Murphy's body.

> That his head was kicked around until it was spiked for public display over the militia barrack gate is probably true enough. That 'the Yeomen greased their boots with his fat during the roasting of his remains' is more a myth perhaps that grew in the telling.[35]

Another account tells how it was thrown into a burning house along with other lifeless bodies. Tradition says that it was recovered by his sister on the night of June 11th and now rests in Castle Ellis cemetery near Blackwater, County Wexford.

Archibald McLaren, a sergeant in the Dumbartonshire Highlanders, later wrote of his experiences in the rebellion. He described the scene after the battle of Arklow as follows

> I confess I was shocked by seeing such a number of miserable wretches brought by their own folly to an untimely end; some were shot through the head, several through the breast, others had half their face torn away by cannon balls, some were stripped naked by the soldiers while others were suffered to lie in their rags, because they were not worth taking. I remember to have heard two wounded rebels in a ditch, consulting how to make their escape, but two Yeomen with their swords, put an end to their consultations. Dead men and horses were lying in heaps in the fields on the roads and in the ditches. As I was returning to the Barrack, my nose was accosted with a disagreeable smell, upon enquiry I found it to proceed from the body of Father Murphy, whose leg and thigh were burnt into the very bone. I could eat no meat for several days ...[36]

The fact that an experienced soldier was shocked by the extent of the carnage indicates the horrors to be seen in the battle's aftermath. Fourteen-year-old Mary Byrne also witnessed these scenes. In later life she was to recall how she saw

> dead bodies ... lying on the road and the pigs tearing them like anything, all blood from their mouths and flys. The bodies were thrown

on the sands and the farmers took them for manure until Lord Wicklow stopped them.[37]

This references to pigs feeding on the corpses was confirmed in an account by a Gordon Highlander.[38] It is interesting that Lord Wicklow showed his humanity in this regard. He was captain of the North Arklow Yeomen and had taken part in the battle, but he was also known to have been a liberal landlord. He obviously took neither pleasure in the conflict nor revenge in victory. Unfortunately, it would appear that not all the victors shared his respect for the dead.

All these corpses had to be buried before the heat of the day played on them and accelerated their decomposition. Those at the upper end of town were brought across the river to the sandy terrain of Ferrybank. In the Fishery, the bodies were laid out on the sand near the Togher, 'and buried in slit trenches by conscripted labour'.[39] At least, digging mass graves should prove no problem in the surrounding dunes. But not all the fallen insurgents had been killed, many were badly wounded and lay among the dead. Those who were found alive were summarily court-martialled and hanged from the tall trees in St Mary's Cemetery, now the Park in Main Street. Such trials and executions continued for several days.

7

'gloomy, dark suspicion': 1798 - 1820

The rebellion was over by the end of July. The belated arrival of French troops in Mayo in August was nothing more than a farcical finale to a terrible tragedy. During the course of the insurrection the aims of the Society of United Irishmen got lost in the mayhem of war. The hoped for brotherhood of all Irishmen, Catholic, Protestant and Dissenter, was ignored and sectarianism ran amok. What had been planned as a war of independence from British rule had degenerated into civil war. It would be ludicrous to say that all insurgents were Catholic and all loyalists were Protestant. Nothing is ever that clear-cut, but for many of the foot soldiers and civilians distorted clarity was more easily grasped than blurred lines of demarcation and the preceived correlation between religious affiliation and political allegiance was copperfastened for many, many decades to come.

Terror did not end with the last full scale battle or skirmish. Loyalist Protestants feared a resurgence of rebel activity. The presence of Michael Dwyer and his followers in the heart of the Wicklow hills fuelled that fear, and the general state of latent panic made every stranger a potential rebel. Catholics feared indiscriminate reprisal. The various corps of yeomenry in the Arklow area, as elsewhere, considered themselves to have been given *carte blanche* and they availed themselves of that to the fullest. More than twenty Catholic chapels in County Wicklow or on its borders were burned by loyalist groups between June 1798 and March 1800.[1] It has been suggested that some of the most anti-Catholic elements in this region had formerly been Catholics, or were the children of apostasised Catholics.

It was due in part to the fact that in the 18th century and especially in the latter part of it, a number of Catholics had conformed to the Establishment[2] for material reasons, and having thus conformed, showed a particular bitterness towards members of the Church from which they had seceded.[3]

Fifty-five-year-old Rev Edward Bayly decided he would remain in Dublin. Just five days after the battle, he wrote to Lambart saying 'never more will I return to live in that country [county?]'[4]. He'd had time to think about the fate of Lamberton House and was perhaps thinking that he might suffer a similar fate should he be seen again in Arklow. He wrote again on the 19th and prophetically outlined the tensions that would exist in the town for some time to come.

The worst effects of it will be the total want of Confidence which must possess the mind of even the most liberal man. The dreadful depravity of principle that has been so unhappily exhibited will check the natural generous movements of the heart, & compel us to wrap ourselves up in gloomy, dark suspicion – for whom can we now trust?[5]

Bayly had, of course, long since wrapped himself in 'dark, gloomy suspicion'. It was he who had written that 'I understand that the Roman Catholics to a man are sworn United Irishmen'. As for 'the natural generous movements of the heart', he had little time for the 'old Magical Words – Conciliation, Concession, & Reform' and believed

the inveterate spirit of Democracy, when it has taken possession of the mind, is of all Daemons the hardest to exorcise.[6]

Edward Bayly did not return to Arklow, at least, not on a permanent basis. Instead, he took up the position of rector in the County Kilkenny parish of Goresbridge.[7] His son, Henry Lambart Bayly, succeeded him as rector of Arklow in October 1799 and held the office until his death in 1827, at the age of 53.

Rev Bayly's opposite number was Fr William Ryan, who had been parish priest since 1772. He was seventy years old at the time of the rebellion and had been at least semi-retired since 1796, when Dr Troy, Archbishop of Dublin, sent twenty-eight-year-old Fr Daniel Murray to assist him as curate. This was the Daniel Murray of Sheepwalk whose brother Thomas was the informer known as "W.A.B.". He was later to succeed Troy as Archbishop.[8] Now in a position to take things easier, and the fact that his house had been burned either during the battle or the following day, Fr Ryan had taken up residence with relatives a few miles outside the town.[9] In the aftermath of the rebellion, perhaps it would have been safer for him to have returned to the town, because on the night of December 14th a group called on him and he was

> ... murdered at his Johnstown residence where he lived with the Bergin family. His killers were strongly suspected of being members of Thomas Atkins' Arklow Southshire Cavalry who shot him through the head, although some blamed the Castletown corps. Ryan had received death threats from four members of Atkins' corps and had survived a previous attempt on his life by them at Cooladangan but the press related the incident as a robbery at the hands of a 'well armed ... banditi ... with blackened faces ... [who] after pinioning the servants, plundered it of every article of value'.[10]

Not satisfied with having killed the retired parish priest, the group later made its way into Arklow to rid the town of its curate as well. They surrounded the chapel,[11] but some of the parishioners had already warned Fr Murray of their approach.

> Hastily taking off his vestments, and having concealed the sacred vessels, he was able with the help of his parishioners to get out through a window at the back of the church. Although fired on by the soldiers he luckily escaped being hit, and having been given shelter further up the town, he succeeded in making his way up along the bank of the Avoca river, and crossing near Shelton arrived safely in Sheepwalk, his family home. Here he was given a horse and made his way via Glenealy to Dublin.[12]

The murder of Fr Ryan and the attempted murder of Fr Murray indicate the little regard in which their pledges of allegiance – Ryan in April, Murray in May - were held. Fr William Ryan was buried in the tiny graveyard of Kilninor near Ballyfad, where local lore states many of the insurgents wounded in the battle of Arklow had also been buried. His epitaph reads

> Here lies Rev William Ryan pastor of Arklow for 26 years
> In religious ways he spent that time
> And led his flock in truths divine.

His home was open to the poor
No one repining left his door
His heart was open, truthful and free
To high and low of each degree
Of filial piety give him his due
This stone declares it to be true
But truth to tell what him befell
Shot through his heart lying in his bed
By merciless robbers on the 14th December
in the year of grace 1798, aged 70

For the next ten months Arklow was without a priest. It was deemed too dangerous. Archbishop Troy knew that it would take a particularly strong man to take on such a task. In October 1799, the same month in which Henry Lambart Bayly became rector, Troy found someone prepared to accept the position of parish priest, Fr Nicholas Kearns. In a letter dated October 12th, Dr Troy wrote to Mr R Marshall of Dublin:

> I have prevailed upon a clergyman to go to Arklow, which had been without a priest since last December, when the Rev. Mr Ryan was murdered. He went there with a strong protection from Government, which recommended him also to General Eustace and Col. Cowper of the Sligo Militia. The latter behaves as becomes a lover of peace, but candidly told the clergyman, Mr Kearns, that he could not control the violence of the Yeomanry. Mr Kearns was obliged to lodge at the Inn. Every Catholic and well disposed Protestant, however willing to accommodate him, refused it from dread of consequence. He cannot go out at night nor far from the town, and his life is threatened and his person insulted most opprobiously. Thus circumstanced, I cannot insist on his remaining there, nor can I expect that any clergyman will venture to replace him. Mr Smith, a Protestant of the town, offered his barn to Mr Kearns to celebrate Mass in it, but without effect, as he was threatened with death for his humanity. Mr Kearns officiates within the walls of the old chapel which was burned, protected by a military guard ordered by Col. Cowper.[13]

Despite the danger and inconvenience, the open hostility and tension, Fr Kearns did stay, keeping as low a profile as necessary until the situation eased.

Apart from the great loss of life during the rebellion,[14] a great deal of damage was done to property. On October 6th, 1798 an Act of Parliament established the Commission for the Relief of Suffering Loyalists, 'inviting those who had suffered financial losses in the service of government to solicit compensation'.[15] It is important to note just who qualified, loyalists who had been in the service of government and had suffered financial loss. Known rebel activists or sympathisers were not eligible. No surprises there, but neutrals would not be compensated either. This made the whole thing very vague. While officers and enlisted yeomen might be obvious candidates, what of people who fought with the militia or the army as civilians? What about people whose furniture was used to erect barricades? Those whose crops had been taken to feed government troops? What of loyalists who had no official standing but may have helped the government with information? A case might even be made for repentant rebels who confessed all they knew. This last possibility was probably what prompted Thomas Murray Snr of Sheepwalk to submit a claim for £537, although his family had been tainted because of Thomas Jnr's ("W.A.B.") United Irishmen activities. Murray Snr probably felt that as his son had turned informer, the government might look on the family has having rendered loyal service.

Unfortunately, while it is easy to discover who claimed what and for how much, it is more difficult to learn if their claims were granted. The claims were published soon after they were lodged, but the wrangling over them meant that payments were piecemeal over an extended number of years. Many claims were disgarded because of lack of supporting documentation, such as properly sworn Affidavits, or lack of evidence as to the nature of the loss and the degree of loyalty of the claimant.

There were ninety-six claimants in the Arklow area, totalling £5,000, of which no less than £2,130-17-9 was claimed by the Rev Edward Bayly for the loss of Lamberton House, furniture, cattle, wine, library and plate. When comparison is made to other claims, it must be assumed that either Lamberton House was a mansion of grace, elegance and immense proportions, or arithmatic wasn't the rector's forte. For example, a local fisherman named William Hunt claimed £4-18-0 for two nets, a pig, clothes and fowl. Admittedly, he hadn't lost his home, but George Kearnes Snr had, as well as nets and furniture, and his claim came to a total of £12-2-0. Richard, George Jnr, and Thomas Kearnes all claimed for destroyed houses and none of their claims exceeded £60. And what of Mary Sherwood? She suffered losses both in Arklow and at Tomacork near Carnew, having two houses, furniture, clothes, wine, whiskey, corn flour, oatmeal, potatoes and pasture ground stolen or destroyed and her claim came to £61-1-10.[16] I could not find how much, if any, of Bayly's claim was approved, nor do I know the result of the Murray claim.

*

One of the most far-reaching consequences of the rebellion was the Act of Union. Ireland had long been subjugated by Britain, but from time to time, and particularly from the beginning of the eighteenth century, a puppet parliament had been allowed to sit in Dublin to take care of domestic affairs. This new piece of legislation was designed to unite Britain and Ireland into a single entity. Under its provisions, the parliament in Dublin would be abolished and Ireland would be ruled directly from London. In theory, the people of Wicklow, Mayo or Donegal would have the same status as the people of Essex or Kent. To bring this about, the Dublin parliament would have to vote for its own abolition and Westminster would have to vote for the Union. The required Dublin votes were secured through a blatant combination of cajoling, threats, and bribes.

Plans to bring the Act of Union about were first mooted as early as July 1798, and one of the first Irish peers to know of it was the Earl of Carysfort, John Proby. Proby was a brother-in-law of one of England's leading political figures, the Marquis of Buckingham, a former Lord Lieutenant of Ireland. Buckingham was not a man to hold a secret and he mentioned the proposal to Proby.[17] Perhaps the reason behind this indiscretion was more than just a fondness for gossip. Buckingham was aware that Carysfort's right to nominate two members to parliament for Macreddin would disappear with the Dublin parliament's demise and, forewarned being forearmed, the more time Carysfort had to prepare a case for compensation for the loss, the greater his chances and degree of success. If he were not generously recompensed why should he vote in favour of the Act? And generously recompensed he was, to the tune of £15,000, plus another title to call his own. Already an Irish peer (as the Earl of Carysfort) Proby was awarded an English peerage to go with it, Baron Carysfort of Norman Cross near the old family home at Elton near Peterborough. Not surprisingly, on mature reflection, Carysfort supported the Act as 'wise, politic, and advantageous to the two countries'.[18]

The Howards were also in favour of this political marriage, although several other Wicklow landlords were not. In 1799, one of Wicklow's two Westminster parliamentary seats was up for grabs, its last holder, William Hume, having been murdered. Hume's son, William Hoare Hume was an obvious candidate, but he was challenged by Captain Hugh Howard, a brother of the Earl of Wicklow. He had the support of the Howard and Proby families, but Hume had the backing of Lord Fitzwilliam and the other powerful magnates in the county. With such formidable support, it was a foregone conclusion that Hume would win. Hugh Howard attributed his failure to take the seat to his support of the pending Act of Union, but this may have been an oversimplification. 'Fitzwilliam had made sure that his tenants did not back Howard over other issues'.[19]

While politicians and other vested interests prepared to turn Ireland into a bartered bride, Fr Kearns continued to say mass in the ruins of the chapel in Old Chapel Ground and was no doubt concerned with a new development in the religious life of the town. This was the emergence of Methodism. Adam Averrell was an itinerant or travelling Methodist preacher who first visited the town in late 1798. It would appear that he rented a room for meetings.[20] Those who followed his lead were termed Primitive Methodists, people who had been Anglican but felt the need for a more fundamental approach. They espoused many of John Wesley's teachings, but continued to celebrate the sacraments in their parish churches.[21] Sometimes missionaries from Wicklow town or elsewhere would arrive and hold a service wherever they could. When they were faced with opposition or lack of co-operation they seemed to overcome such difficulties with relative ease. For example,

> On one occasion Rev J. Kelly visited Arklow with Mr Lanktree and on arriving they sent to request the use of a corn-kiln for a service, but were refused. Mr Kelly then proposed to make it a subject of prayer, after which they applied personally to the owner, who at once consented; and Mr Kelly preached there with much freedom and power.[22]

Perhaps it was the emergence of this new competition that prompted Fr Kearns to write to Lord Cornwallis, the Lord Lieutenant of Ireland, reminding him of the three chapels which had been destroyed 'in the violence that took place after the rebellion'.[23] The chapel at Arklow had been destroyed in the battle of June 9th or the following day,

Castletown chapel was burned by yeomen on November 11th, 1798, and the chapel at Johnstown suffered the same fate on April 20th, 1799.[24] There is no record of a reply, but even if the letter was acknowledged another year was to pass before work began on replacing these chapels. In the meantime, the Methodists were making serious inroads.

> At Arklow the audience was numerous; a few Romanists cursed the missionaries, and were about to resort to violence when some soldiers interferred and secured quietness. A young clergyman listened for a short time, and then tried to get the church wardens to stop the service, but they declined. Then he applied to the military authorities and they also refused to interfer. When thus he could get no one to assist him he sent word to the servants of God not to come again to the town, or they would not get off so well.[25]

It does not say if the young clergyman was Catholic or Protestant, but both the main churches were worried about losing members of their congregations to the new denomination in their midst.

By early 1803, things were at last beginning to move in regard to building a new chapel in Johnstown. Archbishop Troy and the Earl of Carysfort, who seldom visited his Arklow estate, were in correspondence. On March 18th, Carysfort wrote from his London home at Great Cumberland Place to Troy, saying that he had allocated seventeen acres of land at Johnstown for a chapel and a parish priest's accommodation. He had

> hoped to make it 20 acres but it was not possible without inconveniencing adjoining holdings but 17 is still more than enough to satisfy the needs of one person ... [and would] ... contribute to the decent appearance and situation of the parish priest. As the land is meant to support the Office and not the Person, it must of course, be held during pleasure, that is from year to year. It would perhaps not be easy to find a strictly legal, and proper mode, to put it on a more permanent footing. But supposing that it were practicable, I cannot think it would be prudent. I have fixed the rent at the lowest Rate that has been bid for any part of the Land.[26]

Carysfort, or his agent, must have also been in direct communication with Fr Kearns, because on March 27th, Kearns wrote to Troy outlining the same proposal and asking the archbishop's advice. Dr Troy decided to deal directly with Carysfort and wrote to him on the 29th, stating that while he was grateful for the offer he would much prefer a longer lease period as consecutive yearly leases lacked inducement to develop and improve the holding. In other parishes in the archdiocese, the archbishop and trustees held property on longer leases. I can find no further correspondence concerning this, but it must have been resolved because a chapel was built in Johnstown later that year and was in service until the early 1970s, when the present church was built.[27]

The fact that moves were being made to build chapels once more would indicate that the level of hostility towards Catholicism in the area had eased, and this assumption is borne out by a letter from Fr Kearns to an unnamed cleric in August 1803. Although the addressee is unnamed, it was more than likely Archbishop Troy, as the letter is kept in his papers in the Dublin Diocesan Archive.

> Rev Dear Sir
> There is not in Ireland a more tranquil Neighbourhood than this. Not but the White negro drivers would wish to be at their work again; but it won't do, for positive orders are given to the contrary – Col. Pack who luckily was here and had command of the County at the [illegible] – used to give orders to the picketts that if a dog barked they should not throw a stone at him – Shall not see you this year – if you stay away – let it not be from any apprehension of disorder.

The following month, Fr Kearns again wrote to the archbishop stating that work could begin on building a new chapel in Arklow. By this stage, permission had been obtained from Carysfort to site the new church in a more prominent position in the town, ironically directly across from the military barracks at the top of Main Street, on the site of the present Catholic church. The choice of site might reflect the on-going worries that the new chapel would be a target for yeoman vandalism and the proximity of the barracks would act as a deterrent. We have seen how, on the evidence of Fr Kearns' and Dr Troy's letters, the regular army unit in the town had guarded Fr Kearns as he said mass in the ruins of the old chapel.

Kearns was determined that nothing should prevent the building of the church and he was anxious to quash rumours of rebel activity in the area. In his three and a half years in Arklow, he had risked too much and endured too much to have the growing acceptance of Catholic rights endangered by unsubstantiated stories.

Most Rev Sir

The difficulties which hitherto prevented the commencement of Arklow Chapel are at length overcome. You will, therefore, be pleased to pay the amount of Govt. money in your hands for this object to Mr Cornelius McLaughlin, Usher's Quay – Miles O'Neill his father-in-law being appointed treasurer.

Having seen a paragraph in an English paper stating that the Rebels were seen exercising by night near Arklow, I request you will wait on Government and flatly contradict this assertion. It is true that Affidavits were made to this effect, but I had reason to believe that these Affidavits (if they were transmitted to the Government) would have been accompanied with observations destroying their credit – if this has not been the case – I do assert that the Affidavits (to say the best) were visionary – and after enquiry public and private, I stake my every credit on this assertion. I am very anxious on this head and if you do not or cannot take the trouble of the application – I must do it myself; there were two Affidavits sworn before Messrs Atkins and Coates Juniors – one affirming a rebel meeting by night at Balnattin[28] within a mile of Arklow; the other affirming a similar meeting six miles from Arklow near Ballycoog – at a place called Coates's Bridge – the deponent in the first case was a soldier of the City Cork Regt. who went to bed supperless – and his deposition was backed by that of a Mrs Cavana – and a Mrs Newsom. This Affidavit after a most minute enquiry I state to be visionary – the second at Coates's Bridge was made by a Mrs Willoughby a woman of infamous character, I do state to be false, and probably malicious. I again request your interference – and further direction. Trifling as this matter may appear it might be attended with consequences which I think it my duty to prevent. Were the facts grounded I should be the first to give you notice of them. Nothing can be further from the truth.[29]

So, tensions had eased but suspicion on both sides was still rife. For example, Lambart Bayly received a letter at about the same time as the above correspondence was penned.

I hear from all quarters the army in Ireland is the best and in a better state than ... at any former period ... Sea Fencibles[30] are intended to be adopted ... but I could not help expressing great doubts of the loyalty of the men, for instance, how would you like to put arms into the hands of the Arklow fishermen ...[31]

By 1805, however, the situation was quiet enough for tourists to venture here once more and to record their impressions. John Carr was an experienced travel writer who had published accounts of his wanderings throughout Europe. He had an ear for a good story and used anecdotes as well as description to add colour to a place.

> By the time we reached Arklow the night had closed in upon us. Our inn was not the most comfortable in the world, but tolerable; one side of the lower part of it was occupied by a shop for the sale of groceries, wine, whiskey, etc. This union of the characters of shop and inn I found very frequent in Ireland. Here we got excellent wine. The waiter assured us that the beds - for we dined in a double-bedded room - were well aired and added: 'for one gentleman slept in both of them last night'. I thought I had caught a bull for the first time, but upon a moment's reflection I found that the gentleman, after sleeping in one bed might have been disposed to try the other, and so it proved ... A short distance from the town we passed by the spot where a very bloody and decisive battle was fought on June 9th, 1798 against the rebels ... ... We saw nothing particularly worthy of notice at Arklow except the castle which is ancient and in ruins. The morning after we crossed the bridge, which has nineteen arches, through which the Avoca falls into the sea, which is close adjoining, it is low water and a number of fishing vessels lay on the yellow sands. The learned Bishop Pococke who has distinguished himself for his Travels in the East, has observed that Arklow, with its sands, steeps and glens, seen from the promontory, where the prospect has the best effect, presents a striking resemblance to the hill of Mount Sion at Jerusalem.[32]

In the same year as the above was published, Rev J. Robertson also brought out his account of what to see and do in Ireland. To him the prospect of the Avoca Valley,

> is magnificently terminated by the elevated position of the town of Arklow and the extensive sea covered with trading vessels

but he added that the harbour was capable of great improvement.[33]

That sectarianism had not gone away was obvious in 1807 when the following notice was attached to the door of the church

> In the Presence of Almighty God, I do voluntary swear that I will be true and Loyal when called upon under the Oath of a Disturber against King George and his Forces. That neither hopes nor Fears, rewards or punishment shall induce me Collectively or Individually to give Information against any of those members but be ready when called

upon to aid and assist to kill Protestants and be ready on all occasions
to rise up for my brethren and to get arms.[34]

There was also a report of an attack on the home of a Protestant family,
and rumours of administering an unlawful oath in the area.[35]

Perhaps not surprisingly several Protestant families in the locality felt
that life in Arklow had little to offer and decided that the time had come
to cross the Atlantic. Emigration from Ireland had been on the increase
throughout the eighteenth century, but even by the beginning of the
nineteenth the numbers involved were miniscule compared to the
deluge that was to take place in and after the 1840s. The usual profile
of pre-Famine emigrants was younger sons of Protestant businessmen
and farmers whose parents observed the custom of primogeniture – the
first born son was the main beneficiary so that the property or business
would not become fragmented. Younger sons were given a cash

Notice pinned to church door, 1807

payment, sometimes just enough to help them on their way across the Atlantic to seek their fortune in America.

Between 1805 and 1811 several such families left this area for upstate New York. This group settled in the township of Pratt's Hollow in a countryside remarkably similar to the one they had left. The names Tuke, Kinch, Philpot, Stedman, Tackaberry and other names associated with the Arklow area can still be found there.[36] Members of some of these families later moved across the border into Ontario and some of their relatives back in Ireland decided to join them there rather than go to New York. One of these was Benjamin Tackaberry, who had a more interesting journey than he bargained for.

Together with his family, Tackaberry (listed as Tuckerbury on the ship's passenger list[37]) sailed for New York from Dublin on the emigrant ship *Belisarius*. Why he should opt for getting to Ontario via New York is open to question. He could have entered the Canadas via Quebec, but his choice of route was not unusual at that time. This was the year before the outbreak of the 1812-1815 war between Britain and its former American colonies and relations between Britain and the young United States were at their lowest ebb. The British navy deemed it their right to board American vessels on the high seas and take off any British citizens they chose and impress them into the royal navy. The Americans regarded such behaviour as nothing less than piracy. Whatever about the royal navy impressing British citizens on British soil, it had no right to do so on board an American ship bound for an American port. One of the reasons the royal navy committed these acts was to deter the emigration of dissatisfied Irish people to the United States, where their possible enmity towards Britain might channel them to fight for their adopted country in the looming war. Shipping companies in Ireland, such as Joseph Elly in New Ross, had been urging government to subsidise emigration to Canada instead so that British subjects would still be on British soil and not lost to the potential enemy.[38]

In mid-Atlantic, the *Belisarius* was hailed and boarded by the officers and men of the British sloop-of-war HMS *Atalanta*.[39] Most of the passengers, including Tackaberry and his family, were taken off. Seventeen of the men were pressed into service on the *Atalanta*, the rest were carried to the port of Halifax in Nova Scotia. Forty-three of these were then sent to the Townshend estate on Prince Edward Island (then called St John's Island), but Tackaberry was able to prove that he was a loyal subject who had no intention of settling in the U.S., and he was allowed to proceed on his way when he explained that his final destination was in Ontario, then known as Upper Canada.

Before leaving the topic of emigration it should be mentioned that, even apart from the practice of primogeniture among Protestants, religion played a big role in emigration. There may be some truth in the supposition that some Protestants left the country because they felt that the growing tolerance towards Catholicism was ill-advised. Perhaps they could see a time in the not too distant future when Catholics would achieve the political and religious freedoms accorded to mainstream Protestantism. Perhaps they disagreed with Catholic emancipation on idealogical or economic grounds. Perhaps Methodists found the catcalling they were often subjected to by Catholics was more than they could take. All these possibilities reflect the 'total want of Confidence' and 'gloomy, dark suspicion' prophesied by Edward Bayly. On the other hand, perhaps they just felt that life in the U.S. and Upper Canada had more to offer.

One thing is sure, it was easier for Protestants to emigrate and they had a vociferous lobby on their behalf. When shippers like Elly sought government subsidy for getting people to Canada they were careful to point out that it should apply to Protestant emigrants only, or at least by preference. Elly submitted two lists comprising 991 families (5,502 individuals) from south Leinster who wanted to go to Canada. One list was of 710 Protestant families whom he praised without reservation as having defended the country in 1798, and 281 Catholic families who were acceptable but with the

> order, neatness and economy which generally designates the religious
> persuasion to which they belong.

He also mentioned the bad feeling the Protestant families had towards the Catholics, looking on them with a 'dissatisfied and jealous eye'.[40]

One Arklow Catholic on the move was Fr Kearns who was transferred to Rathfarnham in 1810. In his eleven years as parish priest of Arklow, he had re-established the Catholic parish. The congregation had moved from the ruined walls of the old chapel into a new, if not overly elaborate or commodious, church on Parade Ground. Although the Penal Laws were still enforced to varying degrees, there was an implicit acceptance of the Catholic Church's right to exist. Throughout the country, Catholics were becoming more confident as the horrors of the rebellion slipped from everyday memory into the pages of history. They were 'beginning to make their voices heard with meetings and committees springing up everywhere'.[41] Dr Troy obviously felt that Fr Kearns had earned the easier posting at Rathfarnham. In his place came Fr Edan Redmond.

There were two cemeteries in the town at this time, one Protestant and one Catholic. It is impossible to say when interments began in each of these, but the oldest extant headstones in both date from the early eighteenth century. It was ironic that the Catholic graveyard shared the grounds of the old abbey with the Protestant parish church, while the Protestant graveyard lay in religious isolation in Main Street. It is not surprising then that when it was proposed to build a new Protestant church the location selected was the Main Street site directly opposite the Protestant graveyard, the site now occupied by Church Buildings.[42] Francis Johnson, who also designed St George's Church and the Castle Chapel in Dublin,[43] was commissioned to design the new church which would carry the name of its predecessor, St Mary's. It was a handsome building with a square tower and minaret, but it seems to have been structurally inadequate. This inference is drawn from the fact that it was originally built around 1810 at a cost of £1,384-12-3¾ and was enlarged in 1823 at a cost of £1,200.[44] Such a major refurbishment suggests that the church was virtually rebuilt just a little over a decade after it was originally erected. This explains why some sources quote 1823 as the year that this St Mary's was built. The fate of the church it replaced, the old St Mary's at the abbey, is uncertain. Some accounts say that it was later used as an ordinary house. In her article on Methodism in Arklow, Dorothy White states that there was a Methodist chapel in Arklow from 1822 and, as this date almost coincides with the rebuilding of St Mary's in 1823, it is possible that the Established Church allowed the Methodists to rent or buy the old St Mary's. This possibility gains credence when we consider the fact that the rector had already supplied the Methodists with a schoolhouse.[45]

*

In 1812 the port of Arklow was described as not deserving the name of a harbour at all.[46] Despite the appalling lack of infrastructure, some maritime related industries were forging ahead and in that same year

Arklow's first recorded locally built schooner, the *William*, left the stocks.[47] At this time, Arklow was also the centre of the county's fishing industry and the only manufacture in the town was also connected with the fisheries.

> Six tons of hemp are manufactured each year employing not less than one thousand women and children.[48]

The women received between 6d and 9d (3c – 4½c) per day, the children got half that. Every pound of hemp made seven fathoms of net, and each herring net consisted of seventy-five fathoms. Arklow nets were used extensively along the coast and the surplus was sold in the Dublin and Liverpool markets.

There were two herring seasons. One began in May, the other in November, each lasting about six weeks. These attracted boats from Dublin to Wexford. Others came from the Isle of Man and Wales. In the summer season, large vessels from Dublin and Liverpool lay at anchor in the bay, purchasing the catches of the smaller boats. Rev Bayly estimated that £24,250 in revenue was generated annually through the Arklow fisheries.[49]

He made these comments in William Shaw Mason's *Statistical Survey of Ireland* (1816). Bayly had spent his life in the town and knew it intimately, so it is particularly interesting to have his detailed pen picture of Arklow at that time. It is a counterbalance to the fleeting impressions of tourists, it is substance rather than mere captions beneath imaginary postcards. It was such an excellent piece that large chunks of it were reproduced verbatim several times by other writers, not all of whom acknowledged Bayly as the original source. Thomas Cromwell's piece on Arklow in 1820 relied heavily on Bayly's work, but he did add some details of his own, for which reason I have decided to reproduce Cromwell's description of Arklow in full, in Appendix 1 of this book.

Nevertheless, the opinions of outsiders also have their place in this story of Arklow and, apart from individuals publishing their own accounts of their travels in Ireland, some commercial publishers also brought out tour guides. One of these, *The Traveller's New Guide Through Ireland,* appeared in 1815. In its reference to Arklow, it mentioned the barracks and the bridge, as usual, then added

... there are numerous fishermen's cabbins, irregularly built on the wide extended flat between the town and the sea; from this suburb of the village an intricate communication meanders among the sandhills until it arrives at the base of a rocky perpendicular hill, abruptly commencing where the most extraordinary marine saturated sand deposits terminate, which road leads to Courtown ... ... A judiciously constructed pier would render this town a place of considerable traffic, whence the internal wealth of the country might be readily conveyed by water, but alas not even a shelter is afforded for the protection of its numerous fishing boats, perpetually exposed to the inclemency of an irritable and turbulent sea; the noble proprietors of the adjacent soil ought to exert their influence to remedy this local impediment to national prosperity. Here Nature has profusely scattered her bountiful munificence, but, as yet, has received no collateral aid, support, or assistance.[50]

The 'noble proprietors of the adjacent soil' spent the vast majority of their time in England or elsewhere. As absentee landlords they were not instigators of improvements, but to give them their due they usually contributed to campaigns designed to benefit the area. One of these was the construction of an earth bank along the north side of the river to stop the flow spilling off in that direction. The earls gave £100 each towards the cost, the remaining money needed was raised in the town. This paid for a retaining embankment of eighty-four perches (420 metres)[51] and its success should have encouraged the 'noble proprietors of the adjacent soil' to invest further, but they obviously felt they had done their bit.

Other accounts, much of them saying the same thing, followed with predictable and often boring regularity. Anne Plumtre, who had her description of Arklow published in 1817, did add a little extra.

From the point where the road to this mountain diverges from the sweet vale of Avoca, this beautiful vale gradually expands, the hills sloping away till on approaching Arklow the country becomes nearly a flat. A new road[52] has lately been made through this part of the valley, at the foot of the hills, instead of going over the summits. It winds through Lord Carysfort's woods, having the beautiful woods of Shelton, the seat of Lord Wicklow, on the other side of the river. At the latter place are some of the best oaks to be found in Ireland. There is something picturesque in the town of Arklow as approached on this side, standing on a slope above the river. Having stopped here a sufficient time to bait the horse, to eat my own dinner, and to make a walk upon the beach, which affords nothing particularly worthy of remark, I proceeded along the coast road to Wicklow.[53]

The following year, "An Irish Gentleman" shared her admiration of the valley, but this macho individual didn't want his masculine interests to be confused with a woman's romantic nonsense, so he called his narrative *The Scientific Tourist Through Ireland,* and his style has the ring of a fairground stallholder about it.

> See Bridge of nineteen arches over the Avoca; modern church; Barracks in commanding position; ruins of Castle, an odd Tower forming part of the Barracks; and general appearance of the town picturesque. See the mausoleum near to it to the memory of the Howard family, conspicuous on a lofty hill.

No namby-pamby romanticism about this man. All good pragmatic stuff which would interest the scientific-minded and those with an appreciation of engineering genius, barked out in a no nonsense imperative tone. But aware that others had less admirable interests he conceded:

> The picturesque and poetic tourist may amuse himself with tracing the romantic scenery of the Avoca and Avonmore ... Kilcarra Castle, three miles from the sea is the seat of the Earls of Carysfort, lately ornamented with towers and castellated front in a retired spot on a gentle declivity, with romantic glen. The new mail coach [road] leading past this district affords many views of fine scenery. Shelton is the beautifully situated mansion of the Earl of Wicklow at the base of a range of hills luxuriantly clothed in wood. Here are some of the finest beeches and chestnuts in Ireland. House ancient but modernised.[54]

This reference to Kilcarra (until recently Poulahoney Lodge and soon to be Glenart) Castle and Shelton Abbey both having undergone modernisation probably reflects the optimism that accompanies the beginning of economic growth. The hunting lodge at Poulahoney was enlarged and given a facelift to make it resemble a castle, while Shelton House underwent major renovation in the Gothic style and renamed Shelton Abbey, although it had never been a religious foundation. This was a fad of the time, a harmless nonsense lampooned by Jane Austen in her novel *Northanger Abbey* (1817). Such appellations were considered to give a family seat mystique and pedigree based in a distant past. It has been suggested that the growing number of *nouveau riche* in England, whose money was made in the industrial revolution, wanted the "respectibility" of traceable lineage, and that the trappings of heritage helped create the required illusion. Words such as 'castle' and 'abbey' were purloined and stuck on the names of refurbished homes. Perhaps the Probys and the Howards felt they too needed this dubious legitimacy, or perhaps they just liked to keep up with ephemeral fancies. Whatever their reasons, a lodge became a castle and a house became an abbey.

Not everyone was so concerned with ostentation. There were those who prized spiritual riches much higher, and the more evangelical of these were making increasingly greater inroads in Arklow.

> Concerning Arklow, Mr Andrew Taylor states that his work here has greatly prospered, leading to a blessed awakening, during which the old members were revived, many additions made to the society and the congregations such that at times the accommodation was insufficient for those who desired to attend.[55]

Did this 'blessed awakening' indicate gratitude for better times, or a seeking of solace in hard times? One way or the other, it was a trend that continued, for in 1819 it was reported

> The gracious revival in Arklow was followed up by a visit from Messrs Taylor and Tackaberry when 60 persons were awakened to a sense of their sinfulness, and joined the society. Thus the membership, which at the previous Conference had been only forty, was now increased to 200. Concerning one of these additions, a sergeant whose backslidings were healed, Mr Tackaberry states that such a change in the countenance of the man and in so short a time he had hardly ever witnessed. Reilly in writing to Ouseley says 'I cannot express my astonishment at the work in Arklow, since you and brother Noble were there. The most extraordinary conversions which I have ever seen or heard of, have taken place.[56]

Another reference to the progress of Methodism in Arklow at that time gives a hint that all was not well, and indicates that many of the fishing families were destitute. The fish had been scarce and Mr Reilly conducted a service on the beach specifically to pray for good catches. These prayers, we are told, were answered immediately and the following morning

> a man more earnest and grateful in feeling than correct language, hastened to the house of the servant of God, exclaiming: 'The herrins is

come! The herrins is come!' The fact was so; and to this day it is
gratefully remembered by the people of the town, as a marked answer
to prayer.[57]

The families who fished for a living were totally dependent on the
success of the season and, at times such as that described above, hunger
was inevitable. Also, the cramped housing conditions and the congested
and often filthy laneways were breeding grounds for disease. As in
other towns throughout Ireland and elsewhere at that time, Arklow was
regularly visited by outbreaks of cholera, typhus and other ailments
attributable to unsanitary living conditions, poor personal hygiene and
lack of nutritional diet. The presence of the large marsh was also
deemed a source of ill-health and many inhabitants were afflicted with

pleurisies and agues, which however are seldom fatal, when treated
with the necessary attention.[58]

The government was becoming increasingly aware of its responsibilities
in the sphere of public health and at the beginning of the nineteenth
century the duties of the Wicklow Grand Jury, the precursor of the
County Council, had been greatly widened. They were empowered to
establish medical dispensaries and fever hospitals around the county.
Arklow's fever hospital was built in 1818 and stood in what is now St
Mary's Road. The dispensary was built about the same time. The
Medical Officer, the doctor appointed for the purpose, attended the
hospital three days a week and medicines were dispensed to between
300 and 400 patients in the course of a year. The hospital would serve
the town well, or as well as its meagre facilities would allow, until the
1920s and was demolished in 1935.[59] Despite these ailments and
hazards longevity was not unknown in Arklow. Thomas Cromwell cited
the case of a woman who died at 110 just a few years prior to his visit
to the town in 1820, and that her youngest son was eighty. He also
stated that in 1814 the combined ages of a five-man crew in a herring
boat was 335 years, an average age of sixty-seven!

*

And so the first two decades of the nineteenth century closed on
Arklow. The political and religious sectarianism which the United
Irishmen had sought to eradicate was alive and well and as invidious as

ever. There were no outbreaks of physical violence after about 1803, but the general air of distrust was ever present. Psychological and social barriers were plain to see. Such divisions may not have been the cause of the lack of economic development of the town in those years, but they certainly were not conducive to the common good. Some hints of a better future could be detected here and there. Boatbuilding was becoming more important, and the mines continued to benefit the town. Public health was also being looked at seriously for the first time. Perhaps the long awaited watershed would come in the next thirty years.

8

**Long delayed development:
1821 - 1850**

One aspect of life in Arklow which has been only briefly touched on is education. In Chapter Five, I referred to the Charter School which was established in 1748 on the corner of Coolgreaney Road and the Yellow Lane. It was little more than a slave labour camp in which unprotected children were exploited. It was closed down in 1812. The time has come to take a closer look at the development of education in the town.

The Penal Laws had made it impossible for Catholics to receive an education in keeping with their religious beliefs. Protestant children, on the other hand, had no such impediment, although the quality of both subject matter and teaching ability varied greatly from school to school. Catholics could attend these schools if they converted to Protestantism, and societies to promote Protestant education sprang up around the country. The Kildare Place Society, the Erasmus Smith Board, and other supposedly philanthropic agencies grant-aided schools that would not only educate children to 'levels appropriate to their stations' but would also inculcate the Protestant faith irrespective of the child's religion. Perhaps their approach was best summed up by Hugh Boulter.

> There are a great number of Papists in this Kingdom, and the obstinacy with which they adhere to their religion occasions our trying what may be done with their children to bring them over to our Church, to teach the children of the Papists the English tongue, and the principles of the Christian religion.[1]

To promote both the discontinuance of this 'papist obstinacy' and to spread the 'English tongue', Catholic children who entered these schools were to be removed as far as possible from the influence of their parents. The vast majority of Catholic children who received any education at all did so in the local hedge schools. The name 'hedge schools' has become one of the touchstones of Irish history. Even those with only vague ideas of what they were, recognise in the term a denial of civil rights. It is an iconic phrase that encapsulates the systematic repression of the majority by the few. It recalls how Catholic teachers and pupils had to work clandestinely behind hedges. To have the luxury of a building in which to teach and to learn would have been to invite the closure of the school and the possible imprisonment of the teacher.

By the beginning of the nineteenth century, things had eased a great deal. A blind eye was turned to houses being used as schools, but even after the Relief Acts of 1782 and 1793 they were still illegal as

> Catholics could not legally teach unless they took an oath of allegiance and received a licence to teach from the Protestant Bishop of the Diocese[2]

which few Catholic teachers were prepared to do. Although now indoors, many of these schools were still known as hedge schools, because of their origins. They were also known as 'pay schools' as the only remuneration the teacher received was what the pupils, usually the children of poor parents, could afford to give.

A report dating from 1825 lists eighteen hedge schools in Arklow parish, fourteen south of the river and four to the north. Typically they were mud-walled, thatched cabins, like the majority of dwellings in the area and many were described as wretched. James Ball, a Catholic, taught in one of them near the chapel in Parade Ground. He received about £12 a year for instructing thirty-two male students and eighteen female. By comparison Daniel Lapham (probably Laphan, as he conducted classes in Laphan's Lane which now connects Lower Main Street with Castlepark car park) was raking it in on about £34 yearly for teaching forty-eight students. John Harrigan was also doing well, getting £30 from fifty-four students, thirty-six of whom were male and eighteen were famale. Rose Gafney's reputation as a teacher allowed her to make £33 a year with just twenty students, only eight of whom were male.[3]

Just up the road in Parade Ground, parish priest Edan Redmond no doubt relished the growing confidence of the Catholic Church in

Ireland. While many of the Penal Laws were still on the statute books they were largely ignored in daily life. Despite the aforementioned Relief Acts of 1782 and 1793[4], some of the professions were still barred to Catholics but property rights were no longer actively infringed. The rise of a commercial class which included many Catholics saw the financial position of Catholic parishes improve dramatically. The movement for full Catholic emancipation was gaining momentum with each passing year and the relationships not only between the various churches but also between the Catholic Church and government were better than they had been for many, many years. The Catholic hierarchy would soon become an accepted and almost equal part of the social and political establishment, rather than be seen as merely an agency through which a dispossessed and despised peasantry could be kept under control. It was not a time to rock the boat and certainly not a time for a return to any activity that smacked of political subversion or social agitation.

Colonel Joseph Hardy was the man responsible for keeping things in order in the Arklow area, and in January 1822 he reported that the number of Ribbonmen[5] in the Arklow area was not great. The following month he reiterated that his district was 'still uncontaminated'.[6] Nevertheless, there were some things happening about which he was not happy. In March 1822, nine smugglers from the area were convicted at Wicklow, and the ominous appearance of placards around the town caused him to call on the local magistrates to be more energetic in enforcing their authority.[7] The following month, 'the posting of a seditious notice on the gate of a farmer near town' was reported.[8] Fr Redmond fully espoused this policy of clamping down on sedition and proved it in 1823. He had heard that a blacksmith named Skinner, who had recently moved into the area, was swearing recruits into a secret society. So many blacksmiths had been involved in recruiting and making weapons for the Society of United Irishmen twenty-five years earlier that a blacksmith "being up to no good" was almost axiomatic. Redmond immediately informed the Earl of Wicklow who had the man arrested.[9]

The whole question of law and order was in a state of change at that time. From medieval times, local Norman lords, such as the Butlers, assigned constables to enforce laws and collect tithes and taxes. Their powers were fairly limited and lack of supervision made them amenable to corruption. In 1787, the Lord Lieutenant of Ireland introduced a new system by which a chief constable was appointed to each barony, and the local Grand Jury was empowered to appoint sixteen sub-constables. It had little effect. Then, in 1814, Robert Peel set up the Peace Preservation Force to police areas deemed in drastic need of close supervision and control.[10] This was the model from which future police forces developed. It was refined in 1822 when the Irish Constables Act was passed. It was still based on barony, so was not a national force, and it was to be paramilitary rather than civilian. The Peelers had arrived. Their home in Arklow was to be the barracks at Parade Ground and the small garrison of soldiers who lived there vacated the premises for the new force.

It was also about this time, the early 1820s, that the name of Glen Art came into being. The 1st Earl of Carysfort, John Joshua Proby, was not a resident landlord, but he did spend a few weeks of most years at Poulahoney and it was he who converted the hunting lodge into the fine, castellated mansion several tourists described. He was interested in history and archaeology and was a member of the Royal Irish Academy.[11] In 1824 an ancient manuscript which described the meeting of Art MacMurrough Kavanagh and Richard II (mentioned in Chapter Four) was discovered. Its publication caused quite a stir and Proby was particularly fascinated by the story it told. He decided that the wooded glen in which the enemies met was none other than his own wooded glen at Poulahoney, and so he renamed his estate and castle Glen Art. Usage soon altered this to a single word.

Arklow, c.1820

While Proby toyed with nomenclature, his tenants, or those whose livelihood depended on the sea, had more serious things to occupy their minds. The sand barriers which are known as the Arklow Banks have long been known as a danger to shipping. The list of known shipwrecks over recent centuries is long, the list of vessels which have grounded but were successfully refloated is much, much longer. But we cannot even begin to calculate the number of ships and men who have been lost on the banks and along this coast since time immemorial. Medieval maps clearly warn seafarers of these navigational hazards. It is not surprising then that Arklow was graced with a station of the Royal National Lifeboat Institution in 1826, just two years after the organisation had been established in England.[12]

It was not the first lifeboat station in Ireland - Dublin Bay, for example, had a lifesaving service from the eighteenth century[13] - but it has been generally accepted that it was the first RNLI station in this country. In recent years, however, a doubt has been cast on this claim. The vellum which records the establishment of the Arklow station is dated November 1826,[14] but the station at Courtmacsherry in County Cork would appear to have a record of establishment dated November 1825.[15] Also, while the records of Courtmacsherry show unbroken service, the same cannot be said of the Arklow station. Several serious incidents at sea in this area in the years immediately preceding 1826 had prompted the opening of the Arklow station, but during the few years immediately following few such incidents occurred. While this tragedy-free status was to be welcomed, it did cause the RNLI to rethink its decision and the station was closed in 1830 and remained closed for the next twenty-seven years. During that hiatus, the local fishermen reverted to self-sufficiency in such matters.

The belief that Arklow was the first RNLI station in Ireland is so long-held and ingrained in the local psyche that it is understandable that some local people are reluctant to surrender the accolade. They claim that, despite the older vellum in Courtmacsherry, there is room for doubt. Perhaps there is, perhaps there isn't. But is it really important which was the first Irish RNLI station? Surely the aspect from which pride can be taken is the service a particular station has rendered since its establishment, and in this the Arklow station's reputation remains unscathed. Its coxswains and crew members have been the recipients of awards in recognition of their courage. Between 1826 and 2000,

Arklow lifeboats put to sea almost 400 times, saving hundreds of lives. Some of these will be referred to in later chapters.

Proby had been Earl of Carysfort for thirty-nine years when he died in his London home in 1828.[16] He was succeeded by his forty-eight-year-old second son John who had been born in the family seat at Elton near Peterborough. He seems to have been a more flamboyant character, having reputedly joined the army at fourteen. He served in Germany and Russia and also in Ireland during the 1798 rebellion. He also saw active service in Egypt, Sweden, Sicily and Spain. He rarely, if ever, visited the Glenart estate, leaving it in the hands of his agent.

Others, who had no financial interest in the region, did feel it worth a visit and many of these penned and published their impressions just as so many more had done in the previous fifty years. Few had anything further to add to what had already been written and some were so similar to earlier accounts that I suspect there were a few armchair travellers and plagiarists among them. Most of them lacked that touch of individuality and personal anecdote which would have set them apart. An exception was someone who styled himself "A German Prince", and who are we to argue? He spent four years travelling through England, Ireland and France and his experiences were recorded in a series of letters which were later published in Philadelphia. He describes his first view of Castle Howard, perched above the Meeting of the Waters

> with its numerous towers and battlements, which, unluckily, were just finished and a near approach lost all their imposing effect. I found the castle still buried in sleep, and a servant in his shirt showed me the pictures, among which is the splendid portrait of Mary Stuart. This must be a sparkling likeness; it is clearly of her time; ... the attractive, truly French face, with the delicate nose, captivating mouth, the languishing fire of the eyes ... An excellent road leads from this place through the entire valley to the park at Bally-Arthur.

He continued on towards Arklow and stopped at Shelton Abbey,

> a piece of Gothicry ... The possessors have been absent for years, and a negro who was at work in the garden showed me the rooms, in which are some very interesting pictures ... The civil negro led me across the fields and through a pretty deep ford in the river (whose ice-cold waters did not seem to alarm him) to the town of Arklow, whence I returned along the high road to dinner at Avoca Inn.[17]

Shelton Abbey

Untypically, Henry Inglis was more interested in the modest houses of the poor than in the mansions of the magnates when he visited the locality in 1834. He spent three days at Woodenbridge, eulogising the scenery but criticising the living conditions of the peasantry. He described Arklow as

> one of the poorest looking villages that could be seen. It is entirely supported by the herring fishery during the season, but all the rest of the year it is miserably off.[18]

It has been suggested that Inglis mistook the Fishery for the entire town, leaving him with an incomplete and unfair assessment of Arklow as a whole,[19] but just two years later John Barrow had more or less the same to say. His tone was more scathing rather than sympathetic.

> ... at Arklow we came upon the sea, of which we had occasional glimpses from the road. It is a mean little fishing town, at which poverty evidently prevailed, and beggars were numerous.[20]

Strangely, neither man referred to the new Anglican church the Earl of Wicklow had built as a memorial chapel to the Howard family at Kilbride. This was to mark the elevation of Kilbride to parish status in 1834.

After his visit to Arklow in 1837, Jonathan Binns had more to say. His anecdotes suggest he did actually pass through here. He certainly didn't lift the name of Shelton from a book, because he sang the praises not of Shelton Abbey, but Skelton Abbey. Once could have been a misprint, but when every reference is misspelt the same way the reader must draw the conclusion that the writer either misremembered it or had difficulty reading his own notes.

> In our way to Arklow we passed through Ballyarthur, the seat of the Reverend H Bayley, a truly lovely spot, and alighted at Skelton Abbey the residence of the Earl of Wicklow, which is situated in the beautiful Vale of Ovoca. We walked around the gardens and pleasure grounds, which abound in arbutus, bay, holly, and other luxuriant trees and shrubs. The Abbey is a square building, richly pinnacled, designed by W.R. Morrison. Skelton has long been the residence of the Howards, who were originally of English extraction. King James, after the Battle of the Boyne, rested here in his flight to Waterford. We passed through the domain having the mausoleum of the Howard family on a hill on our left along a flat and swampy tract of land, – *[they obviously approached Arklow along the avenue which cuts through the marsh and leads to Ferrybank]* - and crossed the old bridge of Arklow, consisting of nineteen arches, over the mouth of the Ovoca. The harbour appears extensive, but is reported to be unsafe, in consequence of the number of sand banks. Upwards of one hundred boats are here engaged in the herring and oyster fishery. We ascended the partially ruined tower of the Castle which affords a good view of the town and harbour.[21]

These descriptions suggest that progress, if it existed at all, was slow. The same remarks are passed consistently, but there is little insight into what was going on behind the scenes. They are, after all, merely penned impressions. The tourists came and the tourists went. But things were changing, and changing for the better.

In 1829 came Catholic emancipation and the abolition of the remaining Penal Laws, including restrictions on Catholic children receiving an education that would not entail surrendering their religion. The government was well aware of the number of hedge schools in the country – they had risen from an estimated 4,000 in 1807 to over 9,000 in 1824[22] - and was anxious to take control of these. A new system for

National Schools was introduced, under which teachers would have to be examined to ensure that they were competent to teach, the curriculum would be standardised, and no religion would be promoted above another within the system. This last proposal, aimed at redressing the wrongs of the past, was the one that was to stir the opposition of both Catholic and Protestant clergy. Both regarded schools as the seed beds of religious instruction and the "god-less" schools proposed by the National Education Act of 1833 were not to be envisaged. Not all the Catholic hierarchy denounced the new system, however. Daniel Murray, now Archbishop of Dublin, supported it, albeit with reservations. Because of this, he was appointed a commissioner to the National Board and he pushed the introduction of the new system into as many parishes of his diocese as possible. Here in Arklow, Fr Redmond also supported the new measures and the new Boys' National School was opened on Coolgreaney Road in 1839, ironically the year of Fr Redmond's death.

Not part of the national system but doing very well for itself was Elton Boarding School which occupied the refurbished buildings which had housed the disgraceful Charter School a generation earlier. What had been a child labour camp was now a private school teaching classics to the offspring of the well-to-do.

Nor was education the only activity to be brought under central control in that age of standardisation. The year 1836 saw the introduction of the Royal Irish Constabulary, Ireland's first police force to be organised on a national basis.[23] The vast majority of the old County Constabulary, established a decade earlier, were accepted into the new force and their barracks in Parade Ground became the local RIC station. It was hoped that the RIC would not be seen as overtly sectarian as the County Constabularies had been and by 1841 over fifty-one per cent of the rank and file were Catholics. Institutional sectarianism within

RIC badge - Now in Arklow Community College Museum

the new force, however, ensured that the officer ranks were monopolised by Protestants.

In 1838, one of the most important publications ever produced in Ireland was released. This was Samuel Lewis's *Topographical Dictionary*. It was a mine of information about counties, towns, villages and townlands throughout the country and its importance to local historians has increased with each passing decade since its publication. Like H.L. Bayly's account of 1816, it is a snapshot of Arklow at the time it was written.

> ARKLOW: This place ... seems to have been a fishing station since time immemorial ... It is divided into the Upper and Lower Towns, which latter is called the "fishery", and in 1831 it contained 702 houses. The houses in the Upper Town, which consists of one principal street, are neatly built; those in the Lower Town, which is chiefly inhabited by fishermen, are mostly thatched cabins. The inhabitants are amply supplied with water from numerous excellent springs, but no works have been established to convey it to their houses; and the only improvement that has recently taken place is the macadamising of the principal street, and the laying down of footpaths. ... The principal trade is fishery, which was formerly very lucrative, having two seasons in the year; one in May which had lately ceased, and the other in November which ... has become so unproductive as to scarcely remunerate the persons employed in it. The fishery in 1835 employed about 200 boats in the herring season and in dredging for oysters, of the latter which great quantities are taken off the coast in some years and sent to different parts of England and Ireland. Formerly much of the copper ore from the Wicklow mines, which are situated nearly midway between this town and Rathdrum, was shipped from this port during the summer season, and some trade is still carried on in the importation of coal. The want of a safe harbour in which the fishermen may shelter during bad weather, which for two or three seasons has prevailed on this coast, has been severely felt, there being no proper port between Kingstown – *[i.e Dun Laoghaire]* - and Waterford into which they can run for shelter, and many lives are annually lost. The harbour is accessible only for small boats, as the passage is sinuous and subject to shifting sands.[24]

This report goes on to list the fair days as January 11th, March 22nd, April 19th, May 14th, June 28th, August 9th, September 25th and November 15th, showing that the extra fair days called for by Bayly twenty years earlier had been granted in the interim.[25]

Less than a decade later, the *Parliamentary Gazatteer of Ireland* also gave a lengthy description of the town, a description that in many ways was very similar to Lewis's. It was intended for the use of politicians and civil servants, providing background on cities, towns and other administrative regions. Sometimes, however, the compilers of the articles wrote in most unparliamentary language. The reporter on Arklow waxed lyrical, if damningly, in his description of the 'Lower Town'. It was

> ... a wretched segregation of wretched huts, a huddled assemblage of squalid hovels, a magnified copy of a Hottentot or Caffre kraal, with the putrid increment of the accumulated offals of a slovenly fishery.[26]

We can, I think, take it that it wasn't to his liking. However, when he concentrated on factual reportage rather than poetical imagery, he wrote an account worth recording. Much of it echoed what has already been said, but he was more expansive and up-to-date than the Lewis report, especially regarding the fishing industry here.

> Arklow is the headquarters of the whole coast fishery of the county of Wicklow. The natural harbour formed by the Ovoca within its tide-bar is the only retreat for boats, and is unprovided with either pier or any artificial improvement. All vessels which frequent are built to suit its peculiarities, and even they must all lighten on the outside of the bar. The very fishing boats are obliged to lie off, and watch an opportunity of passing the bar on a rise of the wave; they seldom or never enter without striking; and they are occasionally compelled to run to Wexford, Waterford, or Dungarvan. Even at high water of spring tides, the depth over the bar seldom exceeds from 4 to 5 feet. Yet in spite of such serious disadvantages, the county coast fisheries, in 1836, numbered 1378, and 39 decked vessels of aggregately 1,174 tons, 153 half-decked vessels of 1,425 tons, 57 open sail boats with 246 men, and 14 row boats, with 48 men. The Arklow fishermen are so industrious and enterprising that they not only contrive to overcome the enormous disadvantage of wanting a sheltered or an accessible harbour, but succeed in keeping themselves constantly employed in some one or other of a series of fisheries. They fish for herring and hake between Mizen Head and Cahore Point, but for the last 14 years have had little success in that fishery; they frequent the Isle of Man when there is a fishery there; and, when they are not better engaged, they pursue the oyster fishery from January till September, and find it not only an unfailing employment, but a succedaneum for the agricultural alternative on which most other fishermen in Ireland rely. They load their boats with oysters and proceed to Beaumaris in Anglesey; and having there laid the oysters on banks, they afterwards, at periods when they are in good season, and most in

demand, draw supplies for the markets of Liverpool and Manchester. All materials for boats and fishing-gear are procured from Dublin; sails are purchased in Whitehaven[27]; and, in 1836, boat-building was so brisk that, though 4s 4d[28] per day was paid, a sufficient number of shipwrights could not be obtained. In 1835, the exports from the town, consisting of copper ore, corn, herrings, sheep, swine, and beer, amounted in value to £3,677; and the imports, consisting of coal, oatmeal, salt, slate-stone, iron, tallow, sugar, tea, wines, and spirits, amounting to £6,762 10s.

Roughly around the time that the *Gazetteer* was being compiled, a government commission was investigating various aspects of life in Ireland. Although the primary aim of the commission was 'To inquire into the occupation of land in Ireland', other factors such as wages, diet, rent, and housing were also gone into. The commission was headed by Lord Devon, and its findings have become known as the Devon Commission Report. They turned their attention to the situation in County Wicklow in 1844 and one of their principal respondents in the Arklow area was Michael Hudson of Woodmount, in the townland of Kilbride. He was agent to the absentee Lord Wicklow and managed the Howard properties in the baronies of Arklow and Talbotstown. Hudson's evidence was taken at Bray on Thursday, October 24th, 1844.[29] He said that most of the farms in the area were between thirty and sixty acres, but there were some as small as twenty and as large as 150. Farming techniques had greatly improved in recent years, particularly in tillage, and attempts had been made to reclaim some of the marsh but with little success. Tenants were also encouraged to improve their holdings. For example, if a tenant planned on building a house the estate would supply timber and slates. Also, if a tenant carried out drainage work on his holding, a certain percentage of his rent would be rebated for a year or two until it was deemed that the value of his work had been repaid. Such incentives to improve homes and holdings had proved successful.

On the whole, Hudson painted a rather rosy picture of life on the Wicklow estate. He even offered the opinion that the earl was too lax in enforcing payment of the half-yearly rents on the due dates in March and September, and only the most recalcitrant tenant was evicted for excessive arrears. As a result, relations between the estate and the tenants were good, and there had been no agrarian outrages.[30] His description of the south side of the river, however, was less favourable. It was, he said

Arklow Shipbuilders (Reproduced by permission of the Royal Society of
Antiquaries of Ireland©)

> ... thickly inhabited . There are a great many poor people and a
> superabundance of labourers on that side.

He mentioned that many men in the area were employed in the mines
at Castlemacadam and, although he could give no figures, they
appeared to earn 'a great deal of money'. In truth, the influence of the
mines in the region cannot be overstated. Throughout the 1830s and
40s, the increase in trade in the port, and in the port of Wicklow, was
due mainly to the mining operations. The revenue generated by this
trade also acted as a catalyst for a boom period in Arklow shipbuilding.
Local businessmen realised that even greater profits could be made if
the ships that carried the mineral ore were Arklow-owned and Arklow-
manned. With this in mind, partnerships of local business money and
seafaring expertise were formed.[31] The adze and the axe began
swinging on the banks of the Avoca as never before and they continued
unabated for twenty years.

*

Under the Poor Law (Ireland) Act of 1838, Ireland was divided into 130 administrative Poor Law Unions. The Unions were so called because they were composed of a union of several electoral divisions within a district. Each Union was run by a Board of Poor Law Guardians and the entire network was overseen from London by the Poor Law Commissioners. The main work of the Guardians was to erect and maintain a workhouse (also known as a poor house) in their respective Union. This was to be financed by a local levy on landowners - a 'rate'. Throughout the country, these workhouses had a total accommodation for 100,000 paupers. They were bleak and forbidding. Even the darkest moments of Dickens' novels pale in comparison to the extant records of the various Boards of Guardians. The harsh regime was designed to keep the number of people seeking admittance down to a minimum, thereby keeping the cost to the ratepayers down to a minimum. It should not be forgotten that all the Poor Law Guardians were recruited from the ranks of the ratepayers. When destitute families were admitted to the workhouse they were split up, with men and boys in one wing, women and girls in the other.

> No contact was permitted between married couples. Parents were to have reasonable access to their children without inconveniencing the poorhouse administration.[32]

Inspectors appointed to monitor the running of these workhouses repeatedly reported cases of administrative inefficiency, neglect and corruption. Little was done to improve matters. Under no circumstances was outdoor relief to be given. Applicants had to be totally without means and must enter the workhouse to qualify for help. If the workhouse was full and no more admissions could be made then those left outside could not be assisted.

There were five Poor Law Unions in County Wicklow. In the northeast was Rathdown which was comprised mostly of electoral districts in south County Dublin. The workhouse there was situated at Loughlinstown, and its buildings now form the nucleus of St Colmcille's Hospital. The northwest districts of Blessington and Baltiboys were incorporated into the Naas Union in County Kildare. The southwest Union was centred in Shillelagh. The west came under Baltinglass Union, while the southeast of the county formed the Rathdrum Union. Within three years each union had built its workhouse. Rathdown had

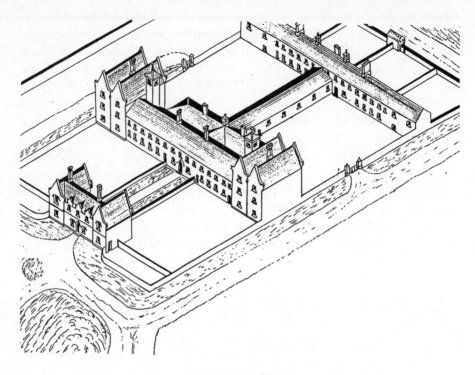

Rathdrum Workhouse

room for 600 paupers, Rathdrum could also house 600, Baltinglass 500 and Shillelagh 400.

Arklow was in the Rathdrum Union, so avoided the necessity of having a bleak workhouse added to the small list of public buildings in the town. There was, however, a small outreach office established here sometime after 1847 when legislative changes allowed for Outdoor Relief to be given to the utterly destitute. It stood in a small lane on South Quay, between the bridge and Doyle's Lane. Because of that office, the lane became known as Union Lane.[33]

The Irish Poor Law was never going to be a great success, but few could have predicted that within a few short years it would buckle under the weight of destitution that came in the wake of the potato crop failures of the second half of the 1840s. Despite the relative prosperity of many Arklow people, and the avoidance of abject poverty by many more, the effects of the Famine were felt to a far greater degree in this area than has been traditionally assumed. There is a misconception that

County Wicklow, along with other eastern counties, somehow escaped the catastrophe unscathed. Over the past ten years, local studies have shown that death from starvation and disease was more common here than is often realised. The workhouses in Shillelagh, Baltinglass and Rathdown were filled to overflowing, while the one in Rathdrum, to which the poor of Arklow might be admitted, also catered for far more inmates that its intended 600. To cater for those who could not gain admission, soup kitchens were opened and government work schemes, such as road-building, could be seen all over the county. Petitions for more help came from County Wicklow just as they came from Mayo and west Cork. County Wicklow may not have had its Skibbereen or its Scarriff, but it would be a grave mistake to believe that the people of the county, particularly the poor people of Wicklow, did not suffer in the horrific years between 1846 and 1850.[34]

The potato blight of 1845 was severe but not unprecedented. Government and private institutions had experience of relieving the level of distress it entailed. The crop failure of 1846, however, was total. Not only did it hit all parts of the country, but its intensity was far greater than the regional blights that afflicted different areas during years of partial blight. What little was salvaged was so scarce that market forces pushed the price beyond the reach of the poor.

The first signs of blight in this area were reported on November 10th, 1845 when the local vicar, Rev Daly, stated that the crop at Kilbride was rotten. Over the following weeks the extent of damage was assessed. It was worrying, but was not yet deemed a major catastrophe. The biggest problem was rising food prices, particularly towards late spring and early summer of 1846. Because it was a seaport and had a fishing fleet, the people of Arklow were considered fortunate, with hopes that the May/June herring season would ease the growing crisis. But as we have seen from the entry in the Parliamentary Gazetteer, this particular fishery had been in decline since the early 1830s and the summer herring catches in 1846 proved dismally disappointing. So disappointing, in fact, that in June many people in the town were described as being in 'extreme distress'.[35] A local Poor Law Guardian, Captain Hore of Lamberton, recorded that 'an eerie silence fell on Arklow as the town's children ceased to play'.[36] Both November 20th, 1846 and April 24th, 1847 were set aside in the parish of Kilbride as 'days of prayer and humiliation for the relief of the great famine'.[37]

Getting food supplies in should have been no problem, but it was.

The lack of proper harbour facilities had often brought cries for development, and these were borne out when it was found that regular relief provisions could not be guaranteed through the port and food had to be carted from Wicklow. Leading local figures protested that the merchants of Wicklow were hoarding supplies and charging exorbitant prices, so they concentrated on getting the food from Enniscorthy. But soon the people of Enniscorthy felt there was not enough food for themselves and they refused to send any out of their region. The carts returned to Arklow empty.

In December 1846, it was estimated that there was enough food in the town to last just four days. To survive the coming months, the fishermen had no choice but to pawn their gear. The new year brought no prospect of better times. The parish priest, Fr James Redmond – he had succeeded his uncle Fr Edan Redmond in 1839 – wrote that thirty of his parishioners had died in the previous six weeks. How many of these were from hunger and how many from fever and other related diseases is not known, but there was a high level of fever in the town as a consequence of the food shortages.[38] As early as October 1846, the Medical Officer for the town, Dr David Wright, had written 'Arklow is overwhelmed with fever'. The demand on the fever hospital was so great that it went into debt and remained in financial crisis for the next six months.

In March 1847, the British Association opened a food depot in Arklow and things eased a little.[39] The Association was not a government initiative but a voluntary group founded by wealthy businessmen who fundraised in England, America and to a lesser extent in Australia. They did, however, work with government bodies and, because of this connection, the London government is sometimes credited with relief measures for which the volunteers of the British Association should be given credit. Despite the best camouflaging efforts of modern revisionist historians, the attitude of the British government towards the 'sister island'[40] was disgraceful and gave rise to John Mitchel's often quoted accusation that while Providence caused the potato blight, British political and economic policies caused the Famine.

In 1847, Arklow and Baltinglass were described by the Poor Law Commissioners – the governing body of the Irish Poor Law – as 'the two great seats of misery in Wicklow'.[41] Of Arklow's population of 3,169, thirty-five per cent were in receipt of Outdoor Relief. This was a measure which the government belatedly and reluctantly introduced because the workhouses simply could not take any more inmates. There were also 650 men employed on relief works in the immediate vicinity of the town. These works included completing the construction of the Rock road; building an embankment along the south side of the river to protect the houses of the Fishery from flooding; completion of the 'great relief work at Lamberton'; improvement of the streets, lanes and sewers of the town; and general improvement of the town's roadways.

By pawning their gear, the fishermen managed to get through the winter, but as the time to redeem their nets and other equipment approached the money had been spent on food. This meant that even if the shoals returned in bumper numbers the fishermen would be unable to get to them. This impasse was overcome by the issue of interest-free loans given by the Society of Friends – the Quakers. They sent £50 to Captain Hore with instructions to distribute it among the fishermen so that they could get back to work. It was received on June 26th, 1847 and allowed 161 nets to be redeemed and to carry out minor repairs on a number of boats.[42] It would appear that the fish were indeed back in good numbers because by November 1st, just four months after the loan had been received, £46-18-0 had been repaid. The outstanding £3-2-0 was accounted for by one man who died before he could repay the 19/- he had received; 18/- worth of nets had been destroyed when a boat was run down at sea; and £1-5-0 had still to be repaid. Surely, a tribute to the honesty of the people involved. This loan was the turning point and the situation in Arklow gradually improved. Arklow's famine experience may not be recorded in ballads, or been as horrific as in other parts of Ireland, but it should never be lightly glossed over.

*

The three decades from 1820 to 1850 were a watershed. Arklow was at last emerging from medieval stagnation and was taking on not just the shape but also the appearance of the town we know today. True, most of the houses of the poor were still small thatched mud-walled cabins, but a rising commercial class invested in their Main Street properties. The Avoca mines were doing well and looked set to continue for some time. The fishing industry was still providing sustenance if not wealth.

Sectarian strife was dormant and civil liberties were more of a reality than they had been. Children were getting some degree of education. The stage was set for Arklow to become a modern town.

9

Signs of Social Change:
1851 - 1880

The 1850s were something of a boom time in Arklow's progress. The commercial life of the town continued to improve. Despite the still largely neglected state of the harbour, fishing and seafaring, mainly in coastal trade, were the mainstays, although the former continued to struggle from one bad season to another. It was the importance of the Avoca mines which proved to be the catalyst bringing slow but steady economic development. Up to 1840 their main product had been copper. Sulphur was a by-product with little market value as most commercial sulphur production was in Sicily. But in 1839 the King of Naples, who was also ruler of Sicily, increased the price of sulphur. Industrial nations such as Britain and France looked for a cheaper alternative supply. The mine owners at Avoca quickly saw their chance and sulphur became the focus of their operations. This change was to lead to several decades of unprecedented profitability for them.

The problem was how to export the sulphur. The lack of a proper port at Arklow was a major handicap and much of the product had to be carted to Wicklow. Also, the Arklow fleet was small, both in the number of vessels and in aggregate tonnage. Local merchants, utilising their growing capital generated from their dealings with the prospering mines and miners, entered into partnerships with local seamen. New vessels were built, and the boatbuilding boom reached its peak between 1852 and 1858.[1]

This burst of commercial activity changed the face of Main Street. As late as 1840 Robert McMicken had summarised the town as containing

68

VALUATION OF TENEMENTS.

PARISH OF ARKLOW.

No. and Letters of Reference to Map.	Townlands and Occupiers.	Immediate Lessors.	Description of Tenement.	Area.	Rateable Annual Valuation. Land.	Buildings.	Total Annual Valuation of Rateable Property.
				A. R. P.	£ s. d.	£ s. d.	£ s. d.
	ARKLOW—*continued.* TOWN OF ARKLOW. MAIN-STREET—*continued.*						
69	Mary Kinsella,	Earl of Carysfort,	House (*in rere*),	—	—	0 15 0	0 15 0
70	Jane Tyrrell,	Same,	House (*in rere*),	—	—	0 10 0	0 10 0
71	William Morton,	Same,	House (*in rere*),	—	—	0 8 0	0 8 0
72	Mary Morton,	Same,	House (*in rere*),	—	—	0 10 0	0 10 0
73	Edward Keeran,	Same,	House (*in rere*),	—	—	0 8 0	0 8 0
74	Eliza Cassidy,	Same,	House (*in rere*),	—	—	0 8 0	0 8 0
75	John Quinn,	Same,	House and yard,	—	—	2 5 0	2 5 0
76	Laurence Somers,	Same,	Ho., yard, & sm. garden,	—	—	2 5 0	2 5 0
77	Edward Keeran,	Same,	Ho., offs., yd., & sm. gar.	—	—	3 0 0	3 0 0
78	John Keeran,	Same,	House and yard,	—	—	0 15 0	0 15 0
79	Mary Coloin,	Same,	House (*in rere*),	—	—	0 10 0	0 10 0
80	John Murphy,	Same,	House (*in rere*),	—	—	0 13 0	0 13 0
81	James Neill,	Same,	House (*in rere*),	—	—	0 5 0	0 5 0
82	Mary Erraty,	Same,	House (*in rere*),	—	—	0 10 0	0 10 0
83	Christopher Howe,	Same,	House (*in rere*),	—	—	0 5 0	0 5 0
84	Anne Dwyer,	Same,	House (*in rere*),	—	—	0 5 0	0 5 0
85	Rose Kenny,	Same,	House (*in rere*),	—	—	0 5 0	0 5 0
86	John Martin,	Same,	House and yard,	—	—	1 0 0	1 0 0
87	James Kinsella,	Same,	House, yard, & garden,	0 0 10	0 5 0	2 5 0	2 10 0
88	Elizabeth Cole,	Same,	Ho., offs., yd., & sm. gar.	—	—	5 0 0	5 0 0
89	John Dunne,	Same,	House, offices, and yard,	—	—	2 5 0	2 5 0
90	Peter Quinn,	Same,	House, office, and yard,	—	—	1 10 0	1 10 0
91	William Cassidy,	Same,	Ho., offs., yd., & sm. gar.	—	—	3 5 0	3 5 0
92	James Burke,	Same,	Ho., off., yd., & sm. gar.	—	—	4 10 0	4 10 0
93	Michael Doyle,	Same,	House & small garden,	—	—	6 10 0	6 10 0
94	Thomas Meates,	Same,	House & small garden,	—	—	7 0 0	7 0 0
95	Peter Kavanagh,	Same,	Ho., offs., yd., & sm. gar.	—	—	3 5 0	3 5 0
96	Letitia Eaton,	William Fitzhenry,	House, offices, and yard,	—	—	9 0 0	9 0 0
97	Rev. Richard E. Eaton,	Same,	House, offices, and yard,	—	—	11 0 0	11 0 0
98	Frances Jones,	John Kinsley,	House, offices, and yard,	—	—	9 0 0	9 0 0
99	Elizabeth Myers,	Earl of Carysfort,	House, office, and yard,	—	—	2 0 0	2 0 0
100	John Kinsley,	Same,	House, office, and yard,	—	—	9 0 0	9 0 0
101	R. C. Chapel,	Same,	R. C. Chapel and yard,	—	—	35 0 0	35 0 0
102	Rev. James Redmond,	Same,	Ho., offs., yard, & garden.	0 1 25	1 5 0	12 15 0	14 0 0
103	Eliza Bradshaw,	Same,	House, offices, and land.	1 1 27	2 0 0	7 0 0	9 0 0
104	William Williams,	Same,	House, offices, and yard.	—	—	9 0 0	9 0 0
105	Mary Neill,	Same,	House,	—	—	0 15 0	0 15 0
106	Patrick Carty,	Same,	House,	—	—	1 5 0	1 5 0
107	John Kinsley,	Same,	Forge,	—	—	0 15 0	0 15 0
108	Ashley Hunt,	Same,	Ho., offs., yd., & sm. gar.	—	—	10 10 0	10 10 0
109	John Tutty,	William Heath,	House, office, and yard,	—	—	3 15 0	3 15 0
110	Michael Redmond,	Same,	House & yard (*in rere*),	—	—	1 5 0	1 5 0
111	Lodgers,	Same,	House & yard (*in rere*),	—	—	2 15 0	2 15 0
112	Michael Browne,	Same,	House, office, and yard,	—	—	4 10 0	4 10 0
113	Michael Quinn,	Eliza Madden,	Ho., offs., yd., & sm. gar.	—	—	6 0 0	6 0 0
114	George W. Reville,	Earl of Carysfort,	House, offices, and yard,	—	—	13 0 0	13 0 0
115	Peter Reynolds,	Same,	House (*in rere*),	—	—	0 15 0	0 15 0
116	Michael Brien,	Same,	House (*in rere*),	—	—	1 0 0	1 0 0
117	John Conran,	Same,	House (*in rere*),	—	—	1 0 0	1 0 0
118	Michael Kavanagh,	Mrs. Fitzhenry,	House (*in rere*),	—	—	1 10 0	1 10 0
119	Anthony Hanrig,	Same,	House (*in rere*),	—	—	1 10 0	1 10 0
120	Patrick Lee,	Same,	House (*in rere*),	—	—	1 10 0	1 10 0
121	Edward Kavanagh,	Same,	House (*in rere*),	—	—	1 10 0	1 10 0
122	Samuel Whitmore,	Mary Kearney,	House, offices, and yard,	—	—	10 0 0	10 0 0
123	Anthony Bolger,	John Kearney,	Ho., offs., yard, & garden,	0 0 18	0 10 0	8 10 0	9 0 0
124	William Kavanagh,	David Goodman,	Ho., offs., yard, & garden,	0 0 16	0 10 0	13 0 0	13 10 0
125	Isabella Holt,	Rosanna Allen,	House, yard, & garden,	0 0 11	0 5 0	4 5 0	4 10 0
126	Daniel Byrne,	Isabella Holt,	Ho., off., yard, & garden,	0 0 11	0 5 0	4 15 0	5 0 0
127	Church,	In fee,	Church and yard,	—	—	45 0 0	45 0 0
128	Patrick Donnelly,	Dorcas Graham,	House, offices, and yard,	—	—	11 0 0	11 0 0
129	David Condron,	John Hatchell,	Ho., offs., yard, & garden,	0 0 16	0 10 0	12 0 0	12 10 0
130	Thomas Hannigan,	Jane Lipsett,	Ho., offs., yard, & garden,	0 0 29	0 15 0	16 5 0	17 0 0
131	Jane Greene,	John Hatchell,	Ho., yard, & sm. garden,	—	—	8 0 0	8 0 0
132	William Beaky,	Jane Hall,	Ho., offs., yd., & sm. gar.	—	—	12 0 0	12 0 0
133	John Kelly,	Susan Crozier,	Ho., offs., yd., & sm. gar.	—	—	10 0 0	10 0 0
134	Mary Tuke,	Reps. —— Price,	Ho., offs., yd., & sm. gar.	—	—	16 0 0	16 0 0

... about eight hundred dwellings, most part mud wall and only one storey, some very small. They are mostly occupied by fishermen and poorer labourers. Very few good houses in the town and less business is carried out from a commercial point of view than might be expected in a town containing about 4,383 inhabitants. The harbour is very bad and will admit vessels of very small burden and that only at high water. Houses are let at a reasonable rate, I have seen them much higher in the interior towns a sixth of its size.[2]

McMicken had been employed by Richard Griffith, the Commissioner of Valuation, to survey 'all the dwellings and public buildings in the town as a rating assessment for Local Taxation purposes'. This was a country-wide project which resulted in the monumental work known as the Poor Law Valuation, or the Griffith Valuation. Because it lists, among other things, the names of the tenant/owner of each property it is now an important source for the family and social historian. By the time the valuation was published in 1854, slated, three-storey houses were becoming numerous in Main Street and would soon line both sides of it. Shops and hardware stores, public houses and coaching inns made it the commercial centre not only of the town, but of the surrounding countryside.

Perhaps it was this economic progress which engendered better social interaction. There was little evidence of religious or sectarian unrest, although the deep-seated distrust of former times had not entirely vanished, it simply lay dormant.

The Carysforts were still 'lords of the land', but the earl seldom visited his Glenart estate. In this relative boom period the holder of the title was John Proby, who had acceded to the title on the death of his father in 1828. Like his predecessors, he had done little to either help or hinder the daily activities of estate and town life, and when he died in 1855 his passing made little impact in the locality. He was succeeded by his brother Granville Leveson Proby, a navy man who attained the rank of admiral in 1857, two years after his becoming the 3rd Earl of Carysfort. He had also held several public offices, including being Member of Parliament for Wicklow between 1816 and 1829. Apart from this, and the fact that he married a granddaughter of the 1st Earl of Wicklow, his interest in Arklow and its environs seems to have been as tepid as that of his forebears. His apparent indifference to the place, as long as the rent revenues were forthcoming, was perhaps for the best. A lack of interest also meant a lack of interference.

Seafaring was still a dangerous business and tragedy was not uncommon. Since the closure of the RNLI station in 1830, local fishermen and coastguards had carried out several remarkable rescues. One such case was when the full-rigged ship *Calypso* was caught in the grip of a severe storm north of Arklow in 1848. Despite the efforts of her eighteen-man crew, she was driven ashore at Mizen Head. Her plight had been spotted by local coastguard James Dillon. By wading through the pounding surf, he managed to get a life-line to the ship and rescued all on board.[3] In the early 1850s came a series of casualties, the most notable being the *Mobile*, an American vessel en route from Liverpool to New Orleans. She went up on the Arklow Bank with the loss of sixty of her passengers. Two years later, in 1854, the Liverpool registered barque, the *Tancred*, was lost off Arklow. A few weeks after that, Arklow fishermen took the crew off the *Robert Kelly* which had grounded on the bank quite near the spot where the *Tancred* had recently gone down. Fortunately, the *Robert Kelly* was later refloated. It was no coincidence that 1854 was also the year which saw the establishment of the Arklow Marine Society for the Prevention of Wrecking and Preservation of Life from Shipwreck. While not intending to provide a full lifesaving service, the Society aimed to encourage the rescue of passengers, crews and property from wrecked vessels. It can be seen from the rules, particularly Rule 8, that all rescue attempts did not stem from the purest motives.

1. That any person may become a member on subscribing to the rules, and paying the sum of one shilling annually; and upon paying two shillings and sixpence annually shall be eligible to serve on the Committee.
2. That each member upon being elected shall solemnly pledge himself to the support of the Committee to carry out the objectives for which the Society is formed.
3. That each member shall pledge himself to refrain from perpetrating any act of pillage, shall refuse to purchase wrecked property, or anything which he suspects of being such, or to conceal or suffer the same to be concealed on his premises.
4. That a Sub-Committee be especially appointed, who shall make such arrangements in case of shipwreck as may tend (under Divine assistance) to preserve life, and secure the property conveyed or cast on shore, or remaining in the shipwrecked vessel.
5. That the Sub-Committee shall use their best efforts to provide that all goods,

merchandise and other property conveyed on shore, shall be deposited in the usual place for the inspection of the legal officers.

6. That a reward, at the discretion of the Committee, over and above the legal salvage, be paid from the funds of the Society to the party who shall be most instrumental in preserving life, or who shall deposit with the legal officers the greatest or most valuable amount of shipwrecked property, the amount of the property to be proved by certificate from the authorities and the reward paid after the demands of the parties to salvage have been satisfied.

7. In order to provide for the remuneration of the Arklow boat Owners who may aid in the saving of Passengers in case of Shipwreck, and at the same time prevent any undue charge being made against the proprietors of the wrecked vessel, we recommend that in all cases requiring the co-operation of the Marine Society, a sum of three shillings per head be allowed by the proprietors for landing the passengers, and the Bonus of Three Pounds to be paid out of the Funds of the Society to the boat which reaches the wreck and returns with a fair number of passengers – special cases to be specially considered.

8. The Committee will not interest themselves to procure remuneration for the crew of any boat which shall use intimidation, compulsion, or undue influence of any kind, to extort money from passengers whom may land from wrecked vessels.[4]

The following year, 1855, the *Lord Mostyn*, a schooner carrying potatoes from Dublin to Cardiff, was lost with all hands somewhere between Wicklow and Arklow. More fortunate were the *Anne, Cyronant,* and *Flint Castle* which all grounded in the same area but without loss of life. Such a lamentable series of wrecks and near-wrecks once more prompted the cry for a permanent lifeboat station at Arklow. In November 1856, the RNLI decided to accede to the request, and the station was re-opened the following year. The Institution's commitment to the region was further displayed by the opening of two other stations in the "Banks Area" – one at Wicklow and the other at Cahore, just south of Courtown.

*

Saving life was one thing, saving souls another, and it was in this pursuit that the parish priest was faced with a dilemma.

The Catholic church which had been built on Parade Ground in 1803 was long past its best and it was decided that a new, larger edifice was needed to administer to the needs of the people. The parish priest at this time was Fr (later Archdeacon) James Redmond, a native of Bunclody (then Newtownbarry) in County Wexford. His uncle Edan

Redmond had served in that position from 1810 until his death on October 2nd, 1839, and it was he who encouraged his nephew to enter the priesthood. James studied in Maynooth College and was ordained in 1827 at the age of twenty-five. His first posting was as curate in the Dublin parish of Blanchardstown, but he was soon transferred to work under his uncle here at Arklow. When his uncle died in 1839, Fr James was appointed as his replacement.

As curate, and later as parish priest, he earned a reputation for caring for his poorer parishioners. He urged them to educate their children, for it was through education that better living conditions would evolve. He also tried to show by example the importance of caring for the sick. Fever of one kind or another was a frequent visitor to the overcrowded lanes. The lack of sanitation, the unhygienic habits and attitudes of many of the poor created breeding grounds for disease. Cholera broke out in the Fishery in 1848. Not for the first time, victims were left to fend for themselves, such was the terror of the other members of the family. This apparent cold-heartedness must be viewed in the light of extenuating circumstances. If children were to survive, a healthy parent could not take the chance of falling victim to disease while tending to a stricken spouse. There was little anyone could do for a victim, and each hour spent exposed to the contagion could leave children orphans or victims themselves. It was an image that was to remain with Redmond for the rest of his life. He also exhorted them to adhere to the teachings of the Church and be more orthodox in their observances. This was a time when papal writ still battled with age-old superstition and ritual for the hearts and minds of the uneducated masses.[5] Attendance at mass and the sacraments was far more lax than they were to become after the 1850s. Catholic bishops were closing patterns at ancient places of pilgrimage, such as Glendalough, after centuries of annual gatherings because of drinking, gambling and general licentious behaviour scarcely in keeping with religious themes.

James Redmond was a forceful character and an ardent writer of letters to politicians and newspaper editors, entering into debates through correspondence on many social and church issues. The temporal and spiritual welfare of his parishioners, however, were his main concerns and he realised that two construction projects were needed to meet their needs. One was the development of the harbour, the other was the building of a new church. In January 1859 he issued the following circular:

It is a matter of grave responsibility to undertake to build a new church in Ireland. The people are generally in such difficult circumstances, that a well defined necessity alone could warrant the additional burden of erecting a large new church. I feel that I can appeal with confidence to such a necessity for a justification of my undertaking.

It was patent to every one passing by on Sundays and festivals, from the large number worshipping outside of the present overcrowded Chapel of Arklow, how necessary it had become to procure a greatly enlarged accommodation. I according undertook, last autumn, to make additions, both in front and rere; but the foundations were found to be so defective, and the walls and the roof in such a ruinous state – the former split from top to bottom in more than one place, and the latter ready to fall in from dry rot – that I found imposed on me the imperative necessity of building an entirely new church. This I have undertaken on a scale to meet the requirements of the large population committed to my care, and to keep pace with the rapid progress of the ecclesiastical architecture of the age.

The church including chancel and bell tower, with collateral porches is one hundred and forty feet long, eighty feet wide in the transept, forty feet wide in the nave, and forty feet high to the wall-plate. It is of the compound Grecian and Italian style, without pillars to obstruct either sight or hearing, and in the form of a Latin cross. It will have a chiselled granite pilaster front, with tower and cupola one hundred feet high. The walls are pilastered, and being faced externally throughout with punched ashlar, show great strength and beauty.

The people have engaged in the work with the utmost alacrity; they are convinced of its urgent necessity; and are proud of its respectable style and dimensions. I not only calculate on the support of my own flock, but I rely confidently on the generous assistance of all who are connected by property, or trade, or kindred, or sympathy, with this Parish. The sooner this aid is given the better, as the state of the old chapel permits no delay. We need all this the more, as the continued failure of the fishery has deprived us, to a great extent, of the important support of the fishermen, who are proverbially generous when Providence crowns their labours with success. I have already received kind countenance and substantial assistance from my good Protestant neighbours, with whom I have the happiness to live on the best of terms; and I sincerely thank God for the happy change which has taken place in my day, when Catholics and Protestants, instead of engaging in deadly feud and battle as of old, live together in mutual benevolence and peace.

Praying for the favour of an early answer, I have the honour to remain etc

James Redmond P.P.[6]

Donations came not only in the form of money, but also as materials and labour. Farmers and carters brought stone from quarries at the Rock (later developed as Parnell Quarries) and the Ballygobban quarries near Aughrim. Other stone, reputedly excess material in the building of Howth harbour, was brought to Arklow by local fishermen.

With Carysfort's consent, the new church was to be built on the same site as the church it was replacing. This presented a problem. It would take a couple of years to erect the walls and roof of the new building, and many decades to complete it internally. What would the congregation do in the meantime? The solution was simple. The new foundations were laid around the old chapel and the walls rose up around it. When the new edifice was roofed, the old chapel was completely encased inside the new one, at which stage its thatch roof was removed and its clay walls knocked down. Then mud and straw were wheelbarrowed out the door of the new, parish church.

It was an imposing building, a reflection of the growing status of Catholicism. Outside, it looked just as it does today, except it would be some years before railings would be erected or the steps put in place. It simply stood on a grassy knoll. Inside, there were no pews, nor altar rails. No mosaic tiles, nor richly decorated ceiling. All that was in place were the bare essentials. What more was needed? Arklow parish church was a three dimensional expression of faith, not only a religious faith, but also faith in the future. Succeeding generations would continue the work.

On Sunday, August 18th, 1861, Archbishop Cullen (Archbishop Murray having died in 1852) arrived to perform the dedication ceremony. *The Freeman's Journal* recorded the event for posterity.

> The ceremonies commenced shortly after eleven o'clock, long previous to which hour the church in every part accessible to the laity was filled with a vast congregation, including all the influential Catholic families of the surrounding district, also a large number of gentry from town, or resident at Bray, Wicklow etc. The interior of the church although as yet in the rough and unceiled, and lacking the architectural decorations which will give grace and symmetry to its aspect, presents now a truly grand and majestic appearance owing simply to its magnificent extent and to the simple grandeur of its design.[7]

The Church of Sts Mary and Peter, consecrated 1861
(National Library of Ireland)

Nor was the new chapel the only sign of changing fortunes. In 1863, the railway came to Arklow.[8] This was indeed a milestone, a clear indication that the town was on the cusp of a new age. Merchants welcomed it as it promised ease of transportation of commodities. The travelling public liked it for its novelty as well as the comfort and speed it offered compared to horse-drawn coaches. There was one fear, however. The mines at Avoca had used the ports of Arklow and Wicklow only because of their proximity. The harbour at Arklow was still primitive to say the least, although sporadic attempts at erecting quay walls had met with some success. Now that the mines were connected by rail to the fine harbour at Kingstown, there was talk of their transporting their ores to there. This would consign the port of Arklow to a bleak future with little prospect of development.

As if in defiance of this perceived threat to Arklow's maritime well-being, the following year saw a new business venture established at the harbour. On the south bank of the river, roughly where Vitra Tiles is now, John Tyrrell opened his boatbuilding yard.[9] He was not the only boatbuilder in Arklow,[10] but the firm of John Tyrrell & Sons was to be the most productive and enduring in the port's history.

Arklow 1861 (Reproduced by permission of the Royal Society of antiquaries of Ireland©)

So, in general, things were looking up for the town. For a thousand years it had languished in poverty, its people existing on the bare essentials, in constant battle for survival. Now it was beginning to look as if Arklow had at last turned the corner. Economic growth was to be welcomed, but only if it was used to drag the town out of the dark ages in relation to human health and community welfare. In modern parlance, wealth should build a society not merely an economy. As if to remind the authorities of this, in 1866 Arklow was hit by a tragedy of considerable proportions which showed that commercial activity was not the be-all-and-end-all of life. The lanes of the Fishery, and those adjoining Main Street and Upper Main Street, were ravaged by cholera. As we have seen, there had been an outbreak in 1848, but the 1866 epidemic was of much greater importance.

The front page of the *Wicklow Newsletter* of Saturday, September

22nd, 1866 carried its usual array of advertisements. Dr Taylor was looking for a 'steady, sober and active ploughman, who knew his business and was not above putting his hand to other matters when required'; blankets were on offer at 7/4d (47c) a pair; and Holloway's Pills were the cure-of-all-ills. The main article, however, was more serious and told of a situation that even Holloway's wonder drug could not cure. It began: 'It is now beyond all doubt that Cholera is in Arklow'.

To understand what the epidemic entailed, it is first necessary to know what cholera is. Doctors define it as an infection of the bowel, causing vomiting, diarrhoea and general debility. It breeds in filth, stagnant pools of water, and untreated sewage. Generally speaking, the more primitive the living conditions, the greater the risk of cholera, and in 1866 living conditions in Arklow were very primitive, especially in the poorer areas. The typical house of the poor was a mud-walled, single-roomed cabin topped with thatch. It was dark, smokey, and the damp rose up through the mud floor, which was carpeted with a layer of sand from the beach. The lanes were packed with these dwellings and the filth of everyday living was allowed to accumulate outside the door. Everything was thrown into the lane to rot, or to be washed away by the rain. There were no backyards and the people saw no reason to go further than the door to dispose of their refuse and sewage. The *Wicklow Newsletter*, a Unionist broadsheet published in Wicklow town, had campaigned for several years for something to be done.

Rev Ormsby
(Select Vestry of St. Saviour's, Arklow)

> It is absurd to talk of improving the social conditions of the people when the avarice of some and the culpable neglect of others consign them to such wretched abodes.

The campaign fell on deaf ears.

The absence of a clean water supply was also a major problem. As early as 1854, the Protestant rector, W.G. Ormsby, wrote to the

Rathdrum Board of Guardians in an effort to get something done about the plight of the people in the congested areas with regard to fresh water. He believed that £100 wisely spent could solve the problem, as well as being sufficient funds to erect public toilets at the river. Again, nothing seems to have been done. In fact, nothing was done until eight years later, when in June 1862 a meeting was held in the courthouse. Captain William Proby, Carysfort's younger son, was in the chair and the parish priest, Fr James Redmond, acted as secretary. Two resolutions were adopted. The first was that public pumps were necessary to procure a sufficient supply of water for the inhabitants of the town, especially for the poor and labouring classes. (Many of the better off who lived in Main Street had private wells in their back gardens.[11])

The second resolution was that a committee be formed to raise the necessary funds. The names of the members of this subsequent committee clearly indicate how sectional (not to say sectarian) interests were put aside when basic necessitates were of paramount concern. They were Rev Ormsby, Fr Redmond, Rev Eaton (Protestant curate), William Heath, Peter Boland, George Ruskill, James Gregory, Surgeon Halpin[12], Surgeon L'Estrange, Thomas Mangan, George Kearon, William Philpot, John O'Neill, Michael Troy and Michael Hudson. A fortnight later, another meeting was held and Fr Redmond spoke of the duty of the mining companies to supply water, for 'had they not destroyed the hitherto unblemished waters of the Avoca?' Carysfort not only gave permission for the pumps to be erected but also donated £50 to the costs involved. Henry Hodgson, a local business man closely connected with the mines and with the railway, had one of the pumps erected at his own expense.

Within a short time, four pumps had been erected: one at the crossroads in the Flash, one on Parade Ground, one at Fair Green, and one in Tinahask.

Although Arklow came under the jurisdiction of the Rathdrum Board of Guardians in matters of health, it had its own Sanitary and Dispensary Committee, which was answerable to the Guardians. The above named William Proby was chairman of this committee. Proby was one of a new breed of landlord class, one with something of a social conscience. Admittedly, he wasn't the actual landlord, but his father was and his older brother, Granville, would inherit the estate in due time. But William did take a keen interest in the welfare of his family's tenants. He was also aware of developments taking place on the more progressive estates in England, where what were termed "reforming landlords" were building new houses, schools and churches for their tenants. This new attitude perhaps partly stemmed from the chivalric concept of *noblesse oblige*, but it was also tinged with the growing commercial ethos of give-to-gain. After decades of brutal exploitation, workers were beginning to organise. Employers realised that improvements in living and working conditions were the only way to avoid social upheaval. They had learned that a contented worker is a productive worker. Likewise, some of the landed gentry were coming to the realisation that a contented tenant is a profitable tenant. This may seem a cynical comment, but that does not diminish its veracity. After all, while the Probys had frequently displayed liberal tendencies in their dealings with their tenants in matters of rent, leases, etc, they had invested little in developing infrastructure that would benefit the area in general or the lot of their tenants in particular. It might be said, therefore, that while the Probys had never been harsh landlords, it wasn't until the arrival of William Proby that an active benevolence could be detected.

The Fishery 1861 (Reproduced by permission of the Royal Society of antiquaries of Ireland©)

The way the Sanitary and Dispensary Committee worked was, if a person was in need of medical attention but couldn't afford the fees of a doctor, he applied for a medical ticket which was issued by one of the members of the Dispensary Committee. The patient then went to, or sent for, the Medical Officer, depending on the severity of the illness and type of ticket issued. The Medical Officer for the district was Dr Robert Augustus L'Estrange. He had been appointed to the position in February 1855[13], and his conduct gave rise to several complaints. Most reports were of his neglect and his refusals to visit patients in the home, but there were also complaints against committee members who refused to issue tickets to applicants. On February 10th, 1862, the Protestant curate, Rev Eaton, felt it necessary to write to the Board of Guardians.

> I beg to call your attention to the necessity for some provision being made for the Poor of this town to obtain the benefit of Medical Aid in times of sickness – for some time past repeated complaints have been made to me by the Poor that they cannot obtain Tickets for Medical Aid – I need scarcely say that such a state of things ought not to be allowed to exist in a town containing upwards of four thousand inhabitants.
>
> I should suggest that the Relieving Officer of the District should reside in the town of Arklow and that he should be authorised to issue Tickets to those who might be entitled to them, if they are unable to procure them (as now seems to be the case) from those appointed to give them.[14]

Fr Redmond also found it necessary to complain to the Board regarding two incidents.

> Johanna Brown was confined to her bed last Wednesday from a bad cold and great debility. Her husband, a day labourer, called on Mr Boland, Poor Law Guardian, and a Member of the Medical Committee, for a Medical Ticket. Mr Boland told him he had better means than a farmer and refused him the ticket.
>
> Catherine Canterbury applied to Mr Boland for a Medical Ticket for her husband who was rendered unable to work from a pain in his arm. The reply she got was, first that Mr Boland had not sight sufficient to write the ticket and, second, that she should bring her husband to the hospital.
>
> Query 1, was Mr Boland warranted in refusing Johanna Brown the Ticket?
>
> Query 2, is a man who on his own admission is unable for want of

sight to write a Ticket, a fit and proper person to be a Guardian of the Poor, and a member of the Medical Committee?[15]

In response, the Board suggested that local wardens be appointed to deal with such complaints and offered one of these positions to Fr Redmond. He declined, but Dr Stopford Halpin accepted. Within a matter of weeks, Halpin was able to bring another complaint before the Board. On February 22nd, he issued a ticket to a patient to be visited by Dr L'Estrange, but L'Estrange refused to attend the patient on the grounds that he had not been informed of Halpin's appointment as warden.

An even more serious complaint was made by John Martin. Martin called on Dr L'Estrange and produced a Visiting Ticket, asking the doctor to attend his daughter who was too ill to leave the house. L'Estrange grabbed his bag and followed Martin's lead. Halfway there, however, L'Estrange turned to Martin and demanded payment, to which Martin replied that he had no money to pay him. If he had, he wouldn't need a ticket issued by the Dispensary Committee. L'Estrange refused to carry out the visit and returned to his surgery. Martin immediately went to Dr Halpin, who on seeing the child, said 'she is lost through neglect'.

Halpin reported the incident to the Board, who investigated the matter. Their findings were, to say the least, remarkable. They explained that the reason L'Estrange did not go to treat the child was that the ticket in Martin's possession was the old form of ticket and not the new one. The Board urged Halpin and all other wardens to supply themselves with the new form of ticket! Nor was this the end of L'Estrange's list of neglect. On March 15th, 1862 Halpin wrote to the Board about L'Estrange being given a ticket to visit a woman about to give birth. He called on her at one o'clock, denied that she was near her time – contradicted by the nurse who was present – and left.

Despite all these cases, L'Estrange retained his position as Poor Law Medical Officer for Arklow, answerable to a Board of Guardians more interested in up-to-date forms than in the health of the poor. It was a shambles when dealing with individual cases. What would it be like in an epidemic? They were soon to find out.

In 1865 cholera broke out in Southampton. This sent a wave of panic through the Poor Law Unions of Ireland. Trade between the English port and Ireland was substantial and hundreds of Irishmen passed through there joining and leaving ships. Many of them were from

Arlow. Circulars were sent to all Poor Law Unions in the country and lists of precautions were published. The people were told how to clean their houses properly; how to disinfect their houses with whitewash; how important it was to clear away stagnant pools; and how they should let as much light and air into their homes as possible. Great care was taken to restrict the epidemic to Southampton, but did it have to come from there – or from anywhere else? Couldn't the conditions against which the local newspaper had been campaigning breed cholera from the lanes without outside help?

There are several theories as to how the Arklow cholera epidemic of 1866 started. One of these is the story of a seaman carried off a ship and left to die at Cox (or Cock's[16]) Corner, that is the corner of Harbour Road and Tinahask. He is said to have had cholera. Another version is a returned sailor had contracted the disease on his last voyage and survived. The contagion was still on his clothes when his mother washed them, after which she died, and the disease was spread by those who attended her wake. A third theory is that blankets "from foreign parts" were bought at a fair, the woman who bought them died within a few days of the purchase. Whether this is true or not, the people seem to have believed it, for it is said that when Lady Wicklow tried to distribute blankets during the epidemic, they were refused.

The common thread in these three stories is the contagion was somehow imported into the town and the fact that it could well have been homegrown is not reflected in the folklore. But how it started is unimportant. What matters is that it did break out. There can be no definite date as to when the first case was noted, but September 22nd saw the headline:

> It is now beyond all doubt that cholera is in Arklow, and that a large proportion of the cases have, we regret to record, proved fatal.[17]

It was the speed of death that frightened people most. James Loughlin's wife and mother-in-law died within an hour of each other, and two days later he, too, was dead. Physical courage and strength seemed no impediment to the sickness. Peter Kavanagh, the lifeboat coxswain, is said to have been in good health as he finished his day's fishing in the bay. He went home and within a few hours he sickened and died, leaving 'a poor helpless wife and eight children to deplore his loss'. Kavanagh had been awarded the Silver Medal of the RNLI the previous year for his remarkable bravery and seamanship in the rescue of seamen from the *Tenassarim.¹⁸* His death caused particular despondency. If cholera could strike and kill someone of his calibre so easily, what chance had other people? Many families lost more than one member to it. One young man was well at 10 p.m. and was dead before daybreak. His mother fainted at the news, no-one went near her and she never recovered, then her husband died of the disease, leaving six or seven young children without a parent.

The disease was held in such horror that sons deserted fathers and mothers, sisters left brothers, husbands left wives. Folklore recalls how barricades were placed on the bridge by the Ferrybank residents, and the river was reputedly patrolled to stop anyone swimming across to the north side. The patrols, it is said, were armed. Folklore seldom misses an opportunity to extend the boundaries of hard fact, but even if this story has been embroidered over the years, it reflects the panic that existed during the epidemic. The fear of contagion was so startling that it overrode all bonds. Nobody would go near a corpse. This presented a new problem, for if the bodies were not buried the spread of the disease and other complications would be even more rapid. Volunteers were needed. Fr Redmond and William Proby stepped into the breach, recruiting and organising volunteers and, according to folk memory, actually taking part in removing the bodies and burying them in some cases. Again, this might have been added to with repeated telling, but they certainly organised removals of bodies and burials.

Folk tales tell of two mass graves being dug. One in the Protestant graveyard in Main Street, the other in the Catholic cemetery at the old abbey. A coffin with a hinged lid was put into service. Volunteers would go to the house to wrap the corpse in a sack. These courageous individuals became known as the "Sack-'em-ups". I have heard the term used derogatorily by people who know no better. In fact, any family who can claim the nickname should do so with pride for their ancestors displayed a rare level of courage. The body would then be placed in the coffin and taken to the appropriate grave. The coffin was then laid beside the grave and tilted until the lid swung open and the body fell into the void. It is difficult to draw the line between fact and false memory in such matters and, as we shall see, the eventual death toll would hardly warrant such makeshift procedures, but the very fact that these stories have survived indicates the level of terror which gripped the popular imagination during that terrible time. That volunteers were needed and did carry out onerous tasks is beyond dispute. Unfortunately, the names of most were never recorded and have been forgotten.

Despite their greatest efforts, Fr Redmond felt he would have to look further afield to combat the disease. In Rathdrum was a convent of the Sisters of Mercy which had been established a few years previously. Fr Redmond contacted them and six of the community offered their services in the fever hospital and the refuge, as well as in the houses of the sick.

Admission to the workhouse in Rathdrum was, of course, out of the question. There were 259 inmates there already and had cholera been admitted it would have spread like wildfire. When someone fell victim to the illness, he was brought to the fever hospital in St Mary's Road (roughly on the site where Dr Ann Marie O'Farrell's surgery now stands). The hospital had been built fifty years previously and could not cope with the crisis. It was decided to procure other premises to accommodate the overload. Also a house on South Quay, near to where the dock was later excavated, was deemed perfect for the purpose of a refuge. It was owned by Henry Hodgson, who four years earlier had had one of the public pumps erected at his own expense. He sought no rent for the use of this building. The procedure was, when cholera struck a household the victim was taken to the fever hospital while the rest of the family were taken to the refuge where they stayed until their house had been disinfected. That many of the victims died is recalled in an ominous resolution of the Dispensary Committee which ordered that a receptacle for the dead be erected at the fever hospital. It was to be ten feet by ten feet seven inches and was not to exceed £5 in cost. To avoid the necessity of transporting patients from the lower end of town through Main Street to reach the hospital, a shortcut was devised. It was proposed to cut a small laneway through Hudson's fields at Castlepark. This would link the then cul-de-sac known as Hall's Lane with the fever hospital. The route was direct and therefore much shorter than the circuitous route of Main Street. Robert Hudson agreed to the proposal and the laneway that was to become known as The Ditch came into being. The first half of it is still recogniseable as a narrow lane, but the second half has been built upon.

The epidemic was not publicly announced until late September, but there had been deaths that might have been attributable to cholera for several weeks previously. Some reports put the first cases as early as

July. Cases were recorded in August. According to the *Freeman's Journal* there were eleven new cases on September 17th, seven of which were fatal.[19] It was not until October 6th that the *Wicklow Newsletter* felt confident to print: 'The cholera has, we are called to announce, abated'.

It is difficult to say how many people died of the disease. Figures ranged from fifty-nine to two hundred. As mentioned, perhaps not all the early deaths were officially attributed to cholera, perhaps the people of the lanes and congested areas attributed all deaths in that time to the epidemic. Compared to the loss of life on the streets seventy years earlier in the Battle of Arklow, the fatality toll was miniscule. But epidemics breed panic. In the early summer of 2003 the SARS virus claimed a couple of hundred lives worldwide. Despite the low death toll, it filled the media for weeks, people cancelled travel plans, cities were declared off-limits, and major alerts were sounded. Imagine then the impact of even 100 deaths on a small town of 4,500 in the middle of the nineteenth century.

The 1866 cholera epidemic was arguably a more important event in Arklow's evolution than the Battle of Arklow. It changed the lifestyle of the people, because it brought home with frightening clarity the need for improved living conditions. Perhaps the *Wicklow Newsletter* of December 9th, 1866 summed it up best.

The Ditch

There can be no question that Arklow is a neglected town. Its sanitary conditions have been of the worst possible kind. Its chief proprietor, the Earl of Carysfort, has proved himself a kind and considerate landlord to his tenants ... ... After famine time the tenantry on neighbouring estates were largely evicted, many sought refuge in Arklow. Building sites at nominal rents on the sandy soil of the lower town were assigned and quickly availed of. A disastrous mistake was committed by allowing the cabins in the Fishery of Arklow to be huddled together in confused masses, frequently without any rear accommodation whatever. There is an absence in them largely of all the essentials of health, light, ventilation, room and cleanliness. They are built in a low, dismal and swampy situation, particularly subject to floods and after a severe shower, a collection of stagnant pools. The Fishery water supply is very bad. Dr Cameron analysed the water from the pump and ascertained that it contained five grains of organic matter to the gallon, two grains more than that of the Thames of London. This has been closed as it was the centre of a district whose inhabitants have been decimated by cholera.

I must state here that at least 100 people, young and old, have perished of this dreadful malady within the last three months, almost exclusively confined to the Fishery.

Improvement of the town is of easy execution. The Town has many poor in it, but it is not poor. Whoever shall erect commodious labourers cottages with fair lease on eligible building sites at the upper end of the town, may command his own terms of rent. A scientific system of sewage, and the erection of buildings, with some pretension to order and appearance, and ordinary sanitary rules, would convert into a seat of industry, a town at present neglected and ill-drained.

Our worthy High Sheriff[20], the son of the lord of the soil, when Arklow was first visited by Cholera recognised the duties of property and lost not an instant in organising a Sanitary Committee. He has assumed the position of Chairman.

He has devoted himself and his business abilities to the Committee. He has assisted the people stricken by Cholera by both public and private funds. He has selected an excellent and ample site for a cemetery on his father's property. The Arklow rate-payer owes him a debt of gratitude. He has large schemes in view for the draining of the town. Hopefully there is a bright era in store now for Arklow.

In the hovels, the importance of personal and household hygiene began to be appreciated. This does not mean that the people became paragons of cleanliness overnight, but neither did they forget the horror they had lived through and many conceded that the filth of their surroundings had contributed to, if not created, that horror. Perhaps the most important benefit of all was the arrival of the Sisters of Mercy. The six nuns who had volunteered to help returned to the convent in Rathdrum when the crisis passed, but the admiration which their work engendered in all sections of the community gave rise to a concerted effort to have them return to Arklow on a permanent basis. This effort was rewarded ten years later.

The importance of William Proby has been referred to many times in the foregoing account. He reshaped the relationship between the Carysforts and their town tenants. He saw the conditions of the people firsthand, and they saw in him a member of the ruling class who exhibited distinct signs of possessing a social conscience. There was room for hope, but it was a limited hope. As a younger son he was not

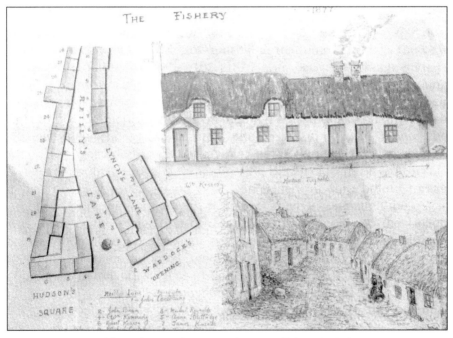

The Fishery mid-nineteenth centry (Brian McKay)

heir to the estate, so how effective could he be, apart from urging his father, and later his brother, to help improve the lot of their tenants?

Fate stepped in. When William's father, Granville Leveson Proby, 3rd Earl of Carysfort, died in 1868 at the age of eighty-four, he was succeeded by his eldest son Granville, who was forty-three. Granville had been an army man, but had embarked on a political career and had held a seat for Wicklow in the House of Commons from 1858 until he succeeded to the earldom. He held several positions during his tenure, including Comptroller of Her Majesty's Household, but as far as one newspaper of the time was concerned

> As Lord Proby in the House of Commons he was well-known as being, perhaps, the most accurately dressed gentleman in that assembly.[21]

Hardly a ringing endorsement of his political acumen or sense of social responsibility, but he seemed harmless enough and on October 16th, 1869 the same newspaper recorded that

> The tenantry of the Earl of Carysfort were entertained by his Lordship at Arklow on Saturday in celebration of his accession to the title and estates.

Just what this new earl intended to do with the estate is impossible to say, but it is probable that he saw no reason to differ greatly from his antecedents in leaving matters in the hands of an agent. Even if he did intend to improve both the estate and the lot of the thousands of people who paid rent to him for being allowed to live on it, he did not have much time in which to implement changes. In 1872, just four years after he acceded to the title, Granville Proby died in Florence. At some stage, he had a fall from his carriage and this is reputed to have led to his early demise. His younger brother William was now unexpectedly faced with the prospect of becoming the 5th Earl of Carysfort and all his ideas for reform came bubbling to the surface.

Granville Proby, 4th Earl of Carysfort

One of the first things he wanted to do was to replace the congested lanes of hovels with new, two-storey, slated houses set out in uniform rows of well ventilated streets. His long-term aim was to build a model village on the lines of Port Sunlight and Bourneville in England. He was then thirty-six years old, mature enough to see the practical difficulties and young enough to have the confidence and, hopefully, the longevity to overcome those problems. His determination was matched by the general goodwill of his tenants, many of whom remembered the part he had played during the cholera epidemic just six years earlier. The parish priest, now Archdeacon Redmond, was particularly pleased to see William Proby in full charge of the estate. His dealings with him over the previous decade had led him to believe that here was a man who was not only willing to change the conditions of the poor of Arklow, but was also capable of doing so. Redmond drew up the following address to Proby on his accession to the title.

The Address of the Roman Catholic Clergy
residing on his Lordship's Estate in the
Parish of Arklow[22]

WE, the Roman Catholic Clergy, who have the happiness of residing on your Lordship's estate, in the Parish of Arklow, beg to address you on special grounds and from the official knowledge with mingled feelings of sorrow and gladness, sorrow for the loss of your lamented Brother, in the prime of manhood, gladness at his being succeeded by one so well qualified as your Lordship to fill his place, and who has such ancestral and personal claims on all who reside on this estate, and especially in this town.

We do, indeed, my Lord, cherish the liveliest sentiments of respect and gratitude toward your Lordship's family.

Your Revered father was surpassed by none in practical benevolence, princely charity and in all the qualities of the paternal landlord.

Your Lamented Brother won the love and gratitude of his tenantry and the esteem and affection of all who knew him.

As for yourself, my Lord, we are really afraid to address you in language dictated by our feelings of respect and attachment lest we should wound your delicacy.

When pestilence spread dismay and destruction in this town, you took your stand between the dying and the dead. No dread of contagion kept you from the house of Refuge, the Cholera hospital and the graveyard to animate the panic-stricken, to see the destitute cared for, the patients attended to, and the dead decently interred.

And in all this, my Lord, you were most zealously aided by your good

Lady, who spared neither time nor money, nor personal attendance in providing relief for the appalling distress.

It is to your Lordship we are indebted for the sanitary provisions, which under God, have preserved this town from the late visitation of Small-pox, which was so destructive elsewhere and was formerly so prevalent in Arklow.

By your thoughtful and energetic influence, my Lord, the Old Church yard, full to repletion, and dangerous to the health of this town, was closed, and the present ample and beautiful cemetery was opened, giving accommodation as consoling to the living, as respectful to the dead.

It now only remains for us, my Lord, to pray that the Giver of all good gifts, may vouchsafe to your Lordship and to your amiable Countess, good health, long life, and all happiness in time and eternity.

With feelings of deepest respect, we have the honor to remain

> Your Lordship's faithful servants
> James Redmond, P.P. Archdeacon
> Joseph Deighton, R.C.C.
> James Dunphy, R.C.C.
> Frederick A. Donovan, R.C.C.
> Nicholas Barry, R.C.C.

As chairman of the Sanitary and Dispensary Committee, William Proby had indeed been instrumental in having the old graveyards at the abbey and Main Street closed. Not only that, he also used his influence with his father, and then his brother, to have a large tract of land donated as a new cemetery. This is the current cemetery, and it is only in recent years that its name has been changed from the New Cemetery to St Gabriels, after 120 years of use. The new cemetery had several major advantages. It was large and open, and best of all, it was a mile from the town centre.

Now that he was earl, William Proby lost no time in firming up his plans and in taking the first steps to bring them to fruition. In the Fishery, the first stage of the new housing scheme got under way and a straight row of fourteen houses was completed in 1875. These were to the west of the substantial building mistakenly called the Charter School[23] which had been erected a few years earlier, and faced eastwards. Two years later two more phases were finished and ready for occupation. One was a north facing row of four running at right angles to the first row, thereby forming an L shape. The other was a row of twenty-four houses on the other side of the Charter School facing west.

The three phases of forty-two houses in all were collectively named St Michael's Terrace, but were to become known locally as Proby's Row. Each house had

> ... a fairly large room to the front ... a stairs led off this room and under this was a large cupboard which provided space for fuel and other odds and ends. A window in the back of the houses provided light for the cupboard. A door led off this room into a small scullery and another led off the scullery into a small backyard. Attached to the scullery was an outside toilet. A gate enclosed the yard and some of these gates survive today. In later years the tenants took over the wasteground at the back of the houses and developed large gardens.
>
> Upstairs each house had two bedrooms divided by a wooden partition with a fireplace in each room. However, a pair of houses at each end of the terrace had three bedrooms.[24]

St Michael's Terrace or Proby's Row built in 1875

These were fine family homes compared to the mud cabins they were planned to replace, but few things in life are error free. In his article Michael Byrne points out

> The middle four houses *[in the row of twenty-four]* are narrower than the rest. It seems that the builders started work at each end and when they got towards the middle they found their measurements to be somewhat inaccurate. With less room than planned, at least two feet had to be taken off the width of the four middle houses.[25]

The following year, 1878, work on a new civic centre for the town got under way with the building of a hall intended as a town hall, but political and sectarian squabbles led to its never being used as such. That hall is now the Marlborough Hall in St Mary's Road. Schools and school teachers' houses were later built alongside.[26]

Improving living conditions and civic amenities was just one aspect of Proby's plans. He also wanted to make it easier for the fishermen and seafarers to make a living at their chosen trade. The 1871 Census recorded that of 352 vessels in the county Bray had one, Greystones two, and 132 were to be found in Wicklow. The remaining 217 were Arklow owned and Arklow based. Only six of these Arklow boats were described as being in trade, with an equal number of pleasure craft. Two were in government service and the rest were fishing. How this figure of a mere six trading vessels was arrived at needs to be explained. Many of the boats were dual purpose and if the Census was taken during a busy fishing season, most of the part-time coastal traders would have been engaged in fishing and would, therefore, have been classified as such.

As we have seen, at various times during the nineteenth century piecemeal attempts to improve the harbour had been made. They were half-hearted to say the least. The mining interests, which had control of the harbour area,[28] not only refused to make the necessary improvements but also refused to allow anyone else to make them. Now in a position of financial, social and political power, William Proby not only managed to break the stranglehold of the mining operations, but also secured a £13,000 government grant to develop the port. It was nowhere near enough, but it was a start. That was in 1876, but even a year later little had been done which would justify the money being drawn down and the "harbour" still consisted of a series of dry stone and concrete walls. Flimsy piers had been extended seaward, but these were washed away in a storm in 1877. Despite this disappointing setback, it seemed that nothing could deter him from continuing with his plans for a new town. But the loftiest of aims often call for unpalatable measures, and therein lay the seeds of discontent that was to make Arklow a byword for mindless sectarianism.

Proby had to finance his ambitious schemes and the best way to do it was to raise rents. The nature of these rents needs to be explained. Most of the cabins of the lanes and poorer areas throughout the town were privately owned, as were most of the better houses and shops of Main Street, so no rent for these buildings was owed to the estate. The rental mostly referred to the ground on which the buildings stood. The proposed new houses, however, would be estate built and owned and therefore liable for rent charges on both the buildings and the ground on which they stood. The ground rents the Carysfort tenants paid were much lower than those on neighbouring estates and in neighbouring counties. So, Proby believed it was not unreasonable to expect the tenants to pay more, particularly as it was they who would benefit directly from the new housing schemes. With this in mind, he employed John Townsend Trench of Kenmare to draw up a Valuation List so that a new scale of rents, more in keeping with the norm, could be imposed. Trench was not only a competent valuer, he was also a very talented watercolourist. Not content with merely listing the names of tenants and the estimated value of their holdings, he decided to make a visual record of the town, street by street. Starting at Coolgreaney Road, he sketched every building for which ground rent was payable to the estate, that is almost the entire town. On 217 pages, each measuring approximately twelve inches by twenty, Townsend Trench drew and coloured the houses, shops, forges, pubs, schools and public buildings of Arklow as they appeared in 1877. Most pages have blocks of four or five adjoining buildings, but some of the more detailed and architecturally interesting structures, such as the two main churches, courthouse, and RIC barracks are given pages of their own. The details on these testify to the accuracy with which they were drawn. Anyone who studies them will find characteristics that are often overlooked when viewing the actual buildings. There are no detectable flights of fancy or unwarranted flourishes. He drew what he saw. If he included a detail on the drawing, that detail existed on the original building. For example, on the small row of houses at Vale Road, he appears to have

St. Mary's, Main Street, 1877

included too many doors, but the ghosts of the "extra" doors, which were blocked up at some stage, can still be detected in the plasterwork of the row as it stands today.

These pages were bound in heavy, leathered boards and this cover was embossed in gold. For many years it has been in the possession of the Fogarty[29] family, and Anthony Fogarty has recently donated it to the National Library of Ireland. It is a wonderful record, one which allows us to take a virtual tour of Arklow as it appeared in 1877, and the Fogarty family are to be commended for their generosity in passing it on to the National Library.

At a remove of 127 years, we have the luxury to appreciate the Trench Valuation Report both as an historical record and as a work of art. But would we appreciate its aesthetic value so eagerly if we were not safe in the knowledge that we are unaffected by its recommendations? The people whose houses were included in it knew that such inclusion would entail a rent increase. Few expected that increase to be so drastic. Before Trench set to work, Proby was getting £316-7-11 a year in rent from the townspeople. By the time Trench finished his valuation, he arrived at £1,067-0-9 as a more realistic, market determined figure.[30] This represented a hike of more than 300 per cent. The fact that the rents had been below the average for so long was not taken into consideration by many of those who lived in the hovels, they simply saw a massive rise, and the good relationship that had existed between the estate and the tenantry was heading for rough

John Townsend Trench Valuation Book 1877

waters. They may have shared, or at least indulged, Proby's dream of a model village, but they didn't want to finance it.

They turned their resentment on the three completed rows of St Michael's Terrace, and dubbed them 'Cowld Town', a corruption of Cold Town. Bad as living conditions in the cabins had been, at least they were warm. The embers of last night's fire were raked each morning and fanned to life for the new day. The thick mud walls and thatch had absorbed the daily heat over generations and reflected it back into the room. Proby's new houses had never had a fire in the grate, and it would take many weeks or months or even years to permeate the cold concrete walls. And how could a thin roof of tongue-and-groove timber dressed in slate be expected to trap the heat as efficiently as layers of thatch? The new houses, icons of modernity in the eyes of their promoters, suddenly were reflections of coldhearted rack-renting in the eyes of many of the cabin dwellers. They felt such houses could never be homes. The new model village would always be Cowld Town, and the relationship between the tenants of the Fishery and William Proby entered into a Cold War that would never see an armistice.

*

In the same year as the Trench Valuation Report was compiled, 1877, the people of Arklow, especially the poorer people of Arklow, lost one of their greatest champions. Since his becoming parish priest in 1839, James Redmond had shown time and time again that he did not regard his pastoral duties as being limited to religious affairs. On May 14th, after almost fifty years of service to the town as curate and pastor, seventy-five-year-old Redmond died. One of the local newspapers[31] mourned his passing and eulogised his life in the purple prose of the time. Allowing for the hyperbole then fashionable, there can be little doubt that Redmond was not only well respected, but was also well liked. The following is a description of the ceremonies surrounding his interment.

> On Thursday the Funeral Office, High Mass, and interment took place in the presence of an immense assemblage of people, the coffined remains being exposed to view on a catafalque. The clergy attended in large numbers to assist in the closing offices of the Church over their departed brother. After the Absolution, at the end of the Mass, a scene took place which will not be easily forgotten by those who witnessed it. When the lid of the coffin was about to be screwed on, and the features of the deceased being exposed for the last time, the grief of the entire congregation was extremely affecting. The cries of young and old, not only of the children and women, but even of the hardy and stern fishermen, were heartrending in the extreme. Well might the widow and orphan weep. He who had been their warmest friend for many years was now forever excluded from their view. He who had unknown to any but the Omniscient eye of Him above relieved their wants and removed their troubles was gone, and all the poor people knew his place could never be supplied. The procession through the streets was the largest ever witnessed in this county, fully ten thousand people attending it. While the coffin was being lowered into its last narrow resting place, the cries of the people were renewed. Such grief can only be excited by the loss of one whose every action in life was marked by the love he bore for others.

It is difficult to imagine the route of the funeral 'procession through the streets' because Archdeacon Redmond was buried in the centre aisle of the church he had been responsible for building.[32] Perhaps there was a final circuit to bid farewell to the town and people he had served so long and so well.

Whatever the details of his departure, Archdeacon James Redmond was going to be a hard act to follow, but the man who stepped into his shoes was every bit as strong, every bit as charismatic and every bit as long lived.

10

Parnell, Priests and Preachers:
1881 - 1895

The man who took over the Catholic parish of Arklow on the death of Archdeacon Redmond was Fr James Dunphy, a native of Rathdowney in Offaly. He had been ordained in 1857 and was immediately posted to Arklow. Twenty years later he became parish priest and is unique in Arklow history as the only priest to spend his entire career, from 1857 until his death in 1914, in the parish.

Redmond had achieved a great deal in building the new chapel, but its construction had incurred a tremendous debt and there was still a great deal of work to be done. There was also the pressing need for the provision of schools. The work of the Sisters of Mercy during the cholera epidemic of 1866 had shown what an asset they would be to the town. Archdeacon Redmond was particularly anxious to persuade them to establish a convent at Arklow. The convent at Rathdrum was a branch of the convent at Athy, Co Kildare.[1] Permission had to be sought there, but unfortunately none of the correspondence has survived. Nevertheless, we know that Redmond's approach was successful and the Sisters of Mercy established a convent here in January, 1876. Six nuns, led by Mother Alphonsus Kelliher, moved into a small, two-storey house on Parade Ground and they started visiting the sick and the poor. It is interesting to note the state of religious instruction among the poor of Arklow at that time, for the convent records show that among the eighty-five people on the visiting list (many of these were visited on a regular basis, so that the number of actual visits made in the year far exceeded this figure), seventeen were deemed in need of instruction, forty-seven were fairly well versed in Catholic doctrine, and twenty-one were 'very well instructed'. This was considered quite a high standard at a time when older people had received little formal education in their youth.

Although the nuns did not come to Arklow to run a school, they knew that education was the key to social improvement. One of the tenets of the Order was 'where a religious woman presides, peace and good order are generally to be found'.

> They first opened a junior boys school in a stable loft behind their house and gradually girls were admitted. The numbers in the school were relatively small, yet it was the only educational venture of the Sisters for their first two years in Arklow. The school grew into the 'Angel Guardians School' ... ... It had a gentle and encouraging character. With much stress on good conduct and good manners, and with particular emphasis on Christian doctrine. The Sister in charge kept order there with a few taps of her pencil. This school continued until 1955.[2]

The main school at that time was the schoolhouse which Fr Edan Redmond had constructed on Coolgreaney Road in 1839. It catered for both boys and girls. Now, with the presence of the Sisters of Mercy forty years later, Fr Dunphy felt that the sexes should be kept separate and came to an arrangement with Carysfort for a site for a new girls' school and convent house. The site he had in mind was immediately behind the church, but this presented a difficulty in that the site was already occupied by a Protestant school. This difficulty was quickly overcome, however, because Carysfort had plans to develop the Chapel Lane as

St Mary's school and covent, opened 1881

part of his model village and the existing schoolhouse which had been built in 1823 was not part of those plans. Carysfort leased the site to the parish priest, the archbishop and Thomas Murray (a trustee) in perpetuity at a rent of £1 per annum. In 1878 a new Protestant school, Carysfort School, was erected on a site less than a hundred yards south of the old school, which was then demolished, and work began on the convent house and Catholic girls' school. The foundation stone for the new convent was laid on October 5th, 1879 and was blessed and opened on St Patrick's Day, 1881. The nuns moved from the house they had occupied on Parade Ground and Fr Dunphy purchased it as a curate's residence.

Throughout the 1880s, Dunphy showed himself to be as dynamic as his predecessor. The chapel in Arklow was the parish church, but there was also a chapel in Castletown and another in Johnstown. The former had been built in 1806, the latter in 1803, as replacements for those burned in the aftermath of the 1798 Rebellion. The one at Castletown was so dilapidated that he set about building a replacement. This was dedicated by Archbishop McCabe of Dublin on June 8th, 1884. Dunphy was a man who firmly believed in the adage 'waste not want not' and he had the old church repaired and converted into a parish hall and, in this role, it served the community well for the best part of a hundred years. Now disused, this building still stands in Castletown graveyard. Also at Castletown, he built a house for the curate, a house for the teacher and rebuilt the national school.[3] He was later to build St Peter's Boys' National School on Harbour Road for the children of the Fishery. James Dunphy, in short, was something of a whirlwind. Like Fr Redmond before him, he was socially active and took a particular interest in the harbour. In his endeavours to have it developed he joined forces with a young Liberal politician who hailed from Avondale at Rathdrum, Charles Stewart Parnell.

In many ways, Wicklow and Arklow are almost twin towns. They both spring from Viking origins, they are both small seaports, throughout the centuries they have both been roughly the same size, and they have both battled to survive and develop. A touch of sibling rivalry was bound to come to the fore every now and then and the late 1870s early 1880s was such a time. This rivalry was to become a wide and deep chasm after the general election of 1892, of which more in due course. Both ports needed well planned and well financed investment, both had applied for major public funding, but because they were so near each other geographically, it was unlikely that both would benefit from government largesse.

Parnell and William Corbet, the Nationalist MP for the East Wicklow constituency, backed the Wicklow project. Gladstone needed the support of the Irish Liberals at that time and the best way to secure that support was to keep Parnell happy. So, in 1880 a £50,000 Treasury loan was made available to build a breakwater and steamboat pier at Wicklow.[4] The success of the Wicklow campaign was strongly resented by the Arklow lobbyists, led by the Conservative Earl of Carysfort, William Proby.

Buoyed up by their success, Parnell and Corbet turned their attention to Arklow. If they succeeded here, where Carysfort had failed, it would be a double coup – economic and political. It would be easy, but disingenuous, to portray these events as petty point-scoring between rival political figures. For his part, although Carysfort ultimately failed in his quest to improve the harbour, his genuine, if sometimes tunnel-visioned, concern for his tenants had been shown many times. Parnell's commitment to the welfare of the people is also beyond question, and he had another reason for seeing the port of Arklow developed. He had business plans of his own which would benefit greatly from a good harbour at Arklow. The Parnell-Corbet campaign for Arklow was successful. They secured a £20,000 loan and a grant of £15,000 to buy out the mining interests in the harbour and work finally began on building proper port facilities.

Confidence in the future benefits of these improvements encouraged greater investment in the local maritime industry. By 1882 there were seventy-nine vessels trading out of Arklow. The older, less economic vessels were replaced by larger ones capable of making longer voyages and carrying greater volumes of cargo. Parnell, whose prowess in parliament had done so much to secure the necessary funding, made a personal contribution of £2,000 to the port. This was matched by Carysfort.

Like many successful men, Parnell packed more into his relatively short lifetime – he was only forty-five when he died – than most of us would dream possible. Even when he was immersed in political and social reform, leading the Irish MPs in the loose confederation dubbed the Home Rule Party, and generally acquiring the deserved sobriquet 'Uncrowned King of Ireland', he still managed to pursue his business interests.[5] An abiding passion of his was geology and he carried out several mining and quarrying experiments on his Avondale estate, but without much success. He was aware of the potential profit to be made from extensive quarrying at Arklow Rock and, now that the harbour was to be improved, he turned his attention to it more fully.

The Rock is made of dolerite, 'the remnant plug of an ancient volcano'.[6] It had been long known that the durability of this material made it ideal for road and harbour construction but it was this hardness which made it difficult to quarry. Throughout the nineteenth century some of it had been used in the piecemeal construction of quay walls in the harbour, but too much investment was needed to quarry the stone on an on-going commercial basis. Now that transportation infrastructure was being developed locally, and major street construction was taking place in cities on both sides of the Irish Sea and the near continent, Parnell decided the time had come to engage the services of an engineer to assess the quality of the stone and the viability of commercial operations at the Rock. There was one problem. The Rock was on the Carysfort estate.

Parnell and Proby were not the best of friends at this time. The latter regarded the former as a traitor to his class and his country. In Carysfort's view, it was the duty of landowners to uphold the link with Britain, not to associate with social agitators and malcontents in misguided attempts to establish Home Rule for Ireland. Parnell's success in securing investment in Arklow harbour where Carysfort had failed also rankled and with each passing year the relationship between the two men was on a downward slope. It was unlikely, to say the least, that Proby would grant permission to Parnell to have the inspection of the Rock carried out. Folklore records that this dilemma was overcome by Parnell having the inspection carried out under cover of darkness. The report was favourable. In fact, the stone from Arklow Rock was considered to be as good as, if not better than, Guernsey stone, which was deemed top-of-the-range. Thus armed, Parnell contacted Proby to arrange a lease agreement. Business was business and personal and political animosities were put aside as Parnell agreed to lease the Rock for a period of thirty-one years.[7]

The demand for 'setts', squared stone slabs for paving and kerbing, in Dublin city and suburbs meant the financial risk was worth taking. The City Corporation of Leeds and other English councils were also interested in paving their streets and bedding their roads with Arklow stone. Dressing stone to an acceptable degree of quality, however, is a highly skilled craft and experienced sett-makers were enticed over from Wales both to produce the setts and to train local stone cutters. The product was good and sales soared, but even greater profits could be made if waste could be reduced.

> The mode of quarrying was simple. Holes were drilled in the hard rock to the depth of fourteen feet or thereabouts, and into these powder was put, the explosions resulting in the separation of great regular-shaped blocks of stone from the parent rock. These blocks were split up by workmen with the aid of small drills and wedges and the stone was then passed over to the sett-makers who shaped them in blocks of uniform size for paving purposes.[8]

This process produced a great deal of waste material and it was decided to invest in two steam crushers which would grind the chippings and general spoils to dust which could then be used to make cement or macadam. This by-product was to prove very profitable.

Getting the product to market posed a few problems. Although the harbour was at last being properly constructed, there was still the hurdle of getting the stone from the quarry to the port. Because of their weight, the cost of carting setts and other products the one mile along South Beach would have been prohibitive. The solution was to build a narrow-gauge railway from the quarry to a specially built private jetty adjacent to the new south pier. A train of three wagons at a time, each containing twenty-eight hundredweight (one-point-four-two metric tonnes) of setts or macadam, would leave the quarry near the top of the Rock, freewheeling down the incline towards the beach. Its speed was controlled by a brakeman standing on a small platform. The momentum carried the wagons to about halfway along the beach, at which point horses were harnessed to them and the journey completed to the timber jetty.

Arklow stone was shipped to Liverpool and Birkenhead, Cardiff, Swansea and Bristol. By the beginning of the 1890s, the quarries were also supplying customers in Germany and Gibraltar. The Irish market was also substantial and should have been relatively easy to supply, but such was not the case. The railway line between Arklow and Gorey passed within a mile of the quarries at the Kish. Confident that this facility would ease distribution problems within Ireland, the quarry company had a private siding and loading platform built at the Kish bridge and carters were employed to bring the stone to there from the quarry. Unfortunately, the railway company, the Dublin, Wicklow and Wexford Railway, proved to be less than efficient. They did not have enough goods wagons to meet the demand so that delivery to customers, such as those in the city of Dublin, was erratic. Sometimes, an order could be left lying at the quarries or at the siding for weeks. Shipping from the port was far more reliable, but was cost effective only if the final destination was also near a port. For example, when setts were needed for the construction of the Howth tramway it made sense to ship the order from Arklow to Howth by sea.

An estimated £750 wages per week was injected into the local economy. Sett-makers earned twenty-five shillings a week, labourers received thirteen shillings.[9] Between sett-makers, labourers, carters, schooner crews, dockers, and a host of ancillary jobs, the Parnell Quarries were a great boon to Arklow.

An aside before leaving the quarries for the time being, the kerb stones in Arklow are products of the Rock and date from the period

Parnell Quarries (Courtesy Pat Power)

under review. One of these in Bridge Street deserves mention. It rests outside the front door of Number 4, opposite the Bridge Hotel. It was originally nearer the Main Street end, but when new brick paths were laid in the early 1990s, the late Seán Treacy requested that it be placed outside his house, where he would guard against its disappearance. On it is carved the crude outline of a schooner and some letters, possibly the name of the sett-maker/lunchtime carver, but these are too eroded to be legible. It is best seen on a wet night, when the rain-filled grooves contrast with the sheen of the street lights. Some of the stones edging the North Quay are similarly marked. One bears the name 'Weadock'. It is tempting to imagine a stonecutter, sandwiches eaten and work not yet resumed, doodling with maul and chisel.

While the success of the quarries was a major boost to the town's fortunes, it was not the only place of industry here at that time. In 1872, John Morrison read a paper to the Newcastle Chemical Society dealing

Arklow Manure Works (Pat Power)

with his establishment which had been built on the north side of the river here in Arklow. He called the factory the Arklow Chemical Works Limited,[10] but a photograph taken in the early 1890s clearly shows it as the Arklow Manure Works. It produced bone meal, sulphuric acid, bleaching powder, washing soda, artificial manure and soap. It provided much needed employment in a town whose dependence on the fishing industry was becoming increasingly precarious. While fishing could still provide good seasons, the periods of enforced idleness or poor catches seemed to become more crippling and fishermen had to venture farther than ever before to eke out a living.

Morrison's paper is a very detailed, very lengthy, and at times, very scathing description of the town and its people. For example, the town

> ... contains about 5,000 inhabitants, many of them able to read capital letters or carefully written figures, and most of them consumers of 'mountain dew' or 'potheen' when they can get it.[11]

While disparaging the townspeople, he liked to make himself the hero of his own despatches and he records how he personally had to work on the 110 foot high chimney because Arklowmen were too scared to go up so far. This, of course, was patent nonsense. Arklowmen sailed the world in square-rigged ships, reefing in topgallants, royals and skysails as they beat their way around places such as Cape Horn. Perhaps what Morrison meant was that Arklowmen refused to up so far for the wages he offered. But he does make some interesting comments, such as the one which echoes a tourist's comment in 1815, regarding the lack of interest in the town's development on the part of the 'noble proprietors of the soil'.[12]

> In my ignorance of the customs and prejudices of the country, I omitted to cross the hand of a certain county magnate, in consequence of which negligence the undertaking was denounced far and wide as one that would spread ruin and devastation on everything within a radius of at least ten miles.[13]

The agents of lords Wicklow and Carysfort also made it clear that they would have to be paid 'a small gratuity' if the project was to go ahead. Admittedly, this does not mean that either of the earls were involved in this chicanery, but if they had been resident and looking after the interests of the people who kept them in luxury, their agents would not have had such a free hand. The poorer people and the priests, on the other hand, were very eager to see this important development take place.

> The latter would allude to the undertaking at the altar on Sunday mornings (perhaps certainly from pecuniary motives) in the most glowing language, they visited the works frequently, and they seemed ever ready to do us a good turn or give us any assistance in their power; and in the most priest-ridden country in the world, the moral influence of the Roman Catholic Clergy possesses immense weight.[14]

One important side benefit of this enterprise was the creation of 'a gas works for town supply and succeeded in illuminating most of the urban area'.[15]

In 1882, there was a small workshop making straw covers for bottles. Clay bottles, particularly the larger ones, were often dressed in a straw cover for protection. Empty clay bottles, jars and demijohns were notoriously easy to crack and break if they clashed together, particularly in transit. A workshop had been established in Arklow to make the protective covers and this proved a valuable source of income for women and girls. On December 9th, 1882, however, the Rathdrum Board of Guardians passed the following resolution

> That it being proposed to the Board that there is some difficulty in providing a site for a temporary Workshop for the Straw Bottle-cover Manufacturer in Arklow, which has afforded during the last twelve months great relief by giving employment to numbers of women and girls, and owing to this difficulty this source of relief is now stopped ... the Clerk of the Union be directed to write to the agents of the Landlord and request him to grant some temporary site in a convenient position.

The following week Carysfort's agents, Trench and Taylor, denied that Carysfort had refused a site to the Straw Bottle-cover Manufacturers. He had, they said, offered the house in which the work was being carried on and also a donation of £10 if the work were carried out under strictly commercial principles, but this offer was rejected by the manufacturers. Even Fr Dunphy got involved in the argument. He said that the reason the house offered by Carysfort was rejected was that the tenant was 'under ejectment', but the current lease still had another six months to run. The Guardians decided to ask Carysfort for an independent site on a more clear cut basis. Unfortunately, no more mention is made of the Straw Bottle-cover Manufacturers in the Guardian records.[16]

So, overall, things were looking fairly good on the employment front, with only the fishing becoming increasingly uncertain. In October 1886, the fishermen were to receive a major setback when a storm wreaked havoc with the local fishing fleet.[17] The *Wicklow Newsletter* reported

> Arklow, having struggled against a series of adverse circumstances will take many a long day to get over it and will depend upon the kindness and goodwill of the outside world. Many industrious families will look in vain for bread during the rigours of the approaching winter.

The river swelled to its widest and highest in living memory, tearing old hulks from their moorings near the bridge and sweeping them downriver at a tremendous rate. They hit into newer, functional boats and vessels in the congested river, breaking them from their moorings and pushing them seaward. It was 4 a.m. but the river walls were lined with people, watching their boats being carried downstream, between the piers and out into the open sea. The lifeboat was launched from the new purpose-built house on part of the site now occupied by Vitra Tiles. The floor of this house was a steep slipway which extended directly into the river for speed of launch, but the violence of the flow at this point was such that a direct launch was impossible. The crew and helpers manhandled the boat, the *Out Pensioner,* down to the end of the pier to launch her from the beach. Five times the men timed their push forward to take advantage of a receding wave, and five times they were beaten back onto firm ground. The sixth attempt proved successful. As well as the lifeboat crew, the *Out Pensioner* carried upwards of thirty volunteers to take rescued boats to safety.

When the long night was over and the storm had abated, the totting up of costs began. Twenty-three of the fishing boats had been either damaged or completely wrecked, putting more than 170 men out of work. One of the boats had been repaired just four months previously at a cost of £40. The owner had had to borrow to pay that bill, now he was left with nothing. The total damage was estimated to be £3,600. A subscription list was opened and over the following weeks, the *Wicklow Newsletter* kept its readers abreast of the growing fund. Local musicians and vocalists organised concerts, £50 was sent by the Shipwrecked Fishermen and Mariners Royal Benevolent Society, a sum

which Queen Victoria matched. Concerts were held in Wicklow and
Gorey as well as in Arklow. Most of the music was provided by the
Original White-Eyed Christy Minstrels, who must have been wonderful
if their music was even half as good as their name. Within three months
£1,516-10-8 had been raised. There was still £2,000 of a shortfall, but
seldom had the community come together so wholeheartedly.
Unfortunately, this spirit of unity was not to last. Stupidity is not easily
eradicated and it raised its head in the wake of a concert held in the
Marlborough Hall on December 27th.

Mr J.K. Twomey, 'a man well thought of in the musical world', was
Master of Ceremonies, introducing twenty-two different acts. The songs
chosen were bound to strike a chord and everyone joined in the singing
of 'The Mariner', 'Anchored', 'Pull Away', 'Man the Lifeboat', and the
'Midshipmite'(sic). When the hall was opened in July 1878, it was
named after Lord Marlborough, Lord Lieutenant of Ireland, who
performed the ceremony.[18] In fact, the new terrace of houses (now
called St Mary's Terrace) was also named Marlborough Terrace. Lest
anyone forget this noble connection, the Marlborough coat-of-arms
hung above the stage in the hall. It had never been properly secured
and was in constant danger of falling from its position and causing
injury. The caretaker removed it for the duration of the concert, as he
had done in the past. William McPhail, editor of the Unionist *Wicklow
Newsletter*, heard of its removal and complained to the organisers. Dr
Michael Molony, apart from being the town's Medical Officer, was
chairman of the committee. He wrote to McPhail, his annoyance at the
editor's petty-mindedness clearly in evidence.

> The success of the concert has demonstrated that people of all parties
> here can unite and pull together for a good project, independent alike
> of religious and political 'lines of cleavage'. This is a step in the right
> direction and indicates that even in Arklow modern progress is
> beginning to make itself felt. It is, therefore, to be regretted that you
> should have sought to make political capital out of a very trifling
> incident, more especially as the matter was fully explained by me to
> your representative on the evening of the concert.

Molony was a remarkable man and I'll return to him in due course. This
was the one and only hiccup in a cross-community enterprise. Perhaps,
as Molony hoped, things were changing. Perhaps the town's long
history of sectarianism was finally on the wane. Perhaps Protestants and

Catholics were finally becoming Christians. Unfortunately, the good doctor spoke too soon, and the following twenty years were to show just how unrealistically optimistic his prognosis would prove to be.

The 1880s saw a dramatic change in William Proby's attitude towards his town tenants. Pat Power has described him as 'Yesterday's Janus'[19] and it is an apt description. Like the double-faced god of Roman mythology, the pre-1880s Proby and the post-1880s Proby were like two totally different men. His early years had been remarkable for his sincere concern for the poorer tenants, his

William Proby, 5th Earl of Carysfort
(Select Vestry of St. Saviour's, Arklow)

later years would mark him out as a stern, highly conservative landlord who was indifferent to the trials and tribulations of his tenantry. What brought about such a profound change in this man? People do change their views as they get older, but his change was so total, so breathtakingly sudden and complete, that there has to have been reasons for it. And there were.

As the decade progressed, his personal antipathy towards Charles Stewart Parnell deepened. Parnell's growing support in Arklow, particularly after his successful campaign to improve the harbour and in creating employment at the Rock quarries, might well have made Carysfort rethink his goodwill towards the people of the cabins. Perhaps he looked on their allegiance to Parnell as a betrayal, or at least gross ingratitude. But there was something else, something that angered him so much that he was to abandon his plans for a model village and to pump the increased rents into making Glenart castle and grounds into one of the finest country seats in the county.[20]

He built gate lodges at Lamberton, Ballyduff, Glenart and Kilcarra, and set about creating excellent gardens. The less than wholehearted welcome the people had displayed for the new houses of St Michael's Terrace - 'Cowld Town' – and their grumbling over the increased rents, certainly helped to sour Carysfort's outlook and make him face in a new direction. Attitudes became entrenched and as the 1890s dawned a new dimension entered the scene and the rift became irrevocable.

Apart from his wish to be an "improving landlord", William Proby was also interested in the growing practice of street preaching.[21] This involved prayer-meetings and sermons conducted publicly. The local rector, Rev Richard Hallowes, was also enthusiastic about this and he took on the task of organising these public events. In many instances, he was the main preacher and it was he who planned the route and the various places along the way where he and his followers would stop and preach.

On Sunday, April 6th, 1890, Rev Hallowes, accompanied by Revs Harpur, Hoffe and Harrison held the first event on the streets of Arklow and the following week they published a circular stating why they felt such open air preaching was good for the whole town. It would, they said, help heel the growing sectarianism between Protestants and Catholics in Ireland. In the light of subsequent events, the irony of this statement is unsurpassed.

From the first, the police reported that these services would inevitably lead to riot and disturbance in the town. They based this opinion partly on the fact that on a previous occasion in Arklow some years earlier when religious services of an Evangelical type were established in a tent near the town, sectarian feeling, leading to some disorder and rioting, was aroused.

Glenart Castle (National Library of Ireland)

Despite the stated aim of conciliation, the route and content of these events seemed tailored to spark off a violent reaction. To start, Rev Hallowes would preach to his congregation inside his church in Main Street.[22] Fair enough, no problems there, but afterwards they would all walk in procession into the heart of the predominantly Catholic Fishery and hold services there, then return up Main Street to Parade Ground. Parade Ground not only offered an open space in which to congregate, but it also meant that preaching would take place in front of the Catholic church, the parish priest's house, and the curate's house. This was felt to be deliberately offensive as the thrust of the sermons was not only to show the righteousness of Protestantism, but also to condemn the "superstitions" of Catholicism.[23] The residents of Main Street, Lower Main Street and the lanes leading off them, and the residents of the Fishery below the Togher, strongly resented these incursions. They regarded anti-Catholic remarks as offensive, but worse still was the perception that the preaching was financed by Carysfort and that the finances had come from the dramatic increases in rent. Whether this was true or not – after all, how much finance was needed to stage these events? – is irrelevant. Perception is a far more powerful agent that fact.

The degree of ill-feeling showed itself in both verbal and physical violence between the street preachers, their followers and the local residents. Tensions steadily increased until national attention was drawn to what was happening in Arklow. *The Freeman's Journal* called it 'a scandal to the district' and referred to the Catholic objectors as a 'crowd composed of fishwives and their near relatives' who used 'abusive and blasphemous language'.[24] It was now a regular occurrence and on June 14th, the *Wicklow Newsletter* described the objectors as

> rowdies who were evidently prepared for a repetition of their disgraceful attacks upon the Protestant clergymen.

Predictably, the *Wicklow People* saw it differently and blamed the disturbances on '[t]he conduct of the four Arklow Protestant clergymen', and gave the opinion that the street preachers, supported by the conservative press, were making too much of a little stone-throwing by 'a few thoughtless women' and that the clergymen were 'making almost a mockery of religion'. They further stated that 'many respectable Protestants of Arklow disapproved of the preachers' actions. Most of the press coverage, however, was against the Catholic residents, decrying their religious intolerance. The parish priest, Fr James Dunphy, referred to these reports in his sermon at all masses on Sunday, June 15th 1890, saying that 'there was indeed religious intolerance but that it came from the other side'.[25]

The situation had become so bad that the Residing Magistrate for the area, J.S. McLeod, banned further street preaching. Posters announcing the ban were stuck on notice boards around the town. This did ease things a little. Catholic residents stayed indoors the following Sunday and Rev Hallowes restricted his open-air preaching to the yard of the Protestant school-house, that is the Charter School in the Fishery, now Wicklow Vale Emporium. Hallowes had argued against the ban, stating that no human authority had the right to dictate when and where the word of God could be preached and he let it be known that the street preaching would continue as before. He also appealed to the Attorney General who ordered that the ban be lifted as he felt the magistrates had exceeded their authority, as he was not satisfied that they had 'reasonable grounds for such a procedure'. This was despite the fact that the local constabulary had to be augmented by fifty extra men every Sunday in the past weeks. This official sanction heightened tensions further. Catholics boycotted Protestant shops and individuals of both sections of the community were attacked. Greater peacekeeping enforcement was needed and each Sunday throughout July and August, 180 extra police and military were drafted in.

This high level of policing had the desired effect. The preachers were not allowed to cause an obstruction and the Catholics, at the behest of the priests, stayed indoors. The next six months were reasonably quiet, but other moves were afoot to stop the street preaching. It was decided that if the authorities would not take the preachers to court, a civil case might do the trick. A legal challenge was brought by four individuals against Revs Hallowes and Harrison, who were charged with having taken part in an unlawful assembly and having obstructed the public highway. This was deemed such an important case that it was referred to the Lord Chief Justice for advice. He felt that the street preachers had a legal right to carry on, but not the moral right. He failed to see why the services could not be conducted in the church or in a remote field, rather than on the public highway. When it was pointed out to him that the practice was carried on extensively in England, he replied 'Oh, England is a different country altogether from Ireland'. Nevertheless he was aware that the same laws applied, but while the preachers had the legal right, he felt that

> if a Catholic priest did this in the town of Belfast, I think the moral opinion at least would be against him as distinguished from the legal.

The case of obstruction was thrown out, but the preachers were requested to exercise better judgement in future.

They didn't, and they were again before the magistrates in March 1891 charged by four more individuals for obstructing the highway. One of the cases was proved and the preachers were fined £1 each. They refused to pay and were committed to prison for fourteen days. Hallowes appealed to the Chief Secretary of Ireland, Arthur Balfour, who was later to become British Prime Minister, on the grounds that the magistrates were biased. Balfour dismissed the appeal and shortly after a directive was issued that

> measures be taken to prevent the holding of open-air services in the town of Arklow in such a place and manner as to cause obstruction of the kind which occurred on Sunday, the 1st March.

Hallowes was informed that services could be held outside the town and, that if he selected a suitable site, the Lord Lieutenant would direct that all necessary protection would be made available to him. The cost of extra police and military up to the end of February 1891 had been £2,587, and as Hallowes was not prepared to back down, the cost continued to rise.

A very detailed account of the preaching on March 29th was published in the *Freeman's Journal* of April 1st. About a hundred soldiers were drafted into Arklow from Dublin to augment the hundred police already in the town. After a service in the church, the preachers and a small crowd, mostly of children, moved outside to the church gates, watched by about fifty police from across the street. More supporters joined the band until they numbered about two hundred and after some passages of scripture were read aloud, the congregation headed down the Main Street, followed by the fifty police. They went down Lower Main Street and into Tinahask until they came to the Charter School. All the doors of the houses were tightly shut, the inhabitants following Fr Dunphy's advice not to get involved in any disturbance.

As the procession passed each house, the people inside beat the doors to drown out the singing. On reaching the school, Rev Hallowes began his sermon. The police asked him to move on, which he refused to do and challenged the police officer to arrest him. His followers all moved into the school, perhaps as a pre-arranged strategy so that none but the preachers would be arrested. The police moved in on Hallowes who dodged them and jumped on the low wall, then jumped down again, then ran behind the police. The police did not want to arrest him, fearing that by doing so they would make him into a martyr. They formed a circle around him and walked back up Tinahask, forcing him to move with them. The scene would have been worthy of a place in a Keystone Cops classic. Hallowes' followers emerged from the school and followed him and the police back up the street. The doors of the houses remained shut, a feature which fascinated the writer of the account, himself a Methodist open air preacher in Dublin, but who disagreed with Rev Hallowes' methods.

> I stopped and asked permission to go into one of the houses (the houses are of a very poor sort, chiefly fishermen's cottages). I found five women and seven men in the house. I said, 'Well, boys, what are you all doing here?' They replied, 'We are shut up here because we do not

Preachers and followers in Lower Main Street (Pat Power)

> like to create a disturbance by going outside, and we do not wish to
> hear Mr Hallowes' lecture.' I asked, 'Do you always spend your Sundays
> like this?' They replied, 'Yes, since we got the order from the priest to
> stop indoors, and this is the way we have to spend our Sunday
> afternoon, instead of being out to get the fresh air, in consequence of
> Mr Hallowes' procession.'

The procession made its way back down to the Charter School again.
This time the preachers and the congregation all went inside. After a
few minutes, Hallowes asked the congregation to stay in while he and
his curate, Rev Harrison, went back outside to preach. He was back in
after a few minutes and they all headed back up the street again, until
they reached Parade Ground, which was already occupied by the
military. Undeterred and unmolested, Rev Hallowes preached for half
an hour, but his congregation was unable to hear him, for they had
been forced to remain in Main Street by the police. At four o'clock the
proceedings came to an end. Hallowes went home, the congregation
scattered, the military and extra police headed back to Dublin and other
bases, while the local police returned to barracks. The whole event
bordered on the farcical.

Even more farcical was the incident of July 19th when Rev Harrison
refused to move on when requested by the police. He locked one arm
around a lamppost, while holding his bible open in the other hand,
from which he read aloud. In the struggle to prise him from the
lamppost the bible was torn. Harrison made strong protests about
police brutality, not against his person but

> against the Word of God, which he held in his hand, being rudely
> crushed and torn, some leaves being entirely pulled out and torn in
> pieces by police acting, as their inspector informed him, in accordance
> with strict orders from Dublin Castle.

And so the slapstick comedy persisted month after month. More court
cases followed, this time mostly claims brought by Hallowes' supporters
against the police. At one of these, the local magistrate was William
Proby. Proby spent some part of each year at Glenart and when he did
so he sat on the bench as magistrate. He said that in the early weeks of
these disturbances, when the Catholic population turned out *en masse*
to abuse the preachers, he would have vigorously defended Hallowes'
rights, but since the people had shown that they were now willing to

let the police handle it, he felt that Hallowes had lost the moral ground and should reconsider his actions. Again, Hallowes would not be swayed.

On one occasion, January 3rd, 1892, at the conclusion of his sermon he pointed to the Head Constable and said

> You had better put on your spectacles, and you will better be able to see ... That man is going to hell with sin; let him put that in his pipe and smoke it.

This worsening situation between the preachers and the police led to physical exchanges, of shouldering and pushing, accusations of the clergy hitting out at police officers, counter accusations of police brutality. Such weekly fun and frolics brought the Catholics out onto the streets once more, not to take part but merely to watch the forces of government do battle with the forces of evangelical Protestantism. For over two years, this pathetic situation had been reported on nationally as well as locally. The Arklow Question, as it became known, was discussed and debated in the corridors of power, causing legal and administrative dilemmas in Dublin Castle and beyond. Such was the level of interest that on one occasion, the *Wicklow People, Wicklow Newsletter, Freeman's Journal* and *Dublin Evening Mail* all sent reporters to cover the events. A small group of professional photographers also arrived armed with cameras and negative wet-plates to record for posterity the regular Sunday show on the streets of Arklow.[26] A series of over twenty images was taken, showing the progress of the procession. One of the photographs taken that day, from an upstairs window of the Charter School, shows the crowded footpaths, a line of soldiers either side of the road, a line of RIC men in front of them and the band of street preachers and their congregation walking towards the school. Perhaps that image, more than any other, sums it all up. A copy of it hangs beside the window from which it was taken in what is now Wicklow Vale Emporium.

On this occasion Hallowes really played to the gallery, leaving the police no option but to remove him from in front of the Charter School and place him under house arrest for a few days until tempers cooled. After a few weeks he again returned to street preaching and continued to do so for several years, but the crisis point had passed. His arrest had made him a subject of ridicule among the Catholics, and his friends and advisers talked him into using less inflammatory speech in his sermons.

In the December 1895 issue of the *Arklow Parish Magazine,* which he edited, he stated

> There has not been one Sunday, or Fair Day, from 1894 to the date of writing, that the Gospel has not been preached in our streets[27]

but the numbers of his followers had greatly decreased as had the numbers who came out to hurl verbal abuse at them.[28] While all this was going on, other events were also taking place; events in which the local Catholic clergy were to show themselves no less narrow-minded.

Rev. R. C. Hallowes
(Select Vestry of St. Saviour's Arklow)

*

Parnell, the man who had taken the cause of the Irish people so far in the House of Commons, died on October 6th, 1891. This man who had sacrificed so much for his beliefs and who had been hailed the Uncrowned King of Ireland was torn to pieces by the very people he had helped. His crime was not his affair with a married woman, Kitty O'Shea. His crime was that the affair was now publicised because of Kitty's divorce, and Parnell was cited as co-respondent. It was Victorian hypocrisy at its lowest. The British establishment loved it for they knew that Irish parliamentary politics were irrevocably weakened. Some Irish MPs, such as Tim Healy, loved it because it gave them career opportunities they would otherwise not have had. Protestant clergy and society saw it as vindication of their condemnation of Parnell as a turncoat. Catholic clergy, including those who had looked upon him as God's gift to Ireland, suddenly forgot all he had done and branded him a fornicator and a threat to anything in a skirt. None was more bitter in this new-found revulsion that James Dunphy, parish priest of Arklow.

Dunphy had been a champion of Parnell. They shared an abiding interest in the development of the harbour, the promotion of the Land League and other movements for social reform. But all this was cast aside because Parnell's private life now filled the pages of newspapers.

The very people who should have supported Parnell in his time of need, not only deserted him, but turned on him and tore him to shreds. If Carysfort had reason for thinking his tenants ungrateful wretches, he should have been thankful that he wasn't in Parnell's shoes.

Of course, not everyone spat on Parnell's memory. There were those in the Home Rule party who remained faithful to him. There were those up and down the country who defied the rantings of their spiritual leaders and refused to forget Parnell's achievements. Arklow was the only place in the county to have an anti-Parnellite organisation,[29] and under Dunphy's pastoral guidance, the people of Arklow disgraced themselves in the 1892 general election.

It was the first general election to be held after Parnell's death. East Wicklow had long been an unassailable Home Rule constituency, but now that the party was split into pro- and anti-Parnellites, there was a chance for the Unionists to take the seat if they could find a strong candidate. Robert Halpin was a native of Wicklow town and one of the best known seamen of the nineteenth century. He had earned an international reputation in his telegraph cable laying days and now was something of lord of the manor in Tinnakilly House in Rathnew.[30] His interest in developing Wicklow's maritime industry was beyond dispute and it was hoped that this, coupled with the tattered state of the Nationalist political machine, just might get him elected. Facing him were William Corbet, long time holder of the seat and still staunchly Parnellite, and a stranger about whom little was known named James

C.S. Parnell (Courtesy Pat Power)

Fr James Dunphy, P.P.

Sweetman. Sweetman was an anti-Parnellite Home Ruler and the priests of the county urged their congregations to elect him instead of Corbet. No one was more adamant on this point that James Dunphy. He cracked the whip and the people of Arklow fell into line.

The election took place on July 7th, 1892, with the following result – Sweetman 1,433, Halpin 1,225, and Corbet 1,115, and it was the Arklow votes that swung it. The *Wicklow Newsletter* condemned the Arklow fishermen for failing to use their own judgement and for

> blindly following the dictates of their clergy to vote for a stranger in the
> county ... Arklow is undoubtedly a stronghold of the clerical party.[31]

William Corbet was also greatly disappointed at the ingratitude of the Arklow voters. At a farewell speech in Wicklow's Market Hall he said that he could understand the motives of the people who had voted for Halpin, but that he would never, could never, understand the motives of those who had voted for Sweetman.

Because of Arklow's betrayal of Parnell, the aforementioned sibling rivalry between Wicklow and Arklow entered a new stage, a deeper, more bitter resentment that was to last for a long time to come. Had Parnell been of a vindictive nature, his ghost might have taken pleasure from the fact that within four years of his death his quarries at the Rock, an important source of employment in the town, went into decline. It limped along until 1919, but the goods years ended around 1895.[32]

*

One of the local people who refused to turn his back on Parnell was Dr Molony. Michael J. Molony has somehow slipped through the fingers of history, but he deserves to be remembered. He was not a native of Arklow. In fact, he spent only the last six of his thirty-one years here, yet when he died in October 1892 he was honoured by a group of volunteers who organised fundraising to erect a fitting monument over his grave. The epitaph says it all.

> *North side, upper panel:*
> This / monument is raised / to perpetuate the memory of / Doctor
> Michael J. Molony / for several years Medical Officer / of Arklow
> Dispensary District / whose unselfish devotion / to his professional
> duties / endeared him / to all classes of the community / and also as a

tribute to / his inviolable integrity / his simple honesty / his unswerving
independence / and his genuine zeal for the sick poor / committed to
his care / Born 1st January 1861 / Died 22nd October 1892 / R.I.P.

North side, lower panel:
An upright honest man lies buried here
Gentle he was, and courteous, good and brave
A faithful friend, unselfish and sincere
He trod the path of honour to the grave
His record 'Good', his name without a stain
This marble monument shall long endure
To tell he lived and laboured not in vain
True to his God, his country and the poor

Who was this paragon? And how did such a young man earn such high
regard in so short a time?

The son of a doctor, he was born on January 1st, 1861, probably in
Galway.[33] He received his early education in Rockwell College and
Blackrock College, attended Queen's University, and took his final
exams in the College of Physicians and Surgeons in Edinburgh,
graduating in 1882, at the age of twenty-two. He worked in Camberwell
and Islington in London, and was then appointed a member of a
specially commissioned medical team to various locations in Britain, to
report on the health of poor districts. On the death of Dr Stopford
Halpin in 1885, who had been Medical Officer for Arklow from 1883,
Molony succeeded to the position.[34] All accounts of his time here marvel
at his energy and commitment not only to his job, but to the community
in many aspects. In 1886, he was vice-chairman and treasurer of the
Arklow Amateur Aquatic and Athletic Sports Committee. He also chaired
the fundraising events for the fishermen whose boats and gear were
destroyed in the same year. During the Coolgreaney evictions of 1888,
Molony treated the tenants with skill and compassion, urging the
authorities to leave the old and ill unmolested. He was an ardent Home
Ruler and Land Leaguer, an uncompromising supporter of Parnell, and
had no time for sectarian squabbles.

When many of the Catholic clergy turned on Parnell, Molony spoke
out against their hypocrisy, for which he was castigated from the
Arklow pulpit and when he died, his friend, Fr Monaghan of Barndarrig,
read the funeral services. Molony had been raised a Catholic and may
well have remained one until his death, but the ill-feeling that existed

The Molony Monument

between him and the local clergy because of his steadfast defence and support of Parnell, seemed irrevocable. Folklore recalls that Fr Dunphy refused to visit him or to allow any of his curates to administer the last rites to him, but very strong proof of such refusal is needed before such serious charges can be accepted at face value. Perhaps Molony himself didn't feel the need for the services of a church in which he might no longer have believed. A great deal more research needs to be carried out before any accusations and counter-accusations can be verified. Perhaps they never will be.

What is certain is that Molony's name became a political/religious football in the weeks succeeding his death. Revs Hallowes and Harrison visited him on his death bed, giving rise to claims that they tried to convert him in his most vulnerable hours. Both men denied this, stating that if Molony had wished to convert to Protestantism at that time, or at any other time, they would gladly have acceded to his wishes, but he expressed no such wish and so they did not baptise him into their Church. They merely called to see him and to sit with him as friends and admirers and to offer what consolation and comfort they could.

As I say, there is a great deal of work to be done concerning Michael Molony. He deserves to be rescued from the void and have his story told. For now, it is enough to say that between his death on Saturday, October 22nd and his funeral on the following Monday,

> upwards of three thousand people visited the chamber of death ... There could not have been less than five thousand present on the occasion *[of the funeral]*, and no creed nor class was absent.... He united to his skill as a physician the charity of a loving heart and a kindly disposition, and a long time will elapse ere his place can be filled. The people of Arklow may indeed well say in their hearts today: - 'He was a man, take him for all and all; we shall never look upon his like again'.[35]

Not a bad endorsement for one so young with just six years spent in the town.

*

In 1891, the government established a body to develop the economy of the more impoverished areas of the west. This was the Congested Districts Board. One of the areas earmarked for such development was the Aran Islands off Galway. Surprisingly, the islanders had little knowledge of or skills in fishing on a commercial basis and it was decided to establish a training scheme to rectify that situation. In fact, at that time, 'most of the Inishmore men could be described as farmers who did a little fishing'.[36]

> Seven Arklow boats which had been mackerel fishing for years on the Cork and Kerry coasts were subsidised to make an experimental fishery at the Aran Islands. Five other boats from Connemara and Aran joined to make an experimental fleet of twelve.[37]

The seven Arklow boats were the *Shamrock, Red Rover, St Veronica, Archdeacon, Signet, Mystical Rose* and *True Light*. To facilitate the experiment an ice hulk was moored at Kilronan pier on Inishmore to preserve expected catches. On the first day 6,000 mackerel were caught. As the locals learned the required skills and began working in partnership with their trainers, the twelve boats were operated as a unit and the size of the catches increased dramatically. On one day alone, 73,000 fish were landed,[38] and over the short season 300,000 mackerel were caught.

> The Arklow boats made in addition to the subsidy, an average of £316 per boat for the season of about three months, while the five local boats, with fewer days fishing and with inexperienced crews, made an average of only £70 a boat.[39]

Nor were the fishermen of Arklow the only ones from the town to benefit from this new departure. John Tyrrell & Sons had built most, if not all, of the Arklow fishing boats involved in this enterprise and they proved so well suited to the task on the west coast that orders were placed with them for more boats to be built for the islanders. One of these was a nobby named *Father O'Donoghue*, after the parish priest of Kilronan who had done so much to bring about this development on Inishmore. Fr Dunphy in Arklow had also been enthusiastic about this project and it is not unlikely that both men had worked together to bring this mutually beneficial enterprise about. It is said that during the successful years, such as that initial season, Fr Dunphy travelled to the Aran Islands to see how things were progressing, but also to 'collect a few "shiners" *[gold sovereigns]* from the Arklow boats to defray the expenses of his parochial engagements'.[40] Some of the early years, however, were far from successful.

> After the 1894 season the Arklow crews were so poor that a collection had to be made to get them home, and only one of the Aran boats was not in debt.[41]

Nevertheless, the Aran Islands fishery had been firmly established and lasted until the 1920s. An unexpected Arklow legacy to the Aran Islands was the marriage of two Arklowmen to island women. They were James Doyle and Henry Lynch. Their descendants still live on the islands. Doyle became a net maker and Lynch's son was at one time coxswain of the Aran lifeboat.[42]

11

The Early Kynoch Years:
1895 - 1910

The last quarter of the nineteenth century had seen significant economic improvement in Arklow, particularly around the port. The trading fleet was bigger than ever, the mines at Avoca gave direct employment not only to people who lived in that vicinity, but also indirect employment to carters and dockers here in Arklow. As more vessels were needed to transport the ore to England, more sailors were needed to man them. Shops did increased business. The opening of Parnell Quarries at the Rock was also a boost, as was the Arklow Manure Works. Nevertheless, despite the disingenuous mantra of politicians and financial commentators then as now, rising tides do not raise all boats and there was still a great deal of distress in the town. In 1892, the editor of the *Wicklow Newsletter* reported the following opinion of the Arklow Dispensary Committee,

> There is no place in Ireland so much calculated to try the abilities of a dispensary doctor as Arklow. The population of the town itself, not to mention the poverty in which the great majority of the inhabitants live, might well induce the Board of Guardians to consider the advisability of appointing two doctors for the district. Despite the remarkable energies of the late Dr Molony, it not infrequently happened that cases of the most urgent nature were neglected for hours. Thus the poor were obliged to suffer keenly, owing to the exceptional labour the dispensary doctor had to undergo, and this lamentable state of things is bound to continue as long as a population of 4,000 people is depending solely upon one medical officer.[1]

There were other doctors in the town, of course, but these had private practices and the vast majority of people were not in a position to pay for medical attention. The dispensary doctor was appointed to give free medical services to the poor. Some of this distress stemmed from the fact that the local herring fishery, which had been the town's economic mainstay for so long, dwindled from about 1880 on.[2] The fishing fleet now made their way to other fishing grounds at various times of the year.

In the early years of the 1890s, the town was buzzing with the possibility of a new factory being established. It promised to be much bigger than anything already in operation (with the exception of the combined statistics of the various mining companies), although no one dared to put a figure on the numbers it would employ. Even the most optimistic forecasts were to pale into insignificance.

In 1891, a Liverpool based company made enquiries as to finding a site suitable for a factory that would manufacture explosives.[3] Because of the hazardous nature of the work, the site would have to meet certain criteria. It had to be large, it had to be removed from a residential area (if possible) and yet be accessible for both the workforce and for movement of goods in and out. Most important, the terrain had to be such as to contain explosions. Sand hills would be perfect. Three sites along the Wicklow coast were considered: one at Dunbur, just south of Wicklow; one at Brittas Bay; and the mile long North Beach at Arklow. The Brittas Bay site was chosen and purchased from the local landowner and plans to commence construction in April 1893 were under way, but red tape and legal problems put the whole thing on hold.

This delay gave a rival company, Kynoch & Company of Birmingham, a chance to slip in with plans of their own. Kynochs had been established forty years earlier and was anxious to expand into Ireland. When Thomas Troy, a prominent Arklow businessman and chairman of the Town Commissioners, learned of Kynochs' intentions, he contacted them through the offices of Irish members of parliament. Other leading figures in the town lent their weight to the campaign, especially the parish priest James Dunphy. They argued that no site was more suitable than North Beach, pointing out the sandy nature of the terrain, the existence of dunes and sandhills, the proximity of a working port, and the availability of a workforce. Kynochs agreed that the site was very suitable and set about getting the required permission. The Kynoch chairman was Arthur Chamberlain, a member of one of the leading Tory families in England. His brother Joseph was later to become Colonial Secretary and his nephew Neville was Prime Minister from 1937 until 1940. Such political clout can be a help when the appropriate party is in power, but when the rival party holds the reins it can be something of a hindrance. And so it was in 1894 when Kynochs sought permission to establish a factory at Arklow. The Liberals were in government, not the Conservatives, and several barriers were erected to thwart the application. The Liberals, however, were not in a very strong position. They needed the support of the Irish MPs to stay in power and it was made clear to them that if Kynochs were not allowed to set up in Arklow, the support of the Irish Party could not be depended upon. So things looked good no matter who was returned at the next election. The Conservatives would probably back it because of the Chamberlain involvement, and the Liberals would back it because they needed the support of the Irish MPs. The barriers were taken down and the way was cleared for Arklow's Kynoch Era. The Liberals lost the 1895 election and the Tories formed the new government, a position they retained until 1905.

North Beach, where Kynocks was located

The Liberal Party weren't the only ones to raise objections to the new Arklow factory. At home, residents on Ferrybank felt uneasy about having an explosives factory sitting on their shoulders and, as construction materials began to arrive by sea and rail, the Ferrybankers stepped their protests up a couple of notches. Kynochs didn't like the way things were shaping up and stated that they could not invest in a town that did not give it full backing. The protest continued and the company stopped construction work. This spread the fear that they would abandon their plans, so leading religious and community figures organised a meeting to show the general cross-community support for Kynochs. Town Commissioners, doctors, businessmen and would-be employees were united in their efforts to secure the new factory. Also to the fore were Fr Dunphy and the Protestant curate, Rev J.W. Harrison, religious irrelevancies temporarily put aside for the common good.

This strong show of support, copperfastened by the cries of 'We want work!!', was all the evidence Kynochs needed to proceed with their plans, but they warned that if the company was to remain in Arklow, to the mutual benefit of themselves and the townspeople, continued support would have to be assured. They said that good management/worker relations could only be achieved through 'fair play'. If that was secured, the future for the town looked bright.

The site was ideal. It stretched from the north bank of the river the full length of the beach, about a mile long. At the riverside, Kynochs bought the Manure Works buildings and adapted them for their own purposes. Other buildings, workshops, mixing houses, offices, dressing rooms, toilets, and all the accoutrements of a major manufacturing plant were constructed. Much of it was concentrated near the river end, but sheds of various sizes, depending on their purposes, sprang up here and there. Small mixing houses, in which gun cotton and nitroglycerine were mixed to produce a concoction known as 'Cordite', were purposely small to keep damage to a minimum in case of accidental blasts. The nitroglycerine was produced on site, but was banished to the extreme north end of the complex. Sandbanks were built around these houses to force an explosion upwards rather than let it spread to other danger houses. Some of these sand barriers can still be seen in what is now the caravan park, providing shelter from winter gales and strong summer breezes. Sulphuric and nitric acids were also produced.

Producing these chemicals was one thing, transferring them from one department to another presented a different set of problems. Friction was to be avoided as much as possible, so the acids were transferred to the nitroglycerine department by one of three methods. One was a system of pipes through which the acids were forced by compressed air; the second was by a small canal system; and third, by rail. The canal channels were about three or four feet wide and roughly the same depth.[4] Perhaps even more impressive was the web of narrow gauge tram tracks which crisscrossed the site. The materials were transported along this in metal bogies.

Kynocks (Pat Power)

Cordite was used in munitions and was mainly produced for the British arsenals at Woolwich and Purfleet. It became synonymous with the Kynoch factory in Arklow and many people who worked there referred to the factory as 'The Cordite'.[5] The production of explosives for commercial blasting operations such as mining was also carried on extensively. These included gelatine dynamite, gelignite, and a substance of their own devising called Kynite. The new factory met with immediate success and, even before it was fully operational, plans to extend it to double its original size and production capacity were under way.

The new factory acted like a magnet, attracting employment seekers to the town. The Town Commissioners looked to the future with more optimism than ever before, but they were aware that the changes taking place would have to be controlled if chaos was to be prevented. Shortly after the opening of Kynochs, the RIC dropped something of a bombshell. There were two police barracks in the town at that time. The main barracks was still on Parade Ground, but there was also a sub-station in the Fishery, in St Michael's Terrace.[6] When it was decided to close it down in 1895 there was an outcry. A special meeting of the Town Commissioners was convened to prevent what they considered an act of irresponsible negligence. It was resolved

> That we, the Town Commissioners of Arklow, hereby express our alarm and regret at the report that the RIC station is about to be removed from Tinahask, in the lower part of the town, and, in the interest of the inhabitants, and the general peace and security of the locality, to impress on government the absolute necessity that exists for police being located in this part of the town.[7]

One of the reasons put forward by the authorities for the proposed closure was the population density didn't justify a station there. The Commissioners dismissed this, stating that the 1891 Census returns had been misleading because 800 fishermen and 300 sailors were absent from their homes the night the census was taken.

> The entire of those men have their permanent abode in Arklow (chiefly from the locality from which the RIC station in question is to be removed) and the fishermen are at home, for say, eight months in the year, and the sailors, who are for the most part engaged in the coasting trade of the United Kingdom, at short and repeated intervals.
>
> Scenes of disorder in this part of the town were of frequent occurrence before the police station was established, and it is quite certain that a recurrence of the same will take place, and the Commissioners and inhabitants, especially those of the locality concerned, look with the greatest apprehension on the state of things which is certain to arise should the police be removed.[8]

The Commissioners went on to say that 'the Cordite factory' and the Rock quarries employed 500 men between them, causing an 'increase of 1,000 to the population, and it is absolutely certain that this increase has not attained its maximum'.

As the town of Arklow is considerably over a mile in length and the main or original barracks is situate at the top of the Main Street, at a most inconvenient distance from the lower part of the Fishery (the most densely populated part of the town) it is quite evident the police in the original barracks could not exercise the same supervision over the lower part of the town, or perform their duties as efficiently as if living on the spot.

We therefore in simple justice to all parties concerned, including the police themselves, who are responsible for the peace of the town, respectfully appeal and confidently trust the government may see their way to leave the Tinahask station permanently where it is at present.

The Commissioners desire to point out that their request is to establish two permanent stations in the town, and to leave the numerical strength of each to the discretion of the police authorities.

The appeal fell on deaf ears, but much to the surprise of the Town Fathers, the people of the Fishery did not fall on one another in spontaneous murderous outbursts. They merely got on with their lives the same as people did in other parts of the town.

*

Within a couple of years, Arklow-produced explosives were being exported all over Britain and Ireland, the Channel Islands, and even to South Africa, India, Australia and New Zealand. By 1898 it was one of the biggest explosive factories in the world. It already employed 350 men, women and boys who between them shared a wage bill of £400 each week, a major boost to the local economy, and that does not take into account ancillary employment.

Kynochs also encouraged their employees to spend their leisure time in "worthwhile" pursuits and provided a recreation hall, diningroom, and library to that end.

Concerts, dances and other entertainments are from time to time organised by a committee consisting of some of the leading officials and workmen.[9]

Things were going so well that it was decided to apply to the Dublin, Wicklow, and Wexford Railway Company to construct a branch line that would leave the main line at Ballyraine, cross the river by a specially constructed iron bridge, then down the north bank of the river to the factory. This, however, was deemed a little too ambitious.

But not everything in the garden was rosy and the good relations hoped for between management and workers were to be tested time and time again. The first such test came just three months after production got under way. For all the frills such as the recreation hall, library, dances and concerts, Kynoch & Company could be tight-fisted when it came to wages. They refused to pay men in the danger houses the same money as their counterparts in their English factories. This led to grumbles and ill-will, and the issue was brought to a head in the wake of a tragedy. Thomas Cullen was only twenty-six when he became the first fatality in the Arklow plant. He was drying guncotton when an explosion ripped through the shed in which he was working. In the subsequent enquiry carried out by an Inspector of Explosives it was decided that the blast might have been caused deliberately to enhance the workers' calls for danger money. A number of potentially catastrophic incidents had recently been averted and the management believed that each had pointed to the possibility of sabotage. The inquiry report also expressed the belief that Thomas Cullen's fellow workers had sacrificed him in their campaign for better wages, but conceded that it could have been accidental. Lack of evidence left the Inspector no option but to return a verdict of accidental death.

The management, in the highhanded manner for which they would become known, closed the factory until further notice. They had threatened to pull out of Arklow in response to the Ferrybank protest even before the factory was built, now they were threatening the same thing after just three months in operation, and they were to do this time and time again. They believed that they could frighten the people into submission, but these people weren't so easily frightened. Instead of wilting under threats, the workers submitted a claim for £1 per week for those working in danger zones and sixteen shillings for those outside these areas, instead of the fifteen shillings per week they were all being paid at that time. Faced with this, the management, realising they had invested too much just to pull out of Arklow, changed their stance saying that unless the men returned to work English workers would be brought over to replace them. This stand off was overcome only by the intervention of Fr Dunphy who persuaded the men to return to work.

The damage had been done and was made even worse when Chamberlain launched a vicious attack on the integrity of the workforce, more or less accusing them of harbouring murderers. He warned that the company would rather pay English workers English rates to work in Arklow. This, of course, only bore out the complaints of the Arklow workers. The company expected them to run the same risks as English workers for less money. Chamberlain used the irrelevant argument that Kynochs paid the highest wages in the district, ignoring the fact that his stance simply bore out the belief that an Irish life was worth less than an English life. This was the kind of stupidity that was to make the town of Arklow look on Kynochs as a Jeckyll and Hyde employer. Kind and considerate when it came to Christmas parties for the workers' children, vicious and tight-fisted when it came to paying people what they were entitled to. Expressions used by Chamberlain, such as 'characteristic cowardice on the part of the work people' and 'treachery and malice of the most wicked kind' prompted Fr Dunphy to defend the Arklow people against such a tirade. He rounded off a spirited chastisement with

> I am, and have been since the inception of these works, very grateful to Mr Chamberlain for introducing to our neighbourhood an industry that gives employment to so many people, but I cannot stand by and hear such a gross slander of my people without raising my voice in protest.

Another major problem facing the company was the poor state of the harbour. Despite the construction of new piers and quay walls, the entrance to the port was often blocked by sand. Only small vessels drawing a couple of feet could clear the bar. Fully laden sailing vessels and, in particular, Kynochs' own steamers could not get into or out of the river. In fairness to Chamberlain and his board, they had said at the outset that accessibility to and from the port was vital to the success of the factory. At least twelve to thirteen feet of clearance was required. They appealed to the Harbour Commissioners to secure funding from the Board of Works so that a dredger could be bought to keep the entrance free. When that didn't materialise and the *Anglesey*, one of Kynochs' steamers, could not clear the harbour for twelve days (and then only after she had been lightened), the old refrain was heard again:

> Kynoch & Co. announce that their Arklow works will be closed until further notice owing to the neglect of the Harbour Commissioners.

Admittedly, it wasn't an overt threat to quit Arklow, but the tune was the same even if the words have been altered slightly. Again in fairness, the factory was running out of guncotton which had to be imported. The Commissioners threw up their hands in despair, pleading impotence. The situation eased when a cargo of guncotton and acetone was imported through Wicklow and brought to Arklow under police escort, but it was a stopgap solution and something more satisfactory would have to be arrived at. Kynochs agreed to buy a dredger if the Harbour Commissioners maintained and operated it.

Busy port despite the problems

This measure was no doubt prompted by the deteriorating political situation in South Africa. Throughout the 1890s the Boers, descendants of Dutch settlers, and the British controlled government had been on the brink of war, spilling over into actual hostilities on two occasions. It's an ill-wind that blows nobody good and in 1899 Kynochs were poised to reap the benefits as the third Boer War was about to erupt. But once again political considerations played their part. The Kynoch group won large contracts, but Irish MPs felt that the Arklow factory was getting the short end of the stick. Apparently their tender was above that of rival companies but, for reasons unknown, they were then allowed to resubmit their tender with a price more in line with the average. When this became common knowledge accusations of political and familial skulduggery were sent scudding through the air. Arthur Chamberlain's brother Joseph was now Colonial Secretary. Whether shocked and aggrieved by suggestions that the Chamberlain family could possibly be accused of unsavoury business practices, or whether simply annoyed by the government's decision to alter the specifications of cordite, Kynochs Arklow decided to eschew further government contracts and concentrate on commercial explosives. The cordite department ceased production. This involved the laying-off of about 200 employees, but these were reinstated as soon as commercial orders for mining explosives increased.

*

As the twentieth century dawned, Arklow was fairly busy. The previous year, 1899, one of the finest ecclesiastical buildings in the country, and certainly still the finest building in the town today, was completed. This was the magnificent St Saviour's parish church. The splendour of St Saviour's is not its size. It is substantial, but there are much larger churches to be seen. It is its style, proportions and setting that make it such a beautiful building, and we have William Proby to thank for it.

Once Proby had abandoned his plans for a model village and had turned his attention to developing the castle and grounds at Glenart, his next project was to build a new Protestant church. St Mary's in Main Street was still serviceable, but was long past its best. Architecturally, it was also something of a poor relation in comparison to the Catholic church of Sts Mary and Peter. St Mary's was crammed into Main Street, while Sts Mary and Peter stood in splendid isolation overlooking the nearest thing we have to a town centre. Proby decided to fund the building of a new church, one placed on the highest point of the town, dominating the skyline and overlooking the valley. On May 14th, 1897 the first sod was turned. On June 10th, Proby's wife, the Countess of Carysfort, laid the foundation stone. The church was to be the parish church, but it was also intended as a memorial to Proby's immediate family.

> Lord and Lady Carysfort had very definite ideas about the design of the church. They appointed an architect who had a large restoration practice in London and was thoroughly familiar with early church buildings.[10]

That architect was Arthur Blomfield (one time mentor of apprentice architect and future novelist Thomas Hardy) and he incorporated the features the Carysforts particularly liked in other churches. The 156 foot tower spire would dwarf a less skillfully designed building, but the proportions of St Saviour's are such that nothing dominates to the detriment of the other features. Inside, the attention to detail is of equal quality. St Saviour's is quite simply a beautiful building. It took two years to build and cost £29,500. It was consecrated by the Archbishop of Dublin on August 12th, 1899.

St Saviour's

The Bottom School

Other things were also happening. A cursory glance at the local papers of the time show the mixed bag of events, big and small, that go into the life of any town. They give an idea of what the local talking points were. A new school was opened on Harbour Road, officially named St Peter's for Infant Boys, but known alternatively to one and all as the Bottom School or the Lower School. It opened in 1900 and it was here that generations of four-year-old Fishery lads were initiated into the world of compulsory education. There were four classes, Babies, Senior Infants, First and Second classes, after which the "graduates" had to trudge their way up to the Top School (never the Upper School) on Coolgreaney Road. The Bottom School had three rooms and was designed to accommodate 200 pupils. Having served four years there without remission, I fail to see where 200 pupils could have been accommodated in this structure measuring eighty-eight feet by thirty feet, unless half of them were to be suspended from the rafters. Originally there were to be two classrooms, but by the time I got there in 1958 there were three. The configuration within the original space must have changed because, to my knowledge, there had been no extension built. It was replaced by the new St Peter's in Castlepark in

1970 and the Bottom School became a Senior Citizens' Centre. It has, unfortunately, lain derelict for the past number of years and will probably be demolished in the near future.

The youngsters were not the only ones making the news. On February 3rd, 1900 the *Wicklow People* carried the report of a local wedding. No big deal, except for the fact that the unnamed groom was ninety and his unnamed blushing bride was eighty. It was his third outing and her fourth. The two topics that filled most of the column inches, however, were the on-going centenary commemorations of the 1798 rebellion, and the visit of the queen, the redoubtable Victoria.

Two years earlier had seen massive turn-outs to commemorate the 1798 rebellion. The 1890s were the pinnacle of Irish consciousness in politics (Home Rule and the Land League), in the arts (the Celtic Revival), in sport (the Gaelic Athletic Association), and in general cultural pursuits such as the growing interest in the Irish language and history (the Gaelic League). Throughout the country, but particularly in the counties in which the 1798 rebellion had raged, huge crowds gathered to listen to speeches and watch pageants. Many of these events terminated in the proposal to begin fundraising to erect monuments to the people who fought in the rebellion. In Arklow, where the tide of the insurrection had been turned on June 9th, 1798, it was proposed to erect a monument on Parade Ground, opposite the RIC barracks. Not only was it opposite the RIC barracks, but it was also adjacent to the chapel and this is an important point. By the end of the nineteenth century the Catholic Church had well and truly shaken off its second class status. No longer did it shy away from nationalist identity. So complete was its about-face that the priests who had been involved in the rebellion, some of whom had been threatened with excommunication for their activities,[11] were no longer a cause of embarrassment and were now fated as heroes of the Catholic people. When the time came to choose a representative figure to stand aloft on the monument, Fr Michael Murphy was the preferred option. It will be remembered from Chapter Six, that Fr Murphy's only contribution to the battle of Arklow was to get himself killed after arriving late. I can't help feeling that Michael Dwyer, Esmond Kyan or Billy Byrne would have been far more fitting. Anthony Perry would also have been a good choice. He was, after all, leader of the United Irishmen in this region and was from Inch. But best of all would have been Matthew Doyle from Poulahoney[12] who had organised an Arklow corps based around the fishermen. All of them would have had a far greater claim to the position than Michael Murphy, but it was not to be. I don't wish to diminish Murphy's commitment to the cause of the rebellion. The man died for his beliefs. You don't get much more commitment than that, but I do believe there were other, far more appropriate candidates and I personally feel that the statue of Matthew Doyle should be pointing the way to Dublin.

'98 band

Throughout 1900, the people were kept abreast of just how the fundraising was going. Amounts large and small poured in. Contributions were received from not just outside the county but from across the Atlantic as well. The weekly reports sometimes lay side by side with reports of the preparations for Victoria's visit. For example, Lord Carysfort's talks to the children in the local schools about the visit were reported. A public meeting was held in the Marlborough Hall to decide how best to mark the occasion. Kynochs promised their workers a day off to go to Dublin in the hope of catching a glimpse of her.

They were also in the news for securing a contract to supply the British army arsenal at Woolwich with 2,000 barrels of gunpowder, and the demand for their products was such that they were applying to Wicklow County Council for planning permission to extend the factory. Not only that, it was announced that the new Arklow Terra Cotta Brick & Tile Co Ltd was expected to start operations before the year was out.[13] This was to be located behind the coastguard station at Seabank, on part of the site now occupied by Mountain Bay housing estate. It was hoped that it would employ between sixty and seventy when in full production. Bad news was the collapse of the local herring fishery, and the loss within a few weeks of four local trading vessels, the *Ariel, G.L.Waters, Reserve* and *Ann Humphreys*.[14] The one bright spot in the maritime fortunes of the town was the fact that there were sixty-three Arklow boats engaged in the mackerel fishing off the southwest coast, and there were now up to fifty Arklow fishermen working for the Congested Districts Board as instructors on the Galway and Mayo coasts, teaching the locals how to work the boats the CDB provided, many of which had been built by John Tyrrell & Sons. They also taught net-making and repair.

The heady days of street preaching and riots seemed to have been consigned to the past, but in June 1900 the spectacle of Christians 'hating each other fervently for the love of God'[15] presented itself once more. The *Wicklow People* reported on the great occasion that surrounded the laying of the foundation stone of the Fr Murphy Monument on June 30th. It described, over pages and pages of that edition, how thousands had flocked to the town from all the surrounding counties and further afield. The description is too detailed to go into here. It was a *big, big* occasion with upwards of twenty-three bands. It was a day of joy, of pride, of achievement. In a town riven with latent sectarianism, not everyone was pleased, but commonsense would have dictated that those not in favour of this display of nationalism should avoid it.

Rev Richard Hallowes was not an ogre. By all accounts, his acts of charity to those in need, irrespective of religious allegiance, showed him to be a man of compassion, but he was uncompromising in his beliefs. For ten years he had shown that commonsense had no place in his commitment to spread the gospel. June 30th was a Sunday, and Sunday was the day on which the Word of God was to be preached – in Parade Ground, amidst thousands of people who had gathered to honour the memory of the 1798 insurgents. To understand how propaganda works, it is an object lesson to read the accounts of this occasion in both the *Wicklow People* (Nationalist) and the *Wicklow Newsletter* (Unionist).

> The best of order prevailed, notwithstanding the mendacious attempt of the Arklow ranters to disturb the peaceable assembly. We shall not waste words on these miserable creatures. *[Wicklow People]*

> Rev R.C. Hallowes and his friends were hustled by police and prevented from walking the public streets. *[Wicklow Newsletter]*

Enough time and pages have been spent on painting this picture already. Let us shake our heads in despairing incomprehension and move on.

*

Sometimes brief snippets from a local newspaper give a better "feel" for everyday life than detailed reports of particular aspects. I could have filled the next twenty pages with such glimpses, but the following will suffice to show how the people enjoyed themselves in Arklow between 1906 and 1908.

There has always been a healthy section of Arklow people who have loved to play to an audience. Drama has a long and fine tradition here, a tradition that is alive and kicking. As I write (April 2003) a local group is in preparation to stage Lionel Bart's *Oliver*, while yesterday in the National Library I read of the success of the Arklow Dramatic Class's successful production of Dion Boucicault's *The Shaughraun*, almost 100 years earlier.[16] That earlier group had 'added fresh laurels to their fame' and such was the demand for their talents that they brought it on tour – to Avoca and Barndarrig. Throughout the decades of the twentieth century, other groups such as the Marian Arts, the Arklow Parish Group, Arklow Arts Association, Masquerade, and many others were to follow in their footsteps.

Other cultural activities in Arklow in 1906 included well attended Irish classes conducted by the Gaelic League. Conradh na Gaeilge and Glór na nGael were to continue this up to the present day. The Arklow

Brass Band used to meet in the Foresters' Hall in Upper Main Street, but the room allocated to them was in such bad repair, and without heating, that it was difficult to get a full attendance on cold January nights. It was decided to launch a campaign to raise funds to either improve the Foresters' Hall or to build a new premises. Their efforts were reported on a fairly regular basis over the next year or two. I won't even begin to list the bands and musical groups who have continued to carry the strong musical tradition in Arklow since that time. All types of music from *céilidh* to rock, from bagpipes to folk, from stage musicals to *sean nós*, have had their champions. The Arklow Music Festival, founded in 1970, is the culmination of that great musical tradition in all its many styles.

For the sports fans, hurling and handball seemed the favoured codes. Athletics were also popular and had been for some time. The annual Arklow Amateur Aquatic & Athletic Sports days had been major events in the 1880s.[17] Boxing, too, was regarded as a healthy pastime. While most contests were conducted under Queensbury rules, there were other less structured bouts, such as the one reported in the *Wicklow People* of February 10th, 1906.

> A PUGILISTIC DISPLAY
>
> On Thursday evening last quite an exciting display was witnessed on the Coolgreaney Road convenient to Lord Carysfort's gate lodge. Late that night two tramps had some disagreement, and words soon developed into blows, and in a short time a fierce and determined battle was in progress. How long the affair might have lasted is impossible to say, but from the savage manner in which the parties attacked each other and the punishment they inflicted, doubtless the contest would have been brought to a speedy termination by the forced retirement of one or the other of the combatants. The struggle, however, was brought to a dramatic termination by the appearance of four policemen, who had been apprised of the affair, and who had hurried to the scene. The pugilists were taken into custody, and the next morning were brought before Mr. R. Philpot, J.P., who sentenced them each to 14 days' hard labour; and a very sorry spectacle one of them presented on his departure to the metropolis. His face was bruised in such a shocking manner that it would have been difficult for even his friends to recognise him.

Oh, to have those four policemen patrolling on Saturday nights and R.

Philpot, J.P. presiding on Sunday mornings, it might once more be safe to walk up Main Street at the weekend.

St Patrick's Day, 1906 was marked by a general holiday on which shops and businesses closed and the chapel was packed for the various services. In the afternoon, the Brass Band and the uniformed Foresters marched down the street to add a dash of colour.

> A most gratifying feature of the occasion was the entire absence of drunkenness, a fact upon which the people deserve a word of congratulations, as also the large throng of country people who visited the town during the day.[18]

While this quote speaks well for the sobriety of the town on Patrick's Day, it raises a few questions about the sobriety of the town in general. If such good behaviour was not exceptional, why would the reporter be 'most gratified' by it? Was drunkenness the norm and this display of sobriety an aberration in honour of the national saint? Was some widespread determined effort meriting congratulations made? If so, well done, citizens of Arklow, now for the other 364 days....

But it was not all entertainment. Over the two years in question, the need for a new hospital was raised on a regular basis. The old fever hospital on St Mary's Road was not only antiquated, it was more a cause of concern to both ill and well. Because of its proximity to the railway station, it was said that the arrival and departure of trains and the consequent to-ing and fro-ing of passengers outside the hospital windows was a constant disruption to ill and convalescent patients. Likewise, there was the danger of healthy passersby falling prey to fever as they passed the hospital. This latter fear smacks of a grasping-at-straws approach to procuring a new facility, but it displays the frustration that was being felt. No one doubted the need for a modern centre, the difficulty was, as always, money and also the problem of where to build it. The argument was to drag on for another year or two without resolution. The fever hospital was last used in the 'flu epidemic of 1918, but was not pulled down until the 1930s.

The 1798 Monument was unveiled in Parade Ground in 1903, but many felt that it would not be complete until it was protected by a surrounding rail. The problem was that whatever money had been raised had been used in commissioning the monument itself and the kitty was now empty. By 1906 reports of revitalising the fund to erect railings appeared in the paper. A particularly heartfelt appeal was made by John B. Doyle of Atlantus, Virginia, who regretted that because he resided in a rural area, there was no large population of 'the race of the Celt' whom he could muster to raise the required sum, but that he wished to see the monument completed. To rally support for his expressed sentiments he wrote the following verses:

In old, historic Arklow town
There stands a stately pile,
In memory to the men who've shown
Their love for Erin's Isle;
Who fought for faith and fatherland
In seventeen-ninety-eight;
They met the Saxon hand-to-hand
That memorable date.

Led on by Father Murphy brave,
And Esmonde Kyan, too,
These gallant men of Wexford gave
The Britons cause to rue.
They bravely fought the ninth of June,
In faith and freedom's cause;
'Gainst English domination
And cruel English laws.

They bravely fought that fateful day;
Ill-mingled streams of blood
Had found their way to Arklow Bay
And mingled with the flood.
The noble hero priest who led
This people in the fight,
That day they numbered with the dead,
The dead who fought for right.

Oh well may Arklowmen feel proud,
A statue to have built,
His virtues to proclaim aloud,
Likewise the Saxon's guilt.
'Twill prove he did not die in vain,
And 'twill commemorate
The gallant heroes who were slain
In seventeen-ninety-eight.

But we must work and watch and pray,

And keep the goal in view,
And suffer not ourselves to stray,
But be steadfast and true.
Thus will it be, till we are free,
From Anglo-Saxon thrall;
And Erin's Isle a nation be,
The noblest of them all.[19]

This brings me nicely to the various hues of Arklow's political spectrum. As throughout the rest of the country at that time, the cultural and political movements which had given birth to organisations such as the Gaelic League were taking on a more overt nationalism. Awareness of cultural identity was developing into a political identity, and there was a growing discontent with political subjugation. Local authorities throughout Ireland were becoming increasingly divided along Unionist/Nationalist lines. In Arklow the Town Commissioners were almost equally divided.

Such clearly defined allegiances sometimes led to vigorous debate and sometimes the debate could become distinctly acrimonious. The type of rhetoric used one hundred years ago is little different to the type of rhetoric we have endured from the various factions north of the border for the past thirty years. Whatever one side promoted, the other side blocked. Whatever one side cheered, the other booed. The sterility of such local "government" is perhaps best reflected in an incident of 1907, involving the proposed offshore visit of the Atlantic fleet of the royal navy.

It was announced at a meeting of the Town Commissioners that the fleet would anchor off Arklow between August 27th and 31st.[20] This was considered by some as a major event and Lord Carysfort wrote to the Commissioners announcing his intention of giving a garden party in honour of the occasion.[21] Approaches were made to the Dublin & South-Eastern Railway in the hope of arrangements being made for cheap fares into Arklow over the four days, so that as many sightseers as possible might be attracted to the town. It looked as if it was going to be an occasion for all to enjoy. Three weeks later, the *Wicklow People* recorded that such goodwill towards the British navy was not universal.

> Shortly before noon on Thursday, eight battleships belonging to the Atlantic fleet arrived in the bay of Arklow. The fleet is under the command of Admiral Sir George Henry Curzon-Howe. He is an uncle to

the Countess of Wicklow, being a brother of the Duchess of Abercorn. The ships which had been at Kingstown some days previously left that place on Thursday morning and had a rough and foggy passage.

Long before its arrival, the rain began descending incessantly in Arklow, a fact which had a very dampening effect on the enthusiasm some persons might have had for travelling and witnessing the arrival of the vessels. The result was that nothing like the number of strangers visited the town anticipated by those who had taken in hand the arrangements for a proper reception for this arm of England's power and fewer still availed of the special facilities for travelling offered by the railway company.

However, there were a good many in and about the town whose feelings and enthusiasms were effected in no way by the merciless downpour and they braved the elements to record the welcome which fell far short of what a good many thought would be given.

The arrangements for according a fitting and proper reception of the fleet was taken in hand by a committee some time ago at a meeting called by Messrs Hugh Byrne and A.O. Hood, the agent of the Earl of Carysfort and F.A.S. King.

At a subsequent meeting it was arranged that a series of decorations should be provided for the delectation of the sailors. The few ships that were in the harbour displayed to advantage a number of flags while the Union Jack could be seen floating from the window of one of the cabins in Tinahask, but these were exceptions, no other decorations were attempted. The inclemency of the weather altogether upset the arrangements for the holding of the sports and as a result a bellman announced shortly after noon that the event had been postponed. It was understood, too, that an address of welcome was to be presented to the Admiral on his arrival, but for some reason or other this part of the programme was not fulfilled. And, incidentally, it should be mentioned that some of the commissioners were desirous of having it made known that they absolutely refused to append their signatures to the address on the principle that they could not conscientiously do so until Ireland's just demands were conceded.

However, it is certain that although the address does not bear all the signatures of the town commissioners that it will be presented to Admiral Howe with all due pomp and ceremony, while it is not improbable that the admiral will recommend these loyal adherents in the proper quarters for preferment of some kind or other.

In striking contrast to some cases of supreme hardship in the town some months ago, and in which aged parents were deprived of their means of support by the drowning of their son, a house to house collection was organised and the result was something like £20, mainly contributed by shopkeepers and others, the town landlord and others whose influence might have admitted the deserving object were absent from the list. On this occasion for providing a useless display of fireworks and other paltry exhibitions, a sum of £80 has been raised by subscriptions to accord a fitting and proper reception for his majesty's fleet as in such cases the men were merely looked upon as so many units of his majesty's strength.

Seeing as the fishermen and poor people were left out in the cold regarding these entertainments, a number of prominent men in the town, including some of the town commissioners, started an opposition show and subscriptions were collected for the purpose of organising a fishermen's regatta. It was only when this fact became known that activity on the other side was more advertised, and not a little amusement was created by an up-to-date form of advertising in the shape of a person riding a bicycle through the town to which was attached a large card announcing the time and place of some sporting events in connection with the visit of the fleet.

As a counterblast to this, the opposition party sent out a bellman announcing the time and place of the fishermen's regatta for which substantial prizes were offered.

As the rain descended until late in the afternoon, neither sports could be brought off and a good deal of disappointment was caused to the townspeople whose curiosity had been raised to the highest pitch by the turn things had taken.

The excitement was very much increased when it was learned that posters had been displayed early in the morning at the principal points of observation in the town. The contents were as follow:

VISIT OF THE ATLANTIC FLEET
Grand display of West British Slavery

Irishmen should remember that they are Irishmen and leave the reception of the fleet to the garrison.

The English Navy is part of the system that is robbing and repressing the country. Why should Irishmen honour its visit? Now that the fishing industry has been practically killed in the town, the fleet comes for show and recruiting purposes. The visit of the fleet may circulate a few pounds in the district but how many thousands does the British government take out of it each year?

Arklow men and women should think on this and leave the fleet severely alone.

The police were despatched in all directions to remove this "seditious" announcement. In the warmth of their zeal, however, to fully carry out the order they, strange to say, overlooked for a considerable time, the [gate] piers at the barracks on which shone two posters to considerable advantage and were perused by passersby with the greatest interest long after they had been obliterated in other parts of the town.

In anticipation of vastly increased business, shopkeepers of all trades laid on an extra supply, but the stir in the town on Thursday was little more than ordinary, for whatever sailors visited the town had an overdose of coasting recently with consequently a diminished supply of money. Extra business will amount to little more than victualling the men.

The fleet anchored quite close to the pier head and shortly after they arrived they were reviewed by numbers of the townspeople and a few that had come in from the country, while the ss *Bobby Balfour* ran frequent journeys out for a nominal fare for a goodly number of the people in an interesting though not really enjoyable trip for the sea was inclined to be choppy.

Messrs Kynochs were considerate enough to give their employees a holiday so they might be impressed by the greatness of the British navy as represented by the eight ships[22] on view, and so that they might be further awed by a closer examination they placed the ss *Anglesey*[23] at their disposal.

A few months after this farcical nonsense, the *Wicklow People* highlighted something about which the Town Commissioners of all shades should have been more concerned: 'Want of a water supply – Most backward town in the county'.[24] Perhaps it was a timely reminder of why they were elected to office, because when a smaller flotilla of the royal navy returned exactly a year later, little fuss was made of it.[25]

*

In his book, *The Kynoch Era in Arklow, 1895-1918*, Hilary Murphy points out that the British government seemed determined from the start to put as many obstacles in the way of the new enterprise as possible. For example, when a new type of explosive was invented here, appropriately called Arkite, the company applied for a licence to manufacture it at both its Arklow and Essex plants. The Home Office agreed to its being made in England only. It took a hard battle for that decision to be overturned. Mercury chloride had been used in the making of munitions and the Arklow factory had to import this ingredient. To save costs, they decided to make their own. Whether by coincidence or something more underhand, the government banned its use shortly after. This was in 1906, and was perhaps the most serious blow to the future of the company. The company again cried that they would have to leave Arklow, but this time it was not a case of crying wolf. For once, the company management, the Harbour Commissioners and the Town Commissioners were united against the common enemy, the British Home Office. These combined strands of a united front resolved

> That we learn with wrath and indignation of the almost certain closing down of Kynochs, Arklow, brought about by the prosecution and persecution of Home Office officialdom, animated, we believe, by the old jealousy and hate of the Irish trade: and we deplore the wiping out of a great Irish industry all the more as taking place under the aegis of the Rt Hon Herbert Gladstone, whose father was a lifelong friend of Ireland, and we now call upon the Home Secretary to save Arklow from absolute ruin.

It is interesting that this crisis arose in 1906, shortly after the Conservatives had been ousted from power by the Liberals. Ironically, the Liberals had always been deemed to be more sympathetic towards Ireland than the Tories, but apparently not when it came to Kynochs Arklow. Again the close ties of the company with Tory governments might have prompted it. Both inside and outside the House of Commons, the Irish Party, under John Redmond, pressed their political bedfellows, the Liberals, to reconsider their attitude towards Kynochs Arklow. It was not until July 1907 that the Liberals backed down and the discriminatory actions against Kynochs Arklow were dropped.

Although this particular problem had been overcome, at least for the present, the Kynoch management could not be sure that similar obstacles would not be put in their way in the future. It was decided to develop their interests in the southern hemisphere, particularly in South Africa. As mentioned earlier, Kynochs had been exporting to long-haul destinations for some time, but shipping costs were making such exports uncompetitive. In late 1907, Arthur Chamberlain visited South Africa to investigate the potential for increased business and returned convinced that Kynochs should establish a new factory there. Not only would this be more likely to secure South African contracts, but it would also be easier to supply Indian, Australian and New Zealand markets. Umbogintwini, about fourteen miles from Durban, was chosen as the best location for the new factory and by the end of 1908 most of it had been built. By the summer of 1909 it had begun fulfilling its contracts.[26]

Several of the management team who oversaw the construction and preparation for production phases had been employed in the Arklow plant, but their names, with a few exceptions, would suggest that they were not locals. One of those exceptions was M.A.Troy, who may have been related to Thomas Troy who had done so much to get Kynoch & Co to set up in Arklow ten years earlier. The first Irishman to arrive in Umbogintwini was Mick Hayden, of River Lane, the foreman plumber responsible for all the pipework in the new factory. He arrived in early June 1908 ahead of the main groups.[27] The main Arklow interest in this enterprise were the twenty-two factory hands from the Arklow plant, most of whom were locals.

> They were called the Kelly Gang partly because there were four Kellys among them (John, Joe, Martin and Mike) and partly because they were 'wild Irishmen'. Every other cabin trunk had the initial 'K' painted on it. Besides the four Kellys there were three Kavanaghs and a Knott. Others in the party were Patrick James Cunningham, P. Murray, and H. White.[28]

They left Arklow in November, 1908. An estimated two thousand people turned up to see them off, creating a scene that must have puzzled the passengers who had boarded the train along the line between Wexford and Inch. So, while much of Ireland was still experiencing the phenomenon of the American Wake, Arklow had to be different with its South African Wake. The local '98 Brass Band were there to add their contribution, perhaps their most poignant piece being 'Come Back to Erin', in which the crowds joined in, knowing that it was unlikely that the emigrants would ever see Arklow or their families again.

These people left to start better lives for themselves, their children, and their descendants. They created a vibrant community that fostered the transposition of Irish cultural pursuits in a very un-Irish landscape. Like Irish emigrants throughout the world, they built a village school and a church, and played Irish games such as hurling. There was also golf. They left their indelible mark on that piece of South Africa, where the word Arklow is still an "Opensesame" to a mythical land which few of the present residents have ever visited. In 1975, two daughters of

Inside St Mary's (Courtesy of Pat Power)

W.V. Blewett visited the town of which they had heard so much. Their father had worked in the Arklow factory for some time before heading for South Africa.[29]

Not all had happy experiences, however. Michael Kelly was only twenty-three when he was killed in the first Umbogintwini explosion on December 7th, 1909, just a year after his arrival.

*

It was about this time that Arklow lost one of its most interesting buildings, the Protestant church of St Mary's in Main Street.[30] It had been built in the early years of the nineteenth century and was largely reconstructed in the 1820s. Throughout the century it had served its congregation well and, as parish church, had been at the centre of the street preaching debâcle in the 1890s. It was still serviceable and the reason behind its sudden disappearance from the streetscape is open to question. One explanation lies in an interesting piece of folklore.

Since its dedication in 1899, St Saviour's became the parish church of Arklow Protestants, but many of the parishioners, especially those who lived around Main Street and in the lower end of the town, failed to see why they should pass by the church they had attended since birth to go to the top of the town. This meant that St Saviour's was seldom as full as might have been expected. According to the story, Carysfort was less than happy with this situation. After all, he had personally funded this magnificent church and he considered the poor attendance an insult to him. When the lease on St Mary's came up for renewal (I stress that this tale is folklore and may have no basis in truth at all), Carysfort refused to extend it, with the result that St Mary's could no longer operate and was demolished, leaving its congregation no choice but to attend St Saviour's. It must not be forgotten that St Mary's had experienced major structural inadequacies within a decade or so of its original construction, and eighty years had passed since any major work had been carried out on it. It is highly likely that by the new century the building was passed its sell-by-date, and having two Protestant churches in a small town (and churches are notoriously expensive to maintain) simply made no sense. Whatever the reason, whether from petulance or sound fiscal thinking, the church of St Mary's was no more.

Much of the roof material was salvaged and re-used in the buildings which replaced it, and its memory its partly preserved in the letters CHURCH BUIL.[31]

*

One of the most important eras in the long history of this town came to an end in 1909. The Proby family had owned it for a century and a half, two centuries if the Allen ownership is included. As Earls of Carysfort they had been 'lords of the soil'. None had been so involved in the daily running of the town as the fifth and final earl, William Proby. His name has been prominent in the last few chapters, so it would be pointless to give a résumé of his life here. All that needs to be said at this juncture is that he died in 1909, leaving behind him a legacy of fine buildings and aborted dreams. He was one of the most complex, contradictory characters this town has ever known. As a young man, his genuine interest in the welfare of his tenants cannot be denied and should not be ignored. He was the epitome of the new breed of liberal landlord, the sort who recognised the power he had to do good. But when he changed, he changed utterly. He didn't turn into a rack-renting, evil-incarnate bully-boy, but his indifference to the physical needs of his tenants stood in stark contrast to his earlier concern. His disillusionment and apparent belief that the people deserved nothing more than the squalor in which they lived, might be understood - not justified, but understood – when it is remembered how many sneered at his plans for a model village, turning his vision into 'Cowld Town'. It also rankled him that, despite his best efforts on their behalf to develop the harbour, the people had supported Parnell, until they also turned on him with equal ingratitude. It is easy to see how Proby might consider such people beyond redemption, incapable of gratitude, unappreciative of goodwill. To read his obituaries in the *Wicklow People* and the *Wicklow Newsletter* is, like the accounts of the street preaching which he encouraged and supported financially, an exercise in journalistic spin. The *Newsletter* heaped praise upon praise on him, the *People* reminded everyone of his laudable early years as well as his 'feeling of repulsion towards his tenants' in later years.

William Proby left no children, but he did have a nephew, Douglas James Hamilton, a colonel in the Irish Guards.[32] In 1904, perhaps anticipating inheritance of the Glenart and Elton estates, Hamilton, his wife and children changed their name by royal licence to Proby. He came into the properties on William Proby's death, but he seldom visited Arklow.

*

The decade closed with two important events of a maritime nature. Ever since the storm of 1886, cries for the construction of a dock basin had been repeatedly made and work began on such a dock in 1907.[33] A 500 foot square site on the south bank of river was to be excavated and flooded and a small gap, or "dock gate", cut to allow access. A slip for the repair of vessels was to be incorporated in the southwest corner. The government body with responsibility for the development was the Board of Works, which had to work closely with the Harbour Commissioners. As in most such developments, problems arose right from the beginning with the main bone of contention being at what stage should the work be deemed complete. Even now the whole affair is remarkable for the degree of fudge, but it would appear that the Board of Works regarded the excavation, flooding and opening of the dock as all that was required of them. The Commissioners, however, felt that much more ancillary work was implicit in the agreement. They believed that a rectangular dock, with firm loading wharves around most of it, if not entirely around it, was what constituted a finished dock and they would not take over anything which fell short of that. By 1910, the north side of the dock, the one running parallel to the river, was in place, the earth having being cleared from it to a depth of some fifteen feet. The dock bed sloped from fifteen feet at the north side to a much shallower depth towards the south side. To get an idea of what this looked like, think of the small beach between the present slip and the RNLI station, but extend it the full length of the south side, with just the slip in the southwest corner. While this allowed reasonable berthage on the north side, berthing facilities decreased steadily towards the south. Also, little was done to erect wharves, except on the deep north side. As far as the Board of Works was concerned, Arklow dock was complete and ready to be handed over, suggesting May 4th as the official opening day. As far as the Harbour Commissioners were concerned, the job was only half done and they refused to accept the handover.[34] The Harbour Board demands were, I believe, perfectly reasonable. The catastrophe of 1886 had shown how inadequate a refuge the river was, and with the increased traffic in the port because of Kynochs and Parnell Quarries, it was vital for fishing boats and smaller trading vessels to have access to safe moorings and modern port facilities.

The argument between the two bodies continued and the stalemate was broken when the local schooner *Elizabeth Jane,* skippered by Michael Tyrrell of Bridge Street, became the first vessel to enter Arklow dock. There is a photograph in the harbour office commemorating this event, but there is no report of it having any official sanction. There was no fanfare, no ceremonial cutting of tape of any colour (not even red), no band, no partying. Even the two local newspapers, the *Wicklow People* and *The Wicklow Newsletter* failed to record this milestone in Arklow's maritime history. Even the Harbour Minute Books are silent on this great event. The thunder of minor politicians and civil servants had been stolen by the people who needed the dock most; the people to whom it was a vital necessity rather than a bone to snarl over.

Elizabeth Jane

That same year, 1910, also saw one of the strangest disasters in the Arklow fishing community when a freak storm blew up.

> ... although there was scarcely a breeze, the waves washed against the pierhead with a violence never seen before. In the midst of such conditions two boats – one belonging to Joseph Brown, the *Fisherlad,* and the other to Murtagh Somers, *Mary Immaculate* – left the river with their crews in high hopes, but ignorant however of the awful reality that for most of them, at least, it was to be their last journey to sea.[35]

The people of Arklow had lived with such tragedies since time immemorial and this occurrence served to remind them that, although some things were changing for the better, life for those who depended on the sea was precarious. Those ashore also had their dangers to life, and poverty and poor living conditions compounded these. Epidemics of one disease or another had been regular visitors to the streets and lanes of Arklow. Cholera, smallpox and typhus being among the most regular. It was the last named which struck the town in 1910 but, as it was to have lasting effects on the housing situation in Arklow, I will hold it over to the next chapter.

12

Kynoch-Arklow Ltd:
1911 - 1920

In 1910, the horrors of the 1866 cholera epidemic were recalled when typhus fever broke out, mainly attributable to the dire living conditions of the poor.

> The spectacle of the old horse-drawn ambulance was again seen passing through the streets, conveying patients to the fever hospital and, as in 1866, was sufficient to send pedestrians running in all directions in terror.[1]

Three extra nurses were brought in from the Mater Hospital in Dublin to help the Medical Officer, Dr Hamilton, and instructions were given that people suspected of having the disease were to be removed from their homes to the hospital immediately and their homes disinfected in their absence. All bedding and clothing were to be destroyed. And once again, the epidemic seems to have originated in the congested lanes of the Fishery.

> The lower part of the town in which the outbreak originated is in a very insanitary condition, the particular localities which came under my notice being Proby's Row, Bank Hall, Condren's Lane Lower, where the houses are generally without backyards or sanitary accommodation.
>   The local administration in Arklow is at a deadlock, consequent on the urbanisation of the town which took effect from 1st October 1910. The Urban District Council are without funds and, owing to the time of year at which they were separated from Rathdrum Rural District, they struck no rate for the current year.[2]

The Arklow Town Commissioners had been the local authority for many years prior to 1910, but they had little clout and were part of the Rathdrum Rural District. As the town grew in size and importance, it was realised that Arklow, like Bray and Wicklow before it, would have to be raised to the status of Urban District Council, giving it the power to raise some of its own revenues through rates. This would allow councillors to address some problems directly, and housing was the greatest problem of all. Dr Hamilton told a Local Government Housing Enquiry that 700 of the 1155 houses in the town should be knocked down as they were not fit to live in.

> Many of these 700 houses are only single-roomed and have no back yards or sanitary accommodation ... In River Lane, there are 42 houses with five or six people in each with only one room. I don't believe there is any town in the United Kingdom where there is a greater need for proper housing for the poorer classes than in Arklow.[3]

The typhus epidemic which caused such panic did not prove as devastating as the cholera epidemic of 1866, although several lives were claimed by it. Dr Hamilton believed that had it not been for the fever hospital, and the three nurses sent from the Mater, that the toll would have been much, much worse. But this was the twentieth century and it was scandalous that the housing conditions which gave rise to it could still prevail. Pressure groups such as workers' associations and tenants' organisations were formed to bring about better living conditions.[4] New houses had to be built and the hovels cleared away. As early as March 1910, seven months before their official urbanisation, the commissioners had instructed an architect to draw up plans for new houses on Coolgreaney Road. This new scheme was to become St Columba's Terrace and was only one of several to be built in a relatively short space of time, the others being St Patrick's Terrace and St Brigid's Terrace. It is interesting that among the objections to its construction was one lodged by Lady Carysfort, widow of William Proby who in his young days had dreamed of such development. She complained that £10,000 had recently been spent on the Lamberton entrance and the avenue to Glenart Castle, and that the proposed St Columba's Terrace would detract from it. She was afraid that there would be trespass from children and chickens and fences would be broken down. Her days of calling the shots were gone and the houses were built.

Providing modern, healthy housing wasn't sufficient in itself. There had to be a major change in the attitude of the people. Just as the Sisters of Mercy had tried to inculcate habits of cleanliness after the cholera epidemic, a new push was made to make the populace aware of the importance of personal and environmental hygiene. The key lay in education. Educating adults and older children had been a concern of Wicklow County Council since its establishment in 1898. In the winter of 1904-5 classes to teach cookery, laundrywork, dressmaking, building construction, carpentry and navigation were conducted, attracting a total of 132 students.[5] Such was its success that in June 1905, the council established the County Wicklow Joint Technical Instruction Committee to start formal classes in Wicklow town and Arklow.

There was no single location large enough for the purpose in Arklow, so the classes were conducted in various places around the town, such as the Convent of Mercy, courthouse, Marlborough Hall and a workshop owned by Mr L. O'Toole. Perhaps because of the dispersed nature of the enterprise, the plural form was used and named Arklow Technical Schools. Afternoon and evening classes were offered, with machine construction, carpentry theory, geometric drawing, freehand drawing, and mathematics being added to the list. The student numbers rose to 219, and each year saw an increase both in student numbers and range of subjects.

The advantages of education were obvious and Kynochs encouraged their employees to avail of the new opportunities offered. The two local earls, Carysfort and Wicklow, also supported the initiative, not only in encouraging their staffs to attend classes but also in presenting awards and prizes. By 1907, the Arklow Technical Schools had proved so successful that it was clear new, purpose-built premises were needed. In 1909, the County Council approved a grant application to that end on condition that the Department of Agriculture and Technical Instruction also gave a grant. The condition was met and plans for the new building were under way. The principal of the Arklow school was a qualified engineer named Richard Wake and he was appointed to draw the plans, which were to be submitted and appraised by a leading Dublin architect.[6] While this was in progress, classes continued as before with a new addition to the range of subjects offered - Sanitary Science. The typhus outbreak brought home the message that hygienic living was of vital importance to avoid a repetition. This course was attended by nurses, midwives, teachers, Urban District Council staff, undertakers, plumbers, and members of the RIC and their families.

A site on St Mary's Road was purchased for £100. Wake's plans met with full approval and were put on public display in the Marlborough Hall in April 1914. The tender to build the school was won by local firm T. & J. O'Toole and the school was completed by early summer 1915, at a cost of £2,909. The hunger for education can be seen not only in the number of students, but also in the fact that many volunteered their labour and saved £30 of the construction costs. One apprentice on the construction was John Corrigan, whose nephew James (Sé) Breen was to be the woodwork teacher in the school and its successor, Arklow Community College, for many years.

September 22nd, 1915 saw its official opening, performed by Lady Carysfort. It was a wonderful achievement in a town battling against poverty. The building was also something of a novelty in that it was lit by electricity produced by its own generator. It would be several decades before the town had its own supply.

Opening of Arklow Technical School, 1915 (Courtesy of Mae Greene)

It is poignant that one of the main advocates of the benefits of education didn't live to see the 'The Tech' open. Fr James Dunphy had been a monumental figure in the town's development between his becoming parish priest in 1877 and his death in November 1914, at the age of eighty-six. He had not limited his interests to his role of religious leader, but was always to the fore in any project he believed would bring material benefits to the town. He was autocratic, but many dynamic people are. His position as parish priest at that time would have strengthened his belief in his own sense of righteousness, but on the whole he used his power positively. The one dark cloud that hangs over his memory is his reaction to Parnell's part in the O'Shea divorce, and his consequent turning dog on those who remained loyal to Parnell. It is a major cloud and not one easily ignored, but it should not overshadow his lifetime's service to the community far beyond the call of duty.

*

Just as Arklow UDC was coming into being in 1910, Kynoch & Company decided it was time to concentrate on their English factories and the one in Umbogintwini, and to step back from the Arklow works. But the plant here was still doing well - the net trading profit for the previous year had been £73,047 - and instead of simply closing it, as they had threatened to do on so many occasions, they sold it to an Irish company. At least, they did on paper, for this "Irish company" was in fact a Kynoch subsidiary with the addition of two Irish directors, E.C. Walsh, chairman of Arklow Urban Council, and Stanley Harrington of Cork. This was Kynoch-Arklow Ltd. Part of the deal was that Kynoch-Arklow would get 430 acres of land, plus interest in another thirty acres in Kynochs' possession, plus the leasehold of the North Quay wharf. Also the new company would acquire all the parent company's mining explosives contracts south of the equator (except in Africa). It looked a reasonable deal, and the factory under this new management structure held its own throughout 1912 and 1913, but nobody could have predicted the boom time that lay ahead.

Just as the Boer War of 1899 had helped Kynoch & Company in their early years here, the outbreak of war in Europe was to prove the catalyst for what was arguably Kynochs' apogee in Arklow. Production of commercial explosives was put on hold as everything was geared towards the manufacture of munitions. Ireland, of course, was still ruled by Britain and was expected to fight Britain's wars. Even the Irish Party, whose MPs sat in Westminster, urged Irishmen to enlist in the British forces in the hope that Britain would show its appreciation by offering Ireland the political crumb of Home Rule when the war was over. John Redmond, leader of the Irish MPs, launched this recruiting campaign when he spoken to thousands gathered in a field at Woodenbridge on September 20th, 1914. He repeated the call over the coming months and it was answered to an astonishing degree, so much so that conscription was not extended to Ireland.

Many Arklowmen, urged by patriotism or unemployment, were among the many thousands who donned the uniform. The production of munitions at Kynoch-Arklow was deemed such an important contribution to the British war effort that employees were issued with exemption cards in case of conscription being introduced here. Kynoch workers were more valuable doing their jobs than being used as cannon fodder in the trenchs of Flanders Fields.

Even with the workforce thus protected, the increased demand for munitions necessitated a major recruitment drive. Many of those who had been unemployed in Arklow had enlisted in the army or the navy, making it necessary for Kynoch-Arklow to look further afield. Special trains were laid on to carry new employees from Wicklow and Rathdrum, from Wexford, Enniscorthy, Ferns, Camolin and Gorey. Another train was employed on the branch-line that joined Shillelagh to the mainline at Woodenbridge, picking up workers at Shillelagh (some of these having made their way from Carnew), Tinahely and Aughrim. Most of these new recruits were paid 3/7 per day (23 cent) for a six-day week. The company paid for the use of the trains, so travel for the workers was free, but within a year this led to an unforeseen complication. This daily commuting added three or four unpaid hours to the day for those who lived farthest from Arklow and after a few months it became evident that a significant number of those who travelled from Wexford were not prepared to work Saturdays under these conditions. Many of those who did turn up, did so for only half a day. Apart from the disruption to production schedules, this meant that the company was paying for Saturday trains that were not being economically used. Twenty-six of the most serious offenders were sacked, upon which about 700 of their countymen stormed out in protest. They demanded not only the re-instatement of the twenty-six, but also a pay rise that would bring them up to 4/6 (28 cent) per day, a twenty-two per cent increase, plus the dinner time to be doubled to one hour. The management gave in, except on the wage rise, and anyone who did not accept these terms was paid off.

It had been hoped that the poor industrial relations which had plagued Kynoch & Company would be greatly improved by having Irish directors and restructuring as Kynoch-Arklow Ltd but it hadn't worked out that way. The confidence gap remained unbridged and this latest episode caused the factory manager, Mr Gold, to comment that he could not employ undependable people. He claimed that a major contract had been lost because delivery could not be guaranteed. Even worse, plans to make Kynoch-Arklow into the largest munitions factory in the world had been abandoned. How much this latter assertion was hyperbole is open to question, but there is no doubt that the company's reputation for reliability had suffered a severe setback. Some of the County Wexford workers were taken back after they pleaded their cases that they had not been part of the strike, and their pledges of future good behaviour were accepted.

As the war proceeded, Kynoch-Arklow was invested with a great deal of power in the immediate area. Armed police, and later British soldiers, guarded the entrances to the plant and patrolled the vast site and environs. Patrol boats steamed up and down the bay. Gun emplacements were established at strategic points, such as on Spion Kop at the north end of the beach. When more troops were drafted in to protect this vital and vulnerable factory, the families of coastguard men were ordered to vacate the coastguard station at Seabank so that the soldiers could be accommodated there. To all intents and purposes, not only the factory but the entire town was placed under martial law for the duration of the war. Further disputes, strikes or negligent work practices would not be tolerated. Regulations controlling access to various departments within the complex were tightened and codes of practice strictly enforced. Any evidence of a worker having consumed or intending to consume alcohol, or having smoked or intending to smoke, was enough to carry severe penalties. A pipe or cigarette paper even without tobacco, a match or empty bottle, were grounds not only for dismissal but for criminal prosecution. The local newspapers recorded several cases of employees being sentenced at the local courts to a week's, two weeks', or a month's imprisonment in Wexford gaol.

Such precautions were merely commonsense in such a high risk industry. For some time past, metal fittings were replaced where appropriate. For example, workers in the danger houses were not permitted to wear the hobnailed boots prevalent at that time, because of the risk of metal-studded soles causing a spark on concrete floors. This regulation provided a type of work more common in Holland than on the Irish east coast, wooden clog making. The location of this 'cobbler in wood' is remembered in the name Clogg Alley off Seaview Avenue.

Wooden dowels, or trenells (i.e. tree-nails), were used in the construction of boxes used to transport explosive products, rather than nails or screws, for the same reason. Brass or other non-sparkable metal was used where necessary. Given all these measures, and the constant urging for safety awareness, it is difficult to understand, or have sympathy with, the mentality of those who breached the anti-smoking or anti-drinking regulations in such an environment. There was plenty of time to smoke and drink when the work shift was at an end, and those who had enough intelligence to control themselves in working hours lost no time in quenching their thirst in the proper places. It is said that the bar staffs in the various pubs had the expected rush timed to perfection, with creamy-headed pints set up on the bar, the final settling just finishing as the doors swung open.

Even the publicans were controlled by the dictates of Kynoch-Arklow, or by the military commander for the area. For example, every publican in town had to accommodate three soldiers each. Even more significant was the following notice issued by the military commander in Ireland

> Whereas the firm of Kynoch-Arklow Ltd. is engaged in carrying out important government contracts, and whereas it has been brought to my notice that the indiscriminate issue of liqour to the employees of the company by licensed houses in Arklow, the working capacity of the said employees has suffered, thereby affecting the power of the company to fulfil their contracts, I, Major-General L.B. Friend, C.B., Commanding the Troops in Ireland, hereby warn all owners of public houses in the urban district of Arklow that should reports of excessive sale of liqour be proved the houses implicated will be closed under the Defence of the Realm Regulations.[7]

To restrict such 'excessive sale of liqour', the licencing hours were greatly curtailed. Pubs could open from noon to 2p.m. (later revised to 10 a.m. to 2 p.m.) and from 5 p.m. to 10 p.m.

The fishermen were also affected by the arbitrary control of the government-run factory. They were not allowed to leave or enter the port in hours of darkness, nor could they fish within five miles of the shore. This was a major impediment to making their living from an already precarious occupation, as most winter fishing was of an inshore nature.

By 1916, the cost of special daily trains was proving too great and the company decided instead to erect basic accommodation facilities for non-Arklow workers around the site. To call them hostels would be to bestow on these huts a connotation of cleanliness and comfort they did not deserve. Local lore has it that

> the beds in these huts were never cold because as one set of men went on shift-work another came back to occupy their beds. The huts were so crowded that a rope was placed along one wall so that the men could hang on to it while sleeping on their feet.[8]

This greatly increased activity stretched the harbour facilities to breaking point. Arklow was an important fishing port, its trading fleet had continued to grow in importance and now Kynoch-Arklow had steamers and sailing vessels entering and leaving on almost every tide. Had the new dock not opened in 1910, much of this harbour movement would have ground to a halt. Carters were in constant use, carrying goods from the harbour to the town and outlying districts and vice versa. To ease this traffic congestion, an overhead cable was erected across the river. Buckets capable of holding seven hundredweight of goods, such as coal and timber, were attached to this conveyor-belt system and constantly traversed the river. The south terminal stood near the old lifeboat house, about halfway between the dock and the pierhead, while the north terminal was more or less straight across. The war, it seems, had its benefits. Between 1914 and the cessation of hostilities four years later, Kynoch's steamers crossed the Irish Sea 2,700 times carrying 350,000 tons of cargo. All this activity generated £689,000 in wages, most of it going into the immediate local economy. The vast site had been built on continuously, so that by the time peace was declared there were more than four hundred buildings, ranging from major constructions to small wooden huts, a canal system, roads and thirty-seven miles of tram lines. No wonder the word 'Kynochs' was to become embedded in the Arklow psyche and was to remain an invisible reality long after it had been wiped from the landscape.

*

Dominant and domineering though Kynochs was during those years, there were other things happening in Arklow. The ten-yearly census was taken in 1911 and makes interesting reading. The first government census taken in Ireland was in 1821. Over the decades the range of questions widened so that census returns are now prime sources for the historian and genealogist. In many countries, census returns must be at least one hundred years old before they are open to researchers, but because so many of Ireland's records have been destroyed by war and mishap, the 1901 and 1911 census returns have been available to the public for many years.[9] One striking aspect when comparing the ages of older people in the 1901 and the 1911 returns is the discrepancy of ages. For example, if someone was recorded as being fifty-eight in 1901, we should expect to find that person to be sixty-eight ten years later, but this is seldom the case. It was not the result of vanity knocking off a few years, because in most cases the people seem to claim they were *older* than they really were if we take the 1901 ages as correct. Why? The first Old Age Pension scheme was introduced in 1908 and under its provisions, applicants could receive up to 5/- (32c) per week, as long as they had reached the age of seventy. As civil registration of births was not introduced until 1864, anyone in their sixties in 1908 could say they were seventy or over and there was no documentary proof to show otherwise. Therefore, to qualify for the pension, many people added the necessary years to their ages, causing wide-ranging discrepancies between their ages as recorded in the 1901 census and those recorded in the 1911 census. So, a fifty-eight year old in 1901 was more likely to be seventy-three or four in 1911 than sixty-eight. It was a nationwide phenomenon and Arklow people were just as eager as everyone else to take advantage of whatever additional income they might lay claim to.

*

Life at sea, whether trading or fishing, had always been hazardous, but in times of war even greater dangers were added to the scales.

Germany's development and use of submarines – *unterseeboot* or u-boat – made a devastating impact not only on British navy ships, but also on merchant vessels flying the red ensign. Several Arklow schooners became casualties of the conflict. The *James Postlethwaite, Kestrel* and the *Vindex* were in Hamburg when war was declared in 1914. They were commandeered and used as barges on the Elbe for the duration.[10] Others, such as *Jane Williamson, Detlef Wagner, Ethel, Jewel, Twig,* and *Violet* were sunk. One of the most poignant of these was the *Lapwing*. She sank with the loss of all hands after hitting a mine off the Suffolk coast in 1917. Among the victims were the master Joseph Kearon and his two sons Edward and George.[11] They lived in 'Kylemore' near St Saviour's church.

The crews of the Arklow fishing boats *Elizabeth* and the *Dan O'Connell* experienced the ravages of war in a most unusual way. In May 1915, Arklow fishermen were again following the fishing seasons and were operating around Kinsale in county Cork. On the 15th of the month, the liner *Lusitania* was torpedoed just a few miles off the Old Head of Kinsale with the loss of 1,129 lives. Edward White and James Hagan, captains of the *Elizabeth* and *Dan O'Connell* respectively, immediately put to sea. Hagan's boat was the first to reach the survivors, about forty of them in one of the *Lusitania's* lifeboats. He put one of his men on board to pilot them safely ashore while he headed towards the wreck area.

> ... such a scene was impossible to describe. There were about twelve boats picking up the living and the dead while the first boats were returning to land survivors.[12]

This rescue work was impeded by the royal naval tug *Stormcock.*

> Edward White, the skipper of the *Elizabeth*, was off the harbour mouth of Kinsale when Commander Shee of the *Stormcock* halted him and ordered him to hand over his survivors. White protested, as did Jimmy Hagan of the *Dan O'Connell,* that there were others waiting for rescue at sea. Some of the women on board, said White, were in a bad way; he wanted to get them to Kinsale as quickly as possible. But Shee threatened "If you don't stop we shall sink your boat". The *Elizabeth's* boat from the *Lusitania* was taken in tow by the Stormcock which headed back for Queenstown. Not only had time been wasted, White reckoned, but lives would be lost by the *Stormcock's* action.[13]

This event and the role played by these Arklowmen is commemorated with a special display in the Arklow Maritime Museum.

*

One of the main elements to endow Kynochs with an almost mythical status in this community was 'The Explosion'. Like everyone else who grew up here – even decades after the factory had closed – I heard scraps of half-remembrances and hand-me-down accounts of that horrific event. There had been fatal accidents prior to this; one in 1910 which killed two workers pushing a bogey containing ten boxes of Arkite paste; a small explosion killed two more the following year; and two buildings near Spion Kop were blown to bits in 1915. Admittedly, the 1917 blast was by far the worst, but nonetheless it should not be mythologised.

On the night of September 20th/21st , 1917, about two hundred men and twelve girls were working the night shift. At about half past three, the guard at the main gate was changed and Pte Richard Craig of the Munster Fusiliers began his watch that was scheduled to end at six. Within fifteen minutes of his taking up his station, a brilliant flash lit up the countryside, followed in a second or two by a deafening explosion. Townspeople were thrown from their beds, windows were shattered and the blast could be heard up to twelve miles away. Fr Purfield, a local curate, dressed as quickly as he could and hurried towards the factory. Scores of people, many still in their night clothes, were running across the bridge, frantic for news of relatives and friends.

When they reached the scene, they were confronted by a horrifying spectacle. Several bodies lay in varying degrees of mutilation. Clothes and boots had been blown off and lay scattered among the myriads of broken glass. Four huts, each housing men mixing nitroglycerine and guncotton, had exploded. Three of the huts had vanished completely, leaving only a crater where they had stood. The fourth was a broken shell. A search was made through the rubble for more bodies, several were discovered. The injured, some horribly so, were taken to the factory's small hospital.[14] With the coming of dawn, the searchers began removing the debris, including the pieces of flesh which was all that remained of some of the victims.

What had happened? No one knew, but an inquest was set for the following day.

Colleagues, relatives and friends of the dead and injured filled the large recreation hall in the factory grounds where the inquest was to be held. The building was unable to accommodate all the on-lookers and many were forced to follow the proceedings by looking and listening through the windows. At the head of the room sat two company directors and the representative of the Home Office, Major Cooper Key. The company manager, Mr Udal, stated that he first heard a hissing or tearing sound followed by three distinct reports only a fraction of a second apart. It could, he felt have been an attack from the sea, the shoreline being only a few hundred yards away and u-boats had been active in this area. In fact, a u-boat sank the *South Arklow* lightvessel on March 28th that year, just six months before the explosion in Kynochs.[15] Cooper Key was disinclined to accept that theory as he felt the time factor between the first and third reports would have been longer than a fraction of a second had shells been fired from the deck gun of a submarine from a reasonable distance, say four thousand yards. Both Pte Craig, who had been on guard duty at the main gate which was in close proximity to the scene of the explosion, and George Harvey, captain of the patrol boat in the bay, also believed an attack had not been made from the sea. To make things more confused, other witnesses maintained that the lights of a car had been seen in the vicinity just before the explosion. A buzzing, drumming sound in the air was also heard.

But couldn't the explosion have been caused inside the factory?

Several reliable witnesses testified that all safety precautions had been adhered to. One foreman had been in the ill-fated houses fifteen minutes before the blast and he had seen nothing to indicate lax security measures. It was pointed out that for some weeks before the catastrophe several employees had been found in possession of matches on the premises, but Mr Udal was quick to counter that no one in the danger houses had ever ignored these particular regulations. With such lack of hard evidence and plethora of conflicting opinions, a verdict of unknown causes was returned.[16]

A total of twenty-seven men were killed that night. In Arklow cemetery, an Irish yew tree stands near the monument which commemorates those who died in the explosion. Their names, ages, and places of residence show how important Kynoch-Arklow was to the general area and not just the town. Of the twenty-seven victims only four were from Arklow. Two were from Blessington, two from Tinahely, two from Hacketstown, two from Shillelagh, two from Enniscorthy, and one each from Wicklow, Dalkey, Knockananna, Gorey, Craanford, Ballycanew, Cronebeg, Woodenbridge, Rathdrum, Barniskey, Redcross, and one from county Cork. Oddly, the monument lists only twenty-six names.

Kynoch memorial, Arklow cemetery

The deaths of twenty-seven young men in such frightening circumstances was bound to leave an effect on the town in general and on the factory in particular. The question which played on everyone's mind was: what would have been the outcome had the explosion taken place at half past three in the afternoon, when the full workforce was milling about that area? How many hundreds would have died? How many maimed for life? It did not bear thinking about. But life goes on. Food must be put on the table, bills must be paid and concerns of what-might-have-been were luxuries few could afford. As long as the war lasted, production targets had to be met. As long as wages were offered, worries had to be reined in.

The story of the explosion was planted in the fertile soil of local lore where it grew lavishly. After a few decades many who heard about it at firesides or public house counters got the impression that the bulk of the factory had been devastated, and that Kynochs had little option but to bring down the curtain on this tragic finale. But that is not the case. The factory was back in production within a day or two.

As the early months of 1918 passed and success for the British and Americans seemed increasingly inevitable, production targets at Kynoch-Arklow would have to be revised with consequent reduction in the workforce. This was a worrying enough aspect, especially as other local industries such as fishing and the Parnell Quarries had recently reduced employment numbers. The town of Arklow, with its urban and rural population of 8,000, depended on the munitions factory to a frightening degree. All the fiscal eggs were in one basket and that basket was heading for very uncertain times. When the company made its announcement, it was worse than anyone had feared. It was not a case of reduction, but one of closure.

It was soon obvious that this was no strategic threat, used as a cynical ploy in the never happy management/worker relationship. The plug was going to be pulled, no doubt about that, but the speed with which the process was planned and executed surprised everyone. By March 1,500 workers were to be let go. The parent company in Birmingham cited running costs as the main problem. Everything was dearer in Arklow. In England, coal was £1 (1.27 euro) per ton compared to £1-15-0 (2.22 euro) in Arklow and the Arklow plant required 1,000 tons per week. Wage costs were also higher in Arklow, but this was due to a combination of factors, including the lower ratio of women to men in the Arklow factory. Elsewhere women were employed at much lower rates than men to do the work carried out by men in the Arklow plant. This situation had largely come about because many of Kynochs male employees in England were overseas.

These commercial concerns were valid, and were probably serious enough to close the factory by themselves. But one of the main reasons for the closure was prompted by politics, not economics. Since the 1916 Rising, and especially since the release of internees from Frongoch and other camps, the rise of Sinn Féin, and the growing demands for Britain to honour its pre-war pledges of Home Rule for Ireland, were inexorably leading to a situation in which the British government could not allow an important munitions and explosives factory to remain in operation in Ireland. Kynoch-Arklow had served its purpose in the war years, but it was no longer essential and may now prove more trouble than it was worth.

Needless to say, the people who depended on it were not prepared to let it go so easily. Just as in 1895, workers, management, town fathers, religious leaders, commercial and business people all raised their voices in the demand for the factory to be retained. This time, however, they were not successful. The best concession they could get was a phased closure over two years, but the vast bulk of the employees were let go within months. The factory closed in 1918, after twenty-three years. Only twenty-three years, and yet over eighty years after it ceased production, students of local history continually choose

Kynochs as a theme for school projects. Arklow Pottery, which shall be dealt with in due course, lasted sixty years; NET/IFI was in operation for almost forty years, and I have never been asked for information for school projects on either of these factories. Kynochs is not only part of our history, it has become part of our mythology.

*

The rise of Sinn Féin and the movement towards political independence was cited as one of the reasons for the demise of Kynochs.

Maria Curran

The Rising of 1916 seemed to have little effect on life in Arklow, but the execution of its leaders and the general turning of the tide towards independence could be seen here as elsewhere. Yet it was the more local issue of the closure of Kynochs, and the resultant plunging of the town's economic future into the depths, that prompted political attitudes to harden. The general election of 1918 saw a landslide victory for Sinn Féin and the following year the first Dáil sat in what is now the National Concert Hall in Dublin. This national trend was reflected in Arklow Urban District Council. On January 15th, 1920, Sinn Féin member, and former member of Cumann na mBán, Maria Curran became one of the first women councillors in the country and her appointment to the chair made her the first female council chairman in Ireland.[17]

Her appointment not only reflects her strength of character and the respect with which she was regarded by her fellow councillors, but also the shade of politics of the majority of the members. This is further shown by a resolution passed on March 19th, 1920.

> That this Council hereby acknowledge the authority of Dáil Éireann as the duly elected government of the Irish people and undertake to give effect to all decrees duly promulgated by the said Dáil Éireann insofar as same effects this Council, and that copies of this Resolution be

forwarded to the Republican Minister for Foreign Affairs for transmission
to the Governments of Europe and the President and Chairman of the
Senate and House of Representatives of the U.S.A.

This was heady stuff. Sinn Féin's establishing the Dáil was not
recognised by the British government and was, by British law, a
unilateral declaration of independence – an act of treason. Arklow
UDC's recognition of the authority of the Dáil was also treasonous. The
RIC regularly demanded the minute books of the council, no doubt
hoping to find statements for which councillors could be charged with
sedition. To thwart such inspection, on at least one occasion, Maria
Curran hid the book in the chapel belfry.

Britain could not envisage such wanton disregard of her authority.
Irish nationalists had no intention of stopping their movement towards
independence. It was the old story of the immoveable object and the
irresistible force. Violence would soon erupt and the country thrown
into a state of war and Arklow would not be immune.

There was a local IRA unit in Arklow. Although Kynochs was no
longer producing explosives, there were some stock piles which had to
be guarded by a military detachment and a skeleton workforce. On at
least two occasions the meagre defences were breached. In February
1920, two and a half hundredweight of gelignite was taken in a raid,
and in the following November thirteen hundredweight of TNT was
taken, and much of the remaining stock destroyed by emersion in the
river. No one was hurt on either occasion.[18] But dangerous times lay
ahead.

13

Statehood and Stagnation:
1920 - 1960

It is difficult to imagine the effects the closure of Kynochs had on Arklow. Despite its many faults, the company's presence greatly benefitted the town. Words and phrases such as 'disastrous', 'an outrage' bringing 'starvation to thousands of people', appeared in the local papers. As in all cases of factory closure, especially major industries, the ripples extended far beyond the factory walls. Small suppliers whose main business had been with Kynochs also folded. Hauliers, dockers and all other ancillary enterprises were hit drastically. The ranks of the unemployed swelled and for many there was little option but to head for England or America. The poverty that had been masked to some extent by 'Cordite' wages was now as stark and as frightening as it had ever been. Between 1910 and 1919, Arklow Urban District Council had built 112 houses[1], but this laudable attack on poor housing would also suffer. Kynochs had been by far the area's biggest ratepayer. Its closure meant a devastating blow to public coffers and the much needed urban renewal would have to wait.

Life was made even more stressful and depressing by the deteriorating political situation. British troops, augmented by Black and Tans, indiscriminately searched homes in reprisal for activities such as the raids on Kynochs. Some of these searches were carried out without too much vindictiveness, but other officers and soldiers were not so particular. As is common, instances of heavy-handedness achieved little except to harden people's resolve. Instead of crushing resistence it encouraged it. The following is a brief outline of the uneasy state of Arklow in the early 1920s.

On December 28th, 1920 a large force of military personnel and police surrounded the houses in Abbey Street and made a thorough search of every building. Despite the raid lasting 'a considerable time', nothing suspicious was found, but one of the residents, William Cleary, was taken into custody, brought to Wicklow gaol and later transferred to Dublin. Other arrests had been made in the preceding weeks. Some of these detainees had been released after a short while, but others, like Cleary, were taken to Wicklow gaol. One description of a less hostile house raid was that of Thomas Furlong's home:

> Presses were scrutinised and drawers and beds examined, as was also a statue of the Blessed Virgin. Pictures and photographs taken away, including some snaps of friends in America. As well as a newspaper and some old copies of 'Nationality', as well as some books and receipts of the I.N.G.W.U. Dennis Keogh, who happened to be in the house at the time, was arrested. Furlong said that the officer in charge was very courteous and allowed Mrs. Furlong and family to move about unmolested.[2]

Not all searches were carried out so cordially. Some of the these were for arms, others for people who were on the run, but no specific reason was needed. For example,

> On Wednesday evening about 6 p.m. they [the military] raided the pub of J. O'Rafferty and ordered him to close the premises until further notice. When he asked why, he was simply told that it was ordered by the competent military authority. As far as is known, Mr. Rafferty is not active in politics, and the only apparent reason for the closure is the fact that three young men were arrested there some weeks ago.[3]

On January 25th, armed men robbed the railway station but got little for their efforts as the day's takings had already been banked.

Military raids on homes continued throughout February, most without success, but in one garden on Harbour Road forty-seven sticks of gelignite were found and the owner of the house, John English, arrested. These were probably part of the fruits of the raid on Kynochs some months earlier. Mr English appeared before a courtmartial at Kilmainham courthouse. He was a sailor and was able to prove that he had been away and could not have taken part in the raid and denied all knowledge that his garden had been used as a place to hide the explosives. After fifteen minutes consideration, the court found him not guilty.[4]

In March J. O'Rafferty again had his premises closed and was taken into custody and not released until June. Mickey Greene of Abbey Street was arrested in April, as were many others. One of these was sixty-year-old Martin Stankard of Ferrybank. His crime would appear to have been that he was collecting rates for the UDC. As has been pointed out, Arklow UDC was republican in its political complexion and several of its resolutions had not endeared it to the British authorities. One way of bringing pressure to bear on it was to starve it of finance. Despite his claims of ill-health and his belief that he would not survive imprisonment, Stankard was arrested after only two days as rate collector. His job was taken by Paul Frith who was also lifted within a few days of his appointment.

> The council are again faced with the problem of getting in money to keep the essential services going. The last six months has seen: William Butler, who held the position for years, resign owing to difficulty about commission and lodgements; Mr. D. Keogh held the position for a few days then resigned as he could get no lodgings in the town; Martin Stankard also resigned after two days owing to the reaction of the authorities and the fact that his health could not allow him to undergo prison treatment. When he was arrested last week, Mr. Hurley, though appointed, declined to act; Mr. Frith was elected. The result is that there is a balance of uncollected rates from last year of over £1,400, while the collection for the present half-year has hardly even commenced.[5]

May saw an escalation of republican activity, with another hold-up of the mail train at Woodenbridge, but by far the most serious event was the ambush of a military patrol just south of Inch, when an auxiliary constable was shot dead and a sergeant badly wounded.

In July, Glenart Castle was targeted. The only occupants at that time were the caretakers, Mr. & Mrs. Ralph Prestage. At the inquest in October, Prestage stated that he locked up as usual on Saturday night and discovered the blaze at 6.30 the following morning. He raised the alarm.

> ... a fire in the central hall burnt itself out, but another fire under the grand staircase was unfortunately more successful and practically all the new portion of the castle was burnt out ... The 5th Earl spent enormous sums on the castle, practically rebuilding it and it was one of the finest

houses in Ireland ... There had been the most beautiful and valuable furniture ...[6]

Some of the furniture was 'saved by superhuman efforts of police [and] military'. Fortunately, many of the paintings, some of which were 'of national importance', had been removed before the fire to the main Proby estate at Elton for safe keeping. In September, Colonel Proby claimed damages of £51,000 and the following month a judgement for £37,000 for damage to the house and £9,000 for the furniture was made at Wicklow Quarter Sessions.

Glenart Castle: the portion with the bay windows was the part of the castle most badly damaged by the fire in July, 1921 (National Library of Ireland)

Ironically it was the day after Glenart Castle was set on fire that a truce between the republican army and the British came into effect. Britain realised that its forces could not defeat the IRA any more than the Republicans could beat the British army. The truce was a hiatus in which hope for a negotiated settlement was real, but nevertheless both the British and the IRA continued to plan for extended war just in case agreement could not be reached. According to Frank O'Connor, Michael Collins ordered his men to strengthen their numbers and to train harder than ever before. He also organised bigger and better gun-running, and during August the first shipload of arms reached Arklow.[7]

IRA men could now walk around in uniform without fear of arrest. One encounter reported by the *Wicklow People* in September sums up that rather strange time of non-war.

[an] exchange of compliments took place at Woodenbridge a few evenings ago. Some of the Arklow police who were travelling in the vicinity met an officer of the IRA who was accompanied by a lady. The police saluted the officer which was very becomingly returned. He was in uniform.[8]

The Arklow brigade of the IRA (Courtesy Liam Charlton)

In November, to mark the fifty-fourth anniversary of the execution of the Manchester Martyrs[9], a procession 'much larger and far more striking than anything that has been seen in the town was held in Arklow'.[10] The newspaper report told of 'hundreds' of members of the IRA from Arklow and the outlying districts. A large concourse of men and women joined the procession making it increasingly bigger. In front was a memorial banner followed by the Ancient Order of Hibernians brass band, accompanied by torch bearers. The colourful turnout marched through Main Street to the 'Dead March' and to the 'Soldier's Song' on the return journey.

> It all went off without the slightest hitch and with the greatest order and decorum.

That such an event could take place without harassment or rioting was greatly to be welcomed, but it begs the question, where were all these 'hundreds of members of the IRA' before the truce was called?

*

One non-political event which took place in 1921 must be mentioned, the opening of the Countess of Wicklow Memorial Hospital. The hospital had been part of the Kynochs complex and used mainly for accident victims on site. It contained a male and female ward, accommodating twelve beds. The building was lit by electricity supplied by a five horse power engine and

> being rigged out with every necessary requisite it forms on the whole an admirable concern and one which supplies a long felt need.[11]

Rev Coster was Honorary Secretary and he opened the proceedings as follows:

> I wish to initiate our proceedings by making a brief statement to your Lordship *[i.e the Earl of Wicklow]* as to the memorial Hospital which is to be opened today. It was felt by us all that the memory of Lady Wicklow must be preserved in Arklow whose people loved her and whom she loved so well. When it came to choose a worthy memorial we decided that it would be best to carry out a project which we had in long view and try to establish a cottage hospital for the benefit of the people of this locality. Accordingly, money has been gladly given by rich and poor for this purpose. In the neighbourhood of Arklow itself about £1,000 has been gathered - £500 from the proceeds of a bazaar and nearly as much from the people. Lady Wicklow's private friends gave about £2,500 more and you, my Lord, and your family have added about £3,000 as a nucleus of an endowment fund.

The Countess of Wicklow Memorial Hospital which served Arklow from 1921 to its closure in July 1961 (Courtesy Pat Power)

We have been able to get an excellent site and purchase buildings formerly in the possession of Messrs Kynochs for a reasonable sum. Then we have had many special gifts. The friends of the late Captain Higgins gave us £66 which has been subscribed to his memory to help in the equipment of our little operating theatre and our surgery. Hospital appliances and furniture have been given to us by the authority of the Duke of Connaught's hospital, Princess Patricia's hospital, Mrs. Earnest Gince's(?) hospital and the Red Cross hospital in Lower Mount Street, so that we are able to make a start with all the equipment. I should like to add that we do so with the goodwill of the local clergy of all denominations and also of the local doctors. We were able to secure the services of Miss Deacon as our first matron.[12]

It was perhaps the only positive development in the town at that time.

*

Politics were the main concern. The Treaty bringing an end to the war with Britain and establishing a twenty-six county Free State and a six county Northern Ireland was ratified by the Dáil on January 6th, 1922. A provisional government was established to run the country until elections could be held. The voting to accept or reject the proposed Treaty was narrow, sixty-four votes for and fifty-seven against, and it was soon apparent that men who had fought side-by-side in the cause of an independent all-Ireland republic were forming into two factions. The pro-Treaty party saw the Free State as a stepping stone to full independence, while the anti-Treaty party considered it a sell-out.

The majority of County Wicklow farmers and other groups, such as the Rathdrum Board of Guardians, supported the Treaty. The *Wicklow People* was strongly behind it and claimed that there was 'unmistakeable evidence' that the ratification met with 'unqualified approval'.

The benefits of the brief period of peace were soon evident. Wicklow gaol, so long the manifestation of British retribution in the county, was taken over by the IRA in February and the Arklow barracks was likewise handed over soon after. The *Wicklow People* recorded the Arklow changeover in the following words:

> The first indication of the impending historic change in the administration of the government of the people was the arrival in the town of six large motor lorries which were accompanied by an armoured car which arrived from Dublin and passed into the barracks yard.[13]

The local IRA men, led by Comdt Green, Lt John Kavanagh (who had fought in Dublin in 1916 and was now just released from his latest period of imprisonment to a hero's welcome[14]) and Adjutant Andrew Kavanagh, took formal possession of the barracks a short time later. At three o'clock that afternoon the lorries containing the departing RIC moved out of the barracks yard. Two IRA officers representing HQ staff had come down from Dublin for the official handing over and when one of them learned that the evacuation caused moving difficulties for Inspector Daly's family, he placed his motor car at their disposal. The Tricolour was hoisted on the flagstaff, replacing the Union Jack, a task in which some RIC men assisted. When all was ready, twelve IRA men were drawn up outside the gates and as the lorries filed passed they presented arms in salute to their former adversaries, a salute which the police 'respectfully and generously' returned. A large crowd had been gathering all day to watch this passing of the last vestige of British authority in the town, and the departure of the RIC was witnessed

in respectful silence. There was no cheering on their part, neither was

there any incident to mar the harmony which characterised the entire
proceedings connected with this historic event.[15]

For the next several months the new incumbants of the barracks carried
out policing duties in the town, making arrests where necessary and
taking suspects before the newly constituted court. Most of the charges
were run-of-the-mill, such as those against three young men who stole
half a barrel of stout from a pub. They were sentenced to a month's
hard labour in Mountjoy. A pogrom against Catholics in the North
prompted the boycott of northern goods this side of the border, and the
local IRA policed the railway station to make sure than no northern
products were brought into the town. There were also more serious
matters to contend with, such as several armed robberies from railway
stations and from the mail cars of trains at Woodenbridge and the Kish.[16]

As an *ad hoc* situation, it seemed to work reasonably well, but the
deteriorating relationship between the pro- and anti-Treaty factions was
becoming more pronounced throughout the country. On April 9th, the
anti-Treaty Republicans appointed an Executive, thereby breaking away
from the pro-Treaty Free Staters. Four days later, under Liam Mellowes
and Rory O'Connor, they took possession of the Four Courts in Dublin
in defiance of the majority pro-Treaty faction. The Arklow battalion also
showed divided loyalties. Some of the men approved of the Treaty as
the best deal they could hope for in the interim, others felt that even if
they did not like what the Treaty offered, it had been ratified by the Dáil
and, as soldiers, it was their duty to support it. Others felt that they had
fought for too long to achieve a thirty-two county republic to accept
anything less.

The anti-Treaty Arklow IRA men took exclusive possession of the
barracks, leaving the pro-Treaty men little option but to vacate it and
move into the coastguard station at Seabank. John Kavanagh, who had
been hailed as a hero by all just three months earlier, had sided with
the coastguard station group and within a week of the split he was shot
in the leg by an erstwhile comrade from the barracks group.[17] It was
this, and similar events, which prompted neutrals to take a stand. On
Monday April 24th, the secretary of the local trade union and UDC
member, Charlie Gaule, addressed a large meeting on Parade Ground
asking for the factions to stop and think.

It is deplorable to read daily accounts of young men who had fought gallantly against the common enemy during the reign of terror, now faced each other as deadly enemies. Even in our town we have seen young Irishmen shooting at one another ... The IRA had done magnificent work in ridding the country of the Tans, but now that work is accomplished and it is up to the politicians. They, as usual, have failed and are now producing an atmosphere of further bloodshed ... Thousands upon thousands of workers are unemployed. Business is at a standstill and things will not get better until the political crisis is over. Many Arklow families are living within bare walls without furniture that has long seen its way to the pawnshop.[18]

As if to support Gaule's words, the same paper also told of how a grant of £2,000 from government for unemployment relief works would supply seventy men with two months work. Within a short time, there were 350 applicants for the jobs and that number was expected to climb much higher. Such practical concerns, however, seemed to matter little to the political ideologists.

On April 14th, the *Wicklow People* reported that half way through a case concerning the theft of trees from the Glenart estate, the IRA Adjutant Andrew Kavanagh asked the political leanings of the court chairman. It was, he said, supposed to be a Republican court with a Republican judge, but the chairman had expressed himself a Free Stater. When the chairman said that his political view had nothing to do with the court, Kavanagh ordered his men outside. With this absence of the police, the case was dismissed.

That same week had seen an even more ominous development. A train carrying hundreds of people left Dublin to hear Michael Collins, the pro-Treaty leader and commander-in-chief of the Free State forces, speak in Wexford. During the preceding night, two rails had been removed from the track at the bridge at Ballyraine. It was discovered at eight o'clock that morning and the alarm raised. When a repair crew arrived at the scene, they were confronted by several armed men who confiscated the tools and threw them into the river. The Arklow station master telegraphed the Woodenbridge station and the train was halted there. A Mr Murphy, who was on board the train, telegraphed the station master at Arklow requesting him to ask the officer commanding the Arklow IRA to allow the repairs to be carried out. This mysterious Mr Murphy seems to have been confident that his request would be agreed to, for without awaiting confirmation the train proceeded slowly from Woodenbridge reaching the scene of trouble at about the same time as the Arklow IRA officer, who had indeed ordered the work to recommence. At this stage it was noticed that a number of men armed with rifles had taken up a position close to the line. Despite this, the work was completed and just as the train was about to continue on its way, some of the armed men approached one of the carriages and took one of the male passengers off. They made him kneel and forced him to retract a remark he was accused of having made. It was a very strange affair, but apparently more entertaining than frightening – except for the man taken from the train – because 'During the morning a large crowd of Arklow folk visited the scene'.

Throughout May and June the town continued to have two policing agencies, one in the barracks and one in the coastguard station, each more concerned with the activities of the other than in protecting the populace at large. Pot shots were taken at each other, and gunfire on the streets had bystanders hurrying for cover. In June a number of ex-RIC men who had continued to reside in Arklow received anonymous letters bearing Dublin postmarks warning them that they had forty-eight hours to leave Arklow or be shot in default. Both the Republicans in the barracks and the Free Staters in the coastguard station denied all knowledge of these letters. The Free State troops offered protection to the men involved, but some had already made arrangements to leave.

Tension between the two groups intensified, until it looked like open warfare was inevitable. It came to a head in June. Word from the provisional government in Dublin was sent to Free State troops throughout the country to take possession of all properties held by the Irregulars (the name now given to the anti-Treaty Republicans). This meant that the Free State troops in the coastguard station had to move on the men in the barracks. A twenty-four hour warning to vacate the barracks was issued. This was done quietly, so that the Irregulars could leave the barracks without appearing to back down under the threat.[19] The Irregulars did vacate the premises, but they did so with less than good grace.

> On Saturday the barracks, which for many months past has been occupied by the Irregulars, was burned. On Friday the coastguard troops gave a twenty-four hour warning to surrender the barracks. This was not generally known around the town. At ten o'clock on Saturday the few people who were in the street saw the Irregulars exit the barracks from over the high wall. The fire spread so quickly that it was obvious that oil or petrol had been used and no attempt could be made to save it.

There were two major explosions followed by a louder, more deadly one ...

A large and astounded throng of spectators assembled in view of the fierce conflagration, but it was generally agreed that any effort to cope with the devastating flames would be futile. This was the view of the national troops *[i.e. Free State forces]* who under the command of Captain Coghlan arrived subsequently on the scene.

In a couple of hours all that remained to indicate the existence of the Arklow barracks was the gaunt smoke-begrimed walls to remind passers-by of the costly tragedy that had been responsible for the complete destruction of one of the finest buildings of its kind in Ireland. Indeed so advantageous was its position for the purposes of defence that a large force of attackers would have found it difficult to overcome a small number of defenders.

Arklow was now in the hands of the Free State, or national, troops and government.

*

The armed conflict between former comrades continued for some more months in the cities, towns, villages and fields of Ireland, resulting in the loss of several of the most intelligent and honourable men of their generation on both sides. Even worse, 'civil war politics', the ideological legacies of both factions, were to be the dominant feature of the Irish political scene for generations to come. The dog-in-the-manger attitude of those in power at any particular time was matched by the terrier-like snapping at ankles by those in opposition. The endless, mindless carping ensured that no economic or social progress would be made for almost half a century and the terms 'statehood' and 'stagnation' became synonymous. Admittedly, the economic war with Britain during the 1930s and the outbreak of World War II would have made development extremely difficult for any new state irrespective of its policies or political complexion, but from the start the new Ireland was introspective and narrow. Agriculture was seen as the sole source of economic salvation, and the fact that Ireland was an island was totally overlooked. If the sea entered political consciousness at all, it was seen as a bulwark against foreign ideas rather than as a highway for trade or a store of untapped natural resources. Our trading ships and fishing fleets were ignored, and in small ports like Arklow, where there were neither fields to cultivate nor industries to give employment, the 1920s and '30s offered nothing more than a twilight world of poverty, with

Wrecks in the river (National Library of Ireland)

emigration being the main hope of a better future. New York was a favoured destination.

Small trading vessels and fishing boats[20] were laid up for long periods. Many, such as the *David Rees, Edward* and *Mary Anne*, were doomed never to sail again. Some redundant schooners and brigantines were towed to jagged spots along the coast, such as the Rock and Porter's Rocks, where they were released to be pushed by wind and tide onto the crags to be broken up by the elements. The resultant wreckage was carried away by local residents for fuel. The larger beams supplied materials for building and farm fences. Before a vessel suffered this fate, she was stripped of everything that could be re-used. Masts, spars, ropes, lights, donkey-engines, and deckhouses were all removed and re-allocated to other ships, or to other purposes ashore. Despite this dismal scenario, the sea was the main hope of employment for many young Arklow men.

The only full-time post-primary education available in the town at that time was for girls who could afford to attend St Mary's. Arklow Technical Schools had been growing in strength since their inception, but their courses were not full-time. Francis McNamara, who was principal from 1920 until his retirement in 1949, decided to remedy this. In 1926, he introduced full-time courses to better equip young Arklow men and women to find employment. Navigation had long been a feature of the curriculum, but now more in-depth approaches to the subject were offered, as was a year-long, four days a week course in teaching youngsters the rudiments of being a ship's cook.[21] With the introduction of the Vocational Education Act in 1930, the Tech was in a better position than ever and opened a Day Marine School offering training in navigation, maths, seamanship, signalling, engineering, marine craft, elementary science and geography. Board of Trade examinations leading to a Mate's Certificate could be taken. Students, armed with new knowledge and formal recognition, fished, joined local trading vessels, or signed up with shipping companies in England with which they sailed the world. For seven years this school did excellent work, but interest waned and it closed in 1938.

Why interest should have dropped off is difficult to say, but the slump in shipping had to have been a major factor. In 1934 the government finally realised that, as an island, we needed a commercial shipping fleet. A bounty of 2/6 (just under 16c) per registered ton was offered to shipowners to develop their businesses. Small as the amount was, it was enough to put some of the Arklow vessels back to work. The vessels that had managed to work through the slump also benefitted from the scheme and now showed improved returns. But the large number of idle, and by now rotting, vessels in the river gave rise to comment in the *Wicklow People*. On September 8th, 1934, it complained that because of the lack of industrial enterprise in the area, it was imperative for Arklow to attract the tourist trade and

> [t]he number of disused old vessels in the river for a long time past has been calling forth unfavourable criticism from many visitors to Arklow during recent months. They tend towards the creation of an unsightly spectacle.

Arklow's heyday as a fishing and trading port was well and truly gone, remnants of its once proud fleets were now 'an unsightly spectacle'.

There was one bit of glamour to take people's minds off the miserable state of the economy. On October 30th, 1934, the *Wicklow People* reported that the local schooner *Mary B Mitchell* had been

A still from McCluskey the Sea Rover. *Jack Doyle is is the one with the dagger in his belt*

chartered by the British International Film Company for their motion picture *McCluskey the Sea Rover*. Not only that, but many of the scenes were to be filmed in Arklow bay, using local people as extras. Best of all, the starring role was to be taken by the Gorgeous Gael, Jack Doyle, the boxing champion, singer, bon viveur, and the walking antithesis of bedraggled life in Arklow.[22] Playing opposite him was Tamara Desni.

Shooting lasted for three weeks with the *Mary B*.[23] leaving the harbour each morning with the actors on board. The camera crew filmed the action from another local boat. They stayed out all day, returning in the evening. In the mid-1980s I spent over a year trying to track down a copy of this film. Many of the people who took part in it or who remembered it as one of the bright spots in a dreary time were still alive and would have welcomed a showing of it in town. Unfortunately, I eventually discovered that the last known copies were destroyed in the

1950s as they were beginning to disintegrate and were becoming dangerous to handle.[24]

More down to earth, but infinitely more important to the town's well-being, was the opening of a new factory at the dock in that same year, when Arklow Pottery Ltd came into being.

In many ways, Arklow Pottery was to become the new Kynochs. Within a few years it offered employment to hundreds of local men and women. Skilled, semi-skilled, and unskilled jobs were again available to the unemployed. Young people about to leave school, usually at the age of four-teen, could join the Pottery as general workers or train as

Turning the sod for Arklow Pottery Ltd

kiln operators, mould-makers, decorators, or clerical staff. Ancillary jobs were also created. The clay was to be imported from Cornwall and Arklow vessels were given a much needed boost. Dockers were required to off-load these cargoes. The Tech ran pottery-related courses. To relate the history of Arklow Pottery Ltd would take a book in itself. All that can be said here is that it was Arklow's lifeline throughout the 1930s, '40s and '50s when there was little alternative, and even in the good years of the '60s and '70s the Pottery played an important role in the local economy. Few families had not at least one member employed there at some time or other. Most families had several members working there for many years. Countless Arklow families were reared on Pottery wages. It was impossible to grow up in this town and not be aware of it. The Pottery hooter was Arklow's Big Ben, marking the significant hours of a working day. It blew at eight o'clock each morning, telling its workers that it was time to begin the day's labour, and indirectly warning the workers' children that it was time to get out of bed and prepare for school. It would sound again at lunchtime and again in the evening, when all children playing in Tinahask would have to get out of the way of the Pottery's cavalry of cyclists and platoons of foot-soldiers as they made their way home to eat.

The Pottery, or as it was usally pronounced 'The Pottree', came to hold a place of affection in the minds of the townspeople – even those who griped about having to work in it. It had its good times and its bad times, but it was always there, like a safety net. As long as the Pottery was in operation, there was a touchstone of constancy, hope for the future.

It also brought the name of Arklow to tables throughout Ireland and abroad, particularly the United States. Its story has yet to be written, but a start has been made in various issues of the *Arklow Historical Society Journal*. Frances Neighbour's articles 'Going to Pot' (1999-2000) and 'Tales from the Potter's Field' (1998-1999), and Des Mulhall's 'Arklow Pottery: Working in the Clay End, 1955-1959' (1990-1991) give excellent glimpses of life in the Pottery.

The Pottery also brought new revenue to the public coffers and throughout the 1930s and '40s the delayed process of modernising the housing stock resumed. O'Connell Terrace, Rory O'Connor Place, Connolly Street, Collins Street, and Griffith Street, were built to create a

Arklow Pottery, Ltd., Arklow.

new area that no longer fitted into the Fishery-Brook–Main Street–Flash components which had for so long made up the town of Arklow. Across the Navvy Bridge, Liam Mellowes Avenue was built, nicknamed Abbyssinia because it was built at the time of Italy's war in Abyssinia[25] in the 1930s. These were all good, modern houses, estates which any urban council would have been proud of. Their names reflect a change of focus at that time. No longer were housing developments named in honour of saints such as Columba, Brigid, Patrick, or Kevin, but after people who had figured prominantly in the fight for Irish independence. O'Connell, perhaps, straddled the boundary between religious icon and political activist. The '30s and '40s were still raw with the ill-feeling of the civil war and one of the most satisfying aspects of these street names is that both sides of the conflict are represented in these housing schemes. Collins and Griffith were pro-Treaty, while Liam Mellowes and Rory O'Connor were unreservedly anti-Treaty Republicans. Mellowes had a local connection. Although a native of Galway, he had relatives living at Castletown and he spent a lot of time there as a boy and young man. He was executed by the Free State government in December 1922 and was buried in Mountjoy gaol. His body was exhumed almost two years later and interred in Castletown on October 30th, 1924, as was his wish.[26] By the late 1940s, the council was ready to tackle their biggest project to date, St Peter's Place.

Another important aspect regarding home tenancy or ownership at this time was the change of ownership of the land on which many of the houses stood. Since the early 1700s, the Allens, and later the Probys, were 'lords of the soil' on the south side of the river. In 1941, local businessmen W. Lee and L. O'Toole, operating as Glenart Ltd, bought the Glenart estate from the Proby family, severing the Carysfort connection. Although many of the estate's former tenants still did not own the ground on which their houses stood, and still had to pay ground rent to the new owners, it was a milestone in that the Probys were no longer landlords, its importance more indicative of social change than financial benefit. During the war years vast quantities of timber were felled, and the estate was sold off in lots. The Forestry department were principal purchasers, with the result that much of what had been the Carysfort demesne was now in public ownership. The big question was what could be done with the castle? A suggestion was made that echoed a similar proposal 800 years earlier. Perhaps the Cistercians would be interested in establishing an abbey here? The abbot of the Cistercian abbey at Mount Melleray was invited to make a foundation in the Dublin diocese and Glenart was a possibility. Unfortunately, there were only fifty acres of land allocated to the project and this was deemed insufficient to sustain an abbey.[27]

In 1947 the Vincentian Fathers bought the castle and outoffices to train students for the priesthood. The wing which had been burned in 1921 was replaced with a much larger construction, and Glenart Castle became St Kevin's, Glenart. The first group of students arrived two years later, and for the following twenty years the castle was alive once more.

The enlarged and refurbished Glenart Castle as St. Kevin's, Glenart

The years of the 'Emergency', or World War II as it was known elsewhere, brought its share of hardships such as rationing. No longer a British colony, the Irish Free State remained neutral, although many local men did join up to fight in the British army, navy and air force. Occasionally, Arklow experienced direct contact with the war.

At 1.06 a.m. on June 1st, 1941 a number of bombs were dropped on the town. The first, the only one to explode, fell

in the vicinity of the Wexford and Coolgreany[28] Roads in a field at
Lamberton where thirty houses sustained blast damage.[29]

A second fell in the same area but failed to explode and, according to
both the *Irish Times* and the *Wicklow People* a third fell in the Marsh, it
failed to go off due to the soft ground. The unexploded bomb at
Lamberton was defused and taken by the military to determine whether
its was of German or British origin, as were scraps of the exploded
bomb. The forensic examination determined them to have come from a
German aircraft, a Heinkel He III. This type of aircraft was too small to
carry large bombs internally, and its maximum bomb capacity was two,
one either side of the fusilage. This means that there could not have
been three bombs, unless there was more than one plane. If this had
been the case, the chances are that four bombs would have fallen, not
three, as another Heinkel He III would also have had to release both
bombs to maintain balance. Many of us grew up with the belief of a
"bomb in the Marsh", but Jim Scannell's article certainly seems to
disprove the theory. Nevertheless, the first two were real enough, and
once the country of origin had been identified, the Department of
External Affairs lodged an official complaint and application for
compensation with the German government, who agreed the following
year that recompense from them was due. It was not paid, however,
until 1957.

Two graves, side-by-side in the cemetery, also remind us that the
horrors 'of the war could not be totally ignored here. The twin
headstones commemorate Sgt Alexander Sherlock-Beard and Sgt Jack
Rostern. They were part of a four-man crew of an RAF aircraft. They
were flying off Cahore Point on February 24th, 1942 when their engine
failed. Their plight was watched by Arklow fishermen working in the
area. On impact with the sea, two of the plane's occupants were thrown
clear, but the force of the crash killed both men. The two other
occupants, Sgt Rylatt and Sgt McGarva, were never found. The badly
broken bodies of Sherlock-Beard and Rostern were taken on board the
fishing boat and brought to Arklow, where the police were informed.
Both men were buried here in Arklow.[30]

In his book *Maritime Arklow*, Captain Frank Forde allocated two
chapters to the experiences of Arklow men at sea in the two World
Wars. Many other Arklow people served in other capacities and several

were decorated for bravery in the British sea, air and land forces. It is one of the many themes which needs to be researched fully.

*

Not all was doom and gloom. As mentioned earlier in this book, the people of Arklow have always had the capacity to entertain themselves. Music has always figured prominantly. Brass and reed bands, *céilidh* groups, showbands, rock groups, festivals have all been part of the social scene. So has theatre, both dramatic and musical. In 1941 a new Musical and Dramatic Society was founded which lasted for over twenty years and gave the impetus for other such groups to succeed it. This was The Marian Arts Society. The Marian Arts was a nationwide movement, established to improve the social life of rural Ireland and to help

> ... prevent the depopulation of our rural districts and small towns, whose drabness and inertia offer no satisfaction to the artistic and gay at heart. It would also offer, if run on Catholic principles a potent counter attraction to the insidious and foul attractions of the stage, cinema and literature, where ever these attractions exist.[31]

This was a time in Ireland of over-zealous guardianship of public morals by both elected and non-elected authoritarians. Works of serious literature and theatre were branded as pornography and banned without serious consideration given to their merits.[32] Most, if not all, of our best writers fell foul of the unbelievably strict Censorship Board. Drama fell into either one of two categories, the "immoral" foreign plays staged in Dublin's Gate Theatre or Irish domestic drama dating from the Celtic Twilight in the Abbey, giving rise to the quip that Dublin theatre-goers could choose between Sodom and Begorrah. The above letter shows the prevaling ethos of prudery and it would be easy to dismiss it as another example of cultural insularity. But to do so would be to subject the idea behind it to the same arrogant intolerance which powered the work of the banning brigade. The Marian Arts was a great movement. It offered an outlet for artistic talent, and it did give the community drama and music that no one could find offensive. It showed that there were forms of entertainment other than imported cinema. If it ranted about the "evils" of non-Irish entertainments, it nevertheless brought colour and light-heartedness into a dark, drab time and for that it should be celebrated. It needs no apologies made on its behalf because its immediate and long-term successes showed that it was what many, many people wanted. Its ethos reflected their ethos. If it didn't, it wouldn't have gotten off the ground. The fact that it did not appeal to what might now be termed the 'Dublin 4 Intelligentsia' is beside the point. It wasn't aimed at them.

Sport was also encouraged, and had been actively engaged in and followed over the years. There had been the Arklow Amateur Aquatic and Athletic Sports events as well as horse racing on the beach in the 1880s and 1890s, and the Arklow Gaelic Pastimes Club was founded on Novemeber 15th, 1905.[33] The club hurling team went on to win three senior championships in consecutive years, 1917 to 1919 inclusive, and the junior championship in 1918. There was something of a lull in the 1920s and '30s. Perhaps emigration took its toll on the number of young people available, but there was a resurgence of Gaelic games when the Arklow Geraldines was formed on March 26th, 1940, and the Arklow Rock Parnells came into being thirteen years later. In between the birth of these two clubs was the formation of what was to become the town's premier soccer club, Arklow Town Football Club. Unfortunately, the adherents to the Gaelic codes looked on soccer as a form of west-Britishness which the town could well do without.[34]

By the late 1940s, Arklow had established something of a reputation as a town for dancing in. Venues such as the Marquee which stood on the site of the Ormonde Hall, and the Mayfair now a snooker hall, attracted huge crowds. Big name performers in the world of ballroom and swing included Arklow on their touring programmes. It was all part of Arklow's promotion as a tourist destination. Several major factories in Dublin, such as Jacob's, the biscuit manufacturer, organised day trips and weekend excursions to the town. Many of these visitors stayed in bed-and-breakfast accommodation, bringing new sources of income. Several of these Dublin girls met Arklow fellows, married and settled down here.

By the close of the decade, a new hotel was opened in the area, but it is unlikely that any factory worker would have stayed there. Like many of the landed gentry before them, the Howards of Shelton Abbey found it increasingly difficult to continue living in the style to which they had become accustomed. Rent revenues were nothing like as bountiful as they once were and maintaining a house on the scale of

Shelton Abbey Hotel

Shelton Abbey was proving a losing battle. The Earl of Wicklow decided the time had come to sell it. Like the sale of the Glenart estate to commercial interests less than a decade earlier, this move was a landmark in the history of the locality. The Howards' departure almost coincided with the declaration making the twenty-six county Irish Free State an independent republic in 1949. While such events had little bearing on the day to day lives of the people of the area, it was a momentous time. Shelton Abbey Hotel was not a financial success and in 1950 the house and estate were sold to the Department of Lands. The Department had already established a Forestry Training College at the former home of Charles Stewart Parnell at Avondale, but when Shelton came on the market it was deemed a more suitable location for a training college. Throughout the 1950s and '60s, students from all over the country came to live and study there, although classes in Irish, English and maths were given in Arklow's Technical School.[35]

The two great homes, Glenart Castle and Shelton Abbey, so long the symbols of foreign rule and absentee landlordism in this area, were now respectively a Vincentian seminary and a forestry school owned by the government of the Irish Republic.

Tourism continued to grow throughout the 1950s. Day-trips from Dublin, known as 'The Sea Breeze' tours, brought hordes of people out of the city. They came by train and bus. Those who could afford the luxury of a car, made their own way to Arklow. The dancehalls provided the fun at night, and the beaches, particularly North Beach, with its high sandy dunes proved the attraction on warm summer days. There were boats on the river and riverside walks, but more had to be done to get visitors to come and to stay. In 1958, a major development was opened adjacent to North Beach. The Entertainment Centre boasted a new dance venue, outdoor swimming pool, café, pitch & putt course, tennis court, and boating on the small lake.

Memories of growing up in Arklow during those decades have been recorded by various contributors to the Arklow Historical Society's series of journals. In several issues, Kathleen Gaffney (née Hayes) told 'Yarns from the Fishery' and of 'Arklow 60 Years Ago'. In 1988-1989 Peggy Kelly remembered 'Childhood days in Arklow in the Thirties'; in the 1990-1991 edition, Robbie Tyrrell recalled 'The Games We Played' in the '30s, and Jackie Burke reminisced on Arklow in general in the 1930s and '40s. Captain Danny O'Neill's 'The Changing Face of the Arklow Fisheries' took an in-depth look at the early 1950s. I will not presume to summarise these accounts. They are firsthand reminisences and should be read firsthand to gain an appreciation of life in Arklow in the first half of the twentieth century.

The Entertainment Centre, now the site of Arklow swimming pool and gymnasium

14

Towards a new Millennium:
1960 - 2000

From the moment I sat down to compile this story of the town of Arklow I knew that the most difficult section to write would be this final chapter. As I worked my way through the various eras towards this rendezvous with today, I kept putting the inevitable collision with the present to the back of my mind. The reasons for this apprehension are many. To begin with, it is a very strange feeling to regard an era through which you have lived as being a part of *history*. There is also the unnerving certainty that many readers will have far greater firsthand knowledge about certain aspects of this chapter than I could possibly lay claim to. Despite these concerns, at no time was I tempted to finish the story at 1960. That would have made no sense. The millennium is a nice cut-off point. It lends a roundness to the book. I decided to compromise by simply giving a brief overview of the last forty years without venturing into potentially controversial detail. I am aware that this leaves me open to the charge of chickening out, but to be honest I don't care and have to admit that since making that decision I have not lost one wink of sleep over it. Let some future historian dig deeper into this period at a more remote, and infinitely safer, distance.

*

The 1960s opened optimistically on the jobs front. At Avoca, the mines were once again in production. There had been little activity there since the turn of the century, but World War II highlighted the precariousness of Ireland being dependent on imported artificial manures and it was decided to investigate the viability of working the Avoca mines for minerals that could be processed as fertilisers. Between 1942 and 1947, 16,000 tons of pyrites were extracted for this, but overall the venture proved a failure and work ceased in 1955. But that same year, the Toronto based Mogul Mining Corporation took out a twenty-one year lease on the mines, setting up two operating companies, St Patrick's Copper Mines Ltd and Irish Copper Mines Ltd. Extraction began again in 1958 and by 1960 the mines were once again in serious production.[1]

Tourism in those pre-cheap package holidays to Spain was also robust, the Pottery was going well, and fishing was in a reasonably healthy state. In 1958 the port's nineteen trawlers made it the third biggest fleet in the country.[2] In 1960, news that Roadstone Ltd were interested in restarting quarrying at the Rock brought even brighter hopes. The quarries, which had been started by Parnell, had fallen into disuse since the early years of the century, but now major road construction in England and on the continent created new markets that would make quarrying a viable proposition once more. It was soon obvious that the new owners were prepared to invest heavily as they set about building a new jetty at the Rock from which they could export the stone direct. In this way they could use larger ships and by-pass the old port of Arklow with its perennial dredging problems. Their decision to do so might also have stemmed from the undeniable fact that without major structural and infrastructural development the old port would become obsolete and eventually close to commercial traffic. Over the next forty years, Roadstone would eat away at the Rock, blasting and crunching it into pieces suitable for such diverse purposes as surfacing the autobahns of Germany and protecting eroding coastlines of Europe, including Arklow's own disappearing beaches.

Things were also moving on the education front. For many years St Mary's College had provided secondary education for girls whose families could afford it. The continuing development of the Technical School had extended the range of subjects and style of education since the early years of the century, but there was still a vacuum for teenage boys who wanted to pursue a more academic education. There were two options. One was to go to the Christian Brothers school in Gorey, the other was to attend a small private school, St Patrick's Academy, on Gregg's Hill run by Mr Liam McCarthy. The presence of the McCarthy family there gave rise to that part of Gregg's Hill being called McCarthy's or simply Mac's Hill. As the demand for this type of education grew the

Christian Brothers decided the time had come to establish a new school in Arklow, on the Coolgreaney Road directly opposite the Boys' National School, or 'Top School'. Its doors opened for the first batch of students in September 1961.[3]

1962 was a hiccup year. The government put the Avoca mining companies into receivership. There had been widespread suspicion (and some evidence) that not all the companies' dealings had been above board. These suspicions were strengthened when a ship carrying pyrites for export grounded in Arklow harbour. She had to be lightened before refloating was possible and in the course of this, it was discovered that the cargo was first grade pyrite although the manifest declared it to be of inferior quality. The government, who had invested more in the new companies than the Canadian parent company, ordered an investigation, after which the companies were put into receivership. The loss of the mines was a major blow to local employment. There were quite a few from the town working there, but Carnew, Shillelagh and Tinahely also felt the brunt. This was the period which we might now refer to as the beginning of Ireland's first Celtic Tiger. Political figures and economists such as Seán Lemass and T.K. Whitaker were determined to drag Ireland out of the stagnation in which it had languished for so long and to stem the flow of the country's young people to Britain, the United States, Canada, Australia, New Zealand and wherever else offered them a decent living. Industrial strategies were developed that would transform the national coffers. Part of those strategies was to ensure that workers who were laid off by one employer would not have to wait too long before being taken on by another. Many ex-miners were to benefit from this policy.

Although the attempt to produce fertilizer from Avoca pyrites had failed, the awareness that an Irish-made artificial manure was vital to the nation's agricultural industry had not diminished, and even before the Mogul debacle moves to solve the problem had been taken.

> A site in the Shelton Abbey estate at Arklow was found to be very suitable in view of the proximity of water, road and rail services as well as its nearness to the main fertilizer consuming area in the south-east of the country.
>
> In 1961 the Minister for Industry and Commerce set up a state-sponsored company, Nitrigin Eireann Teoranta, to erect and operate a nitrogenous fertilizer factory at the location at Shelton Abbey, as stated, near Arklow.[4]

Although not mentioned in the above extract, the presence of the port was also to prove invaluable to the company. It was a major undertaking and even the building of it was a daunting task, attracting tenders from Germany, France, Britain and America. The main contract went to a German consortium and work began on the complex in 1963. Although some of the factory was in operation from at least 1965, NET was not officially opened until July 27th, 1966 with the ceremony performed by the Taoiseach Seán Lemass, who had been instrumental in Ireland's economic development.[5]

Within a short period the Fert[6] became by far the area's biggest and most important employer. It would never reach Kynoch's peak of four thousand, but by the mid-1970s there were over 1,500 people employed by the company. Wages offered by NET far exceeded that of other local companies. Overtime, bonuses, and assorted frills filled wage packets as never before with the result that the Fert acquired the sobriquet 'El Dorado'. Its opening had followed on the heels of the closure of the mines, and because there was a perception that many non-Arklow ex-mine workers had been hired by the new factory at the expense of local labour accusations of regional political interference were regularly voiced. Some Arklow people, perhaps disgruntled by having failed to get employment with NET, suggested that the 1798 Monument on Parade Ground had a new role to play. No longer did Fr Murphy point the way to Dublin, he now showed the southwest Wicklowmen the way to the Fert.

The Fert was without doubt a major catalyst in kick-starting Arklow's economic rise. Apart from giving direct employment it spawned a host of service companies. Hauliers, engineering firms, caterers, all found work because of NET. The company's import and export needs took the harbour out of the doldrums for the first time in decades, and such was the company's importance to the port that it had a seat on the Harbour Board. Maritime matters were further revitalised in 1966 when several shipowners amalgamated as Arklow Shipping Ltd, which over the next 35 years was to become one of the most successful shipping companies in Europe.[7]

Throughout the '60s the sense of optimism which both sprang from and encouraged these developments saw a private housing boom. New estates such as Coolgreaney Park, Knockenrahan and Abbeyville bore testimony to confidence in a better future, but in some instances, the more things changed the more things stayed the same. The Tech was a case in point. The numbers of students attending the school mushroomed in the 1960s, so that by 1967 classes were held not only in the 1915 building, but also in a prefab in the yard, and in rooms in the Youth Club premises (founded 1958[8]) the ITG&WU (now SIPTU) hall and in the Marlborough Hall – 'the very hall used by many of the students' grandparents and great grandparents'.[9] One class was being taught on the upstairs landing![10] A site was purchased on Coolgreaney Road.

A mile away, another school was to close the following year, when the Vincentian novitiate at Glenart came to an end after twenty years. It was felt that it might still serve as a retreat house for the laity, but this idea never really got off the ground and Glenart Castle was to lie idle and neglected for the next decade. It was bought by a local businessman who later leased it to Arklow Pottery as a storage facility. As Arklow moved into the 1970s Shelton Abbey also entered a new phase of its history. It was no longer deemed suitable as a forestry college and the Department decided that a return to Avondale House was more appropriate. Shelton Abbey was acquired by the Department of Justice as an open prison. The concept of an open prison was to help inmates of other gaols who were nearing the end of their sentences, to re-acclimatise to life outside the prison system. They were given more freedom of movement, a more active role in decision-making and acceptance of personal responsibility. There were no locks, but unapproved absence from Shelton was punishable by the transgressor's return to a stricter regime prison.

A third place of learning ceased to operate in 1970. St Peter's Boys' School on Habour Road, the old Bottom School, released its last batch of pupils as a new St Peter's opened at Castlepark. It was the end of an era, further evidence of the erosion of the separateness of the Fishery. The new school would still cater for boys from the area, but it was not *in* the Fishery. It was a minor quibble when compared to the advantages offered by the new premises, and there was a great deal of consolation in the knowledge that the old school was to be put to good use as a Senior Citizens' Centre.

Boatbuilding in Arklow entered a new stage in 1970. Since 1864, the principal boatbuilders had been the company of John Tyrrell & Sons. The company was now owned and run by two brothers, Jack and Willie Tyrrell. Tyrrells' yard had established an international reputation for design and building skills, crowned in the early 1960s by their construction of Francis Chicester's *Gypsy Moth III*, winner of the first transatlantic single-handed yacht race. Willie Tyrrell decided the time had come to open a new yard that would concentrate on metal construction and Arklow Marine Engineering came into being.

More good news came in January 1971 when production once more began at the Avoca mines, with another Canadian based consortium in control.[11] This time a closer watch was kept and the mines continued to operate until August 1982, when they closed for the last time with the loss of 227 jobs.

The early summer of 1974 saw the last students leave the old Tech. Over the previous five or six years, work on plans and construction of the new school was carried out and in September of '74 the New Tech opened for business. At least, that's what is was popularly called and would be for some time to come, but its official name was Arklow Vocational School and would later become Arklow Community College. That opening year saw 382 students enrol and this rose to 458 by 1979, necessitating an extension. The evacuation of the old Tech left the school authorities with something of a quandary. What could be done with it? For many years the Arklow branch of the County Library Service had been housed in the courthouse and it was decided to relocate it to the ground floor on one side of the Tech, with the corresponding space on the first floor being used for storage of book stock. The County Council opened offices in some of the other upstairs rooms, leaving the rest of the ground floor vacant, but not for long.

Since the early seventies it was obvious that Arklow was changing rapidly. It was a growing town with a bright future. The old ways were being consigned to the dustbin of history and it seemed that few would mourn their passing. But there was a great deal of Arklow's past which deserved to be rescued. A group of volunteers who shared the belief that Arklow's maritime heritage should be preserved, displayed, and appreciated, came together to see what could be done in this regard. For generations the people of Arklow had lived from the sea, fishing or trading, in coastal waters or around the world. Few houses did not have momentoes from ports across the globe. Models of ships in glass cases or in bottles, scrimshaw, macramé and a host of other maritime related artefacts and skills graced many homes. But the town's growing affluence was beginning to blind younger generations to the richness of this heritage. For many it seemed that such artefacts were merely reminders of less affluent times to which no one wished to return. It is an understandable and widespread phenomenon and it is at such times of change that dislocation with the past can occur, only to be regretted at a later, more confident date. Thankfully, people like Mark Synnott, Nick Tancred, John Kearon, Tommy Myler, Billy Roberts, Bernard Riley, Paddy Doyle and others were aware of the threat to such pieces of the past as old possessions were dumped in house clearances and renovations.

An exhibition was organised to take place in the Marlborough Hall. The committee went from door to door, and even they were amazed at the wealth of material still available. That exhibition was a resounding success, not only in the number and range of artefacts, but also in the numbers of people who went to see them. The need for a local museum was obvious. When two ground floor rooms in the Tech became available, the committee applied for them and were successful. Appropriately, these were the very rooms used for the Marine School in the 1930s.[12] Arklow Maritime Museum opened its doors to the public in October 1976. Over the past twenty-seven years Mark Synnott has remained steadfast in his devotion to it, and it is doubtful if it would have remained open without him.

Even in times of sustained economic growth there are casualties. While new companies are formed and strive in a changing environment, others geared to a different age fade away. One such casualty in 1976 was the Brook Pottery which stood on the site now occupied by Tesco's supermarket. It was one of the few enterprises to get off the ground in Arklow in the 1930s and their main product was terra cotta drainage pipes. The age of plastic reduced their market in the early '70s until the Brook was no longer a viable proposition. Some of their market had been taken by Nu-Plast Ltd at the dock, where one of the many plastic products was land drainage pipes. But this was a time when such closures were of little importance to workers as there was plenty of work to be had.[13] As one door closed another opened, and the biggest door to open at that time was Noritake.

Since the 1930s Arklow Pottery had produced good quality tableware. In the early decades particularly, the standard of their ware was excellent and some of it was aimed at the luxury market. By the '60s and into the '70s, the emphasis had shifted to mass production of good utilitarian earthenware. In 1975, Noritake Ltd, a Japanese company which produced high quality porcelain tableware, decided to set up in

Arklow, not in competition with the Pottery, but in tandem with it. The Japanese company bought shares in the Pottery and introduced trained personnel and techniques into the company. They also built a new factory beside the Pottery to produce their own high quality porcelain products for the luxury market. It was up and running by 1976 and before the decade closed the twin companies employed over 1,000 people. Many came from Wicklow and Gorey, but the vast majority were local workers.

As well as the Pottery and Noritake, Armitage Shanks, Nu-Plast, Irish Fireplaces and Woodfab Packaging were sited around the dock and every evening the exodus up Dock Road was something to behold. Tyrrell's boatyard had secured the contract to build the Jack Tyrrell designed brigantine *Asgard II* as the national sail-training vessel, which was commissioned by the Taoiseach of the day, Charles Haughey, in March 1981. Arklow had never known such a prosperous time. More housing was needed. Local authority and private housing estates filled the gaps between existing streets, and pushed the edges of the town into what had been countryside. John's Villas, Marian Villas, Fernhill, Oaklands, John Paul Avenue (built in 1979 and named in honour of the papal visit that year), Abbey Park, Abbey Heights, Croghan Heights, Lamberton Heights and others all sprang up south of the river. On the north side Templerainey Park, Templerainey Heights and other developments greatly increased the population there.

Despite the huge numbers working in NET, it never captured the imagination or affection that the Pottery commanded. That may have been because the Pottery had been around a lot longer and several generations of families had worked in it. Another reason was the continuing perception that a great deal of the wages paid by NET went out of the town. To what degree that was true is open to debate, but perception is as potent as reality. Another major factor was the level of pollution emanating from NET. This was not a matter of perception, but a visible, undeniable fact. Since its opening, the vegetation in the immediate vicinty of the factory withered and died. By the late 1970s, that part of the valley, once eulogised by travellers, was devastated. At times the smell of ammonia hung in the air. Many NET employees would not drive new cars to work because they claimed that spots would erupt on them within a short time. There was a general belief that Arklow had exceptionally high instances of respiratory and cancer related illnesses and these were attributed to pollution from the Fert.

None of these suspicions were ever proved, but neither was anything done to allay them. The Fert undoubtedly brought an economic benefit to the region and the management were generous in supporting local events and organisations, but its negative aspects did not endear it to the general populace.

Those who seek symbolism might be interested to learn that just as that part of Shelton looked like a petrified forest and Shelton Abbey was home to criminals, the title 'Earl of Wicklow' became extinct. The Howard family, who had purchased the land in the 17th century and who had become Earls of Wicklow, had severed their connection with the area, but had still retained the title. With the death of the last earl in 1979 the title died out. Meanwhile, across the river at Glenart, the erstwhile seat of Lord Carysfort was being used by Noritake and the Pottery as a warehouse.

If the '60s and '70s were the decades of rapid development, the '80s were the years of recession. Almost overnight, it seemed, Arklow went from virtually full employment to being an unemployment black spot. That decade saw the closure of Noritake, Armitage Shanks, Arklow Gypsum (a subsidiary of NET) and Brennan's Bakery among others.

Brennan's had come into existence in the 1920s, a very faint glimmer of light in the otherwise employment blackness of the time and over the decades, until it closed sixty years later, it had given employment to many hundreds. The Brennan family sold it to David Mosse Ltd in 1980 and the number of workers there increased from forty-five to 130, but it closed in 1988.[14] Armitage Shanks was an English company which made bathroom suites. Some of its redundant workers took it over and, after several permutations, emerged in the 1990s as one of the town's main employers as QualCeram.

The Pottery and NET survived, but with drastic cuts in employee numbers and consequent closure of ancillary enterprises. The impact of all this on a town of less than ten thousand people cannot be overstated. Two thousand jobs had disappeared in an astonishingly short period of time and there seemed little hope of new companies springing up to cushion the fall. The establishment of pharmaceutical companies such as Servier, the Soap Company, Iropharm, and other smaller concerns did take up some of the slack, but it was a time of dozens of jobs lost to every one job created. One of the more resilient small local companies was Fennell's Irish Fireplaces[15] which had been established in 1944, which is still going strong in the new millennium.

The local Presbyterian community has not yet been mentioned. It is a small community, but has been a continuous part of Arklow since 1913. For thirty years before that, Presbyterian services in the area had been sporadic. By the early years of the twentieth century many of these services were conducted in the home of Mr J.A. Crammond of Mineview, Avoca. On April 29th, 1913 a meeting was held to see if the community was large enough and committed enough to form a congregation in Arklow. As a result, the Masonic Hall on Ferrybank was used every Sunday evening. In 1914 a new building was erected on the Dublin road. It was a small building but adequate for the congregation which, even by the 1970s, still numbered an average attendance of about thirty people in the winter. The summer months, however, saw the numbers greatly increase with the influx of holiday-makers, and in 1985 the building was greatly extended. It could be said that it was completely rebuilt.[16]

A voluntary partnership of public representatives and local businessmen, supported by the Department of Labour Manpower Service (later FÁS) formed the Arklow Enterprise Centre in what had been Arklow Gypsum, the premises was made available on generous terms by NET. Their purpose was to encourage new buisness.

Even nature seemed bent on kicking the town when it was down. Hurricane Charlie in October 1986 had wreaked considerable damage, but the December storms of 1989 obliterated the beautiful sand dunes of North Beach. The running track, built by St Benedict's Athletic Club[17], was inundated, the perimeter wall having collapsed under the incoming sea. The boating lake/wildlife preserve could not be seen as it formed part of a single body of salt water. The Caravan Park sustained tremendous damage as waves washed all before them, exposing long-buried remnants and artefacts of Kynochs. Kynochs had been aware of the coastal erosion threat and had erected timber protection against it. That barrier had long gone, leaving nothing but the upright piles near the shoreline. These December storms picked up those piles like matchsticks. On the south side, Arklow Golf Links also fell victim to the inundation.

When the sea receded, it refused to revert to its former position. Like an invading army, it held much of what it had taken as if in quiet confidence that it could take more whenever it wished and there was nothing mere mortals could do about it. It was clear that major protection works were needed to avoid further erosion and throughout

Remains of Kynochs bogies and tram tracks uncovered in the storm of 1989

1990 huge boulders, mostly supplied from Roadstone Quarries, were put into place along North Beach and most of South Beach. Those who remembered the dunes mourned their loss, the beaches at Arklow would never be the same.

And so we reach the final decade, and I'll be brief. The 1990s brought mixed fortunes. New companies were set up, but two old reliables closed, the boatyard of John Tyrrell & Sons and Arklow Pottery. The former had been in business since 1864 and had earned a reputation not only for well built boats but also for innovation in design. The demise of the Pottery had been expected for some years, but it had managed to limp along. After the closure of its sister company, Noritake, in the 1980s it seemed to be only a matter of time before the Pottery followed, but the Japanese parent company kept it going for as long as possible. During its final decade its near neighbour, Quality Ceramics, had gone from strength to strength and, as QualCeram, took over the

Coastal protection in the wake of the 1989 storms

old Pottery premises as part of their expansion plans. QualCeram had also acquired the former premises of both Nu-Plast and the Noritake warehouse on the west side of the dock. Before the decade was out, they also acquired the Noritake factory premises on the east side of the dock, beside the Pottery premises and, in partnership with a Turkish company, set up a tile-making factory, Vitra tiles.

New housing estates sprang up, pushing the edges of the town farther and farther into what had been countryside. The old Arklow of Fishery, Brook, Flash and Main Street is now simply a nucleus around which the town has grown. Soon, an A-Z of Arklow will be needed. Templerainey and Seabank in particular saw tremendous growth in population.

The by-pass, first discussed in the late 1960s, finally became a reality, relieving some of the traffic congestion in the Main Street.

CONCLUSION

At the start of the new millennium, Arklow has a population in the region of ten thousand. It is a typical modern Irish town. It has its good points and its bad points. Voluntary clubs and societies cater for all interests and tastes. It has a high rate of employment, despite the recent closure of the Fert (by which time it was known officially as Irish Fertiliser Industries, IFI) and the consequent financial crippling of the port. On the face of it, it differs little from hundreds of towns of similar size throughout Ireland. But as with all towns and cities and villages, it is unique, and what gives it its uniqueness is the story which lies behind its long, often slow, development to become the town we know today.

The title of this book is *The Story of a Town*. All stories should be readable and enjoyable, otherwise why tell them? I have tried to make this tale as entertaining as possible, and if I've succeeded in that well and good, but I also hope that its has whetted the appetite of some readers to dig further, because it was impossible to go into detail on all the vast range of topics touched upon. As mentioned in the Introduction, a great deal of research and publication of Arklow's past has already been carried out, but there is so much more waiting to be tackled. The history of the recent past, which I just skimmed over, needs to be recorded. The stories of Arklow Pottery, Noritake, NET/IFI, and all the other factories need to be written down by the people who knew them best, the people who worked in them. The history of local government in the town also needs to be compiled. Peggy Leonard of New York, a descendant of an Arklow emigrant, has spent several years compiling genealogical data such as headstone inscriptions and census returns and her work will be a wonderful addition to the town's growing library.

The study of Arklow and its past has given me twenty-five years of pleasure. I hope that some of that pleasure has found its way into these pages.

APPENDIX ONE:

[In Chapter Seven, I mentioned the importance of H.L.Bayly's description of Arklow which was published in 1816. This, combined with Thomas Cromwell's description published in 1820, give the most complete description of Arklow and its people at that time. At least eighty percent of Cromwell's article is Bayly's work, but it would be too tedious to separate and nit-pick. Instead I will reproduce it as it appeared in the *AHSJ* 1982, with just the omission of an occasional paragraph already dealt with.]

This town, in the increase of its population, and the improved appearance of the houses, affords a striking instance of a prosperous change within a comparatively short period: about 50 years since, it was merely a fishing-hamlet, consisting of a number of thatched mud cabins, and a single slated house. Now, however, there are upwards of 60 houses of the latter description, each two stories high.

Arklow may properly be divided into two parts - the upper town and the fishery. The latter still consists only of mud cottages, about 250 in number, badly constructed, and irregularly placed, but the former possesses all that decency and respectability of appearance described. The upper town forms one large street, sufficiently wide, with a gentle descent towards the sea: it has in recent years been greatly ornamented by the erection of a handsome 'Church' with a tower and minarets, from a plan of Francis Johnson Esq. to whom the citizens of Dublin are indebted for the designs of those beautiful buildings, St. George's Church, and the Castle Chapel. Arklow church stands centrally in the town, on a rising ground, and is capable of accommodating a numerous congregation. A handsome 'Chapel' has been since built, in an open and convenient spot in the upper part of the town, and adds to the rural appearance of the place.

The 'Barracks', placed in a commanding situation over the banks of the river, are of a size sufficient to accommodate two companies of soldiers: they are surrounded by a wall, which encloses a yard for exercise, and are connected with the ruins of a fine old tower, which, with six others, forming a 'Castle' at this position were destroyed by Oliver Cromwell in his progress southwards. This castle was once in the possession of the Ormond family, who still retain considerable portions of the royalties throughout this country, although the properties to which they were attached have been long since alienated.

The 'Fever-hospital', a small building erected about 14 years ago, is supported by subscriptions, and allowances from the Grand Jury. The physician attends regularly three days in the week, and medicines are distributed to from 3 to 400 patients in the course of the year. Arklow has also its 'Dispensary' established about the same period. The diseases most prevalent in the parish are fevers, pleurisies, and agues, which however are seldom fatal, when but treated with the necessary attention. The inhabitants of the town are chiefly subject to ague, which is attributed to the neighbourhood of a marsh of about 100 acres on its north side — there are some instances of longevity. A few years back, a woman died here at the age of 110 who, in speaking of her children, said her youngest boy was then 80. In 1814, the ages of the crew of a herring—boat, five in number, amounted to 335 years.

About 10 years ago, a Sunday School was commenced in this town, and it has so fully answered the most sanguine expectations of its utility, that it may perhaps be said that no measure adopted for the religious and moral improvement of the lower classes of the rising generation, within the county, has afforded so fair a prospect of producing the desired effect. This school was opened on the most liberal principles: all books, which could be supposed likely to give offence to any religious persuasion, were excluded. Its expenses are defrayed by private subscriptions; but considerable grants of books have been obtained, at very reduced prices, from the committee of the Hibernian Sunday Schools, Dublin, so as materially to forward its benevolent and praiseworthy objects. Two examinations are annually held, when premiums are adjudged for meritorious behaviour and regular attendance, which have the effect of exciting a general spirit of emulation.

The market day here is Thursday, when articles of various descriptions, and in considerable quantity, are exposed for sale. Great irregularity is however visible on these days, in consequence of the want of a market-house, and of some arrangement for the proper distribution of cars and removal of obstructions to the business transacted - but these are generally the things last thought of in Ireland. There are four fairs during the year, held on 14th May, 9th August, 25th September and 15th November. At these much cloth and woollen goods are always sold; together with black cattle, pigs, etc. The inhabitants of the town and neighbourhood, finding these fairs insufficient for the trading purposes of the country, lately framed a memorial, praying the grant of four annual fairs in addition.

The only manufacture carried on in the parish, is connected with the fishery, and consists in spinning hemp, and making herring-nets. This manufacture, though apparently partial, becomes an object of importance when it is considered that it gives employment to a great number of women and children, who would otherwise be idle. Besides, although, at certain periods of the year, large quantities of fish are taken, yet from the well known improvidence of the class of men employed in fisheries, and from the length of time they are frequently prevented from going to sea by stormy weather, the whole population are often indebted to the industry of these women and children for their support: nor are the early habits of diligence and exertion, thus imbibed by the latter, ever entirely forgotten or eradicated.

The inhabitants were indebted to Mr. Plummer of Arklow (a man well known as the promoter and encourager of every laudable and philanthropic design) for the commencement and extension of this manufacture, which was at first presented to his mind by witnessing great distress amongst the dense population of the fishery, during unfavourable seasons, when it only appeared necessary to guide the natural bent of their inclinations, by affording them hemp, and a ready market for their manufacture.

The quantity of hemp now manufactured in the town of Arklow, amounts to about six tons weight in each year; and the number of women and children employed in spinning and knitting is not less than 1,000. Each woman is capable of earning from sixpence to ninepence per day, and the children from threepence to fourpence. Every pound of hemp is supposed to make seven fathoms of net, and each herring-net consists of 75 fathoms. Great quantities of these nets are used in the fisheries along the coast: the redundancy is disposed of in the Dublin and Liverpool markets.

Mr. Plummer also established a 'Rope Walk' in the town, where cordage of a small dimension is manufactured.

The herring fishery on this coast has became an object of considerable importance within a few past years, in consequence of the increased attention that has been paid to it. There are two seasons in the year: one commencing in May, and continuing six weeks; the other in November, lasting an equal time. From 100 to 130 boats are generally collected, from different parts of the coast, including Dublin and Wexford; some likewise from the isle of Man, and the Welsh coast, during the summer fishery, when vessels from Dublin and Liverpool, lie in the bay and purchase for their respective markets: but much the greater quantity of fish is distributed through the interior of the counties of Wicklow, Wexford, Carlow and Kilkenny, by carriers, who find a ready sale, and make a good profit. The usual prices vary from 10 to 20 shillings the maze of 600; but sometimes they are sold at from a guinea to 25 and 30 shillings.

It is a circumstance worthy of observation, that the herring fishery in the bay of Arklow is considered, next to that of Galway, as the best on the coast of Ireland. And as the numerous advantages to be derived from its increase become more manifest, it will probably be considered, at no very distant period, as an object even of national importance.

The total number of boats annually employed is averaged at 214 and the value of the produce at £24,250.

Independently of the herring fishery, the commerce of the place has of late years rapidly improved, notwithstanding the great danger and many difficulties attending the passage of vessels over the Bar of Arklow. It is not probable that these difficulties could, without a heavy expense, be so totally removed, as to permit vessels of burden to pass safely; yet it is the universal opinion of those who are well-informed on the subject, that, if a few thousand pounds were expended in constructing a pier on the northern side of the river, so as to prevent the waters from inclining in that direction, the backwater that, during the winter floods, rushes with overwhelming force from the mountains, would constantly clear the bar of any obstructions, which collecting of the sand might oppose. After the effects of violent floods in clearing the passage, there have been 17 feet of water on the bar, the sand being entirely removed to the surface of the marl, which lies beneath it at that depth; but, from the want of such a pier as has been described, the advantages resulting from such a force of backwater are entirely lost.

The inhabitants of Arklow have however of late years exerted themselves to apply some remedy to this evil; assisted by subscriptions, of £100 each, from the Earls of Carysfort and Wicklow, in addition to what was collected in the town and neighbourhood, they have raised an embankment at the north side of the river, from the bridge towards the sea, which has already proved of great utility, and has answered the expectations which were formed of it. But as their means are totally inadequate to the expense of completing the design, it is hoped that Government may be induced to pay some attention to the improvement of a harbour, which might be made to afford security to numbers of the coasting traders, who have at present no good port into which they can run for shelter, along the whole extent of coast from Dublin to Waterford. As things are now, the shipment of goods here is attended with no slight expense and trouble. Vessels are obliged to pass the bar from the town, and anchor in the bay, before they have received half their cargoes; when the remainder is brought to them in small boats: and it not infrequently happens, that they are obliged at last to run from their moorings, with their lading incomplete, for Dublin, should a breeze chance to spring up from the east - the usual imports to Arklow are coal, salt, iron, timber, deals, limestone, earthenware, tar, pitch, hemp, ropes etc. The exports are corn, cattle, etc. Great quantities of barley and oats have been exported to Dublin and Liverpool during recent years: and large storehouses have also been erected. The entire population of Arklow parish, but more particularly of the town, has rapidly increased during the last 30 years, and that, it has been manifested, chiefly through the improvements that have taken place in conducting the herring fishery. Lads of 18 and 19 now procure from their fathers a share in a herring boat; marry; their friends unite in assisting them to build a cabin; and they are enabled by their earnings to maintain a family, that generally increases with each succeeding year. Lord Carysfort has appropriated a large plot of ground, approximating to the sea, for the enlargement of the fishery, and has wisely granted such leases as have proved an inducement to lay out their money in building substantial slated houses etc. the mere appearance of which sufficiently points out the advantages of the system. The proportion of protestants to catholics has not been accurately ascertained, but is supposed to be in the ratio of one to three.

The houses of the parish of Arklow, generally speaking may be said to be neither of the best nor of the worst construction which Leinster affords. They are mud cabins, thatched; but certainly superior to those seen in many other parts. They are divided into two or more rooms, according to the means of their occupiers.

The general appearance and dress of the lower orders may be considered superior to those of the neighbouring counties, with the exception only of parts already described, in the County of Wexford. On Sundays, in particular, the entire population maintains an extremely decent and reputable appearance. There are few of these cottagers who do not possess a cow, or some goats, whose milk affords an agreeable and wholesome addition to their potatoes, oatmeal and herrings. Fuel is their chief want; and indeed that article is scarce along the coast in general; but Lord Carysfort has frequently evinced his benevolence in relieving the inhabitants of this district, during inclement winters, by purchasing large quantities of coal, and selling it to the poor at greatly reduced rates.

The fishermen of Arklow, it must be observed, are a race distinct from the other inhabitants; occupying a separate part of the town, and being solely devoted to their own particular pursuits. Neither will they, even when reduced to absolute distress, employ themselves in any occupations not connected with their favourite element. Their lives afford an incessant variety, which seems the zest of their existences. Sometimes they are enduring all the hardships of the sea-faring life; at others they are sitting at home in perfect indolence for days together. Sometimes they have money in abundance; at others, they are suffering under the bitterest effects of improvidence and poverty. But, probably, in these particulars, they differ little from the same class of men in all parts of the world; and both their defects and good qualities, it is likely, may be traced in all cases to the same cause - a life of chance and adventure.

The landed property here is chiefly divided between the Earls of Carysfort and Wicklow. Fortunately, middlemen are in this union almost unknown; their lordships letting their ground, we believe in all cases, only to resident tenants. The extent of the farms varies from 20 to 80 acres; and as the old leases of three lives, or 31 years, terminate, new ones are substituted for one life, or 21 years; and generally speaking the rent demanded does not exceed the value of the land.

The decrease in the tenure of farms above-mentioned, has latterly become very prevalent in Ireland; and, as it is almost a new system, introduced from the sister island, it may be fair to enquire how far it is likely to prove beneficial or otherwise to the interests of the country. In England, it is practiced with success; because there the tenant, at the expiration of his lease, is almost always preferred, on agreeing to a rent that shall bear a just proportion to any alterations that may have taken place in the character of the times. Besides, on taking a farm, the Englishman finds a comfortable farm-house, which the landlord is obliged by custom to build and repair; his farm too is well fenced, the land in general in tolerable heart, and there exists no impediment to his immediately commencing the tillage of it with profit to himself. His taxes are heavy; but as no man in England can undertake the management of a farm without something like an adequate capital, his means, uniting with industry are equal (excepting only in times of extraordinary distress like the present) to the necessary demands upon them.

But in Ireland the case is indeed sadly reversed. Without capital, without a house to reside in, the peasant takes a piece of ground at its utmost value; if he should find upon it four mud walls, with some thatch, but imperfectly calculated to repel the blasts of winter, it is as much as he can expect. To build, when he has no capital , is impossible; he therefore takes possession of the hovel as he finds it, and stops the broken windows, or the holes in the roof, with the first material that comes to hand. In many instances [a] great part of his farm is covered with furze, which requires a considerable period to eradicate, and great quantities of manure to render the soil where it grew productive; consequently it is with the utmost difficulty (to say the least) that he is able to discharge his rent, and afford the first necessities to himself and his family.

If, after a long course of time, he is enabled by weary exertions to become independent of his creditors, he finds himself grown old, the years of his lease have expired and the only prospect for continuing the maintenance of the perhaps numerous family depending on his own life, and the little sum he may have contrived to set aside. Will he, in such circumstances, expend the savings of many a toilsome year in improving a tenure, which the loss of one old life may snatch from his family?

[Cromwell continues highlighting the plight of the Irish agricultural

smallholder and labourer, comparing his situation with his English counterpart. While interesting in itself, it is getting away slightly from the focus of this book. He does, however, return to specifics relating to Arklow.]

The climate about Arklow, and indeed that of this eastern coast in general, is more genial than in common even in this so genial isle; and being sheltered from the prevailing western blasts, by the range of mountains which traverses the country from north to south, it is remarkably favourable to early vegetation. Until about 40 years back, Arklow was in possession of another eminent natural advantage - a river which produced great quantities of excellent fish, and more particularly Salmon. But the mineral qualities imbibed by the water from the mines before-mentioned on its banks, that at the period spoken of began to be worked to a considerable extent, entirely destroyed all the fish between them and the sea, for the distance of eight miles; and the salmon which now attempt to ascend the stream in the spawning season are frequently taken out dead, or in a torpid state. A proposal has been made, to turn the mineralized waters in another direction, by means of metal pipes, and thereby to restore the river to its native purity, and the fishery to its pristine excellency; but such a project must necessarily lie in embryo, unless undertaken by a company, or by those proprietors whose interests are immediately concerned.

There are few resident gentlemen in this district, the property, as before observed, belonging (with a small exception) to the Earls of Carysfort and Wicklow. The following are among the principal mansions: - Shelton, (before spoken of), the seat of the Earl of Wicklow, is beautifully situated on the north bank of the Ovoca, at the distance of about two miles from Arklow. It stands at the base of a range of hills, which gently rise about it, and are luxuriantly clothed with oak and birchwood. The demesne is highly improved, and studded with magnificent beech and chestnut trees. The house is ancient; though the interior was completely modernised by the late earl: its height is only two stories, but it presents a rather long front to the view. The entire coup d'oeil has a fine effect; and, with the surrounding scenery, forms one of the most characteristic and charming retreats of which this delightful county can boast.

Kilcarra Castle, the seat of the Earl of Carysfort, stands on the south bank of the river, nearly opposite to Shelton, but not within view of the vale of Ovoca. It has been decorated with towers, and a castellated front, by its present possessor, who has expended a considerable sum in its improvement. The situation is very retired, on a gentle declivity, commanding a fine view of a glen, the brows of which are clothed with wood. The house, now so much enlarged, was only a hunting-lodge of Lord Carysfort's ancestors.

Ballyraine is situated within a mile of the town of Arklow, and commands a fine marine view: the house is modern, with a handsome front elevation.

Lamberton, about half a mile distant from Arklow, on its south side, enjoys a beautiful view of the sea, and the richly wooded hills of Shelton and Ballyarthur. The prospect is determined by a magnificent range of mountains; and it is well sheltered from the western blasts by ornamental plantations, which form a striking feature in the country.

Emma Vale, to the south-west of the town, has been lately much improved and enlarged, and forms a very desirable residence: it commands a fine view of Lord Carysfort's extensive woods.

Cooladangan, two miles south of Arklow, and near the borders of the county of Wexford, is lately built, and on a generally excellent plan.

Sallymount, five miles north of Arklow, on the Dublin road, is well sheltered with thriving plantations, which are the more ornamental in a spot otherwise bare of wood.

Emoclew, a neat and prettily situated lodge, near the town of Arklow, towards the south, possesses a fine marine view, and an equally fine one inland and of the mountains.

APPENDIX TWO:

ARKLOW POPULATION FIGURES
1841 – 2002
Courtesy of the Central Statistics Office

Year	Population	%age +/-	Houses	%age +/-
1841	3,254		538	
1851	3,300	1.39 % +	588	9.29 %+
1861	4,760	44.24 % +	908	54.42 % +
1871	5,178	7.74 % +	1,030	13.44 % +
1881	4,777	7.16 % -	1,095	6.31 % +
1891	4,172	12.66 % -	1,087	0.74 % -
1901	4,944	18.5 % +	1,125	3.5 % +
1911				
1921				
1926	4,535			
1936	4,680	3.2 % +		
1946	4,915	5.02 % +		
1951	5,203	5.86 % +		
1956	5,292	1.71 % +		
1961	5,390	1.85 % +		
1966	6,083	12.9 % +		
1971	6,948	14.22 % +		
1979	8,451	21.63 & +		
1981	8,646	2.3 % +		
1986	8,388	2.98 % -		
1991	7,987	4.8 % -		
1996	8,519	6.66 % +		
2002	9,955	16.85 % +		

Overall, Arklow's growth in population has been steady over the past 160 years, but some interesting variations can be detected and these usually reflect wider circumstances in the town. For example, the 44.24% increase between 1851 and 1861 suggests that Arklow, like towns throughout Ireland, experienced considerable influx of people leaving the countryside in the wake of the Famine. The decreases between 1871 and 1891, and again in the 1980s, follow the pattern of other towns in those periods of high emigration. The 1871 to 1891 figures in particular suggest this, as there were 1,006 fewer people inhabiting fifty-seven more houses. The building boom of the 1850s and 1860s, when 442 houses were built (a 75% increase) was followed by large numbers of people leaving the town over the next twenty years. The town obviously was not capable of absorbing the post-Famine influx, and yet more houses were still being built. The sudden change of fortunes by 1901 might be explained by the arrival of Kynochs in 1895, and the 1966 to 1981 figures might also reflect Arklow's high employment opportunities at that time.

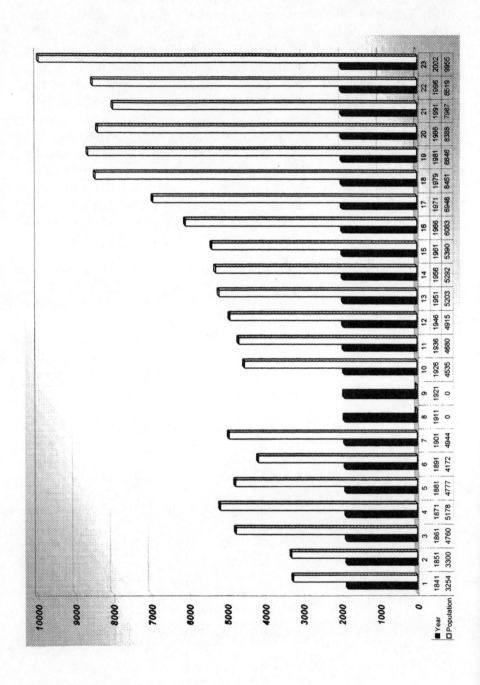

Year	1841	1851	1861	1871	1881	1891	1901	1911	1921	1926	1936	1946	1951	1956	1961	1966	1971	1979	1981	1986	1991	1996	2002
	1	2	3	4	5	6	7	8	9	10	11	12	13	14	15	16	17	18	19	20	21	22	23
Population	3254	3300	4760	5178	4777	4172	4944	0	0	4535	4680	4915	5203	5292	5390	6083	6946	8451	8846	8388	7987	8519	9955

SOURCES:

Chapter One:

1 Price, L. *Place-Names of County Wicklow* p.vi
2 ibid. p.xi
3 ibid. p.viii
4 Orpen, G.H. 'Rathgall, County Wicklow' pp.41-57
5 I have no idea what this means, I'm just quoting the learned Mr. Orpen.
6 This is another version of the name Theoblad Fitzwalter, whom we shall meet later on.
7 Stout, G. 'Wicklow's Prehistoric Landscape' p.12
8 Kinahan, G.H. 'Proceedings' in RSAI *Journal*, xvi (1883-4) pp.224-232
9 Ó Lionáin, F. *Croghan to the Sea* p.7
10 Fitzpatrick, M. www.excavations.ie Wicklow 1997:615
11 ibid.
12 www.excavations.ie Wicklow 1997:614
13 www.excavations.ie Wicklow 1997:618
14 *JRSAI* vol.xl, p.61
15 Tuomey, T.C. 'Description of a Cromleac and Ogham Monument' pp.187-194
16 *JRSAI*, vol. X, (1868-69) pp.175-6
17 Anon. *AHSJ* 1984 p.47. Submitted by Seamus O'Duinn.
18 I was told this by an elderly local on July 4th, 2002 when I went out to make sure that it still existed. A crop of young barley made it impossible for me to verify if it is still there or not.
19 Price, L. 'The Ages of Stone and Bronze in County Wicklow' p.32
20 ibid. p.37. For an earlier description see Tuomey, op.cit
21 Stout, 'Prehistoric Landscape' p.6 map.
22 Kinahan, G.H. 'Sepulchral and other Prehistoric Relics' p.152
23 Power, P. *The Kilmichael Bowl*
24 Stout, 'Prehistoric Landscape' pp. 20, 22-3

[25] Eogan, G. *Hoards of the Irish Later Bronze Age* pp.173, 312

[26] Corlett, C. & Medleycott, J.(eds) *The Ordnance Survey Letters* p.123

[27] Power, P.J. *The Arklow Calendar* p.7

[28] O'Cleirigh, N *The Archaeological Heritage of the Barony of Arklow* p.3

Chapter Two:

[1] Smyth, A.P. 'Kings, Saints and Sagas' p.46

[2] Wallace, M. *100 Irish Lives* pp.17-18. Also Boylan,H.(ed.) *DIB*, p.363

[3] Smyth, A.P. 'Kings, Saints and Sagas' pp.51-2

[4] Ordnance Survey Letters, 19 January 1839, reproduced in Corlett & Medleycott p.88

[5] Ó Lionáin, *Croghan to the Sea* p.13

[6] Price, *Place-Names* p.467

[7] Irish Folklore Commisssion S 923: 185-6, quoted in Lynch, G. 'And the Saint Blessed the Well' p.4

[8] Quoted in Price, *Place-Names* p.vi

[9] Price, *Place-Names* p.xv footnote 28

[10] O'Cleirigh, *Archaeological Heritage* p.7, quoting Price.

[11] ibid.

[12] Price, *Place-Names* p.x

[13] Ó Corráin, D. *Ireland Before the Normans* .

[14] ibid. p.46

[15] ibid. p.53

[16] Severin, T. *The Brendan Voyage*

[17] Ó Corráin, p.71

[18] ibid. p.81

[19] O'Cleirigh, p.8

[20] Ó Corráin, p.83

[21] Etchingham, C. 'Evidence of Scandinavian Settlement in Wicklow' p.114. Etchingham favours the identification of Inber Dee with Arklow based on the Avonmore being called the Dée.

[22] Price, *Place-Names* p.xxi

[23] Etchingham, pp.120-1

[24] ibid. p.128. Also Price, p.xx

[25] Price, *Place-Names* p.xx

[26] ibid. pp. xxi-xxii, 459, 472, 484, and 490

[27] Ó Corráin, pp.105-7

[28] *JRSAI* xxxii (1902) p.71.

29   Christensen, A. E. 'Vikings in the Irish Sea' pp.16-7
30   Shetelig *Viking Antiquities in Great Britain and Ireland,* vi p.104.

Chapter Three:

1   De Rosa, P. *Vicars of Christ* p.56
2   Quoted in Furlong, N. *Dermot, King of Leinster and the Foreigners* p.165
3   Price, *Place-Names* p.xxvi-ii
4   Furlong, F. 'Ormond Deeds Relating to Arklow'   p.31
5   Power, P.J. *The Arklow Calendar* p.21
6   de Breffny, B. *Irish Family Names, arms, origins, and locations* p.67
7   Murphy, D. Rev. *Cromwell in Ireland* p.363
8   Power, P.J. *The Arklow Calendar* pp.117-8; also Price, lxiii
9   Furlong, F. 'Ormond Deeds'
10   ibid
11   Quoted in Lydon, J.F. 'Medieval Wicklow – "a land of war"'   p.155.
12   Price, *Place-Names* p.xxxiii
13   Corlett & Medleycott (eds) *Ordnance Survey Letters* p.124
14   ibid. p.122
15   Keeley V. *Archaeological Consultancy Report* October 1998
16   de Rosa, P.   *Vicars of Christ* p.573
17   Lydon, J.F. 'Medieval Wicklow ' "a land of war"' p.153
18   The descriptions Norman, Anglo-Norman, Norman-English, and English really refer to the same dominant faction. The different wording signifies how the Normans became the Anglo-Normans, who became the English with the passage of time.
19   Frame, R. 'The Justiciar and the Murder of the MacMurroughs'   p.223-9
20   Price, *Place-Names* p.liv
21   Frame, 'Murder of the MacMurroughs'
22   Lydon, p.163, quoting from Frame, 'Murder of the MacMurroughs' p.224
23   ibid.
24   ibid. p.172.
25   Power, P.J. *The Arklow Calendar* p.30; also Price, lxiii
26   The forms Cavanagh and Kavanagh are used interchangeably throughout most of the sources. At the risk of being accused of inconsistent spelling, I will use the variant spellings as indicated by the sources.
27   Sullivan, A.M. *The Story of Ireland* p.179
28   ibid. p.180
29   Greene, M. 'The Dominicans in Arklow'

[30] Quoted in ibid.

[31] de Rosa, *Vicars of Christ* p.129

[32] Quoted in Greene *'Dominicans'*

[33] ibid.

[34] Ronan, M 'The Ancient Churches of the Deanery of Arklow, County Wicklow'

[35] The name Ormond might be spelled with or without an 'e' in this book. The form used depends on the relevant sources.

[36] Price, L. 'The Byrnes' Country in County Wicklow ..' pp.41-62

[37] Furlong, F. 'Ormond Deeds' p.31

[38] Price: 'Byrnes' Country' p.54

[39] Quoted in Murray, P.J. 'The Glenart Estate'   no page number

[40] Price: 'Byrnes' Country' p.56

[41] ibid.

[42] Murray, 'The Glenart Estate'

[43] Price, 'Byrnes Country' pp.58-9

[44] ibid. p.62

[45] Finlay, J. 'Wicklow's Local Government, 1613-1920'   p.26

[46] Price, L. 'Byrnes Country ...' p.55

[47] de Courcy Ireland, J. *Ireland's Sea Fisheries* p.21

[48] For an excellent account of Phelim's revolt see Andrew O'Brien's articles 'Phelim MacFeagh's Revolt 1597-1599' pp 78-86 and 'Distressed Country – Wicklow in 1599' pp-36-43

[49] 'Proceedings of the Earl of Essex' *The Carew Manuscripts* pp.308-312.

[50] ibid.

[51] ibid.

[52] ibid.

Chapter Four:

[1] Donnelly, B. 'From Grand Jury to County Council ..' p.855

[2] De Courcy Ireland, J. *Ireland's Sea Fisheries: a history* pp.14, 15, 17, 21

[3] Price, L. 'Byrnes' Country in the 16th century'   pp.58-9

[4] Loeber, R. 'Settlers' Utilisation of the Natural Resources'   p.274

[5] ibid. p.278

[6] Power, P.J. *The Arklow Calendar* p.48

[7] Loeber, R. 'Settlers' Utilisation ..' p.274

[8] ibid. p.289

[9] Beckett, J.C. *The Making of Modern Ireland 1603-1923*   p.88.

10 Boylan, H. (ed.) *DIB*

11 G.E.C. (et al) *The Complete Peerage* London 1945

12 Power, P.J. *Arklow Calendar* p.49

13 Beckett, *Making of Modern Ireland*   p.89

14 ibid

15 ibid.

16 Power, *Arklow Calendar*

17 Loeber, 'Settlers' Utilisation ..' p.289 quoting the original source as TCD ms 811, f.177

18 Murray, P.J. 'Shelton Abbey and Estate', and Price, *Place Names* p.474

19 Power, *Arklow Calendar* p.50

20 Murphy, D. *Cromwell in Ireland*   pp.141-2, also Power, p.50

21 For an example of this new slant see Reilly, T. *Cromwell: an honourable enemy*

22 Murphy, D. *Cromwell in Ireland* p.106

23 ibid. p.142

24 *A collection of some of the massacres, etc. committed on the Irish in Ireland since the 23rd December, 1641* quoted in Ó Lionáin *From Croghan to the Sea* p.25

25 MacLysaght, E. *Irish life in the seventeenth century* p.285

26 Murphy, D. *Cromwell in Ireland* p.167

27 ibid. p.185

28 Lynch, Dr John, Archdeacon of Tuam *Cambrensis Eversus* 1662, quoted by Ó Lionáin, p.25

29 O'Cleirigh, N. 'Mother Kevin', *AHSJ* 1985. pp.35-40

30 Murray, P.J. 'Shelton Abbey and Estate'   no page numbers.

31 O'Reilly, Stan J. 'The Hearth Money Rolls for the County of Wicklow, 1668' pp.41-46

32 Loeber, R. 'Settlers' Utilisation ..' p302, note 84.

33 For a comprehensive history of map-making in County Wicklow see Power, P. 'A Survey: some Wicklow maps 1500-1888' pp.723-760.

34 ibid. p.727

35 *Handbook on Irish Genealogy* - No author named. p.22

36 Quoted in Forde, Frank *Maritime Arklow* pp. 257-8

37 Ronan, M. 'The Ancient Churches of the Deanery of Arklow, Co. Wicklow'

38 Inscription on the Howard Monument (the 'Pyramid') in Old Kilbride graveyard. See Power, P. *Old Kilbride Churchyard and Mausoleums, Ferrybank, Arklow* revised edition, October 2001

39 Greene, M. 'The Dominicans in Arklow' no page numbers

40 Murray, 'Shelton' says the former, Power, *Arklow Calendar* p.56 says the latter

41 This was the date of the battle as recorded in the Julian calendar. Britain did not adopt the Gregorian calendar until 1752 and all dates had to be adjusted by eleven days, making the 1st of July into the 12th.

42 Power, *Arklow Calendar* p.56

43 Edmund Burke quoted in *Catholic Encylopaedia: penal laws* www.newadvent.org/cathen//11611c.htm

Chapter Five:

1   MacLysaght, E. *Irish Life in the Seventeenth Century* pp.294-5

2   Connolly, S.J. *Priests and People in Pre-Famine Ireland 1780-1845* p35-38

3   www.newadvent

4   ibid.

5   Neill, K. *An Illustrated History of the Irish People* p.73

6   Murray, P.J. 'The Glenart Estate' no page numbers

7   See ibid and Power, *Arklow Calendar,* p.55

8   Power, P. 'Maps 1500-1688' p.736

9   Registry of Deeds Lib 83 pag 331 No.59124 registered 28th December 1736

10 Power *Arklow Calendar* p.121

11 Power 'Maps' p.736. Also NAI M6233

12 For the workings of the Grand Jury see Donnelly, B. 'From Grand Jury to County Council..' and Donnelly, B. *For the Betterment of the People* Wicklow County Council 1998

13 Cantwell, B. *Memorials of the Dead: South-east Wicklow* Ennereilly Graveyard. The headstone can be seen in situ, but access to the graveyard has been restricted in recent years.

14 Shepherd, E. 'Avoca Mines' p.18

15 George T. Stokes (ed.) *Pococke's Tour in Ireland in 1752* p.159

16 Murphy, T.P. *Charter School Education in Ireland with special reference to Arklow Charter School 1748-1812.* Med thesis, July 2002, Education Department UCD. p.32

17 ibid. p.16

18 *DNB* vol.x 1917

19 Journal of the Irish House of Commons, vol.9 App. CCLXXX

20 ibid. vol 12, App.CCXLI

21 Hutton, A.Wollaston (ed.) *Arthur Young's Tour in Ireland 1776-1779* p.94

22 Anon. *A Tour Through Ireland*   p.31

23 Perry , G 'Reynolds and the Royal Academy' 247-268

24 Short, M. *Inside the Brotherhood* pp.115-124

25 Letter from the Archivist of the Grand Lodge of A.F.&A. Masons of Ireland, Freemasons' Hall, Dublin to Jim Rees, dated 21st November 2002

26 Power, P. *Report on Kilbride* p.6

27 These details are written from personal experience. In 1986, Pat Power and I were given permission to recorded these, and other, details inside the mausoleum. They can be found in Pat's report.

28 Knight, S. *The Brotherhood* pp.38-45, and Short, M *Inside the Brotherhood* pp. 91 and 112

29 Shepherd, 'Avoca Mines' p.18.

30 Chapman, W. *Report on the Improvement of the Harbour of Arklow*

31 O'Donnell, R. *Rebellion in Wicklow* p. 60

32 Ó Lionáin, F. *Croghan to the sea* p.72

33 McGettigan, D. 'The Great Wicklow Gold Rush of 1795' pp.12-17

34 ibid.

35 Ó Lionáin, p.72

36 Camden to the Prime Minister in London, quoted by Lionáin. The date of the letter appears to be 8th October 1798, but surely this must be 1795?

37 de Latocnaye *Promenade d'un Francais dans l'Irlande*

38 Holmes. G (1801) *Sketches of some of the Southern Counties of Ireland* p 45

Chapter Six:

1 For perhaps the most comprehensive accounts of the battle see: - Power, P. 'The battle of Arklow' ; O'Donnell, R. *The Rebellion in Wicklow 1798* pp.210-225; Hayes-McCoy, G.A. *Irish Battles: a military history of Ireland* pp.273-313; Bayly. H.L., letter to his father Edward NA ms 2464

2 Letter from Henry Lambart Bayly to his father, Rev Edward Bayly, June 10th, 1798, The Bayly Papers, Representative Church Body Library. Lambart Bayly took part in the battle, this letter is his account as written the following day.

3 Chapman, referred to in O'Donnell, *Rebellion* p.60

4 Exact figures are impossible to arrive at. Estimates range from 10,000 –15,000 combatants on the insurgent side, with several thousand more followers and refugees, and perhaps between 2000-3,000 men on the loyalist side..

5 For a very clear chronology of events leading to the rebellion see Power,

P. 'A Chronology for the Rebellion of 1798'

6   The number of ships and men vary from source to source from 35 ships and 13,000 men to 48 ships and 15,000 men

7   O'Reilly, V. 'Hepenstall – The Walking Gallows'

8   O'Donnell, R. *Rebellion in Wicklow* p.169

9   Bayly to John Parnell, NAI, Rebellion Papers, 620/18A/6

10 Hardy to Edward Cooke, ibid, 620/38/48, January 19th 1797

11 O'Donnell, R. *Rebellion in Wicklow* pp.92-3

12 NAI 620/18A/6 20th August, 1797

13 O'Donnell, R. *Rebellion in Wicklow* p.148

14 ibid. p.158

15 Rees, J. 'The Confession of "A.B."'. Murray was assigned three initials and A.B. should appear as W.A.B. throughout.

16 O'Donnell, R. *Rebellion in Wicklow* p.62

17 21 May 1798 NAI 620/3/32/6

18 O'Donnell, R. *Rebellion* p. 148

19 Murray, P.J. 'Daniel Murray, Archbishop of Dublin 1823-1852' p.19

20 Lawlor, C. *The Massacre on Dunlavin Green: a story of the 1798 Rebellion*

21 Furlong, N. *Fr. John Murphy of Boolavogue 1753-1798* pp.40-1.

22 O'Donnell, R. *Rebellion* p.148

23 The Orange Order was established in 1796 and there were several lodges in the north Wexford/south Wicklow region within two years. The Order was created to defend Protestants against perceived Catholic aggression and to celebrate the Boyne victory of William of Orange over a century earlier. Loyalist gangs in this area were generally referred to as Orangemen.

24 Edward Bayly to Lambart Bayly, June 3rd, 1798

25 Hayes-McCoy *Irish Battles* p.287

26 O'Donnell, *Rebellion*, p.62

27 This was the Charter School referred to in Chapter Five. The children had been removed from harm's way and sent by sea to Dublin, while the soldiers set up this outpost. The school did not re-open until 1801.

28 ibid. p.216

29 Captain Thomas Knox-Grogan of the Castletown Yeomanry. There is a plaque to him in St Saviour's.

30 O'Donnell, *Rebellion* p.217

31 The words attributed to Fr Michael Murphy's trick vary quite a bit, and whether he actually pulled the stunt at all or not is open to question. It is one of the more resilient images of the battle, but that doesn't necessarily

mean it happened.

[32] Quoted in O'Donnell, *Rebellion* p.221

[33] Edward Bayly to Lambart Bayly, June 15th, 1798

[34] *Tryal of Billy Byrne of Ballymanus* p.30

[35] Power, P. 'The Battle of Arklow' p.36

[36] McLaren, A. *A Minute Description of the Battles of Gorey, Arklow and Vinegar Hill*

[37] Rees, J. 'Yeoman Officer's Sword found'

[38] Quoted in O'Donnell, *Rebellion* p.223

[39] ibid. p.224

[40] ibid. p.223

Chapter Seven:

[1] O'Donnell, R. *Aftermath* p.26

[2] That is the Established (or Anglican) Church

[3] Meagher, J. 'Extracts from an article on Father Nicholas Kearns' *AHSJ* 1982, no page number, full article on Father Kearns by John Meagher in *Reportorium Novum* vol.1 no.1 1955

[4] Edward Bayly to Lambart Bayly, June 14th 1798

[5] ibid. June 19th, 1798

[6] ibid. June 20th, 1798

[7] Bayly, H.L. 'Statistical Account of Arklow' p.62

[8] Murray, P.J. 'Daniel Murray, Archbishop of Dublin'

[9] Just where this residence was is debatable. Some sources say Cooladangan (*The People* newspaper 18 November 1898, quoted in Ó Lionáin *Croghan to the Sea*), others say Johnstown (P.J.Murray, a great grand-nephew of Daniel Murray, and Dr Ruán O'Donnell). As the townlands are contiguous, it probably doesn't really matter.

[10] O'Donnell, R. *Aftermath* p.26. The internal quote is from the *Dublin Evening Press* 18th December 1798.

[11] Arklow parish church had been burned either during the battle in June or the following day. Some folklore accounts say that it was burned twice. (Murphy Papers, pp.5 and 9) It must have been repaired to some extent for this account to make sense, yet even as late as October 1799, Murray's successor had to say mass 'within the walls of the old chapel which was burned' – see note 13 below.

[12] Murray, P.J. 'Daniel Murray' pp.12-13

[13] Quoted in Meagher, 'Fr Kearns'. No page number.

[14] The generally accepted figure is 30,000 fatalities in three months

15 O'Donnell, R. *Aftermath* p.13

16 NLI, *List of Claims for the Relief of Suffering Loyalists*

17 Bolton, G.G.C. *The Passing of the Irish Act of Union;* p.61

18 Murray, P.J. 'The Glenart Estate' No page numbers.

19 Bolton, *Act of Union* p.133. It should be noted that only a tiny percentage of tenants – and the population as a whole – were entitled to vote, the criteria being based on property rights.

20 White, D. 'Arklow Methodist Church' p.7

21 Kavanagh, J, 'Early Methodism in Wicklow Town and County' p.5

22 ibid. p.6

23 Meagher, 'Fr Kearns' AHSJ 1982 quoting letter dated 17th February, 1802

24 O'Donnell *Aftermath* p.222

25 Kavanagh, 'Early Methodism in Wicklow' p.7

26 Carysfort to Troy 18 March 1803, DDA 29/9 Troy 1802-3, 54-56

27 For a history of Johnstown church see Ó Lionáin, F. 'The Old Church in Johnstown', pp.50-56

28 That is Ballynattin

29 Quoted in Meagher 'Fr Kearns'

30 Sea Fencibles were water-borne militia, something like a naval FCA.

31 'J.H.' to H.L.Bayly, NLI, Reports on Private Collections vol.4 , p.951

32 Carr, John (1806) *The Stranger in Ireland, or A Tour in the Southern and Western Parts of that Country in the Year 1805* London p161

33 Robertson, Rev J *The Traveller's Guide Through Ireland* Edinburgh 1806, p.292

34 NAI, SOCP. no reference number. I'm grateful to Stan O'Reilly for giving me a copy of this.

35 NAI, SOCP., 1120/97 and 1120/98. Again, my thanks to Stan O'Reilly for bringing these to my attention.

36 I am grateful to Professor Bruce Elliott of Carleton University, Ottawa for bringing this group emigration to my attention. He is currently researching the origins and fates of these families.

37 Anon. *Handbook on Irish Genealogy* Dublin 1980, p.118

38 Elliott, B. 'Emigration from South Leinster to Eastern Upper Canada' in Whelan & Nolan (eds) *Wexford History and Society*, 1987. p.426

39 There is some doubt as to the correct spelling of this ship's name – *Atalanta, Atlanta, Atalante* – I have opted for the last as that is the form used by the British Ministry of Defence Admiralty Library in a letter to me dated 31 August 1999. There is no record of this incident in the ship's

logs, but several American newspapers did cover it. See Elliott, B. 'Emigration...' p.424; and Wilson, D.A. *United Irishmen United States* p.80

[40] Elliott, B. 'Emigration from South Leinster ...' pp.427-8

[41] *Freeman's Journal* 1811, exact date not known

[42] i.e. B.J. O'Beirne's solicitor's offices and *Joanne's* café. Mr O'Beirne's part of the building commemorates the old ties with the church and proudly displays CHURCH BUIL on the wall. For reasons best known to the owners of the other section of the building, the remaining letters, DINGS, have been obliterated.

[43] Cromwell, T. *Excursions through Ireland, etc* London. 1820. See Appenix for his account of Arklow.

[44] *Parliamentary Gazetteer* 1844.

[45] White, D. 'Arklow Methodist Church'. p.7

[46] Wakefield, *An Account of Ireland* 1812

[47] Forde, F. *Maritime Arklow* p.258

[48] Bayly, H.L 'Statistical Account of Arklow' 1814, p.53

[49] ibid. 56-7

[50] Anon. *The Traveller's New Guide Through Ireland* Dublin 1815, p.63

[51] See map accompanying H.L.Bayly's article in Mason's *Statistical Survey*

[52] The mountain is Croghan, the 'new road' is the Vale Road

[53] Plumtre, A. *Narrative of a Residence in Ireland* London 1817, p186

[54] An Irish Gentleman. *The Scientific Tourist Through Ireland* London 1818

[55] Kavanagh, J. 'Early Methodists ...' p.7

[56] ibid, p.8

[57] ibid.

[58] Cromwell, T. *Excursions through Ireland, etc* London. 1820 See Appendix.

[59] Donnelly, B. *For the Betterment of the People* Wicklow County Council c.1998, p.3

Chapter Eight:

[1] Quoted in Power, P. *Arklow Calendar* p.67

[2] O'Cleirigh, N. 'The Hedge Schools of Arklow District' *AHST* 1982, no page number

[3] Report of the Commissioners for Education 1825, quoted in O'Cleirigh, 'Hedge Schools...'

[4] These were introduced to appease Catholic disquiet in times of national danger. In 1782 the British government and its puppet parliament in

Dublin had much of its army fighting the American colonists, leaving Ireland "unprotected" against external invasion or internal revolt. The situation was repeated in 1793 when Britain declared war on revolutionary France. The Relief Acts were crumbs to buy loyalty.

5   Ribbonmen was one of the many names given to members of agrarian societies formed to intimidate landowners, loyalists, informers, etc, etc. They did so by sending death threats, injuring livestock, or setting fire to property. They were also known as Disturbers (as we've seen from Chapter 7) and Whiteboys.

6   NAI, SOCP, 2374, Page 1085

7   ibid. item 11 dated 18th March 1822.

8   ibid. Item 13, dated 2nd April, 1822

9   NAI, SOCP 2509, Page 1151, item 37. Connolly, S.J *Priests & people in pre-Famine Ireland 1780-1845*, p.220

10 McNiffe, L. *A History of the Garda Síochána* Wolfhound 1997, pp.3-4

11 Murray, P.J. 'The Glenart Estate'

12 Morris,J. *The Story of Arklow Lifeboats* Forde, F. *Maritime Arklow* p. 299

13 de Courcy Ireland, J. *Wreck and Rescue on the East Coast of Ireland* p.29

14 This would appear to be the date of the actual opening of the station, but the decision to open a station here was taken on August 3rd, 1825. Morris, *Arklow Lifeboats* p.1

15 Hurley, M. *Home from the Sea: the story of the Courtmacsherry lifeboat, 1825-1995.*

16 Murray, P.J. 'The Glenart Estate' Some sources give his date of death as 1826.

17 A German Prince, *Tour in England, Ireland, and France in the years 1826, 1827, 1828, and 1829, etc ...* Philadelphia , 1833 p 333

18 Inglis, H. *A Journey Throughout Ireland in the Spring, Summer, and Autumn of 1834* London 1835, p.36

19 *Parliamentary Gazetteer of Ireland* 1844, p.69

20 Barrow, J *A Tour Round Ireland Through the Sea-Coast Counties in the Autumn of 1835* London 1836, p36

21 Binns, J *The Miseries and Beauties of Ireland* London 1837 p209

22 Fitzmaurice, J. 'Arklow Boys's National School in Historic Perspective' *AHSJ* 1990-91 p.21

23 McNiffe, L *A History of the Garda Síochána* p.4. Dublin, Belfast and Derry were exempted from this national coverage, with each city having its own force.

24 Lewis, S. *Topographical Dictionary* 1838

25 See Appendix One.

26 *Parliamentary Gazetteer of Ireland*   1846, p69

27 i.e. in Cumbria in the northwest of England

28 At this time a farm labourer's wage was 10d a day or less. See the Devon Commission Report 1844 for general details of wages at that time.

29 His testimony is numbered 1019 in the report, pages 692-696

30 Secret societies such as 'The Ribbonmen' and 'Whiteboys' had been active in many parts of Ireland for decades, injuring the animals or destroying the crops of landlords deemed to be unfair in their dealings with their tenantry. The absence of such activity – and Hudson's testimony is supported elsewhere – suggests that there was no major discontent in the Arklow area.

31 Forde, F. *Maritime Arklow* pp.23-24

32 For an overview of the Poor Law system see Ó Cathoir, E 'The Poor Law'.

33 Many people now refer to Bradshaw's Lane off Main Street as the Union Lane, because of the Trade Union offices there, but this is incorrect. Union Lane is off South Quay, beside Noel O'Toole's carpet and furniture shop and the SIPTU offices are in Bradshaw's Lane.

34 For further reading see Hannigan, K 'Wicklow Before and After the Famine'; Ó Cathoir, E 'The Poor Law'; Byrne, K *From Shade to Sunlight*; and Rees, J. *A Farewell To Famine* and *Surplus People*

35 NAI, Relief Commission, 11/1/4014 (2903)

36 *Freeman's Journal*   December 9th, 1851

37 Kilbride Parish Records quoted in the *Wicklow People* January 1st, 1993 p.5

38 Hannigan, K 'Wicklow Before and After the Famine', p.808

39 ibid. p.807

40 A meaningless phrase often used since the Act of Union in 1801.

41 ibid. p.806

42 Society of Friends *Transactions during the Famine in Ireland in 1846 and 1847* Dublin 1852,   pp 390-1

Chapter Nine:

1 Forde, F. *Maritime Arklow* pp.22-25

2 Quoted in McKay, B. 'Robert McMicken and the Arklow connection – 1840' *AHSJ* 1986 pp.10-11

3 Morris, J. *The Story of the Arklow Lifeboats* p.1

4 This appeared in the *Wicklow Newsletter* dated June 27th, 1857, and is quoted here from Captain Frank Forde's *Maritime Arklow*, pp.310-311

5   For an in-depth study of this battle see Connolly, S.J. *Priests and People in Pre-Famine Ireland*

6   Quoted from an unattributed typed paper written in 1961 as part of the church centenary celebrations.

7   See also Tyrrell, D. 'The Parish Church of Saints Mary and Peter, Arklow', *AHSJ* 1985 pp.52-57

8   For the history of the railway see Shepherd, E. & Beasley, G. *The Dublin & South Eastern Railway* Midland Publishing Ltd, 1998

9   The late Willie Tyrrell told me where the original yard was located. A new yard was opened further upriver, on the site now occupied by Anchor Mews.

10 Forde, F. *Maritime Arklow* pp. 257-274

11 This is evident from the various Ordnance Survey maps produced at that time and from recent excavations during construction work..

12 This was Stopford Halpin, brother of the soon-to-be famous Captain Robert Halpin of Wicklow.

13 Much of the information concerning the Dispensary Committee is taken from the Minute Books of the Rathdrum Board of Guardians 1854-5, pages 188, 302, 407, and 504.

14 Minutes of the Rathdrum Rathdrum Board of Guardians 1862, p.98

15 ibid. p.18

16 I have never seen this written, nor has anyone I have asked over the years, so either spelling is appropriate, particularly as the origin of the name has been lost. I heard this explanation from the late John Hayes, who was born around 1900 and was steeped in the folklore of the area.

17 *Wicklow Newsletter* September 22nd, 1866

18 Forde, F. *Maritime Arklow,* pp.299-301, 303

19 *Freeman's Journal* September 20th, 1866

20 William Proby was High Sheriff of the County.

21 *Illustrated London News* March 6th, 1869

22 The original illuminated address is now in the possession of Mr Allen Proby of Inch, who allowed me to reproduce the text in 'The Cholera Epidemic of 1866', *AHSJ* 1982, no page number.

23 Despite the pejorative label, this building was never a "Charter School" as the one on Coolgreaney Road had been. It was built as a Protestant school in the 1860s, but over the years it has had many re-incarnations, including a fur factory, P&T storage shed, and is now the premises of Wicklow Vale Emporium.

24 Byrne, M. 'St Michael's Terrace – a legacy of the Carysforts' *AHSJ* 2001-2002 p.58

25 ibid. pp.57-8
26 For a full account of the Carysfort Schools see Marshall, M. 'The Three Schools at Carysfort' *AHSJ* 1996/97 pp.30-36
27 For a comparison of the fortunes of the various maritime communities in the county see Rees, J. 'Maritime Wicklow, parts 1 & 2' in *WHSJ* vol.2 no.5, 1999 pp.20-30 and *WHSJ* vol.2 no.6, 2000, pp.45-56 respectively
28 Rees, J. & Charlton, L. *Arklow- last stronghold of sail* p.12; Forde, F. *Maritime Arklow* p.19
29 i.e the Fogartys of P.J. Boland Ltd.
30 Quoted in McKay, B. 'Valuation and illustration of the town of Arklow by J. Townsend Trench – 1877' *AHSJ* 1986, p.9
31 This was probably the nationalist paper, the *Wicklow People*. This extract is taken from an unattributed essay on the life of Archdeacon Redmond which was circulated in 1961 as part of the centenary celebrations of the chapel.
32 Four other priests are also interred inside the chapel: Fr Edan Redmond, died 1839, Fr James Flavin died 1857 – both of whom were either re-interred from their original places of burial or who had been buried in the old church around which the new one was built – and Fr Thomas Murray who died in 1870.

Chapter Ten:

1 Sr. Magdalena, 'A Sketch of the History of the Arklow Convent' .
2 ibid.
3 Fr Dunphy's building programme in the Rock/Castletown area is well documented in Lionáin, F. *Croghan to the Sea.*
4 *Wicklow Newsletter* 29th, 1880; September 4th 1880; December 25th 1880.
5 There are countless biographies of Parnell which show the remarkable energy of the man. Perhaps the most useful, with regard to his Arklow interests, is R.F. Foster's *Charles Stewart Parnell: the man and his family*
6 Nairn & Crowley (1998) *Wild Wicklow* p.123
7 Power, P. 'Arklow Rock Thrived Under Parnell' *Wicklow People* May13th, 1988 puts the date of the agreement as December 1884; Murphy, H. 'City streets were paved with stones from Arklow' *Wicklow People* September 3rd 1975 or 6 (last digit is smudged on the cutting in my possession) says 1882.
8 Murphy, H. 'City streets ... Arklow stone'.
9 Power, P. 'Arklow Rock Thrived ...'
10 Morrison, J. (1872) 'Arklow Chemical Works Limited', the periodical from

which the extract is taken is not known but appears to have been the journal of the Tyne Social Chemical Society

[11] ibid. p.7

[12] See Chapter 7, footnote 50

[13] Morrison, 'Arklow Chemical Works..' p.8

[14] ibid. p.9

[15] ibid. p.13 also Power, P. *The Arklow Calendar* p.96

[16] I am grateful to Kevin Byrne, who has done extensive research in the Minutes of the Rathdrum Guardians, for bringing this incident to my attention.

[17] For a full account see Rees, J. 'The Storm of 1886'

[18] Marshall, M. 'The Three Schools at Carysfort' p.34

[19] Chapter title in the *Arklow Calendar*

[20] In 1883, Proby had an inventory taken of his property and found his estates to total 25,914 acres, worth £31,075 per annum. Co Wicklow 16,674 acres; Huntingdonshire 3,972 acres, Northants 2,270; Dublin 1,250 acres and Kildare 1,748 acres.

[21] I have in my possession a copy of *Memorandum giving the facts as to the STREET PREACHING IN ARKLOW*, HMSO 1892, which details the high point (or low point?) of these events between 1890 and 1892. My account and any quotations in it are taken from this publication.

[22] The one on the site of Church Buildings, opposite St Mary's graveyard, now the Park.

[23] The different accounts in the two local newspapers of the time, the *Wicklow People* (Nationalist) and the *Wicklow Newsletter* (Unionist), reflect the tensions of the population as a whole. The *People* complained of the clergymen's behaviour, the *Newsletter* complained of the people's reaction to the clergymen.

[24] *Freeman's Journal,* May 28th 1890

[25] *Wicklow People,* June 21st 1890

[26] Local historian Pat Power has a set of these images which he uses in an illustrated lecture on this topic.

[27] *Arklow Parish Magazine* vol. VIII, no.96, December 1895, p.2

[28] Power, P. *Arklow Calendar,* p.103.

[29] Foster, R.F. *Charles Stewart Parnell: the man and his family,* p.210

[30] See Rees, J. *Life of Captain Robert Halpin*

[31] *Wicklow Newsletter* July 9th 1892.

[32] Power, P. 'Arklow Rock Quarries', *Wicklow People* May 13th 1988

[33] I am currently researching Dr Molony's life and the debate around his

untimely death. Many details are still to be discovered and the following is a brief outline of research findings to date. I hope to publish a full article on Dr Molony in a future *Arklow Historical Society Journal*.

34 *Wicklow Newsletter,* October29[th], 1892.

35 ibid.

36 Spellissy, S. *Window on Aran* p.43.

37 Micks, W.L. *An Account of the Constitution, Administration and Dissolution of the Congested Districts Board for Ireland from 1891 to 1923* Dublin 1925

38 ibid. p.41

39 ibid. p.42

40 Forde, F. *Maritime Arklow,* pp.248-9

41 Robinson, T. *Stones of Aran: Labyrinth* p.107

42 Forde, F. *Maritime Arklow,* p.248.

Chapter Eleven:

1 *Wicklow Newsletter* December17[th] 1892

2 *Wicklow People* June 6th 1900 p.2

3 This chapter is mostly based on Hilary Murphy's book *The Kynoch Era in Arklow.* Unless otherwise referenced, all statements here are taken from that work.

4 As children in the early 1960s, we used to catch "stingoes" in small sections of canal which could be still be found around the site as recently as the early 1980s.

5 My own grandmother included. There is even a postcard from the time showing Kynochs but naming it, 'The Cordite, Arklow'.

6 I believe it was in No. 5 but am open to correction on this.

7 Quoted in Murphy, H. 'When Arklow had two police stations' *Wicklow People* July 23rd 1976

8 ibid. It is probable that the station was established here because of the street preaching disturbances. The station was adjacent to the Charter School.

9 Quoted (presumably from the *Wicklow People)* in *The Kynoch Era,* p.4

10 Whiteside, L. *St Saviour's Church, Arklow* 1997 p.1. This booklet is a must, particularly if planning a visit to the church.

11 Connolly, S.J. *Priests and People in Pre-Famine Ireland 1780-1845* p. 216

12 See Rees, B. 'Matthew Doyle', pp.42-43. Also O'Donnell, *Rebellion* p.62

13 See Tyrrell, D. 'Arklow Terra Cotta Brick and Clay Company' pp.36-38

14 *Wicklow People,* May-June 1900

15   A phrase, I believe, attributable to Brendan Behan when describing religion in Ireland.

16   *Wicklow People* January 13th, 1906

17   For the full programme for the 1886 events see *AHSJ* 1986, pp.26-29

18   *Wicklow People* March 24th, 1906

19   *Wicklow People* April 14th 1906

20   They did not arrive until Thursday 29th.

21   *Wicklow People* August 10th, 1907

22   The eight ships were HMS *Exmouth, Albion, Cornwallis, Russell, Duncan, Arrigant, Diamond, and Amethyst.* Letter from Naval Historical Branch, Ministry of Defence to author (D/NHB 10/1/7/2G) dated September 19th 1990

23   One of Kynochs' own fleet of steamers.

24   *Wicklow People* December 7th, 1906. A similar heading, this time complaining about the lack of a sewage system, could have been carried in 2003 with equal, if not even greater, justice.

25   ibid. August 29th, 1908. This time the ships were *Venus, Russell, Cornwallis, Albion,* and *Exmouth.*

26   At time of writing, there are preparations under way in Umbogintwini to celebrate its centenary in 2008, and those involved are very conscious of the Arklow connection.

27   The local priest in Umbogintwini in the 1960s interviewed many of the surviving Arklow people. Thanks to the good offices of Anne Tyrrell (nee Sweeney), I have transcriptions of some of these.

28   Murphy, H. *The Kynoch Era* p.32

29   For a sketch of the lives of the Arklowmen in Umbogintwini see Burke, J.'Kynochs in South Africa' . For some reminiscences of workers in the Arklow factory see *AHSJ* 1986 pp.50-51; 1987 PP.57-58;

30   I have yet to pinpoint the exact date of the demolition of this church.

31   See Chap.7, footnote 42.

32   Murray, P.J. 'Glenart Estate' no page number.

33   Forde, F. *Maritime Arklow*, p.284

34   Arklow Harbour Board Minutes, April 18th, 1910.

35   Charlton, L. 'Arklow Fishing Disasters of 1910' pp.46-49

Chapter Twelve:

1   Murphy, H. 'Arklow fever hospital..' *Wicklow People*, day/month not known, 1976

2   Inspector's report quoted in Murphy, 'Arklow fever hospital...'

3   ibid.

4   The *Wicklow People* carried on-going reports of the progress these groups made at that time.

5   Most of the details concerning the Technical School is taken from O'Cleirigh, N. *Ninety Years of Technical Education in an Irish Maritime Town.*

6   Mr C. McCarthy, designer of Dublin's Bolton Street College of Technology – O'Cleirigh, *Ninety Years* ... p.12

7   Murphy, H *The Kynoch Era* ...p.44

8   ibid. p.42

9   They are in the National Archives, Bishop Street, Dublin.

10 See Rees & Charlton, *Arklow – last stronghold of sail;* Forde, *Maritime Arklow,* and Arklow Maritime Museum

11 Forde, F. *Maritime Arklow,* p.184

12 Quoted in Forde, F. *Maritime Arklow,* p.174

13 ibid. p.176

14 This later became the Countess of Wicklow Memorial Hospital and stood on the site now occupied by the Arklow Bay Hotel.

15 Forde, F. *Maritime Arklow* pp.295-6

16 In 1958 the discovery of World War 1 u-boat on Arklow bank again raised the discussion as to whether the explosion was the result of a seaborne attack, but nothing could be proved one way or the other.

17 Tyrrell, D. 'Maria Curran, Pioneer Woman Councillor' pp.10-12

18 Murphy, H. *Kynoch Era* .. p.64-5

Chapter Thirteen:

1   Donnelly, B. *For the Betterment of the People* p.32

2   *Wicklow People* January 1st, 1921

3   ibid. January 15th, 1921

4   ibid. February 26th, 1921

5   ibid. April 30th, 1921

6   ibid. September 24th, 1921

7   O'Connor, F. *The Big Fellow* p.155. Unfortunately O'Connor did not use footnotes to say where he got this information, and I have no other details.

8   *Wicklow People,* September 3rd, 1921

9   Three men executed in Manchester on November 23rd, 1867 for killing a police sergeant as they tried to rescue captured Fenians.

10   *Wicklow People,* November 26th, 1921

11   Hickey, M. & Byrne, M. 'Countess of Wicklow Memorial Hospital', pp.26-30

12   *Wicklow People,* April 16th, 1921

13   ibid. March 25th, 1922

14   ibid. January 28th, 1922, 'A Cordial Welcome Home'.

15   ibid. March 25th, 1922

16   ibid. February 4th, March 4th 1922

17   ibid. April 15th, 1922

18   ibid. April 29th, 1922

19   ibid. July 8th, 1922

20   For information on indigenous fishing boats in Arklow see Myler, T. 'The Arklow Yawl'

21   O'Cleirigh, N. *Ninety Years of Technical Education...* p.27

22   *DIB*, also Rees & Charlton, *Arklow –last stronghold of sail* p.85

23   The pub in Lower Main Street is called after this schooner.

24   Letter from Film Librarian for Elstree Studios to me, dated August 27th 1986

25   Now Ethopia

26   Ó Lionáin, F. *Croghan to the Sea* pp.118-125

27   Murray, P.J. 'The Glenart estate' *AHSJ* 1982

28   As in the case of Ormond and Ormonde, both forms of Coolgreaney and Coolgreany have been used in this book, depending on the revelant source.

29   Scannell, J. 'Arklow's 1941 Narrow Escape', and his follow-up article 'The Bomb that Never Was'.

30   Fitzgerald, S. *The Arklow War Graves*, pp.22-23

31   Open letter of M. Gunson calling for new members, quoted in Loughlin, L. 'The Marian Arts Society Remembered',

32   For a glimpse of how restrictive censorship was see Brown, T. *Ireland: a social and cultural history 1922-1979;* also Carlson, J. *Banned In Ireland;* also Cooney, J. *John Charles McQuaid*

33   Ó Duinn, S. 'Arklow G.A.A.' *AHSJ* 1999-2000, pp.89-93

34   Rees, B. *All For A Game* pp.10-11

35   O'Cléirigh, N. *Ninety Years of Technical Education* ... p.50

Chapter Fourteen:

1   Shepherd, E. 'Avoca Mines', pp.23-4

2   Forde, F. Maritime Arklow, p.254

3   Although the school was blessed by Archbishop McQuaid in 1963, the

first enrolment of students was in 1961. I am grateful to Bernie
O'Halloran, school secretary, for this information.

4   Company document given to employees, no date. p.3

5   ibid.

6   The nickname given to NET / IFI, short for the 'Fertiliser factory'. It was
    more commonly used in the first two decades of its existence than in later
    years.

7   Rees, J. 'The Changing Fleet of Arklow Shipping' *Sea Breezes* October
    1988, pp.680-688

8   See McCarthy, M. 'Brief Outline of the History of Arklow Youth Club',
    pp.54-59; Kavanagh, R. & Mulhall, D. 'This all happened in 1960 in Fr.
    O'Reilly's Youth Club', pp.50-55

9   O'Cléirigh, N. *Ninety Years of Vocational* ... p.49

10 ibid. p.54

11 Shepherd, E. 'Avoca Mines', p.24

12 O'Cléirigh, N. *Ninety years of Vocational.*

13 My personal experience of that particular closure was finishing in the
    Brook on the Friday and starting in Nu-Plast on the Monday.

14 *Wicklow People* September 16th, 1988

15 Byrne, J. 'Irish Fireplaces Ltd.' pp.68-70

16 Bill, A.R. 'Arklow Presbyterian Church – a short history' *AHSJ* 1987,
    pp.44-46

17 See Synnott, B. 'St Benedict's Athletic Club' pp.37-40

BIBLIOGRAPHY

Abbreviations:

AHSJ	*Arklow Historical Society Journal*
DDA	*Dublin Diocesan Archive*
DIB	*Dictionary of Irish Biography*
DNB	*Dictionary of National Biography*
NAI	*National Archives of Ireland*
NLI	*National Library of Ireland*
IHS	*Irish Historical Studies*
JRSAI	*Journal of the Royal Society of Antiquaries of Ireland*
ms	*manuscript*
PRIA	*Proceedings of the Royal Irish Academy*
SOCP	*State of the Country Papers*
TCD	*Trinity College Dublin*
UCD	*University College, Dublin*
WCLS	*Wicklow County Library Service*
WHSJ	*Wicklow Historical Society Journal*

<u>*Manuscript Sources/Oral:*</u>

Bayly Papers, NAI ms 2464
Irish Folklore Commission S 923:185-6, Dept.of Irish Folklore, UCD
Minute Books of Arklow Harbour Board
Minute Books of the Rathdrum Board of Guardians, WCLS
Murphy Papers, a folklore manuscript
Rebellion Papers, NAI, 620/18A/6; 620/3/32/6; 620/38/48
Registry of Deeds Lib 83 pag 331 No.59124
Relief Commission Papers, NAI, 11/1/4014 (2903)
State of the Country Papers, 1120/97; 1120/98; 2347/1085; 2509/1151 NAI
Troy Papers 1802-3; 54-56, DDA 29/9

<u>*Newspapers, Periodicals & Reports:*</u>

Anonymous 'The Grave of the Princess' (poem) *AHSJ* 1984
Bayly, H.L. 'Statistical Survey of Arklow' in Mason S.(ed.) *Statistical Account or parochial survey of Ireland* vol.II 1816
Burke, J. 'Kynochs in South Africa' *AHSJ* 1988-'89
Byrne, J. 'Irish Fireplaces Ltd.' *AHSJ* 2001-2002

Chapman, W. *Report on the Improvement of the Harbour of Arklow and the practibility of a navigation from thence by the Vales of the various Branches of the Ovoca* Dublin 1792

Charlton, L. 'Arklow Fishing Disasters 1910' *AHSJ* 1985

Devon Commission Report, 1844. NAI

Finlay, J. 'Wicklow's Local Government, 1613-1920' *WHSJ* vol.1 no.2 1989

Fitzgerald, S. 'The Arklow War Graves' *AHSJ* 1992-1993

Fitzmaurice, J. 'Arklow Boys' National School in Historic Perspective' *AHSJ* 1990-91

Frame, R. 'The Justiciar and the Murder of the MacMurroughs' *IHS* vol.xviii (1972)

Freeman's Journal as dated in Sources

Furlong, F. 'Ormond Deeds Relating to Arklow' *AHSJ* 1985

Greene, M. 'The Dominicans in Arklow' *AHSJ* 1983

Hannigan, K. 'Wicklow in the Famine years' *WHSJ* vol.1 no.5 1992

Hannigan, K. 'Eye-witness Accounts of the Famine in County Wicklow' *WHSJ* vol.1 no.6 1993

Hickey, M. & Byrne, M. 'Countess of Wicklow Memorial Hospital' *AHSJ* 1999-2000

HMSO *Memorandum giving the facts as to the STREET PREACHING IN ARKLOW* 1892

Illustrated London News, as dated in Sources

Journal of the Irish House of Commons vol.9 App.CCLXXX; vol.12, App.CCXLI

JRSAI vol.xl; vol x (1868-69); vol.xxxii (1902)

Kavanagh, J. 'Early Methodism in Wicklow Town and County' *WHSJ* vol.1 no.2 1989

Kavanagh, R. & Mulhall, D. 'This all happened in 1960 in Fr. O'Reilly's Youth Club' *AHSJ* 1996-'97

Keeley, V. *Archaeological Consultancy Report to Arklow UDC* October 1998

Kinahan, G.H. 'Proceedings' in *JRSAI* vol.xvi (1883-4)

Kinahan, G.H. 'Sepulchral and other Prehistoric Relics, Counties Wexford and Wicklow' *PRIA* vol.xvi, 2nd series vol.II (1879-1888)

List of Claims for the Relief of Suffering Loyalists, NLI

Loughlin, L. 'The Marian Arts Remembered' *AHSJ* 1988-'89

Lynch, G. 'And the Saint Blessed the Well' *WHSJ* vol.1 no.3 1990

McCarthy, M. 'Brief Outline of the History of Arklow Youth Club' *AHSJ* 1990-'91

McGettigan, D. 'The Great Wicklow Gold Rush of 1795' *WHSJ* vol.1 no.2 1989

McKay, B. 'Robert McMicken and the Arklow connection – 1840' *AHSJ* 1986

Marshall, M. 'The Three Schools at Carysfort' *AHSJ* 1996/97

Meagher, J. 'Extracts from an article on Father Nicholas Kearns' *AHSJ* 1982

Morrison, J. 'Arklow Chemical Works Limited' *Tyne Chemical Society* 1872

Murphy, H. 'Arklow fever hospital' *Wicklow People* 1976

Murphy, H. 'City streets were paved with stones from Arklow' *Wicklow People* September 3rd, 1975 (or 6)

Murphy, H. 'When Arklow had two police stations' *Wicklow People* July 23rd, 1976

Murphy, T.P. 'Charter School Education in Ireland with special reference to Arklow Charter School 1748-1812'. Med thesis, July 2002, Education Department UCD

Murray, P.J. 'The Glenart Estate' *AHSJ* 1982

Murray, P.J. 'Shelton Abbey and Estate' *AHSJ* 1983

Murray, P.J. 'Daniel Murray, Archbishop of Dublin' *AHSJ* 1985

Myler, T. 'The Arklow Yawl' *AHSJ* 1986

O'Brien, A. 'Phelim MacFeagh's Revolt 1597-1599' *WHSJ* vol.2 no.4 1998

O'Brien, A. 'Distressed County – Wicklow in 1599' *WHSJ* vol.2 no.5 1999

O'Cleirigh, N. 'Mother Kevin', *AHSJ 1985*

O'Cleirigh, N. 'The Hedge Schools of Arklow District' *AHSJ* 1982

Ó Duinn, S. 'Arklow G.A.A.' *AHSJ* 1999-2000

Ó Lionáin, F. 'The Old Church in Johnstown', *AHSJ 1992-'93*

O'Reilly, S.J. 'The Hearth Money Rolls for the County of Wicklow, 1668' *WHSJ* vol.1 no. 6 1993

O'Reilly, V. 'Hepenstall – the Walking Gallows' *WHSJ* vol.2 no.1 1995; and *WHSJ* vol.2 no.2 1996

Orpen, G.H. 'Rathgall, County Wicklow: Dún Galion and the "Dunum" of Ptolemy' *PRIA* vol.xxxii Dublin 1913

Parliamentary Gazetteer of Ireland 1844

Power, P. 'A Chronology for the Rebellion of 1798' *Arklow Historical Society 1798-1998 Commemorative Journal*

Power, P. 'Arklow Rock Thrived Under Parnell', *Wicklow People* May 13th, 1988.

Power, P. 'The battle of Arklow' *WHSJ* vol.2 no.4 1998

Power, P. The Kilmichael Bowl, and early Bronze Age grave excavation.

Power, P. *Old Kilbride Churchyard and Mausoleums, Ferrybank – Arklow* revised edition, October 2001

'Proceedings of the Earl of Essex' *Carew Manuscripts*

Price, L. 'The Ages of Stone and Bronze in County Wicklow' PRIA vol.xlii (1934)

Price, L. 'The Byrnes' Country in County Wicklow in the sixteenth century; and the manor of Arklow' *JRSAI* vol.lxiv (1936)

Rees, B. 'Matthew Doyle' *AHSJ* 1986

Rees, J. 'The Changing Fleet of Arklow Shipping' *Sea Breezes* October 1988

Rees, J. 'The Confession of "A.B."' *Arklow Historical Society 1798-1998 Commemorative Journal*

Rees, J. 'The Storm of 1886' *AHSJ* 1987

Rees, J. 'Yeoman Officer's Sword found' *AHSJ* 1988-'89

Report on Private Collections vol.4, NLI

Ronan, M. 'The Ancient Churches of the Deanery of Arklow, County Wicklow' *JRSAI* vol.57, 1928

Scannell, J. 'Arklow's 1941 Narrow Escape' *AHSJ* 1990-1991

Scannell, J. 'The Bomb that Never Was' *AHSJ* 1992-1993

Shepherd, E. 'Avoca Mines' *AHSJ* 1986

Society of Friends *Transactions during the Famine in Ireland in 1846 and 1847* Dublin 1852

Sr Magdalena 'A Sketch of the History of the Arklow Convent' *AHSJ* 1983

Synnott, B. 'St. Benedict's Athletic Club' *AHSJ* 1996-'97

Tuomey, T.C. *'Description of a Cromleac and Ogham Monument near Castletimon Church, County of Wicklow'* Proceedings and Transactions of the Kildare and South East of Ireland Archaeological Society *Vol.III (1854-55)*

Tyrrell, D. 'Arklow Terra Cotta Brick and Clay Company' *AHSJ* 1984

Tyrrell, D. 'Maria Curran, Pioneer Woman Councillor' *AHSJ* 1987

Tyrrell, D. 'The Parish Church of Saints Mary and Peter, Arklow' *AHSJ 1985*

White, D. 'Arklow Methodist Church' *AHSJ* 1985
Wicklow Newsletter as dated in Sources
Wicklow People, as dated in Sources

Books:

A German Prince *Tour in England, Ireland and France in the years 1826, 1827, 1828, and 1829,etc* ... Philadelphia 1833

An Irish Gentleman *The Scientific Tourist Through Ireland* London 1818

Anonymous *Handbook on Irish Genealogy* Heraldic Artists Ltd, Dublin 1980

Anonymous *A Tour Through Ireland* London 1780

Anonymous *The Traveller's New Guide Through Ireland* Dublin 1815

Anonymous *The Trial of Billy Byrne of Ballymanus* Dee-Jay Publications 1996

Arklow Parish Magazine vol.VIII, no.96 December 1895

Barrow, J. *A Tour Round Ireland Through the Sea-Coast Counties in the Autumn of 1835*

Beckett, J.C. *The Making of Modern Ireland*

Binns, J. *The Miseries and Beauties of Ireland* London 1837

Bartholomew, Hall, Lentin (eds) *The Enlightenment* OU/Routledge 1992

Beckett, J.C. *The Making of Modern Ireland 1603-1923* Faber & Faber 1981

Bolton, G.G.C. *The passing of the Irish Act of Union; a study in parliamentary politics* OUP 1966

Boylan,H.(ed.) *DIB* Gill & MacMillan 1998

Byrne, K. *From Shade to Sunlight* Rathdrum c.1995

Cantwell, B. *Memorials of the Dead: South-east Wicklow* c.1975

Carlson, J.(ed.) *Banned in Ireland* Routledge 1990

Carr, J. *The Stranger in Ireland, or a Tour in the Southern and Western Parts of that Country in the year 1805* London 1806

Christensen, A.E. 'Vikings in the Irish Sea' in McCaughan & Appleby (eds) *The Irish Sea: aspects of maritime history* Belfast (1989)

Connolly, S.J. *Priests and People in Pre-Famine Ireland 1780-1845* Four Courts Press 2001

Corlett, C. & Medleycott, J.(eds) *The Ordnance Survey Letters – Wicklow: from the original letters of John O'Donovan, Eugene Curry and Thomas O'Conor 1838-1840* . Roundwood and District Historical & Folklore Society, Wicklow Archaeological Society, and Kestrel Books (2000)

Cromwell, T. *Excursions through Ireland, etc* London 1820

de Breffney, B. *Irish Family Names, arms, origins, and locations* Gill & MacMillan 1982

de Courcy Ireland, J. *Ireland's Sea Fisheries: a history* Glendale 1981

de Courcy Ireland, J. *Wreck and Rescue on the east coast of Ireland* Glendale Press 1983

de Latocnaye, *Promenade d'un Francais dans l'Irlande.* Translated as *A Frenchman's Walk Through Ireland 1796-7* by John Stevenson, Dublin

de Rosa, P. *Vicars of Christ: the dark side of the papacy* Corgi edit. 1988 rep. 1991

DNB, vol. X (1917)

Donnelly, B. 'From Grand Jury to County Council: an overview of local adminstration in Wicklow 1605-1898' in Hannigan & Nolan (eds) *Wicklow History and Society* Geography Publications 1994

Donnelly, B. *For the Betterment of the People* Wicklow County Council, c.1998

Elliott, B. 'Emigration from South Leinster to eastern Upper Canada' in Whelan & Nolan(eds) *Wexford History and Society* Geography Publications 1987

Eogan, G. *Hoards of the Irish Later Bronze Age* Dublin 1993

Etchingham, C. 'Evidence of Scandanavian Settlement' in Hannigan & Nolan(eds) *Wicklow History and Society* Geography Publications 1994

Forde, F. *Maritime Arklow* Dublin 1988

Foster, R.F. *Charles Stewart Parnell: the man and his family* Harvester Press 1976

Furlong, N. *Dermot, King of Leinster and the Foreigners* Anvil Books 1973

Furlong, N. *Fr. John Murphy of Boolavogue 1753-1798* Geography Publications 1991

G.E.C. *The Complete Peerage* London 1945

Hannigan, K. & Nolan, W. (eds.) *Wicklow History and Society* Geography Publications 1994. Individual articles under authors' names

Hannigan, K. 'Wicklow Before and After the Famine' in Hannigan, K. & Nolan, W. (eds.) *Wicklow History and Society* Geography Publications 1994

Hayes-McCoy, G.A. *Irish Battles: a military history of Ireland* London 1969

Holmes, G. *Sketches of some of the Southern Counties of Ireland collected during a tour in the Autumn of 1797 in a series of letters* London 1801

Hurley, M. *Home from the Sea: the story of the Courtmacsherry lifeboat 1825 - 1995*

Hutton, A.W. (ed.) *Arthur Young's Tour in Ireland 1776-1779* London 1892

Inglis, H. *A Journey Through Ireland in the Spring, Summer and Autumn of 1834* London 1835

Knight, S. *The Brotherhood: the secret world of the Freemasons* Panther 1985

Lawlor, C. *The Massacre on Dunlavin Green: a story of the 1798 Rebellion* c.1998

Lewis, S. *Topographical Directionary* 1838

Loeber, R. 'Settlers' Utilisation of the Natural resources' in Hannigan & Nolan (eds) *Wicklow History and Society* Geography Publications 1994

Lydon, J.F. 'Medieval Wicklow – "a land of war"' in Hannigan & Nolan (eds.) *Wicklow History & Society* Geography Publications 1994

MacLysaght, E. *Irish Life in the Seventeenth Century* Irish Academic Press 1979

McLaren, A. *A Minute Description of the Battles of Gorey, Arklow and Vinegar Hill*

McNiffe, L. *A history of the Garda Síochána* Wolfhound 1997

Micks, W.L. *An Account of the Constitution, Administration and Dissolution of the Congeted Districts Board for Ireland from 1891 to 1923* Dublin 1925

Morris, J. *The Story of Arklow Lifeboats* Arklow 1987

Murphy, D. *Cromwell in Ireland: a history of Cromwell's Irish Campaign* M.H. Gill & Son 1902

Murphy, H. *The Kynoch Era in Arklow 1895-1918* c.1975

Nairn, R. & Crowley, M. *Wild Wicklow: Nature in the Garden County* Town House and Country House, 1998

Neill, K. *An Illustrated History of Ireland* Gill & MacMillan 1979 (1985 paperback edition)

Ó Cathóir, E. 'The Poor Law in County Wicklow' in in Hannigan & Nolan (eds.) *Wicklow History & Society* Geography Publications 1994

O'Cleirigh, N. *The Archaeological Heritage of the Barony of Arklow* Arklow 1980

O'Cleirigh, N. *Ninety Years of Technical Education in and Irish Maritime Town: the* story of *Arklow Community College* Arklow 1995

O'Connor, F. *The Big Fellow* Poolbeg Press 1979

Ó Corráin, D. *Ireland Before the Normans* Gill & MacMillan 1972

O'Donnell, R. *Aftermath; post-Rebllion insurgency in Wicklow, 1799-1803* Irish Academic Press 2000

O'Donnell, *R. The Rebellion in Wicklow 1798* Irish Academic Press 1998

Ó Lionáin, F. *Croghan to the Sea: a local history of Castletown, Coolgreany and the surrounding areas* c.2000

Perry, G. 'Reynolds and the Royal Academy' in Bartholomew et al (eds) *The Enlightenment* OU/Routledge, 1992

Plumtre, A. *Narrative of a Residence in Ireland* London 1817

Power, P.J. *The Arklow Calendar* Arklow 1981

Power, P. 'A Survey: some Wicklow maps 1500-1888' in Hannigan & Nolan (eds.) *Wicklow History & Society* Goegraphy Publications 1994

Price, L. *The Place-Names of county Wicklow* (7 vols.) Dublin 1945-67

Rees, B. *All for a Game: a history of Arklow Town Football Club 1948-1998* Arklow 1998

Rees, J. *A Farewell To Famine* Dee-Jay Publications 1994

Rees, J. & Charlton, L. *Arklow – last stronghold of sail* Arklow 1985

Rees, J. *Surplus People* Collins Press 2000

Rees, J. *The Life of Captain Robert Halpin* Dee-Jay Publications 1992

Reilly, T. *Cromwell: an honourable enemy – the untold story of the Cromwellian invasion of Ireland* Brandon 1999

Robertson, J. *The Traveller's Guide through Ireland* Edinburgh 1806

Robinson, T. *Stones of Aran: Labyrinth* Lilliput 1995

Severin, Tim *The Brendan Voyage*

Shepherd, E. & Beasley, G. *The Dublin & South Eastern Railway* Midland Publishing Ltd 1998

Shetelig *Viking Antiquities in Great Britain and Ireland,* vi. 1954

Short, M. *Inside the Brotherhood: further secrets of the Freemasons* Grafton Books 1989 (paperback edition 1990)

Smyth, A.P. 'Kings, Saints and Sagas' in Hannigan & Nolan (eds.) *Wicklow History & Society* Geography Publications 1994

Spellissy, S. *Window on Aran* The Book Gallery 2003

Stokes, G.T.(ed.) *Pococke's Tour in Ireland in 1752* Dublin 1891

Stout, G. 'Wicklow's Prehistoric Landscape' in Hannigan & Nolan (eds) *Wicklow History and Society* Geography Publications 1994

Sullivan, A.M. *The Story of Ireland* M.H. Gill & Son, no date

Wakefield, *An Account of Ireland* 1812

Wallace, M. *100 Irish Lives* David & Charles/Barnes & Noble 1983

Whiteside, L. *St Saviour's Church, Arklow* 1997

Wilson, David A. *United Irishmen, United States* Four Courts Press 1998

Electronic

www.excavations.ie Wicklow 1997:614
www.excavations.ie Wicklow 1997:615
www.excavations.ie Wicklow 1997:618
www.newadvent.org/cathen//11611c.htm

INDEX